Solzhenitsyn

Solzhenitsyn

DAVID BURG *and* GEORGE FEIFER

HODDER AND STOUGHTON
LONDON · SYDNEY · AUCKLAND · TORONTO

Contents

Illustrations

A creator is always depicted in his creation, even against his will. You take up a pen and want to be an author . . . because you want to write a portrait of your spirit and your heart.

NIKOLAI KARAMZIN
(one of the founders of Russian prose)

The Man

WHEN ALEXANDER SOLZHENITSYN WAS FIRST published in 1962, a leading Soviet writer declared that "we simply cannot go on writing as before." Since then, he has become not only Russia's most important living writer, but also what a group of admirers recently called "the mind and conscience of our nation." At the same time, he is anathema to the country's ruling establishment, branded "an alien element whose thinking contravenes the sacred convictions of the majority of the Soviet people." This polarization, a measure of Solzhenitsyn's talent and tenacity, has made him a unique figure in Russia and the world.

It also brings a certain unfashionableness to the record of the writer's life. His is a heroic role, and, in the West, conventional heroism is suspect. Too often, Solzhenitsyn's kind of unflagging industry in the service of an admirable cause has been shown to mask baser drives and fears, and it has become almost *de rigueur* for biographers to analyze the selfish instincts underlying virtue.

> For in the fatness of these pursy times
> Virtue itself of vice must pardon beg,
> Yea, curb and woo for leave to do him good.
> *Hamlet*

And if the ideals which inspire Solzhenitsyn's works, protests, and persecution make his heroism fit a faintly obsolete mold, lesser-known elements of his life are like a Walter Mitty fantasy made real. At the age of twenty-eight, he is a labor-camp drudge summoned to work on higher mathematics at a super-secret research institute operated by the security police. At thirty-six, he is an anonymous exile near the Chinese frontier, defeating cancer by supreme physical and mental efforts. At forty-one, he is a provincial schoolteacher whose first submitted adult manuscript is delivered to the Politburo for scrutiny. Since then he has settled down into

1

the role of a writer of rare force, who not only refuses to alter his fiction in response to immense political pressures, but openly challenges the system that generates the pressures and corrupts national life.

In Russia, where the times are less easy than burdensome Solzhenitsyn's courage is regarded as glorious rather than old-fashioned—but, for the moment, so extraordinary that it makes him a kind of living myth in his own country. There it is the secret police rather than biographers who try to debunk his virtue, but years of searching by one of the world's most powerful investigatory agencies have revealed no stain on his honor, leaving resort only to sets of lies. Heroism enjoys distinctly different favor in Russia and the West, but in both places Solzhenitsyn's consistent display of it makes him somewhat implausible—a symbol more than a man. Almost a decade after his first novel appeared, Nikolai Ulyanov of Yale University, himself a refugee from Russia, could argue that Solzhenitsyn does not exist at all, and that his books are written by a secret-police committee working to earn hard currency for the KGB by exploiting sensation-hungry Western readers.

Ulyanov's doubt of Solzhenitsyn's very existence is an unusual explanation for the mysteries of the writer; but mysteries do abound. In these circumstances, something should be said at the outset about the impression he makes on people who know him. Solzhenitsyn is a tall man with a broad chest and shoulders, a slight stoop, and a hint of a paunch on a still athletic figure. Like a character in an Ingmar Bergman film, he makes an impression of bony largeness which exceeds the actual dimensions of his frame. A full russet beard and dark, penetrating eyes are the most prominent features of his long, thin face. The eyes are often narrowed in a slight squint of concentration, and the wrinkles at the corners are more noticeable than elsewhere on his face. Under thinning fair hair, an extremely high, deeply creased forehead imparts solemnity to his reflective moments, but this is contradicted by an animation in conversation and a certain humor evident even during the gravest moments. Prepared for some of the pain of his tragic tales, people who meet him for the first time are surprised to find a quick, cheerful man with a warm smile.

All who describe him remark that before taking full stock of his appearance one is struck by an impression of extraordinary physical energy. A broad, slightly swinging gait, brisk movements, and a vigorous handshake are the introduction to a phenomenon for which the cliché "human dynamo" might have been invented. The energy is so strong and steady that he does not give an impression of weariness even after a day of his exceptionally intense work. If there is a primary explanation of Solzhenitsyn's powers—to survive, to create, to prevail—it lies in his vast supply of this human resource.

The energy has been with him since early childhood—at the university, his forcefulness was spoken of in terms of a speeding bullet—and is expended lavishly in all his activities. Bicycle riding is a favorite form of relaxation and exercise; according to a friend, Solzhenitsyn pedals "furiously" while his thoughts keep pace. He relishes physical labor, especially in simple tasks related to daily living, literally drawing water and hewing wood. Repetitive and disciplined actions help him realign his thoughts after long hours of mental turbulence at his desk. When assigned a sedentary job in prison, he would remove his shirt and rub his body with snow before going to work. Now he enjoys bathing in rivers and streams, from May, when the water is still icy, through to November, when it freezes again. Splashing himself in the sharp spray, he smiles mischievously and invites his shivering friends to join him.

In recent years his energy has been directed almost wholly to writing, and his intense concentration might be better compared to a laser beam than to a bullet. He often writes for twelve to fourteen hours a day, double the stint of most writers during their most industrious periods. The reserves required for this expenditure of mental force are obvious; long-standing friends who are writers too continue to be astonished by Solzhenitsyn's "frantic," "phenomenal," and "incomparable" capacity for work. He lives almost constantly with a writer's creative throes.

Ideally, Solzhenitsyn works in the country and in total solitude. Greenery and a rural atmosphere are so important to him that he has set up makeshift desks in courtyards and gardens when living in a city. His need for solitude leads him to take extensive pains to remain undisturbed when working in his study. He writes his first drafts in ink in longhand, typing out later drafts himself on his old machine. Classical music playing softly in the background does not disturb him, although he himself rarely turns it on. Other noise can drive him to distraction, and a neighbor's radio blaring the mixed diet of ordinary Soviet stations—cheering songs, reports of production achievements, and pep-up propaganda—"sends him up the wall," in the words of a friend. He never watches television.

Solzhenitsyn's day is spent in rigid adherence to the strictest of self-made schedules. His relentless determination to make use of every moment —a childhood trait too, but magnified by a sense of loss of his potentially best writing years to war, prison, and disease—is rare anywhere in the world, and even more so in Russia. With a trace of self-satire he recently boasted to a friend that he had "given my family an hour and a half yesterday—not a bit bad, eh?" With the same self-satire, but also with visible impatience, he sometimes glances at his watch and interrupts a conversation with a visitor. "Oh my goodness—I should have sat down to eat five minutes ago!" Together with energy, Solzhenitsyn has a highly developed talent for organization (demonstrated most clearly as a much-promoted army officer) and the latter is used to marshal and discipline the former into a great effort of self-assertion. As a close friend put it, "He never lets up for a moment. He's always working, planning, thinking—you've never seen anyone keep up such pressure on himself as he does. It adds up to drive, drive, drive." And to a conscious limitation of interests and activities which might interfere with his avowed purpose. Although a very rich man from his Western royalties, Solzhenitsyn draws but a trickle of his fortune, which, together with a trifling state pension, provides for little more than his primary needs. These needs are intentionally humble; more than the minimum attention to material things, he feels, is an empty distraction —one which he was least able to abide even when he was relatively poor and comfort was not so easily scorned.

Other limitations demand more sacrifice. Despite his enduring love for and knowledge of the theater, he seldom goes—or to other branches of the performing arts. His interest in literature is also great, and he often expresses regret to friends that the accidents of his life restricted his reading in earlier years, and the pressures of writing continue to do so now. "My extremely compressed life," he has written, "has greatly limited my opportunities for ordinary reading." Although he acquired a solid grounding in Russian literature during his youth, he regrets especially that his knowledge of Western literature, particularly contemporary writing, is very patchy, and he has almost no formal knowledge of music and the visual arts.

His self-limitations are most severe in his relationships with others. By nature, he is an outgoing man with a strong appetite for people. His instinctive gregariousness and unfeigned curiosity in others' interests and opinions is quickly transmitted and reciprocated, helping him develop what an acquaintance writer calls "a great expertise in drawing out others through his keen interest in them." "In other words," said another friend, "his intense interest in people makes him a rare listener." "Perhaps the greatest misconception about Solzhenitsyn," a third friend has remarked, "is that he's a hermit by nature. The truth is, he loves good company and blooms in it—and makes other people bloom. But he allows himself almost no time for this. It's a conscious sacrifice."

The picture of Solzhenitsyn as inaccessible and somewhat standoffish is indeed widespread, in Russia as well as abroad, and based on the experience of a considerable number of people. With those whom he dislikes, or does not see for other reasons, he can be extremely brusque. With a formal demonstration of politeness barely covering a tense irritation, a door is closed in the face of unwelcome visitors, or a back turned on importuners high and low—and nothing can move Solzhenitsyn to have anything to do with them. Although his disposition is essentially gentle and has mellowed distinctly with his advance in age—"easygoing," "genial," "even-tempered," and "kind" are the adjectives most often used by those who know him well—he occasionally explodes in anger, as often as not out of irritation with persistent interference with his work.

Even with people he chooses to see he restricts his time drastically. On one of his trips to Moscow every fortnight or so (he lives not far from the capital) he may pay a visit to one of his old friends; but after a ceremonial drink and a few minutes of conversation he will excuse himself and hurry away, ending what may be the sum and substance of his social activity for the entire two weeks. No excuse for the quick departure is needed by the friends: they know that on his day away from his desk, Solzhenitsyn has squeezed in as many Moscow appointments as possible, and must hurry on. Even when there is no next appointment, a feeling that he must get back to work begins to gnaw visibly at him within an hour, and he gets up to leave. Rare exceptions are made for special times such as New Year's Eve.

But the exceptions do not extend to lesser occasions. Some time ago, a group of Solzhenitsyn's former prisonmates established the habit of arranging an informal annual reunion in Moscow. In keeping with his attitude toward his imprisonment, Solzhenitsyn was one of the principal initiators: he feels deeply the importance not only of sustaining a sense of fraternity among former prisoners, but of remembering and reflecting—not allowing the lessons of the hard experience to die. After some hours of discussing life and reminiscing about old times, the "veterans" would make their way to a restaurant to end the gathering in a spree of food and drink. Solzhenitsyn accompanied the group to the restaurant, but left them at its doors; despite his role in organizing the reunion and in enlivening the talk and laughter, he had too little time for feasts, which in any case do not appeal to his nature. "To sit through those three or four hours of socializing," explained a friend, "would be a greater strain on him than his real work. He's enormously oppressed by anything that takes him away from his tasks." His fame, too, which he has called a "thick encumbrance," is resented for consuming so much of his time.

As Solzhenitsyn knows and regrets, some Russians who consider themselves his friends are piqued that he makes no excuses for almost never seeing them, and does not bother with the occasional telephone call or other formalities of sustaining friendly contact. His most valued friends are quite happy to fit themselves in with his unyielding sense of dedication and rigid adherence to schedules. But his severe demands on himself once caused disruptions even in his family life.

All this must be put in the perspective of Solzhenitsyn's age, medical history, and notion of his mission. Although rarely troubled now by more than minor ailments, he was gravely ill with intestinal cancer in the mid-1950s and has no illusions about the permanence of a cure from that disease. He senses a calling to share his insights with the world—insights which he hopes may influence the development of mankind and which because of his particular circumstances, few others are or ever will be in a position to share. And even though his capacity for work appears remarkable for a man in his sixth decade, he feels that he may not be able to cope with his task. He has a conscious fear that there may be too little time to complete even those works for which he has made specific plans. For all his great literary production of the past fifteen years, what he calls "the principal project" of his life—which he conceived as a teen-ager and from which Russia's history "distracted" him for two decades—has only just begun. Solzhenitsyn has budgeted twenty years for it, and wonders whether he will have them.

In his estimation of literature's power to influence society Solzhenitsyn expresses a belief which is still very strong in Russia—one which makes his own life illustrative of many fundamental issues of Russian history and society. It is a commonplace that the role of literature and the writer in that country has long been far greater than in Western societies. In the absence of political debate, Russian writers are not merely entertainers but sociologists, political pamphleteers, and voices—often the only ones—of civilized conscience.

But Solzhenitsyn's faith in literature's beneficial influence also illustrates an essential aspect of his individual outlook. In the West, this attitude was most strongly felt in the last century, and many other elements of Solzhenitsyn's personality make him appear a nineteenth-century man. Because he was reared primarily on the great works of nineteenth-century Russian literature, it is not surprising that his literary outlook reflects that age. But in his rigorous sense of duty too he seems consciously carrying forward the literary ethics of an earlier time. "In our age," he has said, "when technology is gaining control of life, when material well-being is considered the most important goal, when the influence of religion has been weakened everywhere in the world, a special responsibility lies upon the writer. He must fill more than one vacated function."

Beyond this, Solzhenitsyn's links to the last century are reflected in his lust for experience. From early in life he has not merely met unusual challenges, but sought them out in a way reminiscent of some of the great rebels and explorers of the Victorian age. In his own ventures, the ethos (if not the reality) of the century of Belief in Progress is repeated. It speaks of Russia's as well as Solzhenitsyn's character that this essentially nineteenth-century outlook has not disintegrated under the impact of world war, concentration camps, and cancer, those most twentieth-century afflictions, whereas many of the most influential writers of the much less ravaged West have moved from a belief in progress to a shrugging resignation about the human condition.

Other aspects of Solzhenitsyn's personality are also at odds with some of the current century's strongest drives. The resentment of an age in which "technology is gaining control of life . . . and . . . material well-being is considered the most important goal" leads naturally to a kind of anticonsumerism. A scientist by training, he fully recognizes technology's power to liberate millions from drudgery; a return to imagined joys of preindustrial society has no place in his ideas. But the excesses of force-fed consumption anger him. In one of his plays he is bitterly sarcastic about a dream to own a "burgundy Super 88 convertible with 350 h.p." He does own a car himself—a wobbly Moskvich with some sixty horse-power and all the wear of eight years on Russian roads. But so long as he is able to keep it running reasonably well, Solzhenitsyn has no desire for something grander. He is a good driver and likes to tinker with the car on the rare occasions when he finds time. His hands are rough like a workman's.

In other respects, his attitude as a consumer, unchanged by his recent fortune, is expressed by an autobiographical character in the same play: ["You don't have to earn a lot, you need to spend little."] Having known hunger and cold, he has a respect for the food and clothing required to sustain life; one of his characters is pictured in puzzled wonder over how his daily half kilo of bread is transformed into thoughts, the most treasured product of his energy. But Solzhenitsyn's scorn for gourmets and dandies is expressed through other characters, and he himself is indifferent to the refinements of good eating. When alone, he is happy to whip up something for himself, and laughs over his less successful efforts.

His attitude toward clothing goes beyond indifference to fine and fashionable things to a positive attachment to old ones. Partly in order to avoid drawing attention to himself, he dresses in inconspicuous urban clothing when in public places. At home, however, he wears old sandals literally to tatters, and, for years after leaving his last labor camp, wrote in an ancient black quilt jacket which had served him well there. His friends say that his love of old clothes reflects not only his frugality and rational commitment to the belief that serviceable things should remain in service, but deeper elements of his personality: an attachment to the old as part of a search for continuity in life; an expression, to some extent, of the traditional guilt of a part of Russia's fortunates, faced with the misery of the masses. For years after he had become relatively well off, Solzhenitsyn could not force himself to take a taxi (which is less a luxury in sprawling Moscow than in most capitals). "He had an aversion to feeling like a lord," a friend explained. "It's difficult to make this sound genuine, the way he feels it as genuine. But when you get to know him, you realize how deep his identification with 'the people' is. Many writers feel *for* them; he feels *with* them too."

Apart from compassion, Solzhenitsyn's consideration for people in personal matters is mentioned as often as his sense of urgency about time. He is not a modest man in the sense of underestimating his own significance. The sober, calculating part of him—several acquaintances describe him as "computerlike" in conversation—records his impact on the world with precision, and the results are used in planning his strategy to assert himself. But his almost obsessive determination to fulfill even unimportant promises derives from his respect for others as well as his demands upon himself. An appointment is a sacred obligation, spurring Solzhenitsyn to arrive precisely on time. He values the others' time as his own, as if they too felt the same compulsion to make maximum use of every moment. "With utter sincerity, he hesitates to meet people," a friend said, "because he's worried about wasting *their* precious time. What you must understand is that his rigid discipline is directed at himself. Toward others, he's almost always tender and warmhearted."

Although the man who made this observation happens to be a writer himself, he is an exception among Solzhenitsyn's small circle of closest friends. A certain number of young writers have sought him out, but he has never wished to become a social part of the literary community, much less to choose his friends from within it. His close relationships with a handful of Russian writers—all talented "liberals"—is grounded wholly in personal affection.[1] Most of the small circle is made up of scientists, former prison and army companions, theater people, and relatives, with these categories overlapping in some instances. Occasionally, when their letters are unusually moving or perceptive, he makes a new acquaintance from among the strangers who write to him.

Naturally enough, it is in the company of his friends that the "private" elements of Solzhenitsyn's personality come alive. "His eyes shine with enjoyment of life," said one. His manner of speaking, which at more formal occasions is exceedingly direct and businesslike, becomes more relaxed. There is a trace of southern accent in his Russian, a mark of where he spent his youth. His voice has a faint pealing quality, as if he takes pleasure in every word of his beloved Russian language.

He is not a man to tell many funny stories or pass on the latest jokes, but he has a keen sense of humor and bursts into exuberant laughter at the stories of others. Subtle wit gives him especial pleasure. But above all, his friends talk of him in terms of the much-abused words "artless-

[1] Death recently ended three such warm friendships with important literary figures. Anna Akhmatova, the "Empress of Russian Poetry," died in 1966; Kornei Chukovsky, the grand old man of Russian letters, in 1969; and Alexander Tvardovsky, the poet and editor, in 1972.

ness" and "simplicity." "For some time," said a Moscow actor considerably his junior, "I couldn't get used to him being a man rather than a symbol. Because he *was* such a dazzling symbol to us all. But when I came to know him well, the opposite happened: he's so simple in his manner, so unaffected and direct—plain, in a way—that it's hard to remember that he's Russia's greatest living man." Another admirer spoke of Solzhenitsyn's "extraordinary simplicity, immediacy, and enormous interest in everything, almost like that of a child."

This side of Solzhenitsyn, seemingly so different from the prickly, uncompromising artist with the saintly ideals and somewhat monkish asceticism, cannot be fully developed in any contemporary biography. A hostile environment prevents biographers from exploring it at first hand—and from examining some aspects of Solzhenitsyn's emotional intensity. The hardship of others, for example, moves him deeply; a tale of injustice or suffering often provokes an instant outpouring of compassion or outrage, distorting his features. But since spontaneity of feeling is a luxury which Solzhenitsyn can rarely afford in his position, he has learned to control his emotions, as he controls his natural gregariousness. "The picture of him perceived by the outside world," said a writer friend with whom he sometimes walks in the countryside, "almost inevitably makes him more calculating than he is. Actually, he feels things quickly and deeply. But he must keep a protective guard around his potential weak spots."

It was this same friend who provided one of the most direct insights into Solzhenitsyn's character. What does the writer like least in life? he was asked. His impatient reply seemed to reflect Solzhenitsyn's own reaction: "Falsehood!" he snapped.

If Solzhenitsyn's nineteenth-century cast makes him a complicated subject for contemporary writers, other elements of his personality impose more substantive difficulties. He will give no encouragement, not to speak of help, to biographers, and has made it clear that he wants no account of his life written while he is alive. His close friends, even those who think his defense of personal life against publicity is excessive, have pledged to compile nothing of this nature during his lifetime. In these circumstances, it must be stated that Solzhenitsyn in no way sanctions this book, and that his wish that his personal life should not be publicly discussed was communicated to one of the authors while he was gathering final information in Moscow during the summer of 1971.

The following December, his attitude had apparently hardened and he issued a statement denouncing as "unceremonious and amoral" biographies containing "information of an extraliterary nature . . . while a writer is alive. . . . The authors gather such information without my knowledge and my agreement, often in dark and roundabout ways by inter-

viewing people who knew me at one time or another but are often not
informed at all. The material collected in this manner is supplemented
with imaginary facts and explanations of motives which must be invented
simply because the true circumstances and motives of my work cannot be
known to anyone, due to the isolation in which I live. Such 'information'
is in no way different from ordinary shadowing."

Biographers cannot ignore this statement, but it should be said here
that none of its points applies to this book in particular, the preparation of
which was never kept secret in Moscow, nor is it based on interviews
with anyone not in relatively regular personal contact with Solzhenitsyn
at the time of the writing. The overwhelming bulk of the authors' information comes from documents which Solzhenitsyn himself has made public
and from interpretations of his work. Rare speculation about his personal
motives—without which the genre of biography could hardly exist—is
clearly identified; and although it contained nothing discrediting, certain
iniormation has been omitted on the advice of Solzhenitsyn's friends.

His categorical hostility to biographies of himself while alive seems to
have been formed by several factors. For one thing, there is a simple resentment of demands on his time and interference with his mission. All
publicity not directly related to his goals is a distraction, and he is not a
man to help biographers without becoming deeply involved in the results.
His job is writing, not being written about; the simplest, surest, and most
sensible policy is to have no truck with the latter. Moreover, the nature
of his writing strengthens this disinclination. He is as much an autobiographical as an imaginative writer; most of his works draw heavily, and
often directly, from his own and his family's experiences. In this sense,
his life is his richest "material," and, as his friends hint, he feels that he
should be the writer to use it first.

Another reason is more general, rooted in a long tradition of Russian
skepticism toward "living" biographies. Indeed, in the absence of an
André Maurois or a Stefan Zweig in Russian letters, the genre itself barely
exists. Instead, strong social as well as literary custom attaches the odium
of intrusion upon the subject's privacy to any biography of a living person. In this respect, Solzhenitsyn's attitude—that a recounting of his personal life would by definition concentrate on the slick, the sensational, and
the secondary—falls wholly into the Russian tradition. One of his friends,
a man who knows contemporary Western literature well and disagrees
with the blanket suspicion of biography as a genre, put Solzhenitsyn's position clearly. "East is East and West is West," he said, in English. "Western writers and Solzhenitsyn have entirely different positions about this—
and although I can explain his to the world, he will probably never relent
in his abhorrence of 'personal publicity.' " In place of "trivial" biographical
material, Solzhenitsyn urges anyone who feels the need to write about him

to concentrate wholly on his works (which contain everything of importance about him) and to limit himself to a critical study of the texts. In this, too, he is wholly in the Russian tradition.

Solzhenitsyn's dislike for the genre itself is reinforced by his natural modesty. Although he does not pretend not to recognize his place in the world, he is embarrassed to the point of distress when people try to fawn over him or gush extravagant praise for his books. According to friends, this is why—despite systematic denigration of his honor and patriotism—he has not only never spoken publicly of his distinguished war record, but has also taken pains to prevent publicity about it. If this degree of personal modesty in the face of that measure of pressure seems somewhat eccentric, Solzhenitsyn's warmest admirers (who themselves would gladly tell the world about his bravery in battle and elsewhere) answer that no truly great Russian writer has been wholly free of eccentricity.

But for all of Solzhenitsyn's idiosyncrasies and rigid convictions, his attitude toward biographical research cannot be understood without reference to "the conditions in which I live," as he recently put it with ironic understatement. The Nobel prize novelist is under permanent siege in his own land, subject to harassment at any moment and intense scrutiny always. His enemies, who have almost the full powers of party, state, and secret police at their disposal (in a country where these powers are vast) work diligently to twist every item of information about him to his disadvantage. Against these forces, Solzhenitsyn has fashioned a unique defense which enables him to survive and write. Integral to the strategy is a life of withdrawal, from which sallies are made only on issues of high national importance and keen personal concern; and, whenever possible, at chosen moments. Some of his friends feel that he underestimates the potential advantages of publicity, but none questions his overall strategic talents, or that his determination to live in obscurity derives from them. All needless risks to his survival as a writer and servant of his mission must be avoided.

In these circumstances, the problems of writing about him are manifest. Few biographers enjoy the advantage of knowing their subjects personally, rather than through letters, documents, and memoirs. But the severe restrictions in Solzhenitsyn's case are curious with respect to a living man. The subject himself cannot be approached, and the official hostility toward him (a rather precise measure of the fear of him) is so strong that no information can be sought openly through institutional channels. In Russia, these include the whole of the literary and academic establishments, from the Writers' Union and editorial boards of literary magazines to the authors of textbooks on Soviet literature and the directors of libraries. Indeed, virtually no critical or documentary material exists in Soviet libraries, and many of them have withdrawn even Solzhenitsyn's few published works. Facts can be learned only through Solzhenitsyn's admirers and friends, of whom the closest are themselves under suspicion and steady surveillance, and who take definite risks in talking to foreigners about the writer.[2] Otherwise, material must be gathered by scrutinizing Solzhenitsyn's fiction and public statements and collating scraps of information in Western periodicals and libraries, thousands of miles from the man himself.

Detective work of this kind inevitably leaves gaps. But a more fundamental consideration is whether to write at all in these circumstances and in the knowledge of Solzhenitsyn's attitude. In this case, the decision to proceed has been made in the hope of dispelling some of the considerable misinformation current about Solzhenitsyn, and in the reckoning that although not all aspects of his life can be investigated now, perhaps they can never be. As for Solzhenitsyn's attitude[3], it can only be said that his achievements have made him a public figure of international importance, and since West is indeed West, biographies of him will continue to be written here. A great writer belongs to the world.

One day, some biographies may be interesting for their revelations of what Russians call, as in the case of Tolstoy, the great writer's "piquant quirks." But at this point, the authors have decided to give minimal treatment to Solzhenitsyn's private life except as it bears on his public position, the interpretation of his works, and the development of his art. But it is precisely while he is alive and at the height of his artistic powers that his role in Russian life should be made clear. Otherwise, his heroic stance and dedication to a seemingly old-fashioned virtue will keep him a remote, and therefore not quite believable, symbol—rather than a living man.

[2] Although the risk for foreigners is infinitely smaller, the Soviet authorities take what reprisals they can on them. One of the authors, George Feifer, who visited Moscow in July of 1971, was, practically speaking, ejected from the country and told that he could "never again set foot on Soviet territory." In considerable rage, a secret police officer explained that this was punishment for gathering material about Solzhenitsyn: "a filthy activity, hostile to the interests of the Soviet people." The author's notes were—illegally—confiscated.

[3] As this book was going to press, Solzhenitsyn's attitude hardened, and he made his position clear by publically denouncing biographies of himself in general, and the present biographers in particular, although he has not read this book himself.

II

Origins

ALEXANDER ISAIYEVICH SOLZHENITSYN BEARS AN uncommonly unwieldy name. For non-Russians, the difficulties of pronunciation are manifest, but the name is curious to the Russian ear too, both in the implications of "Solzhenitsyn" and the juxtaposition of the straightforward "Alexander" with the Old Testament "Isaiyevich." At first hearing, "Solzhenitsyn" seems associated with the verb *solgat,* to tell a lie, suggesting something like "belonging to a lie-teller." The similarity to this word root is so striking that after Solzhenitsyn's major novels had become known, an unsubtle pun circulated in Russia: *"Solzhenitsyn nye solzhot"*—"Solzhenitsyn won't tell lies."

In fact, the name has no connection with this root. For its authentic origin one must thank a philologist from the Russian city of Voronezh who, several years ago, researched the origins of interesting family names connected with the area, among them the rare "Solzhenitsyn." The scholar demonstrated that the name derives from *solod,* "malt," indicating that some Solzhenitsyns, probably in the late seventeenth or early eighteenth century, were involved with brewing.

A note in the Voronezh local newspaper recently mentioned a certain Filip Solzhenitsyn who lived nearby in the early eighteenth century. "Malt" might have been associated with this man as a nickname too, for he was obviously unusually headstrong. Filip Solzhenitsyn had been exiled by Peter the Great to Voronezh, then an outpost on the edge of Russian territory, for having occupied and farmed crown lands near Moscow without permission. This was but one manifestation of his initiative, independence, and, to a degree, rebelliousness. He is thought to be a direct ancestor of the writer.

Filip Solzhenitsyn's radical streak appears to have stayed with the family, and surfaced again in the mid-nineteenth century. By the evidence of the writer's fiction, a man who was his great-great-grandfather was in-

volved in a flare of peasant anger against local landowners or officials in
Voronezh, and once again a Solzhenitsyn was exiled to the country's
expanding frontiers. This time the family settled in the Cossack lands
northeast of the Caucasus Mountains.

Although the exile could not be accepted into the privileged estate of
the Cossacks, the Tsar's most loyal peasant cavalry, this Solzhenitsyn was
given all the farmland and pasture he could work and lived well by the
standards of the time and place. Still, the family remained ordinary
peasants, and until the early twentieth century none of the writer's direct
ancestors on his father's side left the peasantry. And this, curiously enough,
might well explain his Jewish-sounding patronymic, Isaiyevich, "son of
Isai." His father might have been named Isai simply because he was born
on the day dedicated to Isai in the calendar of the Orthodox Church, and
true to old custom his grandfather so named him.

Solzhenitsyn's grandfather grew up in a culture and tradition based
largely upon unreflecting devotion to the church's prescriptions. Christen-
ing his son with a name that had already passed from fashion even among
peasants speaks of a deep respect for orthodox ways. But Solzhenitsyn's
relatives remember not only pious manners but also an inquisitive mind,
which corresponds to the wise grandfather mentioned by several of Solzhenitsyn's autobiographical heroes.

Solzhenitsyn's father, therefore, was of ancient Russian peasant stock
and spent the summers of his early manhood in the fields, as his ancestors
had spent their lives. By that time in Russia, it was not unusual for a
peasant-born man to acquire a practical education. But something in
Solzhenitsyn's father made him uninterested in farming; his leanings
were strongly intellectual, and when he came of student age shortly after
1910, Isai Solzhenitsyn began a year-long campaign to convince his father
to send him to a university. He prevailed at last and was the first member
of the family to break with the long land-bound tradition and to receive
a formal education. It was a reflection of his strong but gentle personality
—in Solzhenitsyn's fiction, clarity and firmness of purpose are among his
prototype's most striking traits—that he eventually won his campaign to
be sent to university without alienating his family.

Isai Solzhenitsyn studied first in Kharkov University in the Ukraine [1]
and later at the Philological Faculty of Moscow University, one of the
city's liveliest intellectual centers. It was natural for a student of literature
to take a strong interest in Tolstoy the writer, but as an indication of his

[1] Enrolling at the university apparently brought some last-minute difficulty to
his long-cherished dream. One of Solzhenitsyn's fictional characters of precisely
his father's age and background was first rejected because the authorities assumed
that a boy with his name could only be Jewish, and that year's quota had already
been filled. The young peasant-intellectual had to produce proof that he was Orthodox
Christian, a submission to a social injustice which long troubled his conscience.

attitude toward Russia's contemporary preoccupations, the young Solzhenitsyn was also absorbed with him as a teacher of life. Tolstoyism was
a kind of nonchurch religion propounding that the kingdom of God resides
within each human soul, and that the way to a true knowledge of Christ
and to salvation was through individual conscience and love rather than
the strictures of an organized church. Tolstoy preached moral betterment
by means of restricting human appetites and simplifying life; his ultimate
goal was to transform the whole of Russia, including the intelligentsia,
into a community of peasants satisfying their own basic needs through
manual work on their own land. Bolstered by the enormous prestige of the
living teacher, Tolstoyism was one of the country's most popular ideological movements at the turn of the century and reached its crest with
Tolstoy's death in 1910. There is strong evidence that Isai Solzhenitsyn
remained a committed believer in the faith when the movement was no
longer fashionable. This testifies to social and moral concerns which accompanied his literary pursuits—in some ways they might even have
interfered with them: apparently Isai suppressed his desire to write poetry
in deference to Tolstoy's notion that the medium was too refined to serve
social and moral concerns.[2]

Tolstoy also preached nonviolence and urged his followers to become
conscientious objectors. But during the first surge of excited patriotism
accompanying the outbreak of World War I, Isai Solzhenitsyn volunteered
for the army. In 1914, his studies uncompleted, he went directly from the
university to the arduous German front, where he would spend the entire
three years of war in the distinguished Grenadier Artillery Brigade. Thrice
decorated, he saved some munition boxes by himself on one occasion when
the battery was ablaze. Later, when "the entire front was collapsing," as
Solzhenitsyn has put it, his battery remained on the front lines until the
Treaty of Brest in 1918. It was an outstanding demonstration of patriotic
devotion.

In the summer of 1917, Isai Solzhenitsyn married in a ceremony performed "at the front" by a brigade priest. Solzhenitsyn's mother was of a
similar background to his father except that, by this time, her family was
distinctly better off. Her father was half Ukrainian and had worked his
way up from day laborer—according to the evidence of Solzhenitsyn's
novels, he spoke broken Russian to the end of his days—to a farmer of
considerable substance who used the most modern methods on his land in
the fertile "black-earth" region not far from the smaller Solzhenitsyn hold-

---

[2] Solzhenitsyn's fictional father—the parallel to his own in terms of time and
place are overwhelming—is shown arguing with his mentor while on a pilgrimage
to the Tolstoy estate. Was not universal love too difficult a goal? the boy asked the
great man. Should not "universal good will" be a more reasonable intermediate stage?
Universal good will is a kind of moral undercurrent in Solzhenitsyn's novels.

ing. This rough and ready man did not begrudge the expense of his children's education and Solzhenitsyn's mother was sent to study at what was called Higher Courses for Women. Because they were private—therefore unfettered—these rather exclusive institutions, resembling private American women's colleges, often maintained broader intellectual horizons than Russia's state-run institutes of higher education.

For Solzhenitsyn's mother, this education provided much more than a finish to a young lady's training. Although her father wanted her to study agronomy in order to be useful on the farm,[3] she was interested in the artistic turbulence that surrounded her. Her formative years took place during the Silver Age of Russian culture in the first decades of this century (Pushkin's time being the Golden Age). The Silver Age was a spurt of experimental artistic creativity. Westerners know it best through the music of Scriabin and the young Stravinsky, the ballet of Diaghilev and Fokine, the theatrical inventiveness of Stanislavsky and Meyerhold, the painting and decorative arts of Bakst and others. But the rejuvenation of poetry—by Alexander Blok and the symbolists, as well as by Akhmatova, Gumilyov, Mayakovsky, and others—moved young Russians even more. They were often permeated by its moods to the point of being "poisoned," as Blok himself remarked.

Solzhenitsyn's mother belonged to this generation spiritually as well as chronologically. Solzhenitsyn's relatives speak of her as a woman with modern leanings, and her prototype in Solzhenitsyn's fiction yearns to become a dancer in the Isadora Duncan style, the most avant garde of the dance movements of the time. In contrast to her family, the spirited girl with the pretty Ukrainian face was not religious. The picture is therefore clearly of an educated young woman of her time, exuberant and kind, whose cultural interests were nevertheless as real to her as any of the more tangible concerns of a girl's daily life.

As well as more personal attractions, these interests drew Solzhenitsyn's father and mother together. The differences between the Russian intelligentsia and the great masses of peasants, workers, and tradesmen are often overdrawn. But it is true that the intelligentsia, that uniquely Russian social stratum, had certain distinct qualities in their outlook and interests. Absorbed by ideas—a consuming interest in art and knowledge—they considered intellectual activity more a way of life than a means of earning an income or climbing the social ladder.

Rather than objective criteria of income and life-styles, it was personal attitudes which distinguished a member of the intelligentsia from, say, a

---

[3] The evidence for this comes from Solzhenitsyn's novel *August 1914*. His friends stress the biographical nature of the family chronicle in the book. The writer himself has revealed almost no direct information about his mother, and his friends are reluctant to talk about even the little they know.

professional man who was not. Both might be honest, capable lawyers. But beyond this, the lawyer who would be considered a member of the intelligentsia would concern himself with the law's role in society and as an instrument of progress, his own personal and professional obligations to society, and the interrelationship of all these considerations in the human condition. The intelligentsia's primary characteristic was its intellectual curiosity and propensity to ask, Why? The newly founded Solzhenitsyn family belonged wholly to this stratum, and in a way their attachment to it was strengthened by both man and wife being first-generation "converts."

But within the intelligentsia distinct groupings persisted. One of the two major categories consisted of the men and women whose sense of social consciousness dominated almost everything else. Although they had largely broken with the life of the great masses, their memories of peasant grievances were strong. This prompted an approach to most issues in terms of betterment for their "younger brothers"—a tendency that turned a substantial portion of the intelligentsia into radicals and revolutionaries, leading many to deny the value of art that did not directly serve the cause of social progress. Isai Solzhenitsyn's study of literature is evidence that he did not share this extreme view, but suppression of his poetic urge in keeping with Tolstoyism suggests his concern with literature as an instrument of social progress. Tolstoy himself ultimately renounced most of his own works, including *War and Peace* and *Anna Karenina*, because they did not serve this purpose.

Solzhenitsyn's mother belonged to a different grouping within the intelligentsia, one which had less sense of guilt and obligation to the suffering masses, especially with the visible improvement in the common people's lot in the early twentieth century and Russia's progress toward greater political freedom and social justice. The primary interests of this grouping were esthetics and culture in all its manifestations.

Thus Solzhenitsyn's parents brought together the two most significant strains of the Russian intelligentsia: one which emphasized art's obligation to improve society; the other which promoted an attitude of, crudely speaking, art for art's sake. Solzhenitsyn inherited both traditions and, in time, his work would be a conscious effort to unite them, for he would lavish equal attention upon esthetic considerations in his writing, and upon its influence in bettering Soviet society.

The end of World War I for Russia came in the autumn of 1917, a few months after the young couple's marriage. The tsarist regime had collapsed the previous March and Soviet society was painfully developing. Amid the furious eruptions of revolution and civil war, Solzhenitsyn's father and mother moved to Kislovodsk, in the foothills of the Caucasus not far from both their parents' farms. Kislovodsk is one of Russia's better-known southern spas, and it is said that Isai Solzhenitsyn went there to recuperate from wounds received at the front. While the civil war raged, there was no hope of resuming his education, and he took a job as a forester managing a substantial tract.

One day in June 1918, he went on a hunt for small game, as was his habit, in the forests of the neighboring hills. While he was reloading his rifle it went off by accident, wounding him fatally. "Poor medical care," as Solzhenitsyn has called it, helped cause his death several days later. A sister-in-law present, among others, at his bedside reported that the dying Isai was convinced he would have a son. Six months later, on December 11, 1918, Alexander Solzhenitsyn was born.

III

Beginnings

FROM THE TIME OF LERMONTOV, ⸢THE elegant little town of Kislovodsk ("Sour Waters")⸥ had been a fashionable resort as well as a spa. But in the ruin and chaos of the postrevolution years, its attractions were more elementary. The civil war took more casualties among civilians than among soldiers; hunger killed many. It was a treacherous time to raise a child, and Alexander's infant years were the period of the hardest fighting, burning, and revenge. Kislovodsk was a better place than most to survive. Although brutal fighting between Red and White Armies raged around the town, climate and location made the northern Caucasus a small island of relative sufficiency in the country's vast land mass of want.

But once a certain order had returned to national life and survival was no longer at stake, Solzhenitsyn's mother left the resort town for the larger world. Alexander was now six years old, and she, although only in her mid-twenties, had resolved to dedicate her life to him—a dedication which included the notion that she should not remarry, for fear of wounding him emotionally. Her son was to be her sole source of fulfillment; for an educated woman, sleepy Kislovodsk offered few opportunities to provide for him.

In 1924, she moved to Rostov-on-Don, where she found work to sustain herself and the child. Rostov was the nearest major city in Russia proper on the main trunk line from Kislovodsk, some 250 miles north. Here Solzhenitsyn would spend the whole of his youth.

A port for both the Don River and the Azov Sea, Rostov was a large, bustling, multinational city. Its faintly Mediterranean flavor in those years was not illusory; the Azov connects to the Black Sea, and through it to the Mediterranean. For exotic atmosphere it was second only to Odessa among Russian cities. Russians and Ukrainians made up most of its Slavic population, but there was also a considerable Armenian community as well as large groups of Caucasian Muslims. And before the revolution Rostov

had long been the capital of the Cossack lands, with their tradition of
military valor and jealously prized, feudallike privileges. Yet the city
lacked style; the sum of these parts did not coalesce into a distinctive
whole. When the mature Solzhenitsyn used one word to describe his
adopted native city, it was "commercial."

This had an unmistakably disdainful connotation all those years later;
but in 1924 it was precisely Rostov's commercialism that provided the
needed job for his mother. The new revolutionary orthodoxy left her
considerably worse off than if she were an average widow with a young
child to support. Although she knew French and English well and was
competent in shorthand and typing, her social origin made her a kind of
pariah in the new Bolshevik order. Were it not for revolutionary fervor,
a woman of her background and education would be expected to work as
a teacher, an editorial assistant or perhaps a civil servant—but these were
precisely the kinds of jobs that the Bolsheviks hesitated to entrust to
members of the old intelligentsia. Shunned by well-paying offices and
enterprises—even a wholly harmless one involved with the construction
of flour mills dismissed her in a way which restricted her future civil rights
—she was compelled to seek free-lance work in the evening. Her house-
work was attended to late at night, making her constantly short of sleep
and no doubt aggravating her frequent colds and subsequent more serious
illness.

In short, the times were ill equipped for merrymaking, as a contemporary Russian poet put it, and the principal goal of Solzhenitsyn's mother
was not to find the "right" kind of job, but any kind. She began working
in Rostov as a shorthand typist, and throughout her shortened life continued to do only secretarial jobs, which earned her a meager living. "She
worked hard," Solzhenitsyn was to remember. "And as she grew older,
she was more and more often ill." Nevertheless, she could not relax her
standards or her devotion to her son—who, like his father, was called
"Sanya" instead of "Sasha," the more customary diminutive for Alexander.

In his turn, Alexander took over some of the tiny household's work
at an early age. He helped daily with the domestic routine and, as soon
as he was able, with the harder chores, such as carrying in the firewood.
Perhaps sensing his mother's total devotion to him and some of the sacrifices it entailed, his sense of obligation to her developed noticeably beyond
that of an average young boy.

Solzhenitsyn now rarely talks about helping his mother in those years
—in fact, he rarely talks about his mother at all: according to friends, her
memory is too sacred for idle reminiscence. But he sometimes chides his
friends' children for not helping their mothers enough. "It was different
when I was a kid," he says half jokingly. "I had to do everything."

It was indeed different when he was a child. To Western eyes, Russia now may seem a consumer's wasteland; then, finding enough food to live was often a severe problem. The boy and his mother lived in a few square feet of a tumbledown house, where they "shared the cares of running a household in those difficult years," as Solzhenitsyn recalled. Some forty years later, when intent to refute notions—calculatedly encouraged by the authorities—that his forebears had been wealthy—Solzhenitsyn stressed in an interview the "extremely difficult" conditions in which his mother had raised him. Not allocated a room by the state, they were forced to pay dearly for "broken-down little huts" rented privately in Rostov. When a room was finally assigned, it was part of a reconstructed stable.

I was always cold. There was a draft. The coal we used for heat was hard to get. Water had to be carried from afar. Actually, I learned only recently what running water in an apartment meant.

By the time Alexander was able to perform meaningful household tasks, Russia had again entered a harsh epoch. There had been seven relatively fat years in the mid-1920s under a policy designed to restore the ravaged economy to its prerevolutionary level. But in 1929, the drastic dislocations of enforced industrialization and collectivization of agriculture began to take hold. The first Five-year Plan was put into effect, financed by ruthless squeezing of tens of millions of recalcitrant peasants. The producers of the country's food were themselves starved and uprooted; agricultural output fell catastrophically and, once again, the Russian people had to struggle for the necessities of life. Like most others, the tiny Solzhenitsyn family was preoccupied with securing its crust of bread. Even for those lean times the family was badly off.

Alexander's mother worked at home and in offices; the burden of acquiring provisions, therefore, often fell to him. Ration card in hand, the ten-year-old boy took his place in line at permanently beleaguered food shops. The waiting consumed many hours, and demanded real physical endurance. Exasperated by chronic shortages, fearful that supplies might be exhausted before their turn came, exhausted themselves by the demands of the times, people often resorted to aggressive language and behavior. Alexander held his ground. This was his first recorded encounter with the harsh sides of Russian life, and one of the qualities it bred in an auto-biographical hero—an inner, dogged "grabbyness, force-bred into him while he was still a boy standing in line at bread shops during the first Five-year Plan"—almost certainly pertains to himself.

There is an unmistakable implication that this aspect of Solzhenitsyn's character was forced upon him to his distaste. But the lessons of practical discipline in coping with mundane problems in adverse circumstances would become a blessing beyond his imagination. Attitudes developed in food shops and other classrooms of Soviet life in the early 1930s prepared him not only for survival in labor camps, but also to stand firm later against the onslaughts of Soviet politico-literary-secret police warfare, which sometimes made the coarse words and elbows of Rostov's bread seekers seem gentle by comparison. Very early, Solzhenitsyn developed a sober appreciation of the "small change" of life which he would need not so much as a writer—Tolstoy, Turgenev, and others could survive without it—but to surmount the daunting obstacles in his passage to writing and publishing.

But struggling for bread was the boy's idea of neither accomplishment nor fun. A photograph taken at the time shows a skinny, close-cropped lad of eleven, with fair hair, fine features, and the unmistakable intelligence derived from his parents. His friendships also reflected the family background. Most were with the children of the high Rostov intelligentsia; it was their homes he visited and their parents whose influence he felt. No less than before the revolution—perhaps even more—the interests of these people were books, ideas, knowledge, and social concerns. When politics were discussed, it was usually in little huddles with nervous glances at the children: will they understand? repeat? give away their parents, even inadvertently? But otherwise—until the blood purges of the 1930s—the atmosphere Alexander absorbed was of books and conversations about them.

In school—his was near the center of the city, attended largely by children of better-educated families—he was one of the best pupils of his class. But here, the intellectual atmosphere was deeply unsettled. During Solzhenitsyn's school years, 1926 to 1936, every aspect of primary and secondary education was subject to fundamental change. Pedagogically, the early revolutionary practices of free discussion in class, self-government by pupils, and a general permissiveness were abandoned; the schools were returned to the prerevolutionary gymnasia's tradition of discipline, with an unshakable authority residing in the teacher. More important were radical changes in many of the subjects themselves. History was the most battered: as Stalin purged them, revolutionary heroes became loathsome traitors overnight; one day only the history of the lower classes was important, the next day a promulgation required memorizing the chronology of the tsars; increasingly elaborate versions of Stalin's role in the revolution were issued, blatantly contradicting the previous versions. . . . In short, the schools were Stalinized.

The paradox was that the "immutable school truths" which every pupil was to remember forever flashed by more quickly than schoolboy crazes: one day crystal radios, the next day stamps. The stream of changes puzzled a number of the boys, but did not disturb many. As his relatives put it, however, Solzhenitsyn was a "boy-intellectual" with a tendency not simply to memorize or study but to "understand the causes of things."

The extreme mutability of the immutable truths led him toward skepticism —not of the revolution itself and its goals, but of current interpretations.

Skepticism, in turn, prompted the first faint mistrust of textbooks. Alexander took the trouble to examine them carefully in the course of his rather fastidious preparation of lessons, even to check the source of some of their quotations. The pages of his history texts in particular were laden with quotations from Lenin, carefully selected and pruned to support the presentation of Stalinist policies as the true inheritors of Leninism and the source of Russia's—and the world's—salvation. When Alexander located the quoted sentences in Lenin's work itself he was apparently surprised by how his texts had twisted them. To one of his principal fictional heroes, Stalin's writings seemed, "even as a kid" in the upper forms, like slop on a plate after reading Lenin. "Every one of his [Lenin's] thoughts is turned coarse and stupid—and he himself [Stalin] doesn't notice how he loses the real gist."

This was an early exercise in what was to be a lifelong habit: returning to original sources. The discernible slant of his textbooks and the excitement of his first intellectual discoveries convinced him that the somewhat laborious process was worth the time—which was already precious to him. His energy was exceptional; he was constantly busy at one or another pursuit, as if he had to be involved in the whole spectrum of activities open to him. Friends remember his most characteristic trait, even then, as the fear of wasting an odd hour.

This did not prevent him from apportioning hours to play. But at a given time, often self-imposed, he would break this off for the next activity: the library, household chores, reading, bicycling. He did everything with relish; what he could not abide was passivity and idleness. In these circumstances, parental guidance was particularly important. Alexander's dexterity in practical matters, the influence of Rostov's streets, the struggle for necessities—all this, in combination with the weaknesses of school guidance and widespread demoralization under Stalinism, might have turned the compulsive boy into an arrogant careerist or a skillful "operator."

But in contrast to the ideological zigzags of school, a reliable compass of ideas and attitudes could be found in the heritage of the intelligentsia. Free dissemination of ideas was already being steadfastly and purposefully suppressed in the 1920s, but the old intelligentsia's humanitarian and humanist ideals had not been entirely snuffed out, and a boy who had contact with them—and was predisposed to assimilate them—could uncover here the sense of direction and purpose he needed. Even the Silver Age, most of whose superb accomplishments had been branded "decadent" and were increasingly unavailable, still lived in the consciousness of its survivors. Solzhenitsyn's mother almost certainly belonged to the circle of those who remembered and admired, and this would explain much about his interests and development.

His father was almost certainly another anchor. Isai's death had a profound effect on the boy's development; his father remained a permanent symbol in his thoughts, perhaps even more commanding than it would have been had the living man supervised his upbringing. It was a symbol of innocence, passion, and pursuit of excellence—of a clean young life cut short before it fulfilled its promise. There was the romance of the young literature student going to war, of the manly discharge of battlefield duties, and of the love which surmounted wartime obstacles to accomplish a marriage at the front. Much later, it was partly in the wake of his father's philosophical devotions that Solzhenitsyn became a Tolstoyan writer in many senses. Like Tolstoy, he was to reveal psychological makeup through the portrayal of characters' reactions to historical situations. Like Tolstoy, he would set himself the task of illuminating the true, underlying forces that moved events in a period of time. And a Tolstoyan ethical code based on the primacy of individual conscience would pervade not only his public activities, but also his work.

That profound feelings of loss over his father's death persisted throughout the writer's life is demonstrated by Solzhenitsyn's laconic public statements about his childhood. In an important interview granted to Western newsmen in 1972, Solzhenitsyn singled out his memory of his father—as he emphasized, only through photographs and the stories of his mother and others—for special mention. He was obviously still pained that the three decorations that he had left from World War I—"which in my childhood were considered the mark of a dangerous criminal"—had to be buried by mother and son lest they be found in a search. Solzhenitsyn also mentioned that his father's grave in a city near Kislovodsk had been leveled by a tractor during the construction of a sports stadium.

> My mother . . . never married again, fearing possible sternness toward me by a stepfather. When I grew up and was able to judge, I came to the conclusion that this sacrifice had been unjustified: in my opinion, sternness encountered at an early age is ordinarily only helpful for a boy.

Here is unmistakable indication of longing for the source of external authority that he lacked, and that had to be found within himself. The desired authority might even be stern—for surovost, Solzhenitsyn's word, has a strong implication of welcome sternness, limited by and applied for the sake of justice. In this sense, he was to become his own father, limiting his boyhood pleasures, disciplining himself with uncommon exactitude, subjugating his entire life to a goal. If there is a central element in his personality, it is this severe self-discipline which sets standards at least as high as could be expected from the most demanding father. These standards no doubt contributed to his later strivings toward ethical maximalism as well as his perfectionism in writing. Moreover, a feeling of incompleteness stimulates some fatherless boys to compensation, which can manifest itself in greater self-assertion and independence. Such a young boy learns to fend for himself rather than await help—and insofar as this analysis pertains to Solzhenitsyn, the self-fathering was also decisive in the development of independence of mind.

From an early age his self-discipline and self-assertion fostered—a goal unusual for a young boy—the desire to write. He himself has remained puzzled by this visitation of purpose at an age usually dedicated to toys.

> A desire to write and an unconscious notion prompted by no one that for some reason I had to become a writer were aroused in me at a very early age—when I was nine or ten and could not possibly understand even what a writer was or for what purpose he wrote.

Alexander's teacher of Russian literature played some part in his "unconscious" incitement. It is easy to teach literature badly in any country at any time, but in the Russia of his school years the thrust of the syllabus was to a kind of vulgarized sociology designed to propagate Bolshevik ideas. Attention was focused on such considerations as what class interests Pushkin represented, the passages of Nekrasov that could be interpreted as foreshadowing the revolution, the extent to which Gorky reflected the struggle of the masses. Despite this obligatory approach, Alexander's teacher was one of those who managed to convey what she felt were the truer values of Russian literature. The entire class was stimulated; Alexander received the special encouragement that good pupils normally draw. For a young boy eager for achievement, literature would naturally have a special appeal. Despite the vulgarization of interpretation, the great works had not lost their attraction; their authors remained national heroes.

Still, Alexander's persistent desire to become a writer at the age of nine can only be called extraordinary. This kind of precocious urge to create is not uncommon among budding musicians, but much rarer in future men of letters. Forty years later, when he had completed the three major novels which established his reputation, perceptive critics noticed a parallel between their structure and that of several works of Thomas Mann. Mann, too, began to write "horribly early," and, as one of his characters observed, quickly felt himself "set apart, in a curious sort of opposition to the nice, regular people." It was a separation caused by "a gulf of ironic sensibility, of knowledge, skepticism, disagreement between you and the others"; and insofar as this gulf is essential to the process of observing and writing creatively, the young Alexander felt it too. The sensibility was another factor in his independence of mind—not wished for consciously, but seemingly fated. The impatient schoolboy began his life of writing.

IV

Emergence

IN LATE ADOLESCENCE AND EARLY MANHOOD, evidence accumulated of Solzhenitsyn's promise. It was not, however, the promise that he would become a major writer and, still less, the conscience of Russia. On the contrary, his achievements lay in areas that might well have got him voted "most likely to succeed" by his classmates—success being measured in terms of making one's way in the "real" world of the establishment and prestigious professions. For at the time of Solzhenitsyn's own graduations— from high school at the age of eighteen and the university at twenty-three —he seemed destined to triumph in terms of the extremely narrow standards of the Soviet establishment of those years.

That his endowments for this kind of success were exceptional had been clear in primary school; during his secondary education, the promise grew into virtual certainty. He had an unusual facility in the natural sciences that gave him a quick understanding of theory, methodology, and practice; what better gifts for a Russian child in the 1930s? Moreover, he chose to study mathematics at the university: another clear indication of success. Mathematics and physics offered the shortest route to a brilliant, safe, and—in all senses—rewarding career. The campaigns of contempt for "bourgeois" scientists and intellectuals that had lasted through most of the 1920s had by now been abandoned and, as so often in Soviet intellectual history, replaced by their opposites. Inculcation of respect, even awe, for the sciences based on mathematical methods ran through the 1930s.

The new campaign was inspired by Stalin himself, who considered mathematics, of which he was wholly ignorant, as the highest and most occult of all the sciences. Stalin's proudly proclaimed intellectual ambition was to make history an equally exact study. He saw to it that scientists were spurred not only by the prestige awarded them but also in more practical ways. Through a system of privileges and material rewards— unusually important in the context of the country's chronic consumer shortages—scientists were relieved of many of the everyday clothing and feeding cares of ordinary citizens. Exceptional students were offered financial encouragement to pursue scientific careers. Solzhenitsyn was one of the first beneficiaries of the latter plan.

He graduated from high school—with outstanding final grades—in 1936, and was accepted for the five-year course in physics and mathematics at Rostov University. The faculty included several excellent teachers of both pre- and postrevolutionary appointment, and they soon took notice of the newcomer with the manifestly original and incisive mind. In 1940, his high standing received impressive official recognition. Solzhenitsyn was awarded one of the first of the Stalin scholarships which were established throughout the country in that year. As was predictable from the name they bore, the scholarships were highly exclusive and intended to reward the highest achievement.

But these grants were not awarded on the strength of academic achievement alone. As with most American scholarships—but again, in a distinctly narrower sense—the recipient had to be an "all-around" student. In Russia, the prerequisite "extracurricular activities" all fell into one pattern, dictated by one interest and serving one cause: participation in the so-called social-community activities of the Young Communist League. Solzhenitsyn satisfied the requirement by editing his faculty's "wall news-paper." This one-page house organ, typed or handwritten and tacked to the wall of a central corridor in the faculty's quarters, was indication neither of literary talent nor of moral excellence. A collection of brief exhortations to study harder, denunciations of academic, moral, and political slackers, and tributes to revolutionary anniversaries and heroes, it represented the students' opinions and interests as the faculty's Party Committee liked to imagine them. No great attention, to put it mildly, was paid to it by anyone except the party propaganda secretary. Nevertheless, in addition to an outlet for energy, the editing of a wall newspaper was perhaps a display of willing political conformism—the only recorded one in Solzhenitsyn's life. It was also solid evidence that the local party organs considered him politically reliable.

Stalin scholarships were a kind of tap on the shoulder by the "selection board" of Soviet success. They opened all political and academic doors to their recipients upon completion of their studies. And while the honored students were still in the university, they were relieved of material cares. The stipend of five hundred rubles a month was over four times higher than that of students in the next category, and more than the earnings of most doctors and teachers. For the first time since Solzhenitsyn could remember, his household was blessed with relative plenty. His mother no longer needed to take on quite such a load of typing, and they could enjoy the luxuries of better food and summer trips.

Yet despite this, despite the obvious indications of accomplishment in all aspects of his university career, Solzhenitsyn was not satisfied simply to pursue it or its adult extension into prestige and relative wealth. For one thing, mathematics was a second choice. The "vague notion" of his childhood that he wanted to be a writer had by this time been transformed into a determination to make literature the kernel of his life's work. Mathematics was a child of necessity—the first, and, as it would turn out, the least formidable in a long series of detours from his chosen goal.

"I intended to pursue a literary education," Solzhenitsyn has written of his alternatives upon graduation from high school. "But Rostov could not provide the kind I wanted, and I could not go off to Moscow because of my mother's solitude and illness—as well as our modest means. Therefore I enrolled in the Rostov University mathematics department. I had considerable aptitude for mathematics, it came easily to me—but I did not feel it was my life's vocation."

But he was not to regret this choice of alternate profession. "My subsequent life showed, however," Solzhenitsyn stated elsewhere, "that without this profession I should not have had a chance to survive to this day [1968] and to write these autobiographical notes." Mathematics and the technologically oriented society's swelling demand for it rescued Solzhenitsyn "unfailingly during all the difficult periods" of the next two decades.

It served him well too because, although his second choice, he did not do a second-best job of it. By his early university years, he had become a somewhat compulsive perfectionist, driven by self-discipline to organize his daily schedules exactly and to work to the limits of his abilities at whatever he had undertaken. (Many years later, when reduced to bricklaying in a concentration camp, Solzhenitsyn never permitted himself to do shoddy work.) The traditional Russian approach was considerably more easygoing.

Solzhenitsyn even developed the habit of eating at a specific time, a minor but telling indication of character since most Russians not regulated by working hours tend to eat at the prompting of their appetites within broad limits for each meal. When the short period Solzhenitsyn had budgeted for his meals had elapsed, he returned to the library, while his fellow students chattered leisurely over their food. Solzhenitsyn often remained in the university library until late evening.

Literature took the lion's share of his time. Solzhenitsyn was writing steadily "throughout my young years," as he put it. None of his youthful work has been published; he now dismisses it as "much rubbish in various genres." Rubbish or not, the genres were indeed varied. Solzhenitsyn wrote short stories, the draft of a novel and dramas, together with a constant stream of poetry. The latter had a particular significance, for, although

Solzhenitsyn is not known as a poet, the art was much more for him than the youthful infatuation it is for many Russian students born of the intelligentsia. Throughout Solzhenitsyn's life, he has written poetry with greater regularity than prose. He developed a great ease at versification, and can write a page of verse in the time that many people require for a well-written business letter.

Very few published examples exist, but on the strength of these few it is clear that Solzhenitsyn has considerable poetic skill. A sense of "the right words in the right order," which Alexander Blok called the essence of poetry, is also striking in the strict and subtle rhythms of Solzhenitsyn's best prose. But although Solzhenitsyn was to call on his poetic talents during the hardest moments of his life, he refuses to regard himself as a poet; and since he allows only works he considers perfect to be published, only a handful of his closest friends see his verses. A request from a foreigner, to see a long poem incorporating reminiscences of his youth, for example, was rejected with vehemence, even though friends say it contains nothing politically or personally sensitive.

The habit of regular writing which Solzhenitsyn developed over a dozen formative years until the outbreak of war in 1941 was the product of purposeful self-training. But in his early manhood Solzhenitsyn felt that this was not enough—that he should undertake a formal study of literary traditions and crafts. In 1939, during his third year studying mathematics, he undertook a second—concurrent—university program in philology. In Russia, philology encompassed a study of literary works, history and criticism in addition to linguistics. For his own program, Solzhenitsyn enrolled in correspondence courses in I.F.L.I.—Moscow's celebrated Institute of Philosophy, Literature, and Linguistics. The institute provided a solid curriculum and professional guidance for Solzhenitsyn's home study, to be tested by examinations in Moscow twice a year.

I.F.L.I. was the most elite and prestigious humanities institute in the Soviet Union at that time. Even during the triumphant Stalinist dogmatism of the 1930s, its students were exposed to more honest scholarship and fewer distortions than elsewhere. An autobiographical character in a Solzhenitsyn play was to refer to the institute jokingly as a "fortress of free thought." Its relative academic freedom was probably partly protected by the enrollment there of many sons and daughters of Russia's rulers.

Precisely these liberal tendencies brought about I.F.L.I.'s disbandment in 1943. By that time Solzhenitsyn had completed only a year and a half of the five-year course. But he was not troubled by his failure to go further; on the contrary, he felt that too much literary sophistication might hinder self-expression. "Looking back now," Solzhenitsyn was to write in the late 1960s, "I have few regrets that I did not receive a literary education, as I do not consider it at all obligatory for a writer; sometimes it even puts him off course."

[This comment was surely made on the basis of his own experience. In his last years of study, he discovered that formal literary training neither facilitated nor improved his own writing. As he grew older, he became more dissatisfied with his youthful "rubbish." A period of difficulty set in: Solzhenitsyn now thinks it "ludicrous to recall," but at the time, he found it "difficult to discover subjects." "I had the urge to write," he says, "but . . . did not know what to write about." Solzhenitsyn attributes these early difficulties to "the paucity of my life experience."]

He has never been the kind of writer who creates material from his inner resources. Only after acquainting himself thoroughly with an aspect of life can he tell its story. Even a work not based directly on personal experience is grounded in voluminous and painstaking research. In comparison with more relaxed students of his intelligence, the intensity of Solzhenitsyn's intellectual pursuits no doubt narrowed his direct knowledge of people, as opposed to academic studies of them. In brief, literary training was not supplying what he sensed he lacked as a writer.

But Solzhenitsyn's difficulty in finding subjects can also be explained by what he was attempting to write. He tried to keep at least some of his early prose within the limits of officially acceptable style and subject matter. This can be inferred from his efforts to have his work evaluated and published. Through friends, he had access to Boris Lavrenyov, an author of romanticized heroic tragedies who had used his talent, obvious in the 1920s, to become a pillar of Stalin's literary establishment. Nevertheless, Lavrenyov still enjoyed some respect in literary and theatrical circles as one of the most effective, if not accurate, chroniclers of the civil war. He was to become Solzhenitsyn's first known professional literary adviser.

The contrast is drastic between Solzhenitsyn's mature style two decades later—the insistence on cool, realistic narration which determinedly avoids embellishments and "colorful" effects—and Lavrenyov's turbulence of language and emotions. But at the time, Lavrenyov's advice was apparently encouraging, for Solzhenitsyn went on to submit some of his finished writings for publication. It was a Russian tradition of some century and a half that most literary works first appeared not in book form, but in one of the "thick" literary magazines. Solzhenitsyn sent his pieces to one of the country's most important, Moscow's *Znamya*. There they were read by Konstantin Fedin, an even more august establishment litterateur. Almost thirty years later the same Fedin would be chairman of the Writers' Union, from which seat he would play an ignoble role in the suppression in Russia of some of Solzhenitsyn's most important fiction. He was not much kinder to the young unknown's early efforts, which *Znamya* rejected.

This early attempt at publication involved considerations inescapable to any Russian writer of the time, and perhaps least of all to a struggling young one. To seek publication meant accepting the limitations of an increasingly rigid literary doctrine. Subjects did exist that lent themselves to honest exploration within the state limit, but they were easy neither to conceive nor to develop. Solzhenitsyn's decision to send his efforts to *Znamya* probably implied that he was accommodating himself to the doctrine, which might well have been a cause of his difficulty in finding themes. The very mention to an editor of some of contemporary Russia's most urgent subjects would have been suicidal.

Solzhenitsyn's coming of age coincided with the Great Purge, the bloodiest years of modern Russian history. "Russia was writhing," wrote the great poet Anna Akhmatova, "guiltless under steel-shod jack-boots and the tires of Black Marias." In the wake of the show trials of Lenin's Old Guard, the makers of the revolution, the secret police shot over a million Soviet citizens outright and dispatched millions more to the killing cold and hunger of concentration camps. Most intelligent Russians were well aware of the horror that surrounded them, but tried to push it from their minds so as to maintain their sanity and concentrate on their own survival. Solzhenitsyn was one of the few who tried to understand, and his efforts to do so were the great secret of his intellectual life. Remarkably enough, he had been disturbed by developments even in adolescence, and the novelist Lydia Chukovskaya, a good friend and public defender of Solzhenitsyn, has written that "he solved the riddle of Stalin as a young man, earlier than others." Solzhenitsyn himself now tells his friends that he had begun to feel doubts about the Communist Party's infallibility even before 1937, when the purges raged to their insane peak.

The adulation of Stalin as an omniscient and omnipotent leader was particularly repugnant to Solzhenitsyn. This is made explicit by a Solzhenitsyn character who says that he most loathed in Stalin the "self-important and didactic tone of his pronouncements. He is quite certain that he is cleverer than any other Russian and that he simply makes us happy when he gives us a chance to admire him." Had there been nothing more sinister about Stalin than this coarse self-glorification, the independent and inquisitive young Solzhenitsyn would have harbored an aversion for him. Still, it was bloody 1937, when Solzhenitsyn was nineteen, that provided the "vital push," as he put it, to his thinking. He believed almost nothing of what he read about the trials and rationale of the purges, sensing that all the confessions were crude fabrications. He understood that the revolution, in which he then wholly believed, and his country, which he dearly loved, had careered agonizingly and incomprehensibly toward darkness.│

Gleb Nerzhin, the central character of *The First Circle*, is in many ways the most autobiographical character in all of Solzhenitsyn's novels. Solzhenitsyn's friends say that Nerzhin's reflections on the purges are a kind of digest of thoughts they have heard him express about himself.

He was only twelve when he opened the vast pages of *Izvestiya*, with which he could have covered himself from head to foot, and read the account of a trial of some engineer-wreckers. The boy disbelieved it straightaway. Gleb did not know why, couldn't grasp it in his mind, but he distinctly perceived that it was all a pack of lies. There were engineers in families he knew and he couldn't imagine these people wrecking rather than building.

And when he was thirteen and fourteen, Gleb did not dash outdoors when he'd done his homework, but sat down to read the newspapers. He knew the names and positions of party leaders, of Red Army commanders and of our ambassadors in every country and the foreign ambassadors in Moscow. He read all the speeches at party congresses as well as the memoirs of old Bolsheviks and each succeeding history of the party; several had come and gone, and they contained differences. . . .

Whether it was because his ear was still fresh or because he read more than was in the newspapers, he detected very clearly the falseness of the inordinate, breathless exaltation of one man, always that one. If he was all, did it mean that others were nothing? Out of sheer protest, Gleb could not enthuse over him.

Gleb was only in the ninth grade when, one December morning, he pushed his way to a newspaper display and read that Kirov had been assassinated. And suddenly for some reason, as in a piercing ray of light, it was clear to him that it had been Stalin and no one else who assassinated Kirov. Because only Stalin stood to gain by it. And he was seized by an aching loneliness: a crowd of grown men all around him, and they did not see this simple truth!

Then these same old Bolsheviks who'd been carrying through the whole of the revolution, who saw their lives only in relation to it, began disappearing into oblivion by the dozens and hundreds. Without tarrying until their arrest, some poisoned themselves in their flats; others hanged themselves at their country cottages. But most often, they allowed themselves to be arrested, appeared in court, and inexplicably repented—reviled themselves volubly with the foulest abuse and confessed to having worked for every foreign intelligence service on earth. This was so excessive, so crude, so beyond bounds that you had to be deaf as a doorpost not to hear the attendant lies. Could it be that people really didn't hear? Russian

writers who dared to derive their origins from Pushkin and Tolstoy
extolled the tyrant with dismally cloying panegyrics. . . .

For Gleb Nerzhin, a silent tocsin pealed throughout his youth—
and an ineradicable decision implanted itself within him: find out
and work out!

Solzhenitsyn had come to an early appreciation of the dangers of
political curiosity. He even felt a premonition that it might suck him into
prison. The suppression of his concern was not easy for him. He may have
made himself put it aside while writing the pieces he would submit for
publication—but as in Nerzhin's case, the inquisitive impulse was too
strong to remain hidden.

Just as he had tried to work out the true image of history earlier he
was now already trying to understand the primary causes of his country's
condition. Before entering the university in 1936, he had conceived what
he now calls "the principal project of my life." It was to be a series of
novels examining a sequence of cataclysmic events and movements in
which the key to contemporary Russia must lie: the collapse of the old
Russia and emergence of the new in the years of World War I and the
revolution which followed. The subject matter reflected a profound curiosity about the true origins of Soviet society—and also a continuing preoccupation with re-creating his absent father, for the epic was to be
centered about the young artillery officer's background and life, with some
episodes only loosely connected with the family, but others directly
depicting a man who is unmistakably drawn from Isai Solzhenitsyn.

Despite his youth, or perhaps because of it, Solzhenitsyn was not
daunted by the formidable task. With his usual quickness in decision,
planning, and execution, he embarked on the study of historical documents.
As early as the winter of 1937 he produced a description of the mid-1914
rout of the Russian armies in East Prussia—the first tangible event, as
Solzhenitsyn still sees it, in the disintegration of prerevolutionary Russian
society. A giant interruption intervened, during which Solzhenitsyn was
first prevented from writing and then felt he must write about the interruption and its causes. But thirty-three years after his first efforts in 1937
—as soon as the burden of his own autobiographical material had been
transferred to paper—he would at last complete the introductory novel in
this most important project of his life.

In addition to mathematics, literature, politics, and an extracurricular
study of German, Solzhenitsyn was engaged in an independent survey of
philosophy. The origins of European thought—of the complex of ideas
that dominated his own thoughts and attitudes—interested him particu-

larly, and he acquired a respectable first-hand acquaintance with the philosophers of classical antiquity. He also tried to penetrate to the inner core of the Marxism that dominated his country. He went to the philosophers who had inspired Marx, Engels, and Lenin, reading Hegel, the father of modern dialectics, and the French utopian socialists, the fathers of modern egalitarianism. A volume of Hegel even accompanied him and his bicycle on a teen-age summer holiday.

The extent of his philosophical interests had also to be masked. Of course I.F.L.I. students were meant to study philosophy—but not to allow their reading to undermine the faith required of all: that Stalin's works embodied the final truth on all philosophical questions. Stalinist teachers observed their students carefully, but Solzhenitsyn learned not to betray his appetite for genuine inquiry.

Apart from mathematics, the only interest that allowed him to express a full and open enthusiasm was the theater, and for a time he seriously considered an acting career. This might offer a kind of middle ground between the abstract dryness of mathematics and the inherent dangers of chronicling his brutal times.

Like most Russian provincial cities of its size, Rostov enjoyed a considerable theatrical life, which included several repertory drama companies and an opera house. Just as Solzhenitsyn was graduating from high school, a star of unusual magnitude was added. Yury Zavadsky, one of the best-known postrevolutionary actors and directors, had been exiled from Moscow for an ideological *faux pas*, but his relatively mild punishment allowed him to continue working at his profession in Rostov. He founded a theatrical studio there, and Solzhenitsyn became associated with it. Solzhenitsyn had already acted in school productions and found the time to become stage-struck. Before deciding to enter Rostov University, he applied for admission to Zavadsky's studio.

The studio was recognized as a full-fledged drama college with university-equivalent degrees. Competition for places was severe: the theater was then an outlet and passion for many young Russians. But Solzhenitsyn passed the rigorous admission tests, only to fail on a technicality. The doctors who screened successful candidates discovered a chronic throat catarrh, making his vocal chords unequal to the steady strain of a stage career.

Solzhenitsyn's disappointment was great; to this day, the theater has remained his second passion, after literature. As in youth, he still tends to see life in terms of stage confrontations in an endless psychological and historical drama, and, when released from imprisonment, his first plan was to shape his concentration camp experiences for the theater. Nor has he himself entirely abandoned all forms of acting. He mimics others with gusto and, more seriously, enjoys reading his own works before audiences. This he does with great intensity, pronouncing each consonant meticulously. His voice falls just below the lower limits of melodrama virtually obligatory when reading aloud in Russia; but its most surprising quality is a youthful intensity that makes him seem very human. However, the authorities now prevent him from reading to public audiences. Significantly, Solzhenitsyn's protests against mistreatment have singled out this deprivation for especial, and noticeably bitter, mention.

In retrospect, Solzhenitsyn's broad range of youthful intellectual pursuits seem more than a jumble of competing activities. Two overriding interests had taken hold of the young man by the time his five university years were drawing to their end, and his old compulsion to drive himself now centered on them. The first was to try to understand the motives of human behavior. Solzhenitsyn explored them personally in a variety of ways open to him: transforming himself into others through acting, examining characters and situations in his writing, and searching, by way of his risky political interest, for the causes of the powerful spasm that seized Russia in his time. Solzhenitsyn's second interest was the study of human thought. While by no means exhaustive, his knowledge of philosophy gave him a rare insight for one of his generation in his land. The fascination of mathematics was its exposure of thought processes in their most abstract and pure forms, free of the interference of emotion-laden subjects.

In both his paramount interests, Solzhenitsyn was moved by a deeper urge: to discover, through his own personal inquiry, the original causes of social developments and individual behavior. The passion which fired this quest was described in a poem by Boris Pasternak, a Russian writer whose own search led him beyond the confines of established Soviet faith.

> I want to push through
> To the very essence of everything:
> Working, searching for my way,
> And in the heart's jumbles;
>
> Straight to the core of days gone by,
> To what made them,
> To the foundations, to the roots,
> The heart of the matter.
>
> Always grasping the thread
> Of lives and events,
> Living, thinking, feeling, loving,
> Attaining the discoveries . . .

The lines apply in all their implications, for Solzhenitsyn's intellectual pursuits did not immunize him to personal aspects of his quest. But, at all times, this quest was far more important to him than the outward success which he took in his stride, and which casual acquaintances took to be the whole of him.

V

Friends and Influences

THE CLOISTERED WORKING HABITS THAT Solzhenitsyn developed as a schoolboy were never accompanied by an urge to seclude himself wholly from
his classmates or adults. Much as he relished his intellectual awakening in
the solitude of his room and the library, he was far from a hermit.
Throughout his life, Solzhenitsyn's forceful personality attracted a circle
of friends and admirers. As a teen-ager in Rostov he was welcome in the
homes of the local intelligentsia. Parents encouraged their children to
enjoy his company, and encouraged Solzhenitsyn himself to borrow their
books. Naturally, however, his most important relationships were with his
contemporaries. Two friendships were to play strong roles in his life,
filling adult decades with sharp twists and ironic consequences.

Solzhenitsyn's last school years were spent with a small group of friends,
all "young intellectuals" with a particular attraction for literature. The
school's literature teacher, who was not much older than her pupils, acted
as a kind patroness for the inner core, which numbered four or five boys
and girls. Of this group, Solzhenitsyn was especially close with a boy
his own age, whom we will call "X." He and Solzhenitsyn were classmates
in school, after which the former, too, went on to Rostov University and
completed his studies at the adjoining Faculty of Chemistry. The relationship of the two young men was something more than that of boyhood
playmates turned university chums. Common intellectual and philosophical interests deepened thir attachment, and the knowledge that
aspects of their curiosity had to be cloaked gave them the kind of trust
in and appreciation of each other that is sometimes harder to achieve in
more open societies.

Solzhenitsyn and X spent some of their summer holidays together, as
well as part of most days in Rostov. X shared Solzhenitsyn's vigor, and the
virtual nonexistence of even the most primitive tourist facilities did not
deter the two from exploring the country. After earlier summer trips to

the countryside by bicycle, the two set out in a small rowboat in the summer of 1939 and made their way several hundred kilometers down the Volga to Stalingrad.

Even for someone with little knowledge of Russia and no desire to write about it, a trip along the Volga is an intensely moving experience. Day after day, the two young students were exposed to "Russian" scenery, a flat expanse which is both homely and sublime, and by conveying something ageless and infinite, induces moods and questions explored by the best of Russian literature. This was one of Solzhenitsyn's earliest extended encounters with the Russian heartland, as opposed to the Caucasian Kislovodsk and Cossack Rostov. Its influence on him was to be demonstrated throughout his life.

From the little wooden boat, the two friends savored the landscapes and their irrepressible associations. At night they camped on the banks or stayed in nearby villages: hotels were unavailable, even if they had been able to afford them. And although ramshackle, the villages held a distinct fascination: the umber log cabins, sagging with years and neglect, were startlingly unlike the whitewashed adobe of Cossack settlements near Rostov.

Solzhenitsyn devoured the new impressions. He had already acquired his lifelong hobby, photography. To pursue it in prewar Russia required great determination: cameras and all ancillary equipment were expensive and very hard to find, and, in the absence of processing laboratories, the photographer was invariably his own darkroom technician. Yet Solzhenitsyn allotted some of his carefully rationed time to surmounting these difficulties. His interest in photography was partially as an aid to memory, for he was eager to fix shapes, shades, landscapes, and faces in his mind's eye. Until this day his walls are covered with his own photographs, often of landscapes and Russian landmarks, like the disused churches overlooking the Volga's melancholy banks and other striking scenes which he photographed that summer.

Solzhenitsyn listened carefully as well as looked. A creative freshness in the use of the Russian language would become a principal resource of his craft, and he was already aware of the potential of regional, social, and phonetic variations in speech as a literary instrument. Voyaging down the Volga, Solzhenitsyn heard the gradual change from the closed northern "o" to the broad southern "ah" as well as the Volga fishermen's smattering of odd ancient words. His observations sharpened a keen sensitivity to language.

But there was almost certainly a less idyllic side to the Volga trip. Collectivization of agriculture was less than ten years old; hardly a village did not show its ravages, in the form of abandoned houses and fields succumbing to scrub. The two friends could hardly fail to notice that most farms suffered from the sullen indifference of their impressed workers. And they probably heard mutters from some of the farmers: hints of state-induced famine, police violence, and the sudden, seemingly senseless destruction of an age-old way of life. Or perhaps laments of lonely grandmothers whose children had been deported thousands of miles in keeping with the policy to "destroy" so-called rich farmers "as a class."

Mere traveling companions might have hesitated to listen to farmers' tales of misery. To take notice of anything that cast doubt on the peasantry's absolute well-being in their collective farms was virtually indulging in "anti-Soviet propaganda." But the two young men "told each other everything," as one of Solzhenitsyn's friends puts it now. Observant and intelligent, X came from a background similar to Solzhenitsyn's and had read much of the same literature and philosophy. The classmates not only shared a deep affection for Russia but also, by now, a conviction that it had recently lurched toward deep unhappiness. They knew that they were committing a crime in discussing the poverty of Stalin's thought and the plight of the peasantry. Solzhenitsyn later said that his path to barbed wire began with school-bench conversations with X. But the shared danger only cemented the relationship.

Friendships of this kind were less rare among young people than among their parents. Frightened nearly to delirium by Stalin's indiscriminate terror, many older people simply stopped talking to one another. Lifelong friendships, even between members of a close-knit family, were abruptly terminated. But some adolescents growing up in the Stalinist insanity of sudden and permanent disappearances were immunized against it, as are islanders to fear of tidal waves. Precautions against earthquakes must be taken, but one tries not to be dominated by eternal panic. Solzhenitsyn and X belonged to the small but discernible category who, after permanent, early exposure to terror, introduced a new strain into the Soviet species. The young Soviet crusaders for human rights who surfaced in the 1960s also belong to this strain. Full appreciation of the dangers they face does not paralyze their brains, tongues, or hands.

The second important relationship of Solzhenitsyn's youth was with his future wife, Natalya Alekseyevna Reshetovskaya. They met at Rostov University, where she, like X, was studying chemistry. She was to live thirty years with Solzhenitsyn—not "with" him in the ordinary sense, however, for they were physically separated most of this time. During some of his hardest years, she sacrificed and endured much for him.

In the beginning, however, their relationship was as ordinary and extraordinary as any first love between two intelligent students. Soon after their meeting on a university stairway, Natasha became Alexander's "steady," although this suggests something too formal and stylized for the social pattern of Russian students. A year or two of seeing each other in the course of their ordinary university day led easily to marriage. Perhaps prompted by a youthful penchant for mystery, they made the ceremony their secret, registering their marriage alone one day in the spring of 1940. There was no need for concealment from either family; both, according to Solzhenitsyn's friends, could only have been pleased. For Solzhenitsyn had married a highly attractive girl next door.

Natalya Reshetovskaya was twenty years old that spring, Solzhenitsyn's junior by a year. She was born in Novocherkassk, a small Cossack town some thirty miles northeast of Rostov. The family had been quite prosperous before the revolution, but this was ancient history to the young daughter. Like Solzhenitsyn, she never knew her father, a young, highly skilled engineer who was killed during the civil war. She was raised by her mother and her mother's three unmarried sisters, the household having moved to Rostov. Like Solzhenitsyn's mother, Natalya's family belonged to the old intelligentsia. However, music rather than literature was the Reshetovskys' passion. Natalya studied the piano from early childhood and pursued her secondary education in Rostov's School of Music. Although she abandoned thoughts of going on to the conservatory and a music career in favor of the university, she was never to lose her love for the piano.

Natalya was a happy extrovert who took pleasure in the company of friends and provoked pleasure with her conviviality. She had chestnut hair, large gray eyes, a roundish, full-lipped face—but more than any handsomeness it was her charm and cheerful energy that attracted people to her. Her self-assured expression indicated that she "knew what she was worth," as the Russians say—not as a flirt, but a girl who could not help but please. Although chemistry was a second choice to music, she was an excellent student, obviously able to adapt herself to an orderly discipline. Throughout her life, she was to retain a strong sense of independence, the product of her individualistic character and the traditions of the intelligentsia. This was symbolized by her decision to keep her own surname when she married Solzhenitsyn (although this is far more common in Soviet Russia than in the West).

Reshetovskaya did not seek an easy life nor an easy marriage. The university years were enough to convince her that Solzhenitsyn would not sacrifice his self-discipline or intellectual drive for a remunerative career; nor his will power, since he had adhered to his rigid schedules throughout their courtship. When the hour struck, Solzhenitsyn would leave her for his next activity. The young bride entered marriage with open eyes—and regretted nothing, for in the eighteen odd months before the war suspended it, the union was happy.

Reshetovskaya shared some of Solzhenitsyn's trips from Rostov. Since

1939, he had been traveling twice yearly to Moscow for his I.F.L.I. examinations. They spent time there with Professor Valentin Turkin, Reshetovskaya's relative and one of the most distinguished Russian film critics, who pioneered the study of cinema as an art form. Solzhenitsyn learned his way around Moscow and around the Turkin library, which, together with the professor's erudition, made a strong impression on him.

But much as he enjoyed these visits to cosmopolitan Moscow, rural Russia moved Solzhenitsyn more during his travels with Reshetovskaya. In the summer of 1940, the young couple took a brief honeymoon that was to exert an enduring influence on him.

They traveled to Tarusa, a picturesque settlement on the high bank of the Oka River some eighty miles south of Moscow. For almost a century, artists and writers had favored the small town as a kind of retreat. The landscapist Vasily Polenov did some of his well-known work here: scenes of fields surrounded by birch groves and sad, serene rivers. Later, Tarusa attracted twentieth-century writers as different as the passionate Marina Tsvetayeva and the subdued Konstantin Paustovsky. Solzhenitsyn and Reshetovskaya did not seek acquaintances among the artistic colony, however, except to visit Reshetovskaya's uncle, a Moscow professor enjoying his holiday. They rented a room near him and stayed a month.

No startling revelations came to Solzhenitsyn during the course of it, but Tarusa's overwhelming "Russianness" became one of those crystallizing experiences that change an artist's life. As on the Volga the previous summer, Solzhenitsyn felt not only an evocation of Russian "secrets" in the countryside, but a hint that the voice of his prose lay somewhere here: that it must somehow be related to Tarusa's humble yet lyric aura. As he put it, he "discovered for myself the only stretch of land where I could become not a writer in general, but a Russian writer."

The discovery was provoked by several observations. First, central Russia provided what he called the right "linguistic environment." In the speech of the natives he found an artless, unself-conscious elegance that opened new facets of the language to a careful listener: unsophisticated sophistication might stimulate his own art. Learning to use language "from the people" rather than from other writers was an old Russian tradition: Pushkin had called upon his colleagues to undertake linguistic apprenticeship "with Moscow's street vendors." In Tarusa, Solzhenitsyn understood.

Central Russia also provided what he called the right "natural surroundings." The sights and sounds of daily life were a constant reminder of Russia's distinct identity. Unlike Dostoyevsky and others, Solzhenitsyn has never glorified Russia's uniqueness or "mission"; but he does feel that a writer must deal primarily with national experience, bounded by his own people's culture, history, and attitudes. A writer, therefore, must plumb national life with all of his senses—but not in Rostov.

Perhaps Rostov was too southern for Solzhenitsyn. It lacked the violent contrast between summer and winter so essential to central Russian life. It was probably also too heterogeneous linguistically. Rostov's cosmopolitanism sharpened the sense of national differences, but dulled the precision of one's own tongue. Moreover, the southern trading port was too removed from the village, which Solzhenitsyn felt was the wellspring of Russian life. Rostov was certainly colorful; its rough waterfront life, multilingual slums, and bands of bold and witty thieves provided an abundance of material for the kind of boisterous, imaginative tale that Isaac Babel told of his native Odessa. But Solzhenitsyn was no Babel. However amusing or brilliant, color for color's sake did not interest him. His goal was to grapple with the pith of Russian life at the depth of the great nineteenth-century Russian novelists. He was now convinced that he must eventually leave his native city in order to absorb the environment they had known.

Nevertheless, it was to Rostov and his mother, ill with tuberculosis and rapidly weakening, that Solzhenitsyn had to return after the honeymon. He and Reshetovskaya were about to enter their final year of university.

The young mathematician graduated in June 1941. His academic excellence would have secured him a postgraduate scholarship as a matter of course, but mathematics would then have consumed the bulk of his time. No doubt to his professors' disappointment, he refused, arranging instead to teach physics in a small Cossack town called Morozovsk some hundred miles from Rostov and his ill mother. The sciences were now only a means of support while writing. Reshetovskaya was taken as a chemistry teacher by the local school, and the couple considered moving to Moscow in the near future to enable Solzhenitsyn to complete his I.F.L.I. degree as a full-time student.

But these plans came to nothing. Solzhenitsyn's formal education ended that summer, and in a way which left him with a lasting feeling that his knowledge, especially his literary horizons, was limited. "My reading consists mainly of what I had time to build up in my youth," he has written. "I know Russian literature tolerably well, but of world literature I've read only the greatest names of the preceding centuries."

Solzhenitsyn's studies were cut short by the event that changed the plans of virtually all Soviet citizens. On June 22, the country was plunged into war.

VI

War

HARDLY A RUSSIAN WAS NOT SEVERELY affected by the almost four years of privation and bloodshed that followed June 22. Solzhenitsyn was not suited to be one of the exceptions. "The validity of war's age-old law was inexorable," he later observed. "Although people did not elect to go to the front, all the keenest and best people found their way there." Despite its ring of front-line soldier's pride, this statement was well founded, as in any country struggling for survival.

Not called up until October 1941, Solzhenitsyn himself was still a civilian during the early Russian debacles which delivered the Wehrmacht swiftly to the outskirts of Moscow. Over a thousand miles of front, from Leningrad to the southern Ukraine, Russian losses during the first months of the war were phenomenal: the best estimates speak of some three million military casualties alone. Solzhenitsyn was lucky to miss these crushing routs.

But at first he cursed his luck. He was drafted from Morozovsk, and because of what he has called, without elaboration, "restrictions due to health," was assigned to a unit of horse transport. But since the young Rostov intellectual could not ride he was appointed, together with other sick, elderly, and otherwise not fully fit Cossacks, to groom ninety horses. The intelligence, pride, and keen ambition of an autobiographical hero were subjected to just this trial in *The First Circle*.

> The war broke out and Nerzhin found himself in a horse transport unit. Clumsy, choking with humiliation, he chased all over the pasture after the horses to bridle them or jump on their backs. He did not know how to ride, how to set up a harness, how to handle the hay with a pitchfork; and even a nail never failed to double up under his hammer, as if in belly laughter over his poor workmanship.

For months Stalin scholar Solzhenitsyn did his duty as a stable boy. His irritation was compounded by the nature of his regiment: he was not only a groom, not only far from the front, but also in a transport unit rather than the cavalry proper. Horse transport was regarded as the army's lowest branch. In request after request to his commanding officers, Solzhenitsyn pointed out that his mathematical background suited him for artillery service at the front. He objected to the illogicality as well as the unpleasantness of shoveling manure. Despite the hard work, it was a soft job by the standards of the Russian Army during war. And safe. But Solzhenitsyn preferred action to safety. Besides, the waste of a trained mathematician to the war effort affronted his rationality.

The stubborn rejection of stable duty brought another facet of his character into clear relief: a compulsion to explore whatever he was engaged in—in this case war—to its outer limits and fullest depths. This trait would resurface often in prison and in struggles with the Soviet bureaucracy. Several times, Solzhenitsyn was to expose himself to mortal danger for the sake of gaining experience, as if still combating the youthful frustration of having too little to write about.

Solzhenitsyn never acted recklessly in these adventures, but with a full and sober understanding of the forthcoming dangers. If examined in isolation his determination to test himself in this way might be seen as a self-destructive urge—although, on the other hand, Solzhenitsyn has a consummate talent in the art of survival, and, having put himself in danger, used all his intelligence, doggedness, and energy to ensure his self-preservation. Both an urge for self-destruction and great skill in self-preservation can of course reside within the same psyche, if in fact these considerations apply to Solzhenitsyn's compulsion to *find out* and to acquire insights for writing. One need not play with death, of course, to become a great writer. But one cannot tell oneself "I know"; one cannot feel he has conquered.

In mid-1942, Private Solzhenitsyn's requests for transfer to the front reached a former front-line officer in his unit. Recognizing Solzhenitsyn's keenness and potential at last, he arranged orders for the stable boy to begin a four-month training course in artillery. Solzhenitsyn's agile mind and facility in applying mathematics to battle problems were noticed early in this training, and he became as outstanding an artillery student as he had been at the university.

But he was never a docile subordinate, as demonstrated by his behavior while still in training. Partly in the pursuit of knowledge, partly to twist the tiger's tail, he would ask his teachers questions about mathematical ballistics problems which he knew them unable to answer. Had his commanding officer been angered, the student might have been

reduced unceremoniously to the ranks. But his superiors were more
impressed than irritated and upon graduation gave him orders for further
training in one of the artillery's most intellectually demanding branches:
the new science of sound-ranging reconnaissance.

⌊His supplementary course was given in Gorky, a major city on the
Volga. The relatively short trip there took two weeks, during which
Solzhenitsyn observed the Russian rear as a wartime traveler. As the
length of the trip indicated, the transportation system was in chaos; the
country in general, much of whose most-developed territory already lay
in German hands, was in the same state. Masses of hungry refugees were
shunted from place to random place in wretchedly packed freight trains.
Yet amid this mammoth disarray, the secret police performed with their
usual precision and well-financed ruthlessness. Formalities of identity
papers and travel permits were adhered to with unrelenting severity.
N.K.V.D. teams cast their nets into the boiling human sea, dragged up the
unfortunates who could not prove convincingly who they were and what
right they had to be where they were, and dispatched their catches to
concentration camps. Solzhenitsyn was appalled, and his short story "An
Incident at Krechetovka Station"—based on an episode told him by a
friend who also traveled at that time—is a gruesome reminder of what
Stalinists did to their own people in the rear, while Hitlerites were
ravaging the tens of millions under their occupation.

⌊Solzhenitsyn left Gorky a highly skilled artillery specialist, and followed
his orders to what was called the Orel Grouping of the Central Front.
"I was made a commander of an instrumental reconnaissance battery,"
he has written, "and throughout 1943, 1944, and early 1945, I was constantly at the front line with my battery, marching from the town of Orel
to Germany." His own statement about his role in the fighting is limited
to these bare facts. To establish the scale of the death and destruction to
which he was exposed, however, little new information is needed; both
have been described by many historians and survivors. From Orel to the
German border was almost a thousand miles, a village-by-village advance
that included some of the bloodiest fighting in the history of war. By
the time Solzhenitsyn joined the front, the Soviet Army was far better
supplied and commanded than at the war's outbreak, but the Wehrmacht
was often still superior in equipment and matériel. The general Soviet
counteroffensive which began on Solzhenitsyn's battlefront in the summer
of 1943 has been called the "military turning point" of the war, as opposed
to the psychological turning point of Stalingrad the previous winter; these
great battles "in the very heart of Russia," wrote a military historian,
caused "a concentrated carnage within a small area more terrible than
had yet been seen." After the massive victories of 1943, Solzhenitsyn

remained in the thick of the fighting as his unit moved westward toward Germany.

Official documents about Solzhenitsyn's war record confirm his steady competence under the heaviest fire. "From the records of Solzhenitsyn's battle activities and the report by Captain Melnikov," one report reads, "it is clear that from 1942 until his arrest, i.e., until February 1945, Solzhenitsyn remained permanently on the fronts of the Great Patriotic War, fought courageously for his country, repeatedly displayed personal heroism, and, by his example, inspired the personnel of the military unit of which he was in charge. In terms of discipline and merit on the battlefield, Solzhenitsyn's unit was the best in his subdivision."

This was written many years after the war, but Solzhenitsyn's coolness in battle was also fully appreciated at the time. One of his two decorations, the Order of the Red Star, was sometimes distributed rather routinely. But the second, the Order of the Patriotic War, was awarded only for the highest personal bravery. Solzhenitsyn's valor and military distinction were also attested to by his rapid advance in rank. By 1945, he had been promoted to the rank of captain, equivalent of a British or American major, and, were he a party member, he might well have reached the rank of colonel.

Many honest, decent men did join the party during the war to associate themselves with what was (for some, *faute de mieux*) the nation's leadership in the struggle for survival. But Solzhenitsyn could not commit himself to this act in naïve enthusiasm; he already knew and felt too much. Most good officers were asked to join; as an outstanding one, Solzhenitsyn was pressed more than once. But he managed to avoid applying without explicitly rejecting the offer, a feat of considerable delicacy. It was not only his maturing mistrust of the party's "infallibility" that kept him away; he had a particular distaste for the party rituals of swearing allegiance, learning party rules by rote, and reciting key phrases in a kind of mumbo-jumbo. He was not a joiner.

Solzhenitsyn has written very little that draws on his years at the front, and seldom reminisces about them to friends. Subsequent "adventures" seem to have pushed the war to a lower priority as a literary subject. Yet he might easily have written half a dozen "safe" heroic novels on the basis of his own battle experience. His reconnaissance missions put him in the most exposed forward positions, in close and constant contact with the enemy. By the middle of the war, Soviet artillery—"the god of war," as Stalin called it—was massive in quantity and punishing in performance; its sheer fire power was responsible for many Russian victories, on Solzhenitsyn's front and elsewhere. But the artillery's auxiliary services, including sound-ranging reconnaissance, were markedly inferior to those of the major combatant nations. Since the Soviet Army did not introduce radar until the very end of the war, sound ranging remained one of the principal methods of pinpointing enemy firing positions. Battery commanders had to place their equipment in the best position for intercepting the sound of enemy guns—often in no man's land, forward of the Soviet advance positions. The risks were great and casualty rates high. Solzhenitsyn has mentioned to close friends that he faced seemingly inevitable death or capture more than once.

⌊Solzhenitsyn knew what he was fighting for; the freeing of Russian soil from Nazi occupation was a goal hardly anyone contested. Yet much about the Soviet Army troubled him. Loyal and responsible officers fought under severe legal and psychological pressures from their own superiors, including the threat of death for failure. Solzhenitsyn found this intimidation unnecessary, insulting, and unproductive, adding, as it did, to officers' nervousness in danger and impairing their judgment⌋

In other words, the rigidity and crude shortsightedness of Stalin's society found their places in the Army too. Apart from police surveillance and the practice of encouraging performance by threat, it was the Army's vast inequality that most fed Solzhenitsyn's developing social consciousness. After facing the same dangers in battle, officers and soldiers separated—the former to enjoy relatively extravagant privileges. To Solzhenitsyn, reared in an egalitarian ideology and sympathetic with at least this portion of its tenets, this brought shame. One of his heroes describes the social disparity from the plebs'—that is, soldiers'—point of view, pointedly reminding his listener that it was then called the "Workers' and Peasants' Army."

> The section commander got twenty rubles a month, but the platoon commander got six hundred—understand? And the officers got extra rations at the front: biscuits, butter, tinned food. And hid from us when they ate it—understand? Because they were ashamed.

Stopping short of incurring wrath for his nonconformism, Solzhenitsyn did what he could to mitigate inequality in his own unit. The strength of his personality allowed him to maintain democratic and friendly relations with his soldiers without sacrificing—indeed, only enhancing—his authority. His own sergeant, an unsophisticated but intelligent man from a well-known provincial city, harbored none of the bitterness of the quote above; on the contrary, twenty-five years later he remained Solzhenitsyn's devoted friend. Throughout their long war together, he and Solzhenitsyn developed a mutual confidence unusual between an officer and an enlisted man in the Soviet Army.

Eyebrows were certainly raised in headquarters over the curious arrangements in Solzhenitsyn's unit, reflected by his soldiers' use of the familiar second person singular to him when their personal relationship warranted. But the young officer was forgiven certain eccentricities for his value in the front line. Known as a man to rely on in action, he had all the makings of superior military leadership: an ability to recognize primary needs and goals quickly and devise realistic and orderly ways of satisfying the one and achieving the other; and the instincts to size up any situation swiftly and take command of it, as he was always in command of himself. Yet for all his military qualities he would have been held back as a professional soldier by his persistent individualism—especially by his frequent rejection of the pleasures of the officers' mess.

In an army where vodka consumption was second only to battlefield courage as a mark of valor, Solzhenitsyn stubbornly refused to drink. This was enough to make him an object of curiosity—sometimes even of suspicion. Nor did he play cards or, ordinarily, participate in the improvised postbattle feasts that were the principal release of most of his fellow officers. On top of this, he was often seen with one of the largish collection of books that accompanied him, or scribbling on a pad—he was sketching characters and plots and outlining thoughts—during free moments. In short, he was that Russian "white crow." Solzhenitsyn adapted his habits and convictions to the Army only insofar as his duty required, and pursued his old personal goals of intellectual inquiry and fruitful use of time as much as possible. Eventually, most of his colleagues understood and respected his individuality.

In the summer of 1944, Solzhenitsyn's unit had fought through the marshes of Belorussia into Poland, and his own luck held. He was alive and well and—remarkably—enjoyed a visit by his wife at the front. Because of wartime travel conditions, visits to the front were extremely difficult, even if relatives risked violating the strict prohibition against them. But Natalya Reshetovskaya managed to work her way through. After Solzhenitsyn was conscripted, she had returned from the Cossack village to Rostov—but as the German armies raced there, was evacuated to Central Asia. When Rostov was liberated by the Red Army, Reshetovskaya returned. Now she was no longer thousands of miles from Solzhenitsyn as she had been in Central Asia, but a mere few hundred kilometers from the Dnieper's western bank, to which his unit had just crossed. In the war-ravaged territory, the lack of civilian transportation was matched by the multiplicity of control posts designed to stop just such escapades as Reshetovskaya's. Yet she produced ruses and stratagems that took her to Solzhenitsyn's headquarters.

A yellowing snapshot taken during the visit has overtones of a Victorian romance. In his smart officer's uniform with the Chinese collar, Solzhenitsyn's self-confidence and good looks are matched by the grace of Reshetovskaya in a longish skirt. They are seated on a fallen log in a wood. In one of his rare lyrical passages, Solzhenitsyn describes a similar visit to his autobiographical hero as he fights across Belorussia.

> Oh women! . . . She made her way to him to the very front, to the bridgehead across the Dnieper. She had forged army papers and wore a man's military tunic that was too loose for her; and field security had constantly interrogated and searched her. She had come through all this to stay with her husband until the end of the war if she could—to die herself if he were killed or survive if he did.
>
> On the bridgehead—lethal only recently, but overgrown with carefree grass in this lull—they snatched back a few short days of their severed happiness. But the armies roused themselves and set out in an offensive; and Nadya had to travel home. Again in the clumsy tunic with the same forged army papers. A one-and-a-half-tonner drove her down a swathe cutting through the forest, and she kept waving and waving to him from the back of the truck.

This was more than good luck; it was to be Solzhenitsyn's last short spell of full happiness in decades. "Who could have told them," Solzhenitsyn writes of Nerzhin and Nadya, "that their separation not only wouldn't end with the war, but was barely beginning?"

VII

Arrest

THE SECOND BELORUSSIAN ARMY GROUP FOUGHT across the German frontier into East Prussia in mid-January 1945. Apart from a brief foray the previous autumn, these were the first Russian soldiers on German soil. Although the earlier thrust had been repulsed by the Germans in fierce battle, the Soviet forces, joined by the Third Belorussian and First Baltic Army Groups, now smashed relentlessly forward. By late January, Soviet detachments had reached the outskirts of Koenigsberg. The Third Reich's collapse was not only certain, but almost in sight.

The reconnaissance mission of Solzhenitsyn's battery made it among the early units over the border—Solzhenitsyn's first and last visit abroad. The war had brought incalculable cost and carnage to Russia: twenty million lives, military and civilian—roughly a tenth of the population—is the generally accepted figure. But within this ghastly context, it had been a good war for Solzhenitsyn.

Just turned twenty-six and a captain in rank, he was recognized by his superiors as a good officer admired devotedly by his subordinates. He had been decorated for high distinction. Most important, he had been lucky on the battlefield. Many of his men had died and his sergeant had been wounded more than once while standing beside him. Solzhenitsyn remained unscathed.

The single serious wound which Solzhenitsyn sustained during those years was not on the battlefield. His mother had died during the previous year—not one of the war's millions of civilian casualties but, at the age of forty-nine, from long-standing tuberculosis, exacerbated by her years of overwork. Buried in Rostov, her grave was to remain unseen by Solzhenitsyn for twelve years, as he wistfully told a journalist. But in 1944, he had no inkling of that distress.

And in contrast to many intellectuals, Solzhenitsyn was unshattered by the special horrors on both sides of the anti-Hitler war. He saw and registered them clearly, but they interfered neither with his equilibrium nor with his military responsibilities. Moreover, he enjoyed that aspect of the front line which moves most men in retrospect: the intense comradeship born of sharing severe hardships and dangers. In a story written almost twenty years after the war, Solzhenitsyn's nostalgia had the ring of a veterans' meeting, and he spoke of tears welling to his eyes when he visited a "depressing" battlefield near a forest where he himself had fought.

> How splendid they were, those friends of wartime days. The spirit that kept us going, our hopes, even that selfless friendship of ours —it has all vanished like smoke. . . .

Solzhenitsyn had not only remained unhurt during his twenty-six uninterrupted months at the front, but in a certain sense had done well for himself. There is even evidence that he later felt some contempt for himself as a young captain who managed to achieve a measure of personal comfort—a greatcoat of fur and transport by personal car—despite the horrors before his eyes. Forcing its way into East Prussia in February, his battery encountered streams of refugees in various states of misery, compared to which he was strong, warm, well fed, and steady of mind. Self-confidence and resoluteness, perhaps even a glint of arrogance, showed in his photographs now.

However, this picture omits one vital element: in the role of a highly competent and self-confident captain of a conquering army, Solzhenitsyn never lost his inherent and driving intellectual curiosity. He was still seeking primary causes as he had since childhood—still compelled to ask, Why? Nor could he keep his reflections wholly to himself.

The portion of the intellectual process that involves imparting and exchanging was suicidally dangerous in Stalin's Russia. Denunciations were rampant and mortal. But even—perhaps especially—in those conditions, *best* friends felt a need to share otherwise uncommunicable thoughts.

Solzhenitsyn's friend was now an officer on a more northern front. But the communication between the two did not cease during the war. During lulls in the fighting, they wrote long, thoughtful letters to each other, maintaining, as much as possible, their candor. Like Solzhenitsyn's, X's skepticism had been aggravated by his war experiences even though he, as a successful officer, had joined the Communist Party. The two men reflected on their observations as freely as possible.

Their letters dealt with a wide range of personal subjects, as well as their old philosophical, moral, and social concerns. Quite naturally, however, war and its meaning predominated. They wrote about its horrors. But more than that: they commented with disappointment and some sharpness about its conduct on their own side.

Among all but a tiny fraction of Russian intellectuals in these years, the overriding goals of the war—the liberation of Russia and Europe and destruction of Nazism—were beyond question. But some of the attitudes and practices of the Soviet Army were not. "Waging war by pouring blood" was a saying of the time. The general policy seemed to be to save equipment, even ammunition, at the expense of men. Moreover, terrible losses were often incurred by massive incompetence, largely caused by Stalin's destruction of the flower of the officer corps in the late 1930s.

Although pleased and encouraged by Nazism's defeats, X and Solzhenitsyn touched on related themes in their correspondence. They alluded to inefficiency and waste, sloppiness and cruelty. Counter to the motto of the day—"War writes off everything"—they mentioned the awful insensitivity and stupidity which had led to disastrous and unnecessary sacrifices witnessed on their respective fronts.

Who was to blame? By 1944, both men had matured into full-fledged anti-Stalinists. In their correspondence, Solzhenitsyn "spoke out against Stalin's cult of personality," as a document put it over a decade later. His adolescent distaste for the country's idolatry of the dictator had turned to revulsion.

For that percentage of Russians who understood the nature of Stalinism, there was often no middle ground. Passion against the "pock-marked devil" sought release, yet all natural forms of it were eliminated, prohibited, or perilous. Some desperate Soviet citizens, having decided that Stalinism was more fiendish even than what they knew of Nazism, went so far as to join the "Vlasov Army," a Russian contingent fighting their own country under German command. Solzhenitsyn did not hold this extreme view, but, like his father before him, he decided that the survival of his country outweighed all political differences. He had, however, been exposed to some of the injustice and vileness that nurtured the extreme view in other officers.

Although anti-Stalinist, Solzhenitsyn and X were Communists in the larger sense. They believed that the revolution was right for Russia; that Lenin not only meant but did well. Indeed, the philosophical framework for their criticism of Stalin was his fundamental distortion, or perversion, of Leninism as they understood it. They took Lenin at his word; they were inspired by his statements in defense of justice, equality, and freedom, untrammeled even by laws.

Theirs was the most common frame of reference for opposition to Stalin. The idealism of many thinking Soviet citizens knew no other foundation than Leninism. And they were encouraged in this not only by Lenin's writings, but also by his last years as Russia's leader when, after the brutalities of the revolution and civil war had receded, the country was advancing toward prosperity and a kind of social justice. For such

men, the cries of "For the Motherland, for Stalin" each time soldiers rose
from their trenches to charge German bullets was a stab in the flesh.
These very soldiers, or their brothers, had suffered most in the famines
caused by enforced collectivization and the general harshness of the
Soviet Army—and men who understood everything about Stalinism could
say nothing to them or in protection of them.

Thoughts such as these found release not only in letters to X, but also
in Solzhenitsyn's diary and the sketches for future short stories. These
private musings would become far more fateful for him than the whole
body of his later work.

It speaks for itself that his inner preoccupations were not only—perhaps not even principally—political or social. In the turmoil of war, the
state of Russian literature continued to disturb him. Thirteen years later,
Solzhenitsyn's wartime literary reflections were officially and cautiously
summarized as criticism of "artistic and philosophical weakness in the
works of Soviet authors and the unrealistic quality of many of them." In
other words, much of Soviet letters—the great outpouring of words,
produced as if to fulfill some Five-year Plan—was hollow, primitive, and
dishonest: Russian literature mummified in the wrappings of state direction. How could Solzhenitsyn become the writer he envisaged in that
dismal artistic environment? In this area of national life, Stalin's coarse
hands caused particular distress.

Of course, Solzhenitsyn and X wrote none of this "in the clear." They
drew on their common past, hopefully comprehensible to them alone, to
develop a private language for their correspondence. Key events and
people, including Lenin and others, were identified by code names. Stalin's
testified to their opinion of him: he was *pakhan*, thieves' slang for an
experienced and dominating gang lord.[1] The disguise was transparent,
but their urge to comment on Stalin's personality convinced them of its
adequacy. A character in a Solzhenitsyn novel jots down a thought one
day which no doubt echoes those of the author himself at this time.

There's a passage in Marx, I remember (find it!), which says that
the victorious proletariat can perhaps do without expropriating the
prosperous peasantry. In other words, he foresaw some sort of
economic means [2] of including the *entire* peasantry in the new
social system. Of course *pakhan* didn't look for any such ways in

[1] For years, it was supposed in the West, on the basis of rumors, that the code
phrase was "the mustachioed one" or "man with the mustache," but Solzhenitsyn's
close friends say that this term, in any case rather obvious, was never used.

[2] In the context, "economic means" implies they might have been used instead
of Stalin's political methods for launching collectivization in 1929. In other words,
Solzhenitsyn's character wanted skillful social engineering based on peaceful in-
centives rather than the brutal police methods by which the Soviet agriculture was
transformed from private to collective ownership.

1929. But has he ever sought anything subtle or well conceived? Why send a butcher to a medical school?

Among other things, Solzhenitsyn could not restrain his disgust at Stalin's abuse of the Russian language—a foreigner's ineradicable imprecision before which philologists and writers genuflected, together with the rest of the nation, in an act of particularly loathsome self-abasement.

Throughout the war and throughout the nation, all Soviet correspondence bore an obligatory stamp: "Examined by military censorship." The correspondence of military personnel, especially from the front, was examined with particular care, not only for disclosure of military secrets, but also for hints of discontent in the armed forces, which was considered exceedingly dangerous. That the relatively simple code of the Solzhenitsyn-X correspondence was unraveled is less surprising than the delay in doing it. Once exposed, however, the censors "locked on." For many weeks they intercepted, studied, and recorded letters from both men before passing them on for delivery. Then the organization called "Smersh" was called in. Smersh (an acronym for "death to spies") had been established at the beginning of the war, largely by regrouping units of the NKVD [3] and renaming them to suggest a high patriotic purpose. Ostensibly organized to combat German spies and fifth columnists concealed in military and civilian organizations, its principal function was in fact exterminating real and imagined anti-Stalinism.

In Smersh's Moscow headquarters, a not inconsiderable operation was plotted with some of the thoroughness and caution due the war itself. The plan was to seize the malefactors simultaneously, thus precluding any possibility of their warning one another. In February 1945, orders were given to dispatch two teams of Smersh agents to the two fronts to execute the arrests. X's went according to plan.

When the team assigned to seize Solzhenitsyn arrived at his front, they found the headquarters of his brigade deep in East Prussia, in the outskirts of Koenigsberg. Solzhenitsyn himself was beyond their grasp. A battle was in progress and the brigade commander, Colonel Travkin, told the agents that he would not permit the captain's apprehension until its completion. Irritatingly enough for the NKVD officers, he was within his rights as a front-line commander of troops engaged with the enemy.

The engagement was particularly fierce and protracted, as evidenced by the death of a Soviet Army group commander near the front. At vast

[3] People's Commissariat of Internal Affairs: the Soviet security service, successor to the Cheka and GPU, but with wider functions. The institution was renamed NKGB (People's Commissariat of State Security) in 1943, but continued to be referred to colloquially by the more familiar "NKVD"—as it will be in this book until the appearance of "KGB" (Committee of State Security), the present appellation, in 1953.

cost and corresponding thoroughness, Koenigsberg, the first German
provincial capital in the Soviet path, had been buttressed into what the
Wehrmacht believed was an impregnable fortress. The German commander, known as "the Lion of Defense," had ordered his troops to
defend the city to the last.

Solzhenitsyn's unit was engaged in a difficult and confused segment
of the front. He has published only one short story about the war, and
even this was set far from any fighting. But despite his disinclination to
reminisce about the front, he has told close friends that this battle was
one of his most dangerous. For a time, his unit was pinned in a pocket
under withering artillery barrages which churned the area into a
strashnaya kasha, a "frightful mess." He sometimes wonders how he
survived.

The battle kept the NKVD officers waiting for days. Impatience
rankled within them, all the more because the NKVD usually had the run
of the Army, plucking whomever it wanted from its ranks. But even
though these officers had briefed Travkin on the political gravity of the
charges against Solzhenitsyn, the colonel continued to deny permission for
Solzhenitsyn's arrest. He had never been personally close to the young
captain; his stubbornness here was grounded entirely in Solzhenitsyn's
military excellence. Travkin valued—and, in the battle, badly needed—his
skills as a veteran front-line officer. Finally Solzhenitsyn's unit fought clear
of the enemy and a messenger was dispatched to find it. Solzhenitsyn was
told to report to headquarters.

The summons was commonplace enough, as was the scene—Colonel
Travkin seated at his desk, with other officers present—when he stepped
through the door. But Solzhenitsyn was promptly asked whether he had
come with his revolver. "I have," replied the captain, his suspicions
aroused for the first time. "Very well, then, give it here." When he had
surrendered his weapon, the NKVD officers ripped off his decorations.
Next they pulled at his shoulder insignia, but by this time Solzhenitsyn's
fighting instinct was aroused. There could be no other meaning to this
assault than arrest, but as Solzhenitsyn was to write of a hero, what was
"insufferable at this fleeting instant" was the "brazenness and gouging
fingers." Although never physically powerful, he fought with his attackers
and threw them off. At this moment, Colonel Travkin intervened and
hinted to Solzhenitsyn about what was confronting him. This required a
certain kind of man: to give an "enemy of the people" the slightest intima-
tion of the charges against him was itself a political crime. Disregarding
the danger to himself, however, Travkin asked Solzhenitsyn if he knew
someone on the northern front. Solzhenitsyn immediately grasped the
implied reference to X and their correspondence—and the gravity of his

position. It was clear that the inherent dangers of his intellectualism had caught up with him. He submitted to the arrest.

The colonel's hint about X was bravery with a practical intention: the knowledge would permit Solzhenitsyn to prepare himself for interrogation. Now Travkin made an even braver gesture, and for no purpose other than to assert his own dignity. He stood and offered Solzhenitsyn his hand.

"Captain," he said, "I wish you good luck."

Shorn of his stars, Solzhenitsyn officially had no rank. In the unwritten law of the day, he was not only no longer a captain, but an enemy of the people—a "dirty counter" (counterrevolutionary). As the operative NKVD saying indicated—"We make no mistakes!"—arrest was virtually synonymous with condemnation. In these circumstances, the slightest show of sympathy for the condemned might easily have delivered the sympathizer to a similar fate. This danger was made more real by the presence at the colonel's side of the brigade's Communist Party overseer, one of whose principal functions was to report ideological deviations or weaknesses among other officers. This is what made Solzhenitsyn call Travkin's handshake "one of the most outstanding acts of courage I saw during the war."

Solzhenitsyn's life would have been in mortal peril were it not for his courage—and luck—in saving his new range-finding equipment from encirclement several months before. For the discovery of written material critical of the war's conduct on top of losing secret equipment to the enemy would almost certainly have brought prompt execution. Nor would there have been much hope of escaping a firing squad now had not Solzhenitsyn's sergeant taken upon himself some vital precautionary measures. Having heard, in Solzhenitsyn's absence at headquarters, that Smersh had come for his officer and old friend, the sergeant hurried to hide some of his personal belongings that might have been incriminating, including some literature of great world importance.

Solzhenitsyn was reading it to understand whom and what he was fighting. This was no more than a continuation of his old drive to understand important phenomena through primary sources—rather than, in this case, the deluge of Soviet articles, cartoons, and broadcasts about German evils. But most authority, Communist or other, suspects a touch of treason in a citizen's wish to investigate "the enemy" from his own sources. And in the NKVD, this suspicion had long before achieved the proportions of mass paranoia, and been institutionalized to crush the slightest deviation from the shifting official position on Germany and other enemies. For them, an officer's possession of German literature would have been clinching and overwhelming proof of betrayal of the Motherland.

[The sergeant managed to hide the unorthodox material before the NKVD officers came to search his things. However, Solzhenitsyn's own incriminating sketches and notes were carried in his map case, and these were confiscated. Upon completion of the search, bureaucratic formalities were observed for Solzhenitsyn's separation from his unit and deliverance to Smersh in Moscow. His escorts seated him in a Lend Lease jeep and set off for the nearest railway station in the Russian rear.]

The jeep's uncertain course told a story about Solzhenitsyn's captors. As strangers to this front, they had no knowledge of its terrain; as non-combatants, little experience of front-line dangers in general. Groping for a safe route out of Koenigsberg, the impatient NKVD officers drove closer and closer to the front. With their background, "the enemy" at that moment meant Solzhenitsyn to them; to the former artillery captain just returned from exhausting battle, the Wehrmacht was still very much the enemy—and a mortal one—whatever awaited him in Moscow. As a reconnaissance officer, he knew the disposition of the combatant forces like his five fingers, as the Russians say. And as the jeep approached even closer to the extremely fluid front, his anxiety grew of driving directly into German fire. Despite his plight, he had no wish to be "liberated" by a German bullet or capture.

"Where are you taking me?" he asked nervously.

"Shut your trap, counter."

Solzhenitsyn took the hint and was quiet while the jeep bounced on toward danger. It materialized suddenly, and, for the NKVD officers frighteningly, in the form of a German outpost. At the sight of it the driver reversed gears and backed away as quickly as possible. From that point on, the officers condescended quite happily to follow the "counter's" directions. Solzhenitsyn led them out of danger, then toward the railway station and first leg of his delivery to Smersh headquarters. His last perception of the war was the receding din of artillery fire at the now-distant front.

His charmed life seeming shattered, he left the war and East Prussia, which "in some strange way was linked to my fate," as he wrote twenty-five years later. The Rostov boy's links with this improbable European backwater were through his father, who fought there in World War I, leading to Solzhenitsyn's first interest in the region and his adolescent attempts to write about it. It was a coincidence of some proportions that the young officer himself fought on that small segment of the huge front, there to be searched out and arrested. Yet another turning point connected with East Prussia would come when he at last returned to the epic of Soviet Russia's emergence after the disintegration of the *ancien régime*.

Secluded in a compartment under armed guard, Solzhenitsyn was transported the eight hundred-odd miles east to Moscow. Back went the train across forests, swamps, and towns through which—and for which—Solzhenitsyn had fought for almost three years. That he had every reason to conjecture that this was his last glimpse of the Russian countryside could only have intensified the tension of the journey. Once in the capital, he was to be conducted immediately to prison. But Solzhenitsyn's friends tell of a sequel to the grim comedy of traveling errors performed at the front.

Like so many NKVD officers, Solzhenitsyn's escorts were of village background and did not know Moscow well. They lost their way en route from the railway station. Regulations prohibited disclosure to prisoners of their appointed destinations—but the officers had again got themselves in a muddle, this one embarrassing if not dangerous. In the end it was Solzhenitsyn who directed them to Lubyanka.

VIII

Sentence

"I WAS ARRESTED FOR MY naïveté," Solzhenitsyn later explained. "I knew that revealing military secrets in letters from the front was prohibited, but assumed that thinking was permissible. . . . Long before this, I'd felt critical of him [Stalin]. I considered that he had departed from Leninism, that he was responsible for the misfortunes of the first phase of the war, that his language was crude. Due to my youthful inexperience, I wrote about all this in my letters. I was clapped into Lubyanka."

Lubyanka was the headquarters of the Soviet security apparatus. At a generous estimate, not one in ten thousand prisoners delivered there under arrest left its "black iron gates" a free man. A correspondingly black joke made the five-story structure Moscow's tallest because "you can see Siberia from its basement." Lubyanka's deep basement had been built to house the vaults of an insurance society, which is one reason—its suitability for interrogation and execution—that the secret police requisitioned the building after the revolution. Another might have been its location: the building stands on Dzerzhinsky Square, near the center of Moscow and the seat of Soviet rule. Solzhenitsyn was escorted past the expansive façade with its "unfeeling" insurance-company naiads "peering down contemptuously at the scurrying little citizens below." Cars delivering prisoners proceeded through traplike gates, to be swallowed up inside. The first sight was of a small courtyard which was "like the bottom of a well, its sides formed by the building's four walls, shooting upward."

As the train rolled slowly back from Koenigsberg to Moscow, Solzhenitsyn had had time to prepare himself for the most feared building in the world—the "nest of legendary horrors," as he described it. The formalities of registration were conducted with unexpected bureaucratic indifference, a normality that was short-lived: the first immersion into the routine of prison life brought utter humiliation. Solzhenitsyn has described the early hours in Lubyanka of a man who had previously been proud and self-confident. A warder is performing the first of the prisoner's countless examinations:

> Like a horse dealer, his unwashed hands prodding inside Innokenty's mouth, stretching one cheek and then the other, then yanking down the lower eyelids, the warder convinced himself that nothing was hidden in the eyes or mouth, and tipped back his head so that the nostrils were illuminated. Then he examined both ears, stretching them out by the lobes, and ordered Innokenty to spread out his hands to show there was nothing between the fingers and to flap his arms to show nothing was under the armpits.
>
> In the same mechanical, irrefutable voice he ordered: "Take your penis in your hand. Peel back the foreskin. More. Right, that's enough. Place your penis to the right side and lift it, to the left side and lift. Right, you can put it down . . ."
>
> When he had thought about arrest before it happened, Innokenty had pictured a furious clash of wits. His inner self was tensed and prepared for a defense of his life and convictions on the highest level. Never had he imagined something so simple, so dull, so inescapable as this. . . .

In processing prisoners, whether in preparation for execution or for forced labor, humiliation served the function of stunning in a slaughterhouse. "The aggregate of this methodical and detailed procedure normally broke the will of the newly arrested prisoner clean through," wrote Solzhenitsyn. He did not go on to describe an interrogation in any detail, however, and when asked about his stay in Lubyanka, his friends are noncommittal. He was interrogated, they say, as all prisoners were in those days—"the usual routine."

The usual routine, however, varied within considerable limits. It often included crude threats and beatings, was sometimes sprinkled with intellectual persuasion by a fastidiously polite officer, was always based on exhausting dead-of-night sessions when the prisoner, robbed of sleep, strength, and all contact with reality, was grilled mercilessly under brutal lights. Confession was the goal. Not merely confession, however, but groveling self-abasement. And, in the self-abasement, incrimination of others. The rationale for this was obvious: the NKVD *had* to produce proof of "anti-Soviet" activity and conspiracies—although not a shred of objective evidence existed except in perhaps one in a thousand cases. No less an authority than Andrey Vyshinsky, Stalin's chief legal theoretician, pronounced that "confession is the queen of evidence."

Solzhenitsyn was the thousandth prisoner: a case against him did in fact exist. Even without further corroboration, the irreverence toward Stalin in his letters and diary was more than enough for severe punishment. Bizarrely—but logically—enough, prisoners in his category were often spared the worst ordeals of interrogation: there was no need to extract a confession of imaginary outrages.

Between interrogations, the Lubyanka offered a carefully conceived routine of dehumanization. Solzhenitsyn remembered "blinding electric lights," "close, constricting walls," and "stonelike indifference in the eyes of mechanical puppets." There was also the suffocating horror of an invention called a "box," in an incomprehensible borrowing from English. Ostensibly used for security while prisoners were shunted within the vast prison, "boxes" were in fact instruments of psychological torture. "Dazzlingly whitewashed and blindingly lit," these cells were so small that "you not only couldn't walk, not only couldn't lie down, but you couldn't even sit down properly.']

And there was the route to one of the cell blocks, over steps well known to world literature: more than one important writer has walked and later described them. Solzhenitsyn's description opens the imagination to the Lubyanka's scale.

> It was there, on the steps of the last flight of stairs, that Inno-
> kenty noticed *how* deeply the steps were ground down. He'd never
> seen anything like it, anywhere in his life. From the edges to the
> middle, they were worn through into broad oval pits, taking half
> their thickness. He shuddered: in thirty years, how many feet! how
> many times! must have shuffled on them to grind the stone to that
> depth. And of every two people who walked there, one was a
> warder—the other, a prisoner.

The inhabitants of this dungeon had no more contact with life beyond its walls—with the crowds a few yards away on a central Moscow square —than characters in a horror film. Natalya Reshetovskaya knew nothing of it. Back in Rostov after her visit to the front, she resumed her studies in chemistry, anticipating the war's obviously approaching end and wait-ing impatiently for the folded triangles of the special war post: Solzhe-nitsyn's letters from the front. Before the spring of 1945, they suddenly and inexplicably stopped.

The dreaded killed-in-action notification, usually delivered within a month of the event, did not arrive. Nor did hints that he might be missing on the battlefield; there was simply no word. During the same triumphal spring of 1945, one of Solzhenitsyn's principal female characters endures the same trial.

> Waiting for a husband to return from war is always hard, but the
> last months before the end are hardest of all; shell fragments and
> bullets, after all, don't calculate how long a man has been fighting.
> It was just then that Gleb's letters stopped.
> Nadya would dash out to watch for the postman. She wrote to

her husband, wrote to his friends, wrote to his commanding officers —they all kept silent, as if under a spell.

In the spring of 1945, artillery salutes smacked into the skies every single evening. On and on and on, they kept capturing cities —Koenigsberg, Breslau, Frankfurt-on-Oder, Berlin, Prague.

But there were no letters. The world was blacking out. Nothing was worth doing. But it was wrong to sink under! If he was alive and returned, he would reproach her for having wasted time. She wore herself out with a full day of work and also prepared for entrance exams in graduate chemistry, studying foreign languages and dialectical materialism. Only at night did she cry.

Suddenly, for the first time, WarMin withheld Nadya's allowance as an officer's wife.

This must have meant—he'd been killed.

Directly after this, the four-year war ended. People wild with joy were running through wild streets. Someone was firing a pistol into the air. And all the loudspeakers in the Soviet Union carried victory marches over the ravaged, hungry land.

For some wives the strain dragged on for years. Reshetovskaya's waiting, however, ended within weeks of Victory Day.

A bureaucratic postcard was delivered to her relatives in Moscow; handwriting in the blanks of the printed form notified them that they were entitled to send parcels to "Cit. Solzhenitsyn, A.I." at a certain box number address in Moscow. Solzhenitsyn had given their name rather than Reshetovskaya's because they, living nearby, would have a better chance to visit and advise him, and perhaps help with food parcels, than his wife in Rostov. After some effort Reshetovskaya's relatives—the Turkins—understood that their promising young relative was a prisoner, and broke the news to Reshetovskaya herself. For Solzhenitsyn's fictional heroine—and his friends say her experience directly reflects Reshetovskaya's—it was a day of rejoicing.

> Not all of her friends and relatives could understand her: she had learned that her husband was in jail—and felt radiant and cheered. Again she was not alone on this earth! . . . It's only from the grave that people don't come back; they do return from hard labor.
>
> Now that there was no death, no terrifying unfaithfulness to *them,* but only a noose on her neck and a boulder on her shoulders, new strength surged into Nadya. He was in Moscow—which meant she must go to Moscow to try to save him. (It seemed that it would be enough just to turn up near him, and already she would be able to start saving him.)

Reshetovskaya was desperate to go to Moscow—to plead and petition, to see Solzhenitsyn, at the very least to *find out* what lay behind the cryptic postcard. Moscow was only seven hundred miles north of Rostov, but the route was virtually impossible. In the months following the end of the war, travel to the capital was so difficult that "our descendants would never be able to imagine it," as Solzhenitsyn wrote. But Reshetovskaya found a way. Instead of pursuing graduate studies in Rostov, she redirected her application to the University of Moscow. As a provincial girl, lacking a superlative record and connections in the capital, she could barely hope for the coveted invitation to take examinations at the country's most prestigious graduate institution. That summer the invitation not only came, but she passed the examinations with distinction enough to be enrolled. "It was one of those inspired summits of life," wrote Solzhenitsyn, "when some kind of beneficent power helps us, and everything becomes possible."

Whatever power had favored Reshetovskaya's winning of the dazzling prize of legal Moscow residence, nothing could help her save Solzhenitsyn, as she so blindly hoped. The bureaucrats of the penal system's "petitioning" offices were supremely indifferent to the fervor of her wish and desperation of her attempts. She spent long hours in classes and laboratories, of course; but the mission of her life was somehow to obtain relief for Solzhenitsyn. First she tried simply to secure a visit with him. At this stage, it was not granted. A process of treading well-worn rounds of bureaus followed: a trial of questioning, besieging, and begging to establish some kind of contact with the hidden prisoner.

Petition in hand, Reshetovskaya presented herself at offices of all institutions theoretically empowered by the constitution and enabling laws to intervene in Solzhenitsyn's case. The list was considerable: the Supreme Soviet, Supreme Court of the Soviet Union, Supreme Court of the Russian Republic, and no less than three attorney-general offices, in its federal, republic, and military divisions. The stark waiting rooms of these offices teemed with despairing—or maniacally optimistic—relatives and tales of family grief, enough to crush the hope of new "recruits" on a single visit. The milling about of prisoners' relatives in these offices— all of them as ignorant and ineffectual as if they had been suddenly rounded up on some street—was a mass tragedy in itself, in keeping with the scale and ruthlessness of the times. Reshetovskaya played her part in it, making her way from one office, and one hope, to the next. "Helpless women paced before the law's concrete wall," wrote Solzhenitsyn. "They lacked wings to take flight and flutter over it. What remained was to bow in supplication at every opening of every tin gate."

The faintest glimmer of hope was grasped at, including the services of lawyers who hinted that portions of their extortionist charges were needed to wield corrupt influence somewhere in the penal leviathan's mysterious nerve center. Even if they materialized, the lawyers' efforts are not known to have helped a single political prisoner. "Politicals" were beyond help because, as a Solzhenitsyn character puts it, they were "not criminals but enemies" and "couldn't be sprung for millions." Reshetovskaya could afford only an odd thousand or two for these members of the bar. She lived on her graduate grant, and accumulated the consultation fees only by sacrificial scrimping. Most relatives knew full well that their money bought no more "influence" than quicker service in some Moscow restaurant, where their lawyers spent the fees on food and drink. But they paid the sums even over years, nct so much to draw a winning ticket but "for the dream that they might."

The one contact between prisoner and family permitted at this stage was a parcel of food, the passing of which usually meant hours of nerve-destroying waiting. Despairing relatives exchanged stories, all variants on the theme of sudden arrest for unimaginable reasons, followed by the endless, hopeless cycle of petitioning. When Reshetovskaya at last reached the head of the line and passed her parcel—wrapped according to regulations—into the little slit of a window, she could not even see the official's face; her little offerings of food were taken by an anonymous pair of hands. She had no way of knowing whether Solzhenitsyn would receive them, not to mention anything more significant about his condition or fate.

Solzhenitsyn's condition was in fact typical for a prisoner under investigation for political crimes. The indictment against him fell into two parts, both under the Criminal Code's multifarious Article 58 which defined "counterrevolutionary crimes." The first part spoke of "propaganda or agitation including incitement to overthrow, undermine, or weaken Soviet rule . . . as well as the distribution, fabrication, or possession of literature of the same content." The second prohibited "any kind of organized activity" directed toward the preparation or commission of such crimes.

In brief, Solzhenitsyn was accused of a kind of thought crime: entertaining and imparting prohibited ideas. The language of the code was so loose that almost any expressed opinion other than the latest "line" could be classified as counterrevolutionary. And the notion of conspiracy embodied in the indictment's second part was so broad that almost any Soviet citizen, whether or not he himself had actually said anything at all, could be seized.

Yet it was official policy to pretend that this terror did not exist. One of the most hallowed Soviet legal illusions was—and remains—that common crime and political crime were not fundamentally different: whether the charge was picking pockets or uttering an inadmissible thought, the law must take its course in exactly the same way. The difference lay principally in the far more meticulous and severe prosecution of political crimes. The pretense, like that of the constitution and the Supreme Soviet playing democratic parliament, was designed to bridge an abyss between Stalinist practices and generally recognized civilized norms; to demonstrate clean hands to the world and perhaps relieve the conscience of legislators and law enforcers. In any event, Solzhenitsyn's alleged offenses, bizarre as they were, were handled according to some of the recognized forms of criminal law and procedure.]

Solzhenitsyn spent his first four months in solitary confinement. During this time, an investigation of his case was conducted, parallel with his interrogation. Since the charge against Solzhenitsyn involved the communication of criminal thoughts, everyone with whom he had had contact was investigated and pressed to corroborate the indictment. Even Boris Lavrenyov, the writer to whom Solzhenitsyn had sent some of his efforts before the war, was questioned. Once a revolutionary dramatist, Lavrenyov had become a prominent composer of paeans in Stalin's cult, with access to the dictator himself. Yet this did not deter the zealous secret police investigators from eagerly probing the ramifications of his brief link with Solzhenitsyn.

[Intense investigations of political prisoners often produced predictable results: someone in the accused's circle of friends and acquaintances was persuaded—or volunteered—to give "evidence" in support of the indictment or additional charges. This apparently happened in Solzhenitsyn's case. Documents published over a decade later indicate that his conviction was based not only on his army writings and correspondence with X, but also on a denunciation—perhaps more than one—of "anti-Soviet fabrications" which someone "alleged" Solzhenitsyn had "uttered" to Reshetovskaya and two friends. His indictment also charged that he "had been conducting anti-Soviet agitation among his acquaintances . . . since 1940." Inasmuch as even the NKVD could not use a personal diary as evidence of "agitation," and since Solzhenitsyn's correspondence with X did not exist in 1940, the date mentioned in the indictment supports the supposition that someone else gave evidence against Solzhenitsyn.]

But more questions are raised than answered by the wording of the indictment. Was there a denunciation—or several? Did it come from a frightened friend under pressure from the secret police? Had an informer reported him before his arrest—perhaps even before the war, while he lived in Rostov—and was this report produced from old files now that Solzhenitsyn was in Lubyanka? Indeed, did the arrest produce the denunciation, or the opposite: did a denunciation lead to Solzhenitsyn's arrest?

Unless and until the archives of the Soviet secret police are opened, these questions are unlikely to be answered. Solzhenitsyn himself seems unwilling to speak of them, although faint hints can be found in his statements to support other evidence of a denunciation. The combined weight of all the evidence justifies the assumption that someone did tell the NKVD that he knew Solzhenitsyn to be "anti-Soviet" before the war. By the standards of the time, the denunciation was highly restrained: mere "agitation" and anti-Soviet sympathies, without ties to the Gestapo or an intention to kill Stalin. But even on its own, this "evidence" would have been enough to cost Solzhenitsyn a decade or more of freedom. It was a useful addition to the NKVD's case.

Whatever the results of the investigation, the interrogation of Solzhenitsyn himself yielded nothing, although not for lack of effort by the interrogators. For four months, armed guards regularly led Solzhenitsyn down corridors of the Lubyanka labyrinth, delivering him to one of many small rooms with tiny grilled windows: the investigation chambers. Solzhenitsyn was seated on a rickety stool facing a small table, and the man behind it—one of a team of such men, whose place in the history of inquisition is assured—attempted to persuade, cajole, terrify, reassure, and perhaps flatter him into confession. It would be easiest, Solzhenitsyn was constantly reminded, if he named other "guilty" persons too. But these efforts produced no results: published documents on Solzhenitsyn's case reveal no hint of self-incrimination, and his friends say that the investigators were stymied by his resolve.

Refusal to besmirch oneself was not so rare as is sometimes supposed. Even in total isolation, even under hard mental and physical torture, a significant percentage of prisoners refused to succumb. Still, they were a small minority. No evidence exists that extreme methods were practiced on Solzhenitsyn, but even without them a special kind of courage and endurance was required to withstand interrogation. Alternation of threats and cajolery was the least painful aspect of a process designed to disintegrate the prisoner's personality.

In the transformation of a former man to "a grain in the sands of the [labor] camps," the first weeks were especially trying. Lubyanka's initial humiliation was superseded by exhaustion, the product of a carefully conceived program of hunger and sleeplessness. Sudden awakenings in the dead of night for hours-long interrogations were accompanied by a meticulously enforced ban on sleep during the day. This brought most prisoners' nerves to the verge of collapse, while demonstrating to them their total lack of rights—personal as well as civil. For the deprivation of so fundamental a right as sleep is likely to destroy other assumptions about one's individuality and right to exist.

Permanent hunger complemented the sleeplessness. Solzhenitsyn later remembered his rations as "the thinnest gruel, buckwheat or oat—half of it water, without a single star of fat on the surface." The combination helped transform the young, self-confident captain into a sallow-faced prisoner of indeterminate age: a shadow of a man, wholly and utterly dependent on his jailers. The jailers counted on a prisoner's despair, exhaustion, and confrontation with permanently ruined life to break him.

But Solzhenitsyn persevered. No doubt the realization that pressure to confess would not affect him encouraged the investigators to shorten their labors to an unusually brief four months. Moreover, although there was insufficient evidence for a regular court, there were other ways to sentence the prisoner.

Solzhenitsyn's "trial" was the work of the same NKVD that had discharged the investigation. It was conducted by a board of three NKVD officers that bore the name "Special Session," but was popularly known as a "troika." Throughout the country, it was troikas that performed the routine work of dispatching millions of citizens to death or concentration camps where the evidence was too scant even for the deeply politicized Soviet judiciary. Procedurally, troikas were elegant in their simplicity: no defense was entertained, nor, ordinarily, was the victim questioned. The decision was reached on the basis of papers supplied to the board; the uncertainty was reduced to the severity of the sentence they would award. For "politicals," this could vary considerably, from three years' confinement to execution.

Solzhenitsyn's case was heard on July 7 by one of the many troikas functioning in Moscow. Two formal charges were lodged against him: that he had conducted anti-Soviet agitation "from 1940 to the day of his arrest," and that he had "undertaken steps" to set up an anti-Soviet organization. The troika had two forms of evidence: Solzhenitsyn's writings and correspondence, together with the allegations that he had "uttered anti-Soviet fabrications." The charges were less deadly than they might have been, especially in that Solzhenitsyn was accused of having attempted to establish, rather than actually founded, an anti-Soviet organization. At a time when a husband and wife indicted together were often condemned as a conspiracy, the Solzhenitsyn-X liaison might easily have qualified as an anti-Soviet organization, with correspondingly heavier sentences.

Providence smiled on another aspect of Solzhenitsyn's case. The evidence before the troika, written in Solzhenitsyn's own hand, demonstrated that he was a particularly "dangerous" breed of anti-Stalinist, one whose opposition to Stalin derived from his own reading of Lenin. As the document which rehabilitated him a dozen years later put it, Solzhenitsyn "spoke out against the cult of Stalin's personality while upholding the correctness of Marxism-Leninism, the progressive character of the socialist revolution in our country, and the inevitability of its victory through the world." He would have been better off had he attacked Stalin from the position of a monarchist or "bourgeois-liberal." The dictator was relatively insensitive to criticism from the few surviving defenders of the *ancien régime,* but enraged by anyone who dared speak of discrepancies between his policies and Lenin's, or between Marxism-Leninism's promises and Stalinism's practices. Solzhenitsyn's was no mere antirevolutionary talk, but heresy of a particularly detested, and feared, variety. Undermining faith in the Infallible Leader, weakening the church from within—these evils had to be extirpated; all the more because they might indeed threaten Stalin's leadership by calling attention to the very strictures which supposedly justified the dictatorship.

Considering the gravity of the offense, the "trial" went relatively well for Solzhenitsyn, again for no predictable reason. Solzhenitsyn's war record could not have been expected to move the board. But, perversely, the modest but genuine evidence against him probably helped: in his case, there was no need for the wildly exaggerated charges lodged against many wholly innocent people on the no-smoke-without-fire principle. Most of all, however, Solzhenitsyn probably benefited from sheer good fortune. Lacking firm guidance in law, the troikas had considerable leeway in fixing sentences, and defendants were often disposed of on the basis of whim and personal prejudice. The unevenness of NKVD justice was illustrated by the cases of Solzhenitsyn and X themselves: at virtually the same time, on virtually identical evidence, a troika in the same city awarded the latter ten years in "corrective labor" camps. In Solzhenitsyn's case, the verdict was kinder: his sentence was eight years.[1] "This was then considered a lenient sentence," he later observed.

"Corrective labor" camps made survival uncertain even in a far shorter period. Still, the two-year difference gave Solzhenitsyn a measurably better chance. He was lucky again, and would remain so for most of his sentence.

---

[1] Since party members sometimes drew heavier punishment, X's membership might possibly have been a factor.

IX

First Encounter

SOLZHENITSYN'S ATTITUDE TOWARD HIS sentence distinguished him in a crucial way from many prisoners. Almost all "politicals" knew themselves to be wholly innocent, and the very absurdity of their "crimes" provoked daydreams of action. They yearned to prove the "crimes" a ghastly mistake, and the hope that they would be righted soon was nourished for months or years. When the bubble burst, so did morale—and this often led to disaster. The full realization of hopelessness was too much to bear.

By contrast, realism would protect Solzhenitsyn's morale throughout his sentence. Since he accepted the logic of his punishment—"I never thought I'd been sentenced without guilt; after all, I did express opinions which were inadmissible at that time"—the charges against him did not seem absurd. Enduring punishment for the right to think and to exchange ideas was easier than "for nothing." Lack of illusions about "mistakes" and false hopes for sudden mercy helped Solzhenitsyn concentrate on the only chance for survival: the most rational organization possible of his concentration camp life. Almost immediately, he learned how difficult survival would be.

After sentencing, he was transferred from Lubyanka to the Butyrka transit jail. He spent several months there in a large cell shared by some seventy prisoners, mostly intellectuals. Among them was Professor Nikolai Timofeyev-Resovsky, one of the world's leading geneticists. To while away the time the professor organized a lecture "club" in the cell. Every morning after the distribution of rations—one of few moments in the day when the transit prisoners did not feel acute pangs of hunger—some of them would meet at the window and listen to one of their number talking on a subject of interest. It was the autumn of the Hiroshima bomb and Solzhenitsyn, a relatively recent physics graduate, gave a talk on advances in the field of atomic energy. He and Timofeyev-Resovsky became friends, but were soon separated, not to meet for twenty years, when the professor would play an important part in Solzhenitsyn's life.

From transit jails prisoners were distributed to a vast network of mines and construction sites, usually in remote areas of the country. But Solzhenitsyn was one of a small minority delivered instead to a small specialized camp whose inmates built housing for NKVD officials in Moscow itself—a stroke of remarkably good luck which Solzhenitsyn lacked the experience to appreciate.

Even in a relatively mild Moscow camp, his first encounter with forced labor "stunned" him. It was a "teeth-grinding struggle for survival," for which he was ill equipped. He had no manual skills, and his intellectual gifts were more a hindrance than a help. Throughout his prison years, Solzhenitsyn often sighed: "If only I were a shoemaker."

He was quickly put to work as a general laborer at a construction site: unloading, carrying, and installing building materials. Unaccustomed to the backbreaking work, he could not fulfill his daily quotas—a constant effort, for camp rations were awarded on the basis of quota fulfillment. But Solzhenitsyn fell into the lowest category, fed principally on thin oat gruel, black potatoes sweet with frost, and half-baked rye bread. Already exhausted by starvation, he could not regain his strength on these rations, nor harden to his work. Many prisoners never recovered from this initial ordeal, but swirled downward in a quick spiral of exhaustion and despair toward an unmarked common grave.

Luckily, Solzhenitsyn was helped over this first hurdle by Reshetovskaya, whose graduate studies had now installed her permanently in Moscow. Sentenced prisoners were allowed visits by close relatives, and their first meeting took place in October, some eight months after his arrest. At this period there was no limit to food parcels for convicted prisoners, and Reshetovskaya took full advantage of this—at distinct sacrifice to herself. The early postwar years were what Solzhenitsyn has called "the time of cheap money and expensive bread." Reshetovskaya had to "deny herself food and to sell her things" for her regular food parcels. However, she rarely saw Solzhenitsyn. Like camp rations, visits from relatives were awarded on the basis of quota fulfillment; Solzhenitsyn seldom qualified.

His strength partially restored, Solzhenitsyn realized that he must acquire a manual skill to escape the grip of unskilled labor; he became an apprentice parquet layer. Almost twenty years later, as a recognized writer, Solzhenitsyn visited a block of flats on which he had worked. It is a distinctive semicircular building with a turret, commanding a view of Leninsky Prospect, one of the principal thoroughfares in the city center. While Solzhenitsyn worked there, the site in a location then called Kaluzhskaya Zastava (Kaluga Gate) was transformed into a kind of miniature labor camp, with barbed wire and guard towers added to the normal construction-project fence. The prisoners lived in an unfinished wing of the house on which work was still in progress, and several signed their initials in wet mortar. Solzhenitsyn has pointed out his own "A.S." to friends.

He did not become a master builder; the daily labor quotas were still beyond his physical capacity. And the camp rules, written and unwritten, were harder to master than those of a manual trade. Solzhenitsyn had been a proud young man, with traces of arrogance; now he had to learn to submit to ignorant, self-willed warders and coarse work supervisors. His intellectual gifts had made him accustomed to the limelight, at least among his friends. But the camp crawled with informers, and any expression of an original, much less an unorthodox, idea might easily be reported, leading to a second sentence for anti-Soviet propaganda. Solzhenitsyn's principal apprenticeship was in silence and self-effacement; he had to subdue the part of him he liked best: his intellectual individuality.

Outward manners too were transformed. Solzhenitsyn had always abounded in energy and his movements were correspondingly decisive and quick. But the thin nourishment required conservation of energy, best accomplished by moving slowly. Solzhenitsyn began acquiring the habits of veteran hard-labor prisoners, who, like seasoned boxers, avoid wasting an unneeded step or word. However, he refused to surrender his conscience, the price he would have to pay to ease his lot.

Great pressure was exerted on prisoners to become informers. The recruitment campaign was launched by a camp security officer, who summoned most prisoners after their arrival. Where camp rules permitted, easy office work or service jobs—best of all, work in or around the kitchen —were offered in exchange for information. Even when this kind of bribery was unavailable, there were always ways to protect volunteers from the most grueling jobs—or, on the contrary, to threaten recalcitrants with them. "Life in the camps," Solzhenitsyn wrote later, "surpassed in its ruthlessness all that is known about the life of cannibals and rats." Dread of protracted pain leading to an anonymous death sometimes made informers even of men who had been sentenced specifically for having refused this role outside.

Prisoners who succumbed to the pressure usually saved themselves physically, but "the price of their survival was the blood of others" and the loss of all moral dignity, of the last shred of self-respect. For their reports led to supplementary sentences, transfer to murderous jobs, incarceration in punishment cells, and sometimes the shooting of fellow prisoners. Survival could transform a man almost literally into a cannibal.

Informers also risked professional hazards if discovered. Considered less than human by other prisoners, they were killed without mercy at every opportunity. Nevertheless, successful recruits—and skillful security officers—kept the operation highly secret, and the chances of being strangled in the barracks were far smaller than of expiring of hunger and exhaustion "on general [camp] duties." Soon after arrival at their camps, prisoners had to decide whether their lives were worth preserving at any moral cost. A surprising percentage—perhaps even a majority—decided they were not.

[Some twenty years later, Solzhenitsyn summed up the quintessential wisdom of ordinary Russians turned prisoner. The camps, he wrote, helped many prisoners understand the worth of their own lives in relation to others. Although some felt that "boot-licking, flattery, and lies" might be tolerated to save themselves, the betrayal or destruction of innocent fellow prisoners was too high a price: "our lives aren't worth that."]

In other words, grave moral compromises were acceptable for the sake of sheer survival—but for survival as a human being with a moral core, a prisoner had to fix a line beyond which he would not step.

Solzhenitsyn's trouble was that he was far from ordinary. Servility, flattery, and lies were perhaps a tolerable price for some, but they nauseated him. His pride and concern for truth were serious liabilities; the minimum standards of decency in the camps fell too far below his own notions of self-respect—and this made his position in the Moscow camp uncommonly perilous. "I did not know how to cope with manual work," he explains, "and I was incapable of moral compromises."

Moral compromise in many variants is one of the principal themes of a Solzhenitsyn play set in another camp some hundreds of miles from Moscow. On the strength of his organizing abilities as a military man, an army captain recently arrested at the front is made the production supervisor of the camp's labor force. Soon he must decide whether to keep the position, in which he can assure a certain level of personal well-being and distribute some comfort to friends and the most desperate unfortunates —but only by adhering to the rules of the corrupt ration-grabbing game, which would continue to inflict severe hardship on the bulk of the prisoners. By instinct, the former captain breaks the rules and is promptly removed.

The play's action takes place in the autumn of 1945, and Solzhenitsyn has written that at about this time he spent part of his sentence in a camp of the same type though nearer to the capital than the play indicated. His removal there from the Moscow construction site was probably caused by the arrival after the war's end of replacements in the form of German prisoners of war called reparation laborers. Judging from the play, the new camp was considerably harder than the Moscow one, although still less severe than its counterparts in the frozen north. Potatoes grew in the ground there, as one of the inmates gratefully remarked, "so no one can call this remote." Another prisoner pointed out that they were lucky to be in a camp where spoons were necessary rather than in a deadly "Goners-ville" branch. " 'Gonersville' is when [the porridge] is so runny you can tip your tin and drink it over the edge."

Nevertheless, this second camp strained Solzhenitsyn's physical resources. He had not yet developed a life-saving manual skill nor an ability to wheel and deal. Like the production chief of the play, he was restrained by his instincts from taking part in gross injustice, even when tempted. In these circumstances, separated from direct help from nearby relatives, a continued spell even in this middle-ground camp might have been fatal, and he himself now believes that he would "never have survived in the camps" had he remained in ordinary ones for the length of his sentence. But, not for the last time, his mathematical training now "saved his life," in his words.

["One fine day," Solzhenitsyn remembers, "an official from the Prisons' Administration office came to our camp and distributed questionnaires among us. I entered [my profession] as a mathematician and physicist. I was then delivered to a research establishment which was inside a prison, and where the standards [of work] were so high that any scientist on the outside would have considered it an honor to work here."

This bolt from the blue came in July 1946, after some nine months of forced labor. The research establishment was the *sharashka* which Solzhenitsyn was to make famous in *The First Circle.*[

‹ X ›

The First Circle

Sharashka IS UNDERWORLD SLANG FOR A rowdy flea market specializing in stolen goods. Many Russians do not know the word's primary meaning, but most scientists and high intellectuals recognize it as the sobriquet for the singular research institutes that functioned under Stalin. Staffed primarily by prisoners, they were operated by and for the secret police. Thus *sharashka* was both ironic and highly precise, for here the NKVD obtained creative research on the cheap. It cost them only food and hostel-type lodgings for the scientists they had incarcerated.

Solzhenitsyn's life in his *sharashka* is reflected almost precisely by *The First Circle,* the novel which his friends say is his most autobiographical. Gleb Nerzhin, a central protagonist, is in some ways a precise portrait of Solzhenitsyn himself; other major characters are so nearly based on real people that only their surnames are changed. Thus Dmitry Sologdin is a skilled Russian engineer in real life (who confirmed in 1972 that the novel is largely "nonfiction fiction"), and Lev Rubin closely resembles Lev Kopelev, a literary critic who was to play a substantial role in Solzhenitsyn's career.[1] Place names are also authentic, and Stalin and his closest aides are portrayed as themselves, every detail of their appearance and setting having been painstakingly researched. In short, much of *The First Circle* is reportage delayed from the 1940s on one of our century's most bizarre institutions: a kind of intellectual broiler farm, where some three hundred scientists, kept like so many battery hens, produced ideas and inventions.

Although the institution as a whole had been born in the early 1930s, the *sharashka* for which Solzhenitsyn was selected had only recently been established. His ascent from the circle of concentration-camp hell occupied

[1] A photograph of Solzhenitsyn with these, his two closest prison friends, was taken several years ago and entitled by them "The Three Musketeers of Sharashka—Twenty Years On."

by general labor camps to the "best and highest" first circle took place
in prison railway cars and Black Marias. Virtually overnight, brutal physical labor was replaced by a quiet contemplative limbo: Solzhenitsyn's old,
prized pleasures of reading, writing, and thinking. Hunger was stilled by
a good diet which included unlimited quantities of black rye bread, still
rationed in Moscow shops and unavailable in the countryside. Prisoners
were allowed to maintain accounts, although not cash, and, for those who
could afford it, groceries were delivered from Moscow's best shops—a
kind of NKVD delicatessen service. And in comparison with the cold,
packed barracks and suffocating, teeming jails he had left, both pervaded
with the stench of open latrines, Solzhenitsyn's new living conditions were
actually pleasant.

[When the prisoners' van passed the barbed-wire boundary, he found
himself in an old country estate whose buildings stood within a park of
century-old linden trees. When the trees were planted, Marfino, as the estate was named,[2] was half a day from Moscow by horse. By the 1940s, the
city limits had expanded to approach it, but without disturbing its pastoral
character. For several months after Solzhenitsyn's arrival, Marfino's inmates were permitted to roam freely in the park; in the evening they
strolled "on dewy lawns." Although this was soon forbidden in a general
tightening of security, prisoners were nevertheless granted three hours a
day for walking.[

Like many nineteenth-century estates, Marfino had its own church—
which was now the inmates' barracks. The church was divided in two by
flooring laid halfway up its walls, and each story was further subdivided
by vertical partitions. Solzhenitsyn found himself quartered in a compartment on the second floor, part of the altar cupola. A wall divided the
cupola in half, and the vaulted ceiling "circumscribed the semicircular
room like the firmament." Five tall Empire windows provided a fine view
of the park and roofs of the neighboring village of Marfino. A drawing
made by one of the prisoners from Solzhenitsyn's window shows a peaceful
cluster of trees in rich autumn foliage. These quarters offered little privacy;
Solzhenitsyn's half of the cupola contained a dozen bunk beds. But in
contrast to the camps, each prisoner had his own bunk without sharing,
and slept on sheets instead of filthy mattresses.

Otherwise, elements of Marfino might have been designed by some
secret police decorator trying to harmonize the establishment's function
with its faintly spooky appearance. Not satisfied with the juxtaposition of
barbed wire and bucolic setting or with a church converted to a barracks,
he had the inmates wear an odd costume: "strange blue one-piece overalls

---

[2] Solzhenitsyn calls it "Mavrino" in *The First Circle*, but although certain details of the
estate seem slightly disguised, it has been confirmed that the setting is Marfino, roughly ten
miles north of the present Sheremetyevo International Airport.

instead of usual human clothes." The sight of these science-fiction robots completed Marfino's prevailing atmosphere of eeriness, which all outsiders sensed when setting foot on the grounds. The ultimate touch was super-secrecy: to mention the very existence of this "enchanted" place was to break a powerful taboo and violate its most strictly enforced law. Sol-zhenitsyn hardly exaggerated when he called it "a magician's castle sepa-rated from the capital and its unknowing inhabitants by a bewitched, free-fire zone."

In substance, Marfino was an institute conducting classified research in various aspects of electronic communications. Although it existed to serve the specific needs of the secret police, nothing more sinister was done dur-ing Solzhenitsyn's first eighteen months there than the development of a kind of walkie-talkie for general police work, for which Solzhenitsyn pro-duced some of the necessary mathematical calculations. Early in 1948, however, Marfino was assigned a new project ordered by Stalin himself: development of telephone scramblers ensuring conversational secrecy even if his lines were tapped. Solzhenitsyn was put in charge of the mathe-matical calculations of audibility tests.

It was as good a prison life as he could hope for. Physical safety was ensured and the option of death by overwork and undernourishment or survival by collaboration had been removed. Since Solzhenitsyn could not have hoped to earn his living by writing in Stalin's Russia, his work in Marfino was similar to what he would have been doing as a free man. The institute was not merely "one of the most enlightened corners" of the prison empire, but of the country as a whole.

Marfino's inmates spanned the whole spectrum of types, characters, and experiences, from "people who had spent fifty days in a death cell and people who knew the Pope and Albert Einstein personally" to workers and peasants caught up in the purges. Most were only too eager to re-lieve the boredom of prison life by recounting the stories of their lives, with or without prompting Solzhenitsyn would spot prisoners with a prom-ise of interesting stories or ideas and invite them to accompany him during the walk period. His genuine interest in people attracted them to him, and he was seldom refused. This arrangement provided a privacy impossible in the liivng quarters, therefore greater frankness. As with Plato and his disciples in their Athenian olive grove, philosophical strolling in their linden park was Marfino prisoners' most intense intellectual preoccupa-tion. Even the more cautious exchanges indoors were in some ways freer than in ordinary life—and always on an exceptionally high level.

These exchanges, usually on philosophical, historical, and political sub-jects, were the principal pastime outside work; they contributed signifi-cantly to Solzhenitsyn's incomplete education and powerfully influenced his intellectual development. Strong clashes of opinion by thoughtful men were important raw material for the future writer. His friendships, especially with X, had been based on a fundamental harmony of ideas, with relatively minor differences in details. But here, honest men disagreed about fundamental issues, something which broadened his tolerance and gave him an opportunity—rare for the hypercautious times—of observing the workings of strong minds in intellectual opposition.

⌊Solzhenitsyn's principal adversary in this sparring was a large man —large in every sense—named Lev Kopelev. Six years Solzhenitsyn's senior, a former university lecturer in German literature, a man of wide general erudition, he was a kind of prototype of the fiery, "know-it-all" Russian-Jewish intellectual, and in fact was noticeably more developed intellectually than Solzhenitsyn. Other elements of Kopelev's personality made him a compelling, if sometimes exasperating, adversary in debate. Animated by his vivid mental images of prerevolutionary injustices, as much in love with the party as is any such stereotype in literature, transfixed by Stalinism's self-contained logic, he was simultaneously an orthodox and an idealist Stalinist. Despite his own case, he felt that Stalin's policies as a whole were correct and necessary for the country and for progress toward a world proletarian revolution. Stalinism and only Stalinism, he believed, could bring this millennium to earth, even if the crude and stupid people who implemented it often made mistakes; even if their mistakes included the imprisonment and brutal treatment of innocent people—indeed, of those who, like himself, sincerely admired Stalin.⌋

By contrast, Solzhenitsyn had hardened in prison to repudiate the whole thrust of Stalinism, including its cardinal element, the forcible collectivization of agriculture. Although his condemnation was still based on his reading of Marxism, Solzhenitsyn, unlike Kopelev, saw in Stalin himself the central source of the crudeness and stupidity which had brought so much suffering to Russia. Solzhenitsyn's view was far from unique at that time, but it had brought him to awareness, unusual even among intellectuals, of the causes of Russia's malady. Moreover, he was losing his faith in Marxism's utopian promises, if not in its usefulness as an instrument of historical and social analysis.

In place of his earlier acceptance of Marxism's basic tenets and his underlying optimism, he was developing a generalized skepticism, supplemented by a personal ethic influenced by Taoist stoicism. He valued skepticism "as a form of liberation for the dogmatic mind," thus tacitly admitting that the Leninism of his earlier years had been too rigid and dogmatic. He felt that "humanity needed skepticism for breaking stony heads and stuffing down fanatic throats."

Tao ethics appealed to Solzhenitsyn as a kind of counterbalance which might help avert the self-seeking cynicism to which skepticism—the realization that the pursuit of happiness in the Marxist millennium had failed in Russia—so often and so easily led. "He who knows how to be content will be content with little," Nerzhin quotes.

Many of Marfino's inmates shared Solzhenitsyn's skepticism; the stoical ethic of self-denial was far less popular. Solzhenitsyn found himself roughly in the center between the dogmatic, ascetic "left" represented by Kopelev and the self-indulgent, cynical "right," in those disillusioned prisoners who considered self-interest the only practicable approach to life. For the first time, he was hammering out his own intellectual stand, borrowing from and resisting elements of conflicting philosophies around him. The opportunities for this kind of intellectual development scarcely existed elsewhere in Russia. Opposition to the absolute "unanimity of thought" disseminated by the party was almost always expressed in the company of narrow circles of friends united by a common outlook, the only foundation for trust.

Had Solzhenitsyn met Kopelev outside prison, it is unlikely that he would have taken the risk to speak frankly to him. An incautious word might have led to quick disaster, and Kopelev's outlook might have suggested that he was capable of reporting to the secret police. Only Marfino's intimacy and unique freedom—living with Kopelev under arrest, sharing a room with him, observing him continuously in all phases of life —made clear to Solzhenitsyn that a supporter of Stalin's general line could be not only intelligent but honest; that fundamental political disagreement among decent men did not necessarily make enemies. It was one of Stalinism's many perversities that Solzhenitsyn found freedom of debate, one of his life goals, only in prison. For his protagonist the luxury of "exchanges of free thought without fear, without concealment," made prison life "not all that black." [3]

Discussion of life and thought raged in Marfino like a nonstop colloquium. Even sharp differences rarely caused estrangement; on the contrary, earnest disagreement was a foundation for trust. For intellectual antagonists were at the same time coconspirators, sharing a booty of free thought; the holders of the most disparate philosophies were guilty of the same "crime." Lev Kopelev was Solzhenitsyn's adversary and also his best friend.

Marfino friendships achieved a rare depth. In the absence of family life, and with the knowledge that the few "free" women employed in the research laboratories were inaccessible or untrustworthy, friendship afforded the only form of genuine human exchange. Solzhenitsyn came to

---

[3] Of course, only the *sharashkas* enjoyed this freedom. Denunciations for "subversive talk" continued to be a regular feature of ordinary camps. Although informers operated in the *sharashkas* too, the operation was conducted on a much smaller and less dangerous scale since the authorities were reluctant to upset their valuable inhabitants needlessly.

see in them "a kind of happiness, the kind we didn't have on the outside." His Marfino attachments were to last indefinitely and play a significant role in his postprisoner life.

Marfino's philosophical debates did not burn themselves out over the years, but were constantly stoked by new intellectual fuel. Despite the inmates' total isolation from the outside world, they had almost as much access to information as employees of ordinary research institutions— meaning, at that time, more than virtually all Soviet citizens. Under the pretext of research needs, they could order almost any book from any library in Russia. Through Western European and American technical journals, they had a glimpse too of the Western world. The Soviet press and radio were constantly available, and, although hardly informative in the ordinary sense, they provided a gauge of Soviet trends. (Labor camp inmates were deprived of newspapers and often of radios.) And despite the strict prohibition and dangers, some Marfino prisoners employed in the radio research department assembled short-wave sets capable of receiving foreign stations. The home-made receivers were often dismantled after each listening session, to prevent discovery during periodic searches and security checks.

The security procedures annoyed Solzhenitsyn more than most other inmates. He was concerned about hiding not equipment but manuscripts. For he had begun to write again. In the Army, he had time only for sketches, apart from his letters and diary entries. In transit prisons, he participated in some collective oral composition: inmate "happenings" which usually reflected prison conditions in wry satire, together with the outside world's naïveté about them.[4] In his labor camps, it was not so much the lack of time as of strength that had kept him from writing. Thus Marfino provided the conditions for his first sustained literary effort after an interruption of over five years.

In addition to the stimulation of its extraordinary intellectual community, Marfino provided the opportunities for creative withdrawal that Solzhenitsyn needed to write. He had his own desk, supposedly for mathematical calculations—and, within limits, control of his time. So long as he completed his tasks, he was left undisturbed. In mathematics—unlike writing—Solzhenitsyn worked quickly, and was left with considerable free

---

[4] *The Smile of Buddha,* a novella inserted into *The First Circle,* is largely a restoration of one such composition. It describes the tragicomic eyewash performed on an influential and benevolent American lady, often thought to represent Eleanor Roosevelt, during her visit to a Moscow prison. Collective oral composition continued in Marfino. Solzhenitsyn has described the inmates staging a trial by NKVD officers of Prince Igor, the hero of a medieval Russian *geste.* The prince is charged with—and duly convicted of—complicity in his own defeat by steppe nomads. If not for their reflection of current reality, these compositions would have made a kind of theater of the absurd.

time. Behind barricades of learned tomes on his desk, bent protectively
over his paper, he worked away at his writing, glancing up at intervals
to ensure that he was unnoticed.

⌊The manuscripts were hidden in Solzhenitsyn's own desk, where he
constructed a cache inside a tier of drawers. Since its volume was greatly
restricted, Solzhenitsyn adapted his formerly bold and broad handwriting,
now writing as tightly as possible, "as if carving with a needle."⌋

⌊The manuscripts were not discovered, but they did not survive: Solzhenitsyn himself burned them in a lavatory several hours before his
deportation from Marfino. He knew that they would be found during the
thorough search at the magic castle's gates, and that they would be confiscated and he saddled with an additional sentence. Still, the ten-minute
burning of his own "books" was hard on him; Nerzhin is described emerging from the act "white-faced and indifferent to everything." In a sense,
three years of his life had been cremated. The "little sheets of paper" that
were reduced to ashes "represented his first maturity—at the age of thirty."⌋

What Solzhenitsyn wrote in Marfino is a matter for speculation. *The
First Circle* is less helpful about this than it otherwise might have been,
for Solzhenitsyn made the semiautobiographical hero a historian, a significant departure from his own background. And in general, he refuses
to discuss his unpublished manuscripts, even those which survived. Yet
he probably grappled with the phenomenon of Stalin in a preliminary way
in Marfino, perhaps laying the groundwork for the Stalin chapters of *The
First Circle,* completed a decade later. As in adolescence and later at the
front, Solzhenitsyn was still gripped with curiosity about "the bloated
gloomy giant." Now, after his voyage from comfortable reaches of Stalinist
society to the most desperate levels, he could reflect maturely about the
dictator, his own experiences supplemented by reading and other inmates' stories.

There was one side of Solzhenitsyn's work, however, which was not
only unhidden, but addressed to the prison administration; if and when
their archives are opened, examples of Solzhenitsyn's writing will probably
be found. This work was in the characteristically Russian genre known as
the *zhaloba,* roughly "complaint by petition."

Russians have been writing *zhaloby* in one or another form for centuries: to tsars, governors, ranking officials, and petty bureaucrats—all manner of overlords. In an autocracy lacking the rule of law, appeal to the
highest authority was often the only hope for justice—most often, for
redress of an injustice inflicted by a petty tyrant within the vast bureaucracy. In medieval Russia, the writing of complaints was a lucrative
profession, and some of the surviving examples, especially from the reign
of Ivan the Terrible, make moving reading. In the last half century of
tsarist rule, the fine art of the *zhaloba* began to lose its edge as conditions

slowly improved, but it revived spontaneously under Stalin's dictatorship.

Solzhenitsyn fitted squarely into the tradition, which he went on to develop. Complaining about infringements of prisoners' minuscule rights —confiscation of a permitted book; the stealing by the cooks of a portion of the flour ration—might seem a quixotic gesture in the context of the larger injustice of the camps themselves. But Solzhenitsyn's determination to fight for these slenderest of rights helped preserve his sense of dignity. His autobiographical hero prides himself on his skill in composing *zhaloby,* and the description of Gleb Nerzhin's complaints fits the style of Solzhenitsyn's protests even in the late 1960s and early 1970s. It was characterized by a deft barracks-lawyer approach which produced a tight amalgam of conciseness and meticulous matter-of-factness—and, throughout, a careful control of underlying anger.

> Nerzhin had a natural gift for unhesitatingly composing complaints in a few stunning words. And of rapping them out in one breath during the short second when the food slot in the cell door opened, or fitting them onto the scrap of tissue paper, fit for a toilet, which was issued in jails for writing petitions. During five years inside, he had evolved a special resolute manner of addressing prison administrators—what prisoners called in their lingo "laying on some classy lashes." He used only proper words, but his arrogant and ironic tone—which, however, no one could find fault with—was the tone of a superior talking to a subordinate.

It was a skill which decisively influenced Solzhenitsyn's style as a publicist when he emerged as a public "protester" almost twenty years later.

However, in the 1940s the thought that protest would find even the most tenuous place in Russian life during the inmates' lifetime seemed insane, and Solzhenitsyn was in no way intentionally preparing himself for the day. It was the opportunity to resume his creative writing in something resembling normal conditions for which Solzhenitsyn valued Marfino most of all. And it was the thought of losing this privilege that helped prompt an extraordinary decision taken after some three and a half years in the *sharashka.* In late 1949, Solzhenitsyn prepared to leave the first circle and descend into the "bottomless pit" of the hardest of labor camps.

XI

Descent

EVEN FOR PRISONERS WEARY OF Marfino's zombielike routine, it was rare to leave the castle deliberately for a "proper" labor camp in the hinterland. Solzhenitsyn did not volunteer, but took certain definite actions which he knew carried a clear threat of expulsion. Prompted by moral and personal crises which had been gestating for more than a year, the actions are described, again autobiographically, in *The First Circle*.

For Solzhenitsyn, one of Marfino's most treasured privileges was free time. In late 1949, he was given to understand that he would soon be deprived of it. The institute's stewards had selected him for a new, highly challenging job. Professionally, it was an undeniable compliment. Solzhenitsyn had never extended himself as a mathematician, precisely in order to conserve as much time as possible for his own thoughts. Having completed his tasks, he would delay delivering the results until the time when less able minds would have produced them. But after some years, he was given an assignment in which he could not conceal his intelligence. It was an investigation of a particularly intricate mathematical problem, and, however long he delayed, his simple and elegant solution revealed a penetration essential for more creative research. It was then suggested —meaning ordered—that he become one of the chief mathematicians of a new team being assembled to develop a coding device.

The compliment was unwanted, at the very least because the new job would occupy Solzhenitsyn totally, absorbing all his intellectual energy as well as most of his waking hours. Pondering a similar offer, his autobiographical hero delineates the dilemma.

> Give oneself up to the tentacles of the cryptographic octopus? Fourteen hours a day, without a break, one's head would be usurped by the theory of probabilities, the theory of numbers, the theory of errors. . . . A dead mind, a parched soul. What would remain for reflection? For learning about life?

On the other hand, it was a *sharashka*. It wasn't a camp. Meat
for dinner and butter for breakfast. No rough, lacerated skin on
your hands. No frostbitten fingers and toes. No flopping dead on
your boards like a dumb log in your muddy boots; you get in bed
under a lovely white sheet. . . . Sweet comfort! What good are you
if there's nothing but you?

All rational considerations led to this: Yes, I agree, Citizen
Commander. All considerations of the heart prompted something
else: Get thee behind me, Satan.

But resistance to a major intrusion upon his intellect and to the temptations of a mechanical but comfortable existence were not the only factors
in Solzhenitsyn's decision. Conscience was a longer-standing and more
fundamental issue. Marfino's work involved the prisoner in a larger moral
dilemma: in one way or another, all were helping to make the secret police
more effective. Prisoners' skills were exploited to make more prisoners.
Solzhenitsyn too was contributing a part of his gifts toward this end—
and not in an easily rationalizable way, for he was helping prepare ma-
chines intended to augment Stalin's personal security.

Actually, prisoners could justify their complicity in terms of the alternative: refusal to participate meant a great risk to life. And in Solzhenitsyn's case, by the luxury of partial withdrawal in his own inner
world, with time for thought, valuable conversation, and writing. He could
feel that this might one day compensate for his contribution to Marfino's
goals—but no longer if he had to give mind and body to the new research.

A second crisis of the Marfino years was more intimate. Perhaps the
research institute's hardest punishment was its total isolation from the
"real" world. Reshetovskaya lived a mere hour away in Moscow, but "it
was as if she were on Mars." In the magic castle, unlike his first camps,
he needed no food, and Reshetovskaya's unease grew with her inability to
help him in any material way. Nor could she bring him much comfort.
Visits were never permitted more than once a month, and sometimes as
rarely as once a year. The meetings were held in various Moscow prisons,
to which Marfino inmates were delivered and quickly returned. The purpose was to avoid all mention and clues about the research institute, and
every minute spent with relatives was chaperoned to prevent a whispered
hint about the prisoners' whereabouts and work. It was obvious to Reshetovskaya that Solzhenitsyn's physical appearance had improved remarkably. He was even dressed in ordinary clothes (which were allocated to
prisoners in place of their robotlike overalls for the duration of their visits).
Solzhenitsyn could only assure his wife of his physical and material well-
being. But he appeared from nowhere and disappeared into a void; and
his smile, his face, even his movements, reflected this ghostly existence.

The relatives [of the prisoners] were not to know where their living-dead men lived, whether they had been led in from some place a thousand kilometers away or from the Savior's Gate of the Kremlin, from an airport or the yonder world. They could see well-fed, well-dressed men with soft hands—no longer talkative, smiling sadly and giving assurances that all their wants were seen to and they needed nothing.

These visits had something in common with ancient Greek steles—the slates of the low relief depicting both the deceased and the living who were erecting his tombstone. But the steles always had a thin line dividing the other world from this one. The living gazed fondly at the dead man, while he looked toward Hades: looked with eyes that were neither happy nor sad, but transparent —the gaze of knowing too much.

In some ways, Solzhenitsyn's eerie existence frightened Reshetovskaya more than the known hardships of the camps. Added to this were fears about her position, no easier to bear because they were of a more practical nature. The relatives of "enemies of the people"—wives, mothers, and even children—were persecuted in a variety of ways. Most were excluded from professional training and all but menial jobs, expelled from Russia's major cities and spied upon, even set upon, keeping them in a state of constant anxiety.

Reshetovskaya had avoided persecution only by concealing her marriage from the university, which was possible because her surname was not Solzhenitsyn. But in 1949 her postgraduate studies were approaching their end. When applying for a job, she would be given a long questionnaire including a section about close relatives in prison. To lie was to invite her own imprisonment. Only divorce could avert the threat. Under normal circumstances, it was difficult to obtain, but anyone married to a prisoner had only to apply.

Solzhenitsyn understood the full implications of Reshetovskaya's position. Since his first correspondence with her after his arrest in 1945, he had urged her to divorce him. At first, the thought of even a sham divorce upset her; she felt it would seal their separation, which she refused to accept. It would end even her infrequent visits to Solzhenitsyn, leaving them both alone. Despite the sad tales of other prisoners' wives, she felt her bond to Solzhenitsyn was unique: they, if no one else, would overcome the strains of separation, would outlive the sentence, would return to what they had had.

Yet inevitably they were estranged. They had lives to live in which their love for each was buried under the weight of their separate troubles. Solzhenitsyn had been imprisoned for some five years; they had been

apart—since he went to war—for eight. This was not unduly long in the
Russia of that era—but in their case there had been just one year together
before separation. Both had changed drastically since; both faced the fact
of the change. It was no longer realistic to talk of picking up the old relationship after Solzhenitsyn's release; they could only hope for a new
beginning.

> The horror was just this: there would be no return. *To return* was
> precluded . . . perhaps not a single cell of his body would remain
> as it had been. All that was possible was to show up *anew*. A new
> man would arrive, a stranger bearing the name of her former hus-
> band, and she would see that her first and only man, for whom she
> had waited, withdrawn within herself . . . that man no longer ex-
> isted: he had evaporated, one molecule after another. If they were
> to fall in love with each other again in this second life, that would
> be fine. But if not? . . .

From here, it was but a step to accepting the expedient of a temporary
divorce. But it was still painful to put the thought in words. The exchanges
of Reshetovskaya and Solzhenitsyn are again suggested by *The First Circle*,
when the inmate is visited by a graduate chemist of exactly her age. She
raises the subject with difficulty.

> "I wanted to say. . . . Only you won't be hurt, will you? . . .
> You once insisted that we . . . get a divorce."
> Her last words were very quiet. . . . Yes, there had been a time
> when he'd insisted on this. But now he shuddered. And only at this
> moment noticed that her wedding ring, with which she never
> parted, was not on her finger . . .
> "Good girl! You should have done it long ago," agreed Gleb
> firmly, feeling neither firmness nor conviction and deciding to
> postpone his puzzling until after she'd left.
> "Maybe I won't have to," she said with an entreating tone, again
> pulling her coat over her shoulders. At that moment, she looked
> very tired and worn. "I just wanted to agree on it, just in case. . . .
> Maybe it won't come up."
> "No, why not? You're absolutely right. Good girl," repeated
> Gleb without feeling . . .

Solzhenitsyn could end such confrontations by leaving Marfino. If he
were far from Moscow and unavailable for visits, Reshetovskaya could
go through with the divorce more easily. Desire to relieve her of her dilemma, therefore, supplemented his distaste for the proposed new assignment and nagging moral reflections about being in Marfino at all.

There was another reason for wanting to leave the research institute.
Although he feared the "bottomless pit" of labor camps no less than other

prisoners, Marfino now seemed to him more destructive of his inner self than physical death itself. He felt he was "drowning in a puddle" of stale relationships and stifling routine. A fear of insanity was setting in. In a poem of the time he repeated a famous line of Pushkin: "Prison is watching me from every corner. 'God, let me not go mad.'" However dangerous it might be, he needed new stimulation, *any* kind of change.

This merged with Solzhenitsyn's old instinct to go to "first sources" and to explore whatever he was engaged in to its outer limits and fullest depths. In his brief periods in labor camps and now at Marfino he had escaped something essential in the "mainland" of prison life: the experience of a lone struggle for existence in a cold, remote camp. Just as he would not have a safe war grooming horses and listening to other people's tales, he would not have a "comfortable half-free" imprisonment in the *sharashka* as a prisoner who knew much of prison's most important meaning only from secondary sources.

And something else beckoned him from the camps—an attraction that might seem perverse, but that artists share with other seekers of adventure. Solzhenitsyn wanted an "experiment" of testing himself in confrontation with death. Thomas Mann, whose urge to write in boyhood paralleled Solzhenitsyn's, addressed himself searchingly to the question of what distinguishes the creative personality, and in one of his reflections spoke of "impoverishment and devastation as a preliminary condition" to serious writing. "Good work comes out only under the pressure of a bad life," says an autobiographical Mann character; ". . . one must die in life to be utterly a creator." Mann was speaking here of experiences less literally lethal than Solzhenitsyn was likely to face. But he mentions the awakening, illuminating possibilities of prison. In the case of both writers (and those they represent) there seems to be a craving for "utterness"—being pushed to the limits of human experience; facing the hardest tests of nature and society alone—to provide creative insight. As Solzhenitsyn's fictional protagonist sets out from Marfino to face his ordeal, he speaks of a turning point, which "must bring . . . a hard and long haul to somewhere in Siberia or the Arctic. To take him to death or to victory over death."

All these factors bore on Solzhenitsyn's decision. The final element was timing. He was in his prime, a time when some men, confident of their energy and strength, begin to feel that the predestined time has arrived for them to strike out toward the principal experiences of their lives. From childhood, Solzhenitsyn had thought of life in terms of the laws of drama. In youth, the dramatic elements appeared to fit into the framework of Chekhov and Tolstoy: every man shapes his own life, every destiny is determined by character. Now destiny seemed predetermined, more in keeping with Greek drama; yet every man continued to play his role as his character required. Solzhenitsyn felt that the time for his own major scene had arrived, and that he must play it honestly and well, however the action might end.

> Each person has his special moment of life when he unfolded himself to the fullest, felt to the deepest, and expressed himself to the utmost, to himself and to others.

Only such motivation from a strong, categorical personality can explain a willingness to leave Marfino for a labor camp. Still, at the decisive moment—when Solzhenitsyn refused the offer of the new job—it was to his own surprise. His supervisor was more than surprised: with controlled anger, he made a note to "write off" Solzhenitsyn—to dispose of him, that is, as part of Marfino's inventory. Solzhenitsyn knew what almost certainly awaited him after the refusal, and during the last months in Marfino openly neglected his desk job, volunteering instead for outdoor tasks such as sweeping the park's alleys. Self-respecting scientists hoping for an early release through dedicated research tried to avoid these chores. On Solzhenitsyn, they worked as a sedative.

A portrait sketched by the same fellow inmate who had painted Marfino's park in its autumn foliage (probably Kondrashev of *The First Circle*) showed that Solzhenitsyn looked older than his thirty-one years in his final *sharashka* days. The light brown hair was still thick, but his faded skin was cut by wrinkles around the eyes and mouth and a prominent crease in his forehead. Protuberant eyes set in a gaunt face demonstrated that Marfino's relative comforts had not kept away a "prison look." Solzhenitsyn's hero was also thirty-one as he left that winter for his distant camp, a few months earlier than his creator followed him in real life. "Was it the middle of his life? Almost its end? Only the beginning?"

XII

Щ-232

On a balmy morning in mid-May 1950, Solzhenitsyn was suddenly interrupted while clearing winter leaves from the park, and within hours found himself in transport to an unknown destination. His first leg was to a transit jail where prisoners often stayed months in severely overpopulated cells while offices of the prison empire matched the need for labor in this or that far-flung outpost against the available supply. Solzhenitsyn spent the summer of 1950 awaiting allocation, and it was again growing cold when his long migration to the camps began.

"Transport" was a distinct phase, often the most perilous, of a prisoner's life. Obsessive security during any shifting of prisoners led to search after search of their persons—in this case, after they had been stripped to their underwear in the bitter cold. Throughout their long shunting across the country, the prisoners lived in "gray transit jails with a permeating stink and sealed suffocating compartments of freight cars." The suffocation was caused by the packing of nineteen—in some cases, twenty-three—into a space designed by the tsarist penal authorities for five prisoners or one guard horse. Even in the dead of the Russian winter, the freight cars were barely heated. In place of Marfino's regular meat and butter, Solzhenitsyn and his traveling companions were issued—at irregular intervals—with frozen bread and a lukewarm liquid best described as prison soup. One of Solzhenitsyn's autobiographical characters mentions that at one point in transit, he was without water for forty-eight hours. "When one reads Dostoyevsky describing the horrors of life at hard labor," Solzhenitsyn has written, "one is astonished. How peacefully they served their time. In ten years they didn't face a single move."

Yet in the first days of their new "adventure" at least some of the Marfino deportees felt a kind of elation. Solzhenitsyn was not alone in having taken steps to exchange the *sharashka*'s distasteful ambiguities for the straightforward challenge of the camps. Other prisoners in this position were swept with a sense of release and of pride at having assumed at least some control of their own fate in the most adverse circumstances.

> . . . what awaited them was the taiga and the tundra, the Cold Pole of Oi-Myakon and copper mines of Dzhezkazgan. They would be faced with kicking and shoving, starvation rations of sodden bread, hospitals, and death. What awaited them was only the worst. But their inner selves were filled with peace. They were possessed by the fearlessness of men who have lost *everything*—a fearlessness difficult to attain, but solid.

Emotion of this kind led Solzhenitsyn to speak of "the true greatness of man which I had learned in prison."

Although a strain of fearlessness would endure within Solzhenitsyn and others throughout their prison years, the elation of leaving Marfino quickly evaporated in contact with the realities of "transport." Physical hardship was bad enough, but Solzhenitsyn was also shocked by the reaction of people outside to the prisoners' plight.

For "free" Soviet citizens who witnessed it, transport was as unsettling a time as it was unsettled for the prisoners themselves. Only at railroad stations along the prisoners' routes could most ordinary Russians come face to face with the realities of concentration-camp existence. For some, such stations became the site of their first anti-Stalinist feelings; the regime might have been disliked, mistrusted, or resented before, but the sight of the freight cars and their occupants—gruesome evidence of what had been known only in the abstract—provoked ineradicable revulsion.

Solzhenitsyn did not expect people to protest at the spectacle of prisoners being loaded and unloaded at the stations; no sane man would have betrayed his revulsion, however strong. Something else troubled him: that few witnesses to the ghastly scenes showed even recognition of the prisoners' existence. Solzhenitsyn interrupted his description of transport with an angry indictment of his fellow citizens' weakness and indifference—a passage distinct from his habitually compassionate tone.

> You have all seen [the prisoner] at that moment in our railway stations, but you hurried to sink your eyes like cowards, to turn away like loyal subjects lest the guards' lieutenant suspect you of something wrong and detain you.

There follows a broad picture of what millions of transportees faced at the time. This stage, Solzhenitsyn remarked, was as fateful for a prisoner as a wound for a soldier. As wounds ranged from "slight to grave, curable to mortal," transport too could be "short or long, diversion or death."

The prisoner steps into his carriage, which is coupled to the mail van. Densely barred on both sides, its interior invisible from the platform, the carriage travels with an ordinary train and in its sealed, stifling closeness transports a thousand memories, hopes and fears.

Where are they being taken? This is not disclosed. What awaits the prisoner at his new destination? Copper mines? A lumber camp? Or coveted farmwork where he will manage to bake himself an occasional potato or stuff his belly with fodder-turnips? Will he be laid low by scurvy or dystrophy from his very first month on general duties? Or will he be lucky enough to slip something to someone or to meet a friend and wangle a job as an orderly, hospital attendant, or even assistant quartermaster? And will he be allowed to send and receive letters at the new place? Or will they cut off his correspondence for years, making his loved ones count him among the dead? . . .

Maybe he won't even arrive at his destination? Will he die of dysentery in his cattle car? Or because the train will make time for six days without bread? Or will the guards beat him to death with their hammers for somebody's escape? Or at the journey's end, will they throw the prisoners' frozen corpses like logs from the unheated goods vans?

Freight trains take a month to a Pacific port . . .
Lord bless the memory of those who never arrive.

Solzhenitsyn did arrive. As his train made its way slowly across endless plains, furtive glimpses through crevices in the freight car walls provided a measure of relief: the station names indicated that they were being taken not to the tundra and its permafrost, but somewhere to the southeast. They still did not know precisely where when, cold and hungry, they were herded into the "cutting wind" of the steppe at a small station. The sign informed them that they had arrived in Dzhezkazgan, a town in western Kazakhstan, some 1500 miles from Moscow.

Excepting the extremes of polar regions, deserts, and impassable mountains, this was one of the least populated areas on earth. Hundreds of miles of desolate, virtually uninhabited territory surrounded the town on all sides. It was not for nothing that the local name for the area was "the hungry steppe." Some twenty-five miles north along the railway line was a second Dzhezkazgan: the camp complex. A fifty-mile branch line cut through it to the last station, which was named Karsakpai. The labor camps scattered along the branch line were known collectively as Karlag.

After unloading, Solzhenitsyn was sent to one of them, a spot in this huge empty area that bore the name "Sandy Camp." [1]

The *raison d'être* of the complex was copper mining. It was pursued in conditions which years later prompted Solzhenitsyn to grieve for his comrades, whom the ore was "poisoning to death." He himself never worked in the mines, and learned their human cost only through his fellow prisoners. Thanks to his work experience in the Moscow camp four years before, Solzhenitsyn was assigned to a construction brigade. Parquet flooring had a low priority in Dzhezkazgan; he was again an unskilled laborer here. Before the year was over, Solzhenitsyn was shuffled to another camp within Karlag, and from there to a coal-mining complex some five hundred miles to the northeast. The third camp, still within Kazakhstan, was called Ekibastuz. Solzhenitsyn was to serve out the final two-plus years of his sentence here, and make its atmosphere and living conditions known to the world through the peasant's perception of Ivan Denisovich, his best-known character.

Solzhenitsyn declines to talk about the details of his camp experience, even to clarify the sequences of his several camps—matters he considers private. However, it is clear that he was in Ekibastuz early in 1951, and, although he worked there too as an unskilled laborer, he soon became a bricklayer with a crew assigned to projects within the camp complex. He has said that he is present in his tale of this camp "insofar as I myself rafted timber and laid bricks."

Ekibastuz belonged to a new category of camps solely for political prisoners. In nationality, education, and social background, it was a wholly heterogeneous collection including former admirals and unskilled workers, peasants side by side with urban intellectuals. Sizable representations of nationalities recently annexed to the Soviet Union, especially Balts and West Ukrainians, were sprinkled among the main body of Russians. Many of Solzhenitsyn's fellow inmates were victims of Stalin's "social prophylaxis," a particular form of the terror. Under this policy, entire groups were arrested for what their members might do, rather than individuals for their real or imagined acts. Millions of former prisoners of war, for example, were incarcerated because the Germans might have recruited some of them as spies. Tens of thousands of students were sentenced as anti-Soviet agitators because a few had actually been caught expressing something less than favorable about Stalin. Large groups of other national

---

[1] The rustic camp names in Karlag and elsewhere—"River Camp," "Oak Camp," "Lake Camp," "Meadow Camp"—provoked a wry observation from one of Solzhenitsyn's characters. "You'd think there's some great unrecognized poet in the Ministry of the Interior, on Pushkin's scale. He can't quite bring himself to write a full-length poem and doesn't have the time for verses—but he gives poetic names to camps."

minorities—Chechens, Kalmuks, and Crimean Tartars, for example—suffered similarly.

Thus Ekibastuz provided Solzhenitsyn the opportunity for intimate acquaintance with many kinds of people whom he would not ordinarily have known at any length. The extreme diversity of social backgrounds influenced his outlook and, later, his work. Having lived as a rank-and-file laborer, he became that rare intellectual who spoke about "the people" without guesses, hypotheses, or poses. It required little imagination to see things through the eyes of Ivan Denisovich, that most ordinary of Russian peasants; Solzhenitsyn had lived with his prototypes and listened carefully to them when, under stress, their reactions and emotions were stripped bare. This would become apparent not only in Solzhenitsyn's creative writing but also in his public criticism of contemporary Russian social conditions: both would have a keen sensitivity to the mood of the nation as a whole rather than of its educated minority alone.

All the prisoners in Solzhenitsyn's camp had been sentenced as spies, saboteurs, or propagators of dangerous anti-Soviet propaganda. Actually, far less than one percent were guilty of any crime whatever, even to the extent that Solzhenitsyn himself was guilty—even under the distinctive definition of "counterrevolutionary crimes" in Soviet law. Solzhenitsyn has written wryly about one Ekibastuz prisoner who was believed to be a genuine Rumanian spy. The inmates, especially other sentenced "spies," were agog over this odd creature.

Political prisoners were considered especially dangerous, and guarded accordingly. The camps were constructed like reverse fortresses to keep the enemy in. "Two powerful searchlights swept the camp from the farthest watch towers," Solzhenitsyn wrote, describing an early morning in Ekibastuz. "The border lights were on, as well as those within the camps. There were so many that they outshone the stars." Specially fortified enclosures, inaccessible to prisoners, stood inside the fortress: the so-called lockup, for extra punishment of erring inmates—"the only brick building in the camp, with a high wooden fence around it"—and the bakery, which was "protected from the prisoners by barbed wire." Thus the captives were constantly confronted with physical evidence of their masters' power and their own impotence.

Another special arrangement made clear to them that the watchful power could zero in at any moment; that no one could hope for anonymity in the crowd of black uniforms. Each political prisoner was clearly identifiable by a letter-number designation. To the operators of his camp, Solzhenitsyn had no name: he was prisoner Щ-232. The letters of the alphabet stood for one thousand prisons. Щ, the twenty-sixth letter, indicated that Solzhenitsyn was the 26,232nd (political) prisoner in this single complex. Each prisoner wore his designation, in the form of prominent stencils on his uniform, during all waking hours. Former painters among the inmates were assigned the special duty of renewing the stencils.

Apart from the calculated humiliation of the designation, "politicals" lived under special restrictions such as the one which limited them to sending two letters a year. Compared to ordinary camps the discipline was stricter and the work more exhausting. Solzhenitsyn's camp, however, was not one of the worst, certainly not in comparison to those in the northern tundra. And it had the great advantage of not including professional criminals.

Most ordinary camps had a mixed criminal-political population. There, as in transit jails, thieves and bandits added enormously to the politicals' hardships. Tightly organized on the principle of all for one and one for all, professional criminals mercilessly exploited and terrorized the atomized mass who belonged to no band. They forced others to fulfill their own work quotas, leaving them prey to death by exhaustion, hunger, and cold. Death was all the more likely because they also confiscated the best boots and warmest clothing, together with food parcels, and sometimes half their rations. Younger prisoners were sometimes forced to serve as lackeys and homosexual lovers. In short, the most vicious forms of criminal activity were practiced on the only available subjects, often with the connivance of the camps' administrations where the victims were politicals.

Solzhenitsyn had encountered pros in his first transit prison after Lubyanka, and again in his camps in and near Moscow. His hatred for them exceeded even that for prison-informers. Several of his positive heroes, men of broad general compassion, came to the point of excluding pros from the community of human beings. Solzhenitsyn's personality, especially his difficulty in swallowing personal humiliation, might well have caused him serious trouble had the Ekibastuz camp also contained pros; murdering men who resisted their demands was an act of no consequence to the latter.

Even without the pros, however, climate and geography made survival uncertain. Eastern Kazakhstan was largely uninhabited simply because it was uninhabitable, even by nomads. Ekibastuz lies a few miles from the Irtysh River, one of the half dozen great rivers of Siberia. The town is surrounded by steppeland "so flat," as a local resident put it, "that you can see everything for a hundred miles as if on your palm." This observer, who arrived at roughly the same time as Solzhenitsyn, spoke of a stark landscape broken by barracks and of a water shortage caused by the intense salinity of the earth.[2] He spoke too of the severity of the climate. Summer heat and winter cold reached painful extremes on the vast land

---

[2] Eki-bas-tuz, in fact, means "two heads of salt" in Kazakh. The name is drawn from a local legend.

mass, and both were exacerbated by an almost ceaseless wind. Violent snowstorms called *buran* in Russian were a particular test of endurance, as Ivan Denisovich expressed in his simple way. "When a *buran* begins to blow up in these parts . . . if you don't rig up a rope from the barracks to the mess hall, you lose your way. And if a prisoner freezes to death in the snow—well, he's only dog meat." Hard as they were, however, the storms were welcomed, for they provided respite from the hardest trial: work.

Solzhenitsyn's own writings were to become the classic portrait of life in the camps. But *One Day in the Life of Ivan Denisovich* is an account of a *good* day, and of a man accustomed to manual labor. For Solzhenitsyn and others not so trained, most days were that much harder. In winter, the work often lasted ten or eleven hours in the open; in summer, longer. Winds blew constantly over the naked steppe, intensifying both heat and cold to near the limits of tolerance. The unaccustomed effort of digging and bricklaying at raw construction sites demanded energy unreplenished by the rations, principally heavy bread, thin porridge, and soups of vegetables or fish. While work drained the prisoners' strength, hunger and exposure threatened their health. The inmates' thick cotton jackets provided scant protection against the fierce cold and inadequate relief from the dizzying heat. The thin-walled wooden barracks were also unequal to the elements; prisoners were almost permanently chilled in winter and sweltering in summer. The unprivileged caste who lived and worked "on general duties," as it was known, were called "sloggers." Solzhenitsyn joined them in late 1950.

One Day describes his living conditions with documentary precision. A former naval commander named Boris Burkovsky, who lived in Solzhenitsyn's barracks and appears in the novel as Commander Buinovsky, has said that "the general picture of camp life, as well as many details, was identical to that of the book." Burkovsky has also made clear that many of the novel's characters are in fact portraits from life. Among them are an experienced, authoritative work-crew leader, a privileged former film director, and Burkovsky himself, an idealistic Communist defiantly protesting against camp conditions. Unlike Solzhenitsyn's other "prison" novels, however, *One Day* contains no autobiographical character. For a description of Solzhenitsyn, therefore, one must turn to Burkovsky himself. Solzhenitsyn, he has recalled, was "a good comrade, an honest fellow." He did not stand out from the mass of prisoners, but "was taciturn [and] never got involved in loud discussions." There was no intimacy, little security, and no energy for Marfino's throbbing talk.

Like his appearance, Solzhenitsyn's mental attitude did not stand out sharply from that of many other prisoners. The advancing exhaustion of "general duties" brought him near to exasperation and despair. In accordance with his fundamental principle "not to overdo the horrors of prison life," *One Day* does not record the full extent of his desperation. Solzhenitsyn's intention was to portray "something more frightening—the gray routine year after year when you forget that the only life you have on earth is destroyed." But this decision about what to stress belonged to a later period. While on general duties in Ekibastuz, Solzhenitsyn saw himself as a kind of draft animal being worked to death, heaving a "powerless pickax" to spark against the frozen earth. He shared with other prisoners the certainty that time had stopped and his suffering would be endless.

> The shining world will never be, and never was!
> A hoar-covered cloth wrapped about my face,
> A fight for porridge, a shout from the crew boss,
> Another day—one more day without an end.

Nevertheless, Solzhenitsyn was distinguished from other prisoners by his covert creativity—of which this poem was an example. A new kind of creative urge seized him, almost compulsive in its intensity.

Solzhenitsyn's "writing" in Ekibastuz was in fact not quite that, for had the camp authorities suspected that one of the "drudges" was bearing witness to camp conditions he would have been locked up for long spells in the freezing isolation chamber, after which a second sentence for anti-Soviet agitation would surely have followed. Therefore his creative instinct had to be secret, together with its products. Constant searches of prisoners' persons and belongings precluded normal writing. To others in the barracks, even friends such as Commander Burkovsky, all that could be noticed of Solzhenitsyn's literary inclinations was a highly developed interest in language, something understandably rare among prisoners on general duties. In keeping with his old habit, Solzhenitsyn took pains to study the speech and social manners of his diverse collection of fellow inmates. And Burkovsky recalled that in his spare moments, Solzhenitsyn would often "lie down on his bunk to read a ragged copy of Dahl's dictionary [the Russian Webster, Littré, or Duden], jotting down things in a large notebook."

None of these jottings, however, contained anything faintly incriminating. The camp offered but one secure place for his compositions, the same place that kept the core of his existence secure. For years, Solzhenitsyn retained in the manner of the folk bards of preliterate nations. In other words, he wrote nothing but poetry and kept everything in his head.

Contrary to widespread legend, Solzhenitsyn did not compose and edit in his head: one of his old Marfino companions provided him with a safe place for writing. Transported together, they were delivered by coincidence to the same camp, where his companion was in time put in charge of its machine shop. He had Solzhenitsyn transferred from bricklaying to his work team, and found a warm safe place for his friend inside the shop. Amid the clattering of iron, unobserved by stool pigeons and guards, Solzhenitsyn rewrote his verses until satisfied, committed the day's work to memory, and destroyed the paper. Solzhenitsyn memorized thousands of lines, some of which he occasionally recited to this man and several other trusted inmates. The prisoners were proud that they had a writer of great stature in their midst.

But Solzhenitsyn does not now share the prisoners' high opinion of the work that he did at that time, of which only a few dozen lines were subsequently published. One of the main compositions of the time was a long verse epic called "The Feast of the Victors," which Solzhenitsyn has disowned as too bitter and one-sided, and whose very mention as part of his literary opus he vehemently rejects. Another long poem was entitled "The Way," a lyrico-philosophic reflection on the fate of men in general and of Russian prisoners in particular. Its title suggests that it was connected with Solzhenitsyn's interest in Tao philosophy: Tao means "the way" in the sense of human paths followed in the world. Despite a widely held belief, none of Solzhenitsyn's prose poems was written in the camp: memorization required that all of his composition be in verse.

Solzhenitsyn has decided with apparent finality that his verse falls short of his own standards, that, whatever its documentary value, Russian literature would be better off without it. The only apparent exception to this rule was the release of less than a hundred lines from "The Way" for publication. This was done through a friend, the man who, under the pseudonym of "D. Blagov," has provided the only significant insight into Solzhenitsyn's literary development in the camps.

Blagov,[3] a man of wide erudition, became one of Solzhenitsyn's first and closest encouragers in his postcamp years. His study of Solzhenitsyn, first circulated in the Soviet literary underground in 1964, gives evidence of an intimate knowledge of the writer, not surprising in view of their many years of confidential exchanges. In camp, Blagov has written,

> [Solzhenitsyn] felt an appeal, a calling ... to become the poet of the events taking place around him. In other words, to give them rhythm. . . . He could no longer limit himself to the struggle to sustain his physical life and dignity, which in itself forced a prisoner to exert all his strength. He had to exist in the world of the spirit too, and to create images. . . . But writing was prohibited in the camp. Agonizingly, he tried to memorize his streams of thought and images. To relieve his memory, he sometimes attempted to translate them into verse form, involuntarily becoming a poet. The world of the spirit incessantly pumped thoughts, images, and rhythms

[3] Blagov has subsequently identified himself as Venyamin Teush.

into him, building up unbearable pressure upon his mind and memory.

In confirmation, Blagov quotes verses from the "involuntary poet," without naming Solzhenitsyn directly. However, Solzhenitsyn's authorship has been positively identified.

The lines quoted by Blagov and his description of the prisoner's state of mind make clear that Solzhenitsyn had found a new "theme," if not its final orchestration. His first task upon leaving the camps would be to bear witness to his fellow prisoners' fate. In this sense, Solzhenitsyn's maturity as a writer began in Dzhezkazgan and Ekibastuz.

XIII

Survival

SOLZHENITSYN HAD FOUND HIS THEME within a year or so after arriving in Kazakhstan. It was important enough to need telling to the world, exalted enough—in the sense that it involved fundamental questions of human nature and the human condition—to satisfy his predilection for epic drama. In this respect leaving Marfino for a proper labor camp had not been a mistake.

The desire to fulfill his creative urge had become Solzhenitsyn's principal motivation for survival. Many prisoners lacked such motivation and in their misery found it easier to succumb. Religion was an important support to many. During his imprisonment Solzhenitsyn was consciously non-religious but his calling was as strong as the strongest faith. He had acquired his sense of mission as a writer (which persists to this day), and it gave him the necessary will to resist the temptation to seek an easy relief from his misery in death.[1]

On the construction site the misery was intense. Unlike Solzhenitsyn, another Russian concentration camp author, Yevgenia Ginzburg, does not shun horrors, and her description of the physical state of prisoners gives a sharper picture than anything Solzhenitsyn has written. In the following passage from *Into the Whirlwind* [2] she is describing the prisoners she saw in her camp—not the same one as Solzhenitsyn's, but also involved in mining—from her perspective as a temporary kitchen worker.

---

[1] A prisoner's great difficulty in maintaining the will to live in desperate circumstances was demonstrated in North Korean POW camps at this same time. Having lost the will, inmates in great numbers died for no physical reason but because they quite simply did not get out of bed, or feed themselves. Among those who did survive, some achieved it by forcing themselves into grueling programs of physical exercise.

[2] One of a stream of manuscripts about camp life which came to *Novy Mir* after *One Day*'s publication, this brilliantly graphic, deeply moving memoir was published years later in the West, but never in Russia. Collins-Harvill, 1967.

So I stood and dished out the soup, interminably dipping my ladle into the tubful of gruel, filling the mess tin to the brim and holding it out to each of the disincarnate figures who passed in front of me. They were muffled in rags and bits of sacking. With their black frostbitten rotting cheeks and noses and bleeding toothless gums they looked as if they had issued out of primeval chaos or out of one of Goya's nightmares. I was appalled, but went on mixing and stirring the stew so that it would be as nourishing as possible. Still they came. There was no end to the black procession. They held the mess tins in their numb fingers and, placing them on the end of the long plank table, took the soup as if it were the Host imbued with the mystery of life.

Clearly, under such conditions, Solzhenitsyn's life was in peril for the third time in his thirty-three years—and greater peril than was advisable if he was to fulfill his mission. Thus the offer of transfer to the machine shop offered him a refuge for creative work and a safeguard from threats to his life. Antiquated, noisy, and hot, the shop produced replacement parts for the camp's mining and industrial equipment. Despite his friendship with the chief, Solzhenitsyn's work day was a full one: the crew was strictly limited in that place of warmth and higher rations, and every member had to work hard to meet the common quota. Little less was demanded of Solzhenitsyn in the machine shop than on the construction site; it still represented general duties. Yet the strain of the former was less likely to be fatal to an essentially healthy man than Ekibastuz's scaring cold, and the satisfaction of having creative work as well as a small but perceptive audience powerfully boosted Solzhenitsyn's morale.

Apart from finding a rare warm place to work, a prisoner with a strong resolve to survive had to concentrate his entire attention upon organizing the minutiae of his life. Camp veterans knew that only the severest practicality made this possible, an understanding reflected in one of their fundamental maxims: "Prison is your home sweet home." Wherever consigned, whatever the hardships, one had to strive for the maximum level of comfort and permanence, however low. In the case of Solzhenitsyn and the minority who cared about such things—or were still able to care—this axiom was qualified by another: that no effort to enhance one's own well-being shall be undertaken in violation of one's conscience. But the prisoners who neglected the "small things of life," here very small indeed, were almost certainly doomed—those who thought, for example, that since they would probably spend only days in one or another barrack, it would be a waste of energy to seek out a warmer place therein. The set of attitudes this represented sooner or later led to fatal pneumonia or such weakness that the relentless struggle for the preservation of one's moral self was irretrievably lost. With a trace of irony, Solzhenitsyn has written in

The First Circle of the bond, especially during "transport," between a pair of felt boots and self-respect—or life itself.

> The living creature with the least rights on earth, with less fore-warning about his own future than a frog, a mole, or a fieldmouse, the prisoner is wholly at the mercy of the whims of fate . . . Woe to the limbs that are not shod in felt boots! . . . Without a pair of his own, a prisoner spends all winter slinking; he lies, plays the hypo-crite, suffers insults from nobodies, or oppresses others himself—anything to avoid winter transport. But the prisoner with his own felt boots is dauntless. Boldly he meets his masters' eyes and, smiling like Marcus Aurelius, receives his check-out chit.

With his fundamental practicality in the best of times, Solzhenitsyn was equipped to deal with the worst. In his first camps, he had learned quickly to try to improve his physical arrangements. By 1952, his situation in Ekibastuz's deafening machine shop and jerry-built barracks was as good as could be expected. With only a year of his sentence remaining, Solzhenitsyn was dragging out his time, as Russian prisoners say too, between long days of labor and his incongruous study of dictionaries and quasi-Homeric compositions. The end of his sentence was phantasmal; no prisoner fully believed he would reach it. But as Solzhenitsyn's end crept toward the boundary of the conceivable, he suddenly seemed certain never in fact to attain it. In February 1952, mere months before the date of his anticipated release, death threatened him again. He was "bitten by the crab," as he himself ironically put it. In other words, stricken by cancer.

The disease was as vicious as unexpected. It required immediate and decisive treatment, but in fact was exacerbated by the nonchalance and delays characteristic of inmates' medical care.

This deficiency was not necessarily caused by deliberate cruelty, but by the nature of medical service in the camps. Each camp had its own sick bay, which was headed by a military doctor, usually an officer of the secret police, and staffed by doctors, assistants, and nurses who were pris-oners. As one of Solzhenitsyn's camp characters says, the sick bay is "the key to everything"; its boss was known as "master of life and death." Far more than on the outside, these metaphors about medicine's role described a hard reality.

For, above all, the sick bay meant an enriched diet and a respite from work. To an exhausted "goner" on general duties, even a brief spell there was literally a chance to snatch life from certain death. To fall ill was al-most a blessing; and even better to bribe or simulate one's way into a sick-bay cot. Despite elaborate precautions against this and the slim chance of success, there was never a shortage of prisoners who ceaselessly schemed

—or daydreamed—of ways to be admitted. There was also always a corresponding shortage of hospital beds, even measured by acceptable beds-per-person standards among a well-fed and healthy population.

The natural consequence of this violent imbalance between supply and demand was an arrogant "buyer's market." Pleas for beds were treated with extreme suspicion; even when genuinely and dangerously ill rather than merely exhausted, most prisoners were at least temporarily turned away. Beyond this, the medical units were poorly equipped and lacked proper medicines. Solzhenitsyn's camp did not have the X-ray machine essential for full diagnosis of his cancer. On the other hand, Stalin's terror had ensured that most larger camps boasted a corps of well-trained specialists and consultants: prisoners who had fallen victim to the purges.

Solzhenitsyn's tumor sprouted in his intestines and swelled so fast that he felt its growth "between morning and evening" of the same day. Having overcome the routine obstacles to medical attention, he was prepared by the camp surgeon for a prompt operation. But camp procedures canceled it on the evening before its performance.

One of the fundamental devices for ensuring discipline in the prison empire was a constant shuffling of inmates from one camp to another. In three years, Solzhenitsyn had been in three, but some prisoners were moved that often in a single year. The idea was to prevent "conspiracies," meaning any degree of friendship or attachment, to keep camp populations atomized, precluding the permanence necessary for development of a sense of self, of group, and of leadership. The very act of shuffling (in cattle-car conditions) helped eliminate any residual pretensions to being more than a prison number. To prevent prisoners passing messages with their departing fellows to comrades in distant camps, transports were always announced with no warning whatever.

Doctors were not spared the grueling routine. And the surgeon who was to operate on Solzhenitsyn was a prisoner—whose next deportation took place during the night before the operation. Days were lost while another surgeon was found; more days before he could examine Solzhenitsyn and prepare him for the same operation. A week later this surgeon too was shipped to his next camp—a stroke of minor bad luck, for prisoners usually stayed longer.

But meanwhile, the operation had been performed. Its purpose was to remove the tumor and, once out, to establish its nature. Solzhenitsyn convalesced in the sick bay and had just begun to walk again when he himself was scheduled for displacement to another camp. At the last moment, however, his name was removed from the list—not on medical grounds, but because a camp administrator had discovered that his sentence would expire within months. The general policy was to avoid shifting prisoners with less than a year to serve.

The departed surgeon had cut a slice of Solzhenitsyn's tumor and sent it for analysis to the nearest laboratory, eight hundred miles north in the Siberian city of Omsk. But labeled with neither Solzhenitsyn's name nor his camp, the specimen arrived at the laboratory as if from an ordinary hospital in the village nearest Ekibastuz, whose postal address the latter used. It was not carelessness that had caused this seemingly incredible lapse, but careful observance of regulations drawn up in accordance with an unvarying policy: since the existence of concentration camps was not acknowledged in Stalin's Russia, laboratory technicians in Omsk had no more business knowing the facts than did a United Nations committee or Western trade union delegation.

Solzhenitsyn's incisions healed while the analysis was performed, and, although still in pain, he was discharged from the sick bay and returned to general duties. In the meantime, his friend from the machine shop had been transferred to a punishment camp for participating in a protest against arbitrary disciplinary penalties inflicted upon prisoners. Many of the old crew had gone, and there was no question of returning to the earlier refuge. Solzhenitsyn was assigned to lifting and carrying boxes of liquid concrete whose weight, even without the quotas, was enough to tax the strength of a strong and healthy man. This was not the inspiration of some especially vindictive administrator or guard; like everything else involving Solzhenitsyn's illness and recuperation, the job was entirely in the spirit and practice of all "corrective labor" camps.

The results of the biopsy were returned to the camp in good time: Solzhenitsyn's tumor had been caused by one of the most malignant forms of cancer. Immediate X-ray treatment was prescribed to prevent the cancer's spreading, followed by a second, extensive, operation to remove the diseased sections of his intestines and possibly contaminated adjoining sections. It was the usual course of treatment for dangerous, well-advanced cancer.

But there was no X-ray equipment. Besides, the analysis was still anonymous, and no one in the sick bay bothered to track down the patient concerned. The treatment of the disease, therefore, ended almost before it had begun. From the authorities' standpoint, however, the important consideration was that Solzhenitsyn was again fulfilling a proper work quota instead of occupying a clean cot and consuming extra rations.

Not the least odd aspect of this bizarre medical case was that from his point of view, too, the episode ended happily. Apparently the exploratory operation temporarily retarded the tumor and he was not told the precise nature of his disease. When the pain of his incision subsided, he was still occasionally uncomfortable, but felt he'd made an encouraging recovery. For the time being, the loss of the analysis seemed just another bureaucratic mishap.

XIV

Release

Solzhenitsyn served out the final months of his sentence in Ekibastuz. In February 1953, eight years to the month after his arrest, he was released —and not rearrested, as were many prisoners. But to be discharged from camp in those days rarely meant freedom. Having left the barbed-wire gates for the last time, Solzhenitsyn was delivered directly to a jail. And his destination was not home, but exile.

In Stalin's last years, former camp inmates were lepers, to be quarantined from the nation at all costs. Those who escaped an additional sentence for imaginary "anti-Soviet" behavior in the camps were subject to thorough isolation through a procedure called "deprivation of the rights" of a Soviet citizen. In practice, this almost always meant enforced settlement in a remote village, far from European Russia. Former prisoners were prohibited from crossing the boundaries of their assigned villages without special permission each time. Whatever its other purposes, exile served effectively to cut off information to distant Russian cities about life in the camps.

Some prisoners were condemned to deprivation of rights at the time of their "regular" sentences to terms in the camps. For the annulment of Solzhenitsyn's rights, however, a simple administrative decision by an official of the Ministry of the Interior sufficed, without the formalities of a trial. "Without being sentenced," Solzhenitsyn later observed, "I was awarded exile in perpetuity."

At that time, it was not merely camouflage that the freight cars which transported prisoners were marked "Spec. Eqpmt." To NKVD officials, former prisoners were indeed articles of equipment, although more ordinary than special. Documents which accompanied them were called "way bills," just as for goods, and the human freight was shifted at the whim of the owners. The official responsible for prisoner III-232 decided that he be shipped over a thousand miles southwest of Ekibastuz. Together with other items identified in a clutch of way bills, Solzhenitsyn was herded into a freight car.

Two criteria determined a former prisoner's destination: bureaucratic convenience and security considerations. To prevent "conspiracies" and "mutinies," the concentration of exiles in any one place was maintained at a predetermined level, usually quite low. The second criterion was the need to fill statistical vacancies within these levels. Neither the preferences, background, nor skills of the prisoners were considered. Although no longer prisoners in law, exiles were transported exclusively through the prison transit system. "Over and above my eight-year sentence, I did a month in transit jails," Solzhenitsyn has remarked. "But this is the kind of small change that is embarrassing even to mention among us."

The month in prison transit came to an end in early March 1953. Solzhenitsyn had been delivered to the *aul* (village) of Berlik, in southern Kazakhstan. Berlik stands on the edge of the Sands of Muyun-Kum, in a desertlike steppe sparsely spotted with austere plants known locally as "camels' pricklies." The territory's regional center was called Kok Terek, which means "green poplar" in Kazakh. The poplar was the town's proud landmark: it boasted one. This was the very frontier of civilization. Beyond the small town, for hundreds of miles to the southwest of Lake Balkhash, stretched the desolateness of sand and wind.

The old cliché about standing alone in the desert was a literal reality for Solzhenitsyn at the start of his exile in Muyun-Kum. The *aul* was populated principally by Kazakhs, a Moslem people whose Turkic language Solzhenitsyn did not understand, and whose way of life was as alien to him as Pakistani village life would be to a university-educated Englishman. He was still gravely ill, and knew it.

With all of this, Solzhenitsyn first surveyed his place of perpetual exile with a kind of elation. After eight years of prisons and camps, the harshness of the naked steppe, even the limitations on an exile's freedom, were at first mere details. Solzhenitsyn has described an inmate's emotions on his first free night, suggesting that the place where a person is told that he may now go without a guard—"You may go by yourself"—can become more dear to him than where he was born, "a screaming infant understanding nothing."

> Ah, that first night of half freedom! . . . they weren't [yet] allowed into the village. But they were permitted to sleep on their own in a hay shelter in the yard of the security police building. They shared the shelter with horses who spent the night motionless, quietly munching hay. Impossible to imagine a sweeter sound!

Unable to sleep half the night, the new exile Oleg Kostoglotov paced the yard "like a man possessed," savoring the absence of watchtowers and guards. Head upturned to the pale sky of the early spring night, he "stumbled happily" on the ground—but kept walking, oblivious to his route; it was as if the dawn would see him enter not a "mean, remote *aul*," but "the wide, triumphant world." The music of the southern night surrounded him as he ambled.

From dusk to dawn donkeys and camels brayed and honked in yards and stables through the village—solemn, trumpetlike sounds, vibrant with desire, telling of conjugal passion and faith in the continuation of life. And this marital din merged with the roar of Oleg's breast.

Can any place be dearer than one where you spent such a night?

That was the night when he began to hope and believe again, in spite of all his vows to the contrary.

There was more reason for faith and hope than Solzhenitsyn knew in his wilderness. In those first days of March, Stalin lay on his deathbed. From March 3 the entire Soviet population listened to the steadily worsening medical bulletins.

But without easy access to private radio during his first hours in Berlik, Solzhenitsyn was still isolated from this event that gripped the world. Besides, a vital personal problem was quite literally at his back. Places where former prisoners were settled had a special police officer who supervised all exile affairs. Exiles were required to report to this *komendant* every fortnight, and could not change their residence without his permission. On arrival and until they established and reported a permanent residence, they had armed guards at their backs: Solzhenitsyn's immediate problem.

His eagerness to shed hopefully the last of the tommy guns pointed at him was demonstrated by his speed in finding quarters. By the evening of March 4 he had moved in with an old Russian woman named Katerina Melnichuk and her husband Yakov. The Melnichuks could not rent him a room; their house had but one, and it was crowded with their own family. Solzhenitsyn was established in a corner of the kitchen, on a bed improvised from empty crates. It was late when the arrangements were completed, and Solzhenitsyn went directly to bed. In the morning he would walk the streets without escort for the first time since February 1945.

He did not sleep late. Mrs. Melnichuk woke him early with the news that the loudspeaker was blaring in the street. She was somewhat deaf and couldn't quite decipher its message. Might her lodger step outside to help?

At that time, outdoor loudspeakers usually broadcast during high revolutionary holidays. When they were heard on other occasions, Russians were gripped by an all-pervading dread: war! When Solzhenitsyn left the house to listen, it could not have been without some apprehension. But the message was wildly different. "The radio," as he drily described it, "was broadcasting the news of Stalin's death."

In time, the dictator's demise would change Solzhenitsyn's life, even more than that of most Russians. But none of this was immediately apparent; the status of exiles remained wholly unchanged. Inwardly, Solzhenitsyn "was resigned to the exile being perpetual. . . ." If he had hope, it was not in his mind, but in his heart.

Several days after moving in with the Melnichuks, Solzhenitsyn was summoned to the local office of state security. There, in his own words, he "docilely signed, as did everyone else, the document on perpetual exile." [1] Solzhenitsyn was acquainted with its terms and undertook to live by the complicated rules, whose language alone—"exile in perpetuity" was actually in the text—could induce claustrophobia. With a trace of black humor, one of Solzhenitsyn's heroes interpreted this phrase from the victims' perspective. "If it were a life sentence—well, I suppose my coffin could be taken home to Russia; but since it's perpetual, even that won't be allowed back. . . . I won't be let back even after the sun burns out. Perpetuity is longer."

But Solzhenitsyn accepted his lot with a stoic and strictly realistic resignation. Having survived so much worse, desolate Berlik was a kind of resort whose prospects at times seemed even sunny. "After the camps," he wrote later, "you could not call the world of exile cruel . . . The exile world was far more spacious, easier to live in and more varied." Several years before, while he was a prisoner, "distant, dark exile" had seemed an unattainable dream. The veteran survivor was determined to make the best of his new life—and, as seemed imaginable only a month after Stalin's death, of the life of the country as a whole.

Stalin's last months had been a nightmare for Russia. The bitter Korean war seemed to portend a larger conflict with America and more years of hunger, weariness, and bloodletting. In January, when Stalin had charged a group of Kremlin doctors with poisoning the country's leaders, blood seemed about to flow from internal afflictions too. Throughout the winter of 1952–53, an atmosphere of hysterical fear and frantic mistrust intensified as Russians awaited a new mass purge—another 1937.

But the dread was dispelled in early April by Stalin's successors. The

---

[1] In an interview with Solzhenitsyn—one of the two extensive interviews ever given as such—the Slovak journalist Pavel Ličko reported that Solzhenitsyn refused to sign the exile document. This was one of a few errors of detail in an otherwise reliable and extremely revealing account. Solzhenitsyn corrected the error in a personal letter, adding that "in its essentials, all [the interview] turned out well."

"Doctors' Plot" was officially declared nonexistent, an invention of the secret police. Three months later its chief, Lavrenty Beria, was overthrown and liquidated.

The nightmare receded more slowly in the exiles' outposts than in Central Russia. "Everyone was waiting for important changes," Solzhenitsyn wrote later, "but the changes that crept through were small and slow." Just enough, in other words, to nourish hope, but too little to live on. In any case Solzhenitsyn, no more than his major characters, was not going to indulge himself with illusions.

> He mustn't trust the effervescence of any of those Beethoven chords. They were nothing but iridescent bubbles. He must control his unruly heart and believe nothing, expect nothing from the future, no improvement.
> Be happy with what you've got.
> In perpetuity? Why not? In perpetuity!

Solzhenitsyn took up his new responsibilities. He could expect material help from no one. The Melnichuk family were kind; in particular the elderly woman Katerina took pity on the lodger whose gestures betrayed his recent ordeal. Even she, a poor Russian peasant, was overcome with compassion when she watched Solzhenitsyn eat the last morsel of skin (usually untouched by Russians) of some potatoes she'd boiled for him. She understood that he had known hunger beyond her own experience. The Melnichuks also found Solzhenitsyn so likable that when he was to move away to set up on his own, they would give him a genuine feather pillow, an uncommonly valuable gift. But in their poverty they could not keep him without payment for his board. Solzhenitsyn had no possessions to sell, the usual way of tiding oneself over in hard times. His clothes struck even the Melnichuks as wretched, and he owned nothing but a small wooden suitcase (whose contents, characteristically, were principally books he had managed to accumulate in his camps). The luckier exiles were helped by their distant families. But Solzhenitsyn's mother had been dead for nine years, and his relationship with Reshetovskaya had changed drastically. For, contrary to a later Soviet newspaper article about him, Reshetovskaya did not join him in Berlik. In fact, he knew by now that she was married to someone else.

When Reshetovskaya had asked him for permission to get a divorce in the Marfino period, Solzhenitsyn had reason to encourage her. Even if they were sanguine about surviving their sentences, a certain percentage of prisoners resolved, at whatever sacrifice to themselves, not to drag their women farther along their *via dolorosa*—in Solzhenitsyn's case, a woman whose devotion remained strong over five years of tragedy. Solzhenitsyn's concern for Reshetovskaya was expressed in a memorized prison poem lamenting her "ten years of cold loneliness." (The poem was composed in 1951: the ten years of separation included those caused by the war.) "She sacrificed her youth for me fruitlessly," he wrote. Reshetovskaya was indeed no longer young: she had turned thirty-two at the time of the poem. Since Solzhenitsyn entered the Army her life was hard; after his arrest, it had faint overtones of his own nightmare. But despite Solzhenitsyn's urging that she disentangle herself from him, premonitions of utter loneliness gripped him, as his writings later reflected. And his worst fears materialized: in time the divorce of convenience developed into reality.

It had taken place while Reshetovskaya was a graduate student of Moscow University. Soon thereafter, she completed her studies and was awarded the degree of *kandidat* of science, which closely approaches a Ph.D. degree. Then she found work in a laboratory of the same Moscow University. But, as Solzhenitsyn had foreseen, his "guilt" tainted her too.

In those days, the Soviet Union was a land mass of suspicion and an ocean of questionnaires. Questionnaire after questionnaire was distributed to one or another section of the population, and most often to people in jobs of any degree of sensitivity. The object was to expose not only "spies, wreckers, and saboteurs," but also class enemies (or potential class enemies)—meaning, in practice, anyone with "suspicious" impedimenta in his background. Reshetovskaya had made no mention of Solzhenitsyn or his fate in these questionnaires. But when the facts were discovered—not that her husband, but her *former* husband was in a camp—she was told that she must leave the university laboratory and Moscow.

She was given a choice of several cities for her own much less severe exile. Of these, she selected the small provincial center of Ryazan, some 115 miles to the southeast of Moscow. Although Ryazan has little reputation in the West, its appeal to Russians lies in its antiquity, as one of the first truly Russian cities in the early Middle Ages, and in its associations with Sergey Esenin, the country's most popular twentieth-century lyric poet, who was born nearby.

To Reshetovskaya, Ryazan's appeal was also its proximity to Moscow and some practical advantages: in this city, she was promised living accommodations of her own. And in fact she was allocated a room when she arrived, in a house belonging to the local college where she took up her new job. She set to work again as a chemist and busied herself in building a new life. Her old one seemed irreversibly ended: she had not lived with Solzhenitsyn for ten years nor, because of the perpetual exile, could she resume even a semblance of a normal life with him anywhere in European Russia. Her mother joined her from Rostov. Then a more dramatic change took place: in 1951, she remarried.

Reshetovskaya had had a hard time in her separation from Solzhenitsyn. But time passed and, with her zest for life and outgoing character, she became involved again, slowly, with her new surroundings and new people. She knew, of course, that of those political prisoners who survived the camps few returned from exile. Even if Solzhenitsyn survived, he would be a pariah, and to join him would be to enter a kind of hermit-martyrdom, alien to her personality. In these circumstances she was courted with some determination by a man she had met in Ryazan.

Many rumors circulate in Russia about Reshetovskaya's remarriage. One makes her second husband a party official who showed her documents that seemed to prove Solzhenitsyn's death. In fact, her new husband, like her, was a chemist and *kandidat* of science, a quiet, somewhat shy widower with two young boys. He moved into the small flat in an old log house which she was already sharing with her mother.

Solzhenitsyn is hypersensitive to discussion of his years with Reshetovskaya. For her part, she is believed to be writing an account of the relationship which will treat the 1950–53 period, not the last and perhaps not even their hardest, from her perspective. Until this account appears, it can be said only that she did not inform him for some time of her remarriage, no doubt to spare his feelings. When he did receive the news, their correspondence dwindled almost to nothing. Gleb Nerzhin's sad prediction to his fictional wife of love's inability to outlast prison barriers seemed now to have reached the final stage of fulfillment.

In these circumstances, Solzhenitsyn had to find a source of support immediately. Once again, his mathematical training proved invaluable.

In the winter of 1964–65, the twilight of Solzhenitsyn's brief official favor in Russia, a journalist from a Kazakh youth newspaper visited Berlik to write about him. His article described Solzhenitsyn's hunt for a job through the reminiscences of the man who provided his first one, teaching in a local secondary school.

On a warm April day, Zeinegaty Syrymbetov, acting director of the regional department of education, received an unusual visitor. "Solzhenitsyn, Alexander Isaiyevich. I'm trained as a teacher. I'd like to work in school." . . .

After cautious questioning, Zeinegaty realized that Solzhenitsyn had been a victim of those circumstances which later acquired the name of the cult of personality. And that he did not choose to live in Berlik of his own free will.

Syrymbetov understood that he was taking a certain risk in giving Solzhenitsyn a job in a school. What if someone had the bright idea to interpret this as suspicious sympathy for a former prisoner?

The meeting with Solzhenitsyn took place eleven years ago. Yet Zeinegaty remembers its every detail.

"We were short of teachers at the time," he now remembers, "especially in math and physics. Besides, I had a feeling that if I didn't help this man who had come upon hard times, my conscience would torture me for the rest of my life."

Thus Alexander Isaiyevich Solzhenitsyn became a teacher of mathematics, physics, and astronomy in Berlik's secondary school. . . . On May 3, 1953, after an interval of many years, he entered the classroom again.

In fact, the interval since Solzhenitsyn had last taught in the Cossack town of Morozovsk was almost twelve years. When he began work in a profession for which he had been trained, a link was made to his old life and the foundations laid for a reasonable new one in exile.

XV

Exile

BERLIK'S NEW TEACHER OF mathematics, physics, and astronomy was a sad spectacle. Zeinegaty Syrymbetov remembered his "old fur hat with bald patches, discolored army breeches and high boots worn badly at the heels." Some of his movements betrayed the camp inmate's ingrained tenseness in the presence of warders. "His hands crumpled his hat uneasily," Syrymbetov observed. His face and figure displayed the effects of his incarceration and recent surgery more explicitly. Now even the hair was dull with lack of nourishment, and the face reflected profound physical stress. Elements of Solzhenitsyn's old self survived: like many observers before and after him, Syrymbetov perceived a "sharp contrast" between ragged appearance and self-sovereign manner, and spoke of the characteristic self-confidence and "winning simplicity and charm which this man emanated." It was as if the camps had shriveled the flesh but not the spirit.

But Solzhenitsyn was not appointed on the basis of self-confidence or charm, nor even of his obvious professional qualifications. For a man of Solzhenitsyn's education in a place so short of qualified teachers as this desert *aul*, securing a teaching job might have seemed "only natural." It was far from that. An educated exile was much more likely to be limited to unskilled or semiskilled work; assisting in land surveying, the job of a major Solzhenitsyn character, was more typical, although still better than average. From an orthodox standpoint, teaching gave "enemies of the people" too easy access to a community's opinion makers. Colleagues and impressionable teen-agers ignorant of camp life could be subverted. And if, eleven years later, the local educational director recalled every detail of his first meeting with Solzhenitsyn, it was as a soldier remembers helping an anonymous comrade through a hail of bullets. The employment as a teacher of an unknown Russian "enemy of the people" by a petty official of Kazakh origin was an act of considerable bravery. As the article hinted, Syrymbetov might easily have been denounced by a vigilant Stalinist zealot, which could have cost him at least his own job. If his decision speaks of the impression Solzhenitsyn made in that first interview, it also testifies to Syrymbetov's character.

Stalin's reign had corroded the moral fiber of vast numbers of good "little" people. Under fear of torture, death, and nameless secret-police horrors, many committed acts of treachery and cruelty that would have been wholly alien to them in an ordinary setting. But a certain number resisted; even in the darkest Stalin years, a "conspiracy of decent people" survived.[1] Of these, some developed a kind of immunization and rejected the official ethic of total subservience to the state, for which they substituted personal codes based on decency and conscience. This "counterethic" helped many otherwise doomed "enemies" to survive. When two strangers committed to it met, there was an instinctive recognition and desire to help. But such people were relatively few, and a prisoner or former prisoner had to be lucky, as Solzhenitsyn was in Berlik, to stumble upon one at a critical moment.

The role of Syrymbetov's conscience in helping Solzhenitsyn is significant, for individual conscience, as opposed to any written moral or political code, is the pivot of Solzhenitsyn's ethics. A similar motif underlies one of his major novels, and the central issue of a second is a conflict similar to Syrymbetov's: the demands of conscience against the reflexes of personal security. Here Solzhenitsyn observed the workings of the counterethic in his own case before using it in his fiction.

In the era preceding 1953, exile life featured impermanence as well as discomfort and restriction. Rearrests were frequent, together with sudden change of location, often from the desert's heat to the tundra's ice. But Solzhenitsyn now had reason to believe that his position in Berlik was relatively secure and protected against undue harassment. Not only Syrymbetov's good will but the nationwide easing of terror encouraged the presumption that if major changes came, they would not be for the worse. Exiles had already begun to speculate on rumors of an eventual lifting of their restrictions.

But if Solzhenitsyn did not anticipate further persecution, he still did not permit hopes for miracles of deliverance. He continued to regard his exile as permanent, and even described himself as "content" with this. As a free citizen, he explained later, his record would have hindered him from getting a job. Recognition of an exile's compensations is reflected through his fictional Oleg Kostoglotov—who, of course, knew as well as anyone of exile's deprivations and oppressiveness.

[1] Although reflected clearly, this "conspiracy" is not defined as such in any of Solzhenitsyn's writing. But Vladimir Dudintsev described it in *Not by Bread Alone*, the novel which in three years—after the de-Stalinizing Twentieth Party Congress in 1956—was to become the banner of Soviet liberals.

But he also perceived, as few have, that exile can also bring release—from doubts and responsibilities to oneself. The true unfortunates were not the exiles, but those who had been given passports with the sordid "Article 39" [2] conditions. They spent their time blaming themselves for all their past false decisions, constantly on the move looking for somewhere to live, trying to find work and being thrown out of places.

By contrast, Oleg realized, a new exile kept his "rights intact." Since the selection of location had not been his, he could not be tossed out. Since everything had been planned for him by the authorities, he need not torture himself over missing opportunities for living elsewhere and arranging a more comfortable life for himself. The knowledge that his was the only possible path gave him "a cheerful sort of courage."

Solzhenitsyn went so far as to buy himself a little house. Like most in the *aul,* including the Melnichuks', it was a whitewashed adobe cubicle with three windows, none much bigger than a face, a roof of straw and clay, and a chimney more impressive than anything below it. The doorstep was two stones brought from neighboring mountains. Inside, a large stove had the pride of place, and its maintenance—for heating in winter and cooking throughout the year—was Solzhenitsyn's principal household duty. In the absence of trees or sufficient dung for fuel, Solzhenitsyn gathered his own supplies, largely tough desert bushes which he cut and dragged home. In time, he himself grew some of the vegetables that were boiled on the stove. His tiny house was adjoined by a vegetable garden, which he tended lovingly. Short of police surveillance, his free time was now private—therefore genuinely free.

The move to the new little box, where Solzhenitsyn would remain for two years, was made in the autumn of 1953. The address, number 10 Pioneer Street, might well have pleased him with its realism: Berlik was indeed a pioneering little town. His previous address with the Melnichuks in Garden Street, by contrast, had a socialist-realist flavor, inasmuch as it suggested the promised happy future, rather than the conditions of the "temporary" transition period. Apart from private vegetable patches, gardens here were a fanciful illusion in parched sands which barely supported camels' pricklies and the firewood bushes.

By the start of the new school year in September, Solzhenitsyn seemed well settled in Berlik. A few years earlier, as an inmate, he had thought often of his exile life. Above all, he imagined a time when his long-constricted inspiration would be released into a flow of powerful, if still secret, creation. A poem written in imprisonment about four years before his arrival in Berlik speaks of this yearning to commit to paper what he knew

---

[2] Article 39 restricted work and residence rights of former camp inmates.

and felt, even if the paper itself had then to be hidden. For this alone would relieve his "tortured memory"—the torture not only of what he had seen and experienced during the camp years, but also of the self-imposed burden of memorizing.

> Some day in distant dark exile
> My time will come and I'll free my tortured memory—
> Swaddled in paper and bast within a corked bottle,
> I'll hide my tale under fir needles and drifts of blizzard snow.

At last the time for unburdening seemed to have arrived. Although his exile turned out to be hot, dusty, and glaring rather than dark and icy, it was as remote as Solzhenitsyn had imagined: India and China were nearer than his own Central Russia. He had time enough to begin transferring his thoughts to paper—and now, with his hut on the edge of the *aul*, privacy enough too. Yet it seems that very little, perhaps none, of his known writings was undertaken in his first year after release. Creativity was harder to tap than he had imagined.

At a purely practical level, solitude forced him to carry the full burden of housekeeping, doubly exhausting amid Russia's chronic consumer scarcities. The larger circumstances of his environment too did not help him meet the demands of writing. He had discovered in his youth that he wanted to be a distinctively *Russian* writer, and for this he needed the psychological and linguistic reassurance of living in Central Russia. Its smells, sounds, and landscapes—the very air he breathed there—were his stimulations. Even his native Rostov, although interesting as a multilingual port, had not been Russian enough. This realization was quite naturally forgotten in the camps, but made itself felt again in the Sands of Muyun-Kum.

These several factors—physical and mental exhaustion, a broken family, the uncongenial environment—were quite enough to inhibit Solzhenitsyn's writing. But another legacy of the camps provided the decisive handicap: although the secret composing continued throughout his prison years, he now developed something like a psychological allergy to the act of committing words to paper. Since it was the written word that had caused his arrest and subsequent hardship, it is reasonable to suppose that a subconscious fear of more suffering induced the allergy.

It is succinctly described in a story entitled "The Right Hand." On a visit to a city two years after leaving his last camp, the protagonist notices "a stationery kiosk selling little plastic pencils and tempting little notebooks." However, "I'd already had occasion to possess notebooks in my life and they'd ended up in the wrong places, so I thought it best not to have them ever again." The chances of Solzhenitsyn's own material again "ending up" with the secret police were greatly increased by what he had decided to make his theme. With this psychological handicap to creativity replacing the primarily physical ones during his imprisonment he needed a special kind of rest to absorb humor, compassion, and dignity again— the currents of ordinary life before he could recommit himself to writing.[3]

Without the connubial help enjoyed by many other former prisoners, Solzhenitsyn's "unthawing" would have to be self-generated. As years passed in Berlik, he would gradually restore himself through teaching, friendships with villagers (both exiles and regular inhabitants) and a discovery of the surrounding countryside. The process of reestablishing contact with ordinary life was impeded still more by Solzhenitsyn's general feeling of infirmity. Whether or not a residue of his tumor, his imperfect health prevented him from plunging into activities with his characteristic gusto, and, in particular, restricted his energy in the classroom. In these first postprison months, in fact, he was himself a student as much as a teacher, for he was taking a refresher course in life "outside."

Solzhenitsyn had probably never heard of *univers concentrationnaire*, the term of the French writer and former Auschwitz inmate David Rousset. Rousset first applied his concept to Nazi concentration camps, but Solzhenitsyn's physical and mental condition at this time, together with the literature he later produced, are the strongest available evidence of its universality: concentration camps in any country *are* a world apart. As Solzhenitsyn also noted, prisoners "completely forgot" the reality of the outside world, and it was "unutterably difficult to return to this world." Its rules and habits, even many of its joys, had to be relearned, as if after long amnesia.

As for coping with daily life, even shopping and the handling of money could become unnerving problems. Solzhenitsyn has drawn a memorable scene of a former prisoner, overwhelmed with a kind of vertigo when he finds himself in a shop: he cannot grasp how people remember the size of their shirt collars, much less bring themselves to ask for them. It appears "perversely refined" to the ex-inmate, and sets in motion a chain of mis-

[3] When first published in Russia (1962), the short story entitled "Matryona's Place" was—incorrectly—dated 1953. This was a by-product of Soviet censorship. The story graphically described the poverty of a village called Torfoprodukt—social commentary that would pass the censor only if the action could be shown to relate to the distant past. In fact, the action had taken place in 1956, but it was impermissible to paint this picture of a village only six years before, already in the Khrushchev era. By changing the date to one just after Stalin's death, any shortcomings could be attributed to him.

Solzhenitsyn has stated categorically in a personal letter to a friend abroad that " 'Matryona's Place' could not have been written in Kazakhstan *before* [his italics] I found myself in Torfoprodukt," i.e., before 1956. Thus a relatively minor truth was sacrificed to save the story as a whole—whose point, in any case, is moral, rather than political or sociological.

giving about his own place in the real world. "Why," he asks himself, "should I return to this kind of life?"

Another revealing scene describes the dismaying implications of buying a skewer of shishkebab. Here the character realizes that he no longer understands the scale or proper role of money: extremely scarce in the camps, it had a wholly different meaning than on the outside. His difficulty with the skewer of meat opens his eyes to the abyss between him and the woman he fancies because she belongs to the normal world. This, in turn, shows him what he has forgotten about relations between free and civilized people. Solzhenitsyn's friends have confirmed that these episodes are highly autobiographical.

[One of One Day's most shattering revelations is the prisoner's total solitude. Densely compressed among crowds of fellow inmates, all in the same misery, all poised on the verge of destruction, each prisoner is nevertheless totally and terrifyingly alone. (The single exception in One Day— Alyosha, the Baptist, who communes daily with coreligionists and God— serves largely to prove the rule.) There are no women, nor do genuine friendships flourish: camp provides as little nourishment for normal affection as the Kazakh steppe for fruit trees. Each prisoner is wholly absorbed in his own personal war against death; not a calorie of energy can be wasted on anly relationship, except those which help the fight to survive.

[Although newcomers to the camps occasionally tried to protest in the name of prisoners' rights, veterans understood this as a form of suicide: it could change absolutely nothing, except to hasten the poor, deluded protester's death. All idealism, all humanism, all civilized standards, were victims of the struggle for survival. Even the best of men (even Ivan Denisovich) were sometimes cruel to weaker prisoners. And if the exhausted "goners" in the barracks occasionally provoked a tinge of pity, it never went further: not a finger was lifted to help the wretches. By Western standards, the whole of Soviet Russia in those years was stunningly harsh; but the inner world of the camps was brutalizing almost beyond outsiders' imagination.

This is what Solzhenitsyn had to put aside—not forget, because it needed telling to the world—but abandon as a way of life. Solzhenitsyn had grown accustomed to the pervasiveness of death. Now, in his adolescent pupils, he absorbed the converse: the energy of young life. In them, he saw the dawn of exciting, seemingly unlimited adult experience, the play of ambitions, friendships, and awakening passions—and, in a few pupils, an intense, youthful intellectual curiosity. The contrast between the school's energy, sense of community, and zest for life, and the camps' loneliness and death, was a dazzling, but healthy, shock. He now worked for self-fulfillment, instead of under the threat of death for unfulfilled quotas, and responded to ordinary human interests and demands, in place of "Do this or I'll kill you." Respect and self-respect were the overriding considerations, rather than contempt and self-effacement.

The village, too, helped. Solzhenitsyn gradually adapted himself to community life and its rudimentary forms of socializing: strolling the central streets, enjoying a film, indulging in a drink. He has described the process himself, starting with the exile's elation when he slipped on his single, frayed white shirt at twilight and strolled down the village's main street.

> The wall under the community center's rush roof would have a poster announcing a new "trophy" film,[4] and the village idiot, Vasya, would be urging one and all into the theater. Oleg would try to buy the cheapest ticket in the house—two rubles, right in the front row with all the kids. Once a month he'd have a fling, buy a mug of beer for two and a half rubles and drink it in the tea room with the Chechen truck drivers.

Solzhenitsyn struck up friendships with a handful of his fellow exiles in Berlik. They were people of his own social background—members of the Russian intelligentsia—and of his recent experiences—former camp inmates. He had the good fortune to meet former prisoners whom the camps had not broken—who had retained a love of life that helped restore his own. In Solzhenitsyn's fiction, such a couple appears, somewhat stylized, as the elderly Kadmins—a gynecologist Nikolay Ivanovich, and his wife, Elena Alexandrovna—who helped make Oleg's exile life "full of laughter and elation."

> Whatever happened to the exiled Kadmins, they kept saying, "Isn't that fine? Things are so much better than they used to be. How lucky we are to have landed in such a nice part of the world!"
> If they managed to get hold of a loaf of white bread—how wonderful! If they found a two-volume edition of Paustovsky in the bookshop—splendid! There was a good film on at the center that day—marvelous!

The arrival in the village of a dental technician—even a second gynecologist—was cause for the Kadmins to count their blessings anew. The new doctors would handle the gynecology and illegal abortions, leaving the general practice—with less money but greater peace of mind—to Nikolay Ivanovich.

> And the sunsets over the steppe, orange, pink, flame-red, crimson, and purple—superlative! Nikolay Ivanovich, a small slender

---

[4] Western films captured by the Red Army in Germany in 1945, and shown throughout the Soviet Union for many years after the war.

man with graying hair, would take his wife by the arm . . . and they would march off solemnly past the last house of the village to watch the sunset.

In the camps, "friendship" was almost always an arrangement for mutual advantage: I'll fix you up with tobacco if you get me a pipe. But people like the Kadmins were a vivid reminder that relationships of simple mutual affection still existed. Solzhenitsyn grew progressively closer to them.

There were obstacles, principally in the form of the *komendant* in charge of exile affairs, whose duties included discouraging friendships among his charges. In a ceaseless hunt for potential "conspiracies," he occasionally summoned a circle of exiles, one by one. After interrogation about the nature of their relationships and subjects of their conversations, he carefully compared notes in hopes of uncovering "lies and contradictions." Paradoxically, this served to strengthen friendships by eliminating casual and dispensable acquaintances. Only friendships of genuine fondness and need justified the risks.

Several of Solzhenitsyn's friends were amateur naturalists who took him along, when his health permitted, on exploratory walks into the steppe, within their permitted boundaries. His senses began to open to the distinct qualities of Kazakhstan, which he took to with an enthusiasm and curiosity characteristic of his prewar days. First came a discovery of the exotic in nature, something he had not known before. Relish is obvious in his narrative: he remembered the bitter scent of the steppe's *jusan* "as if it were an intimate part of him."

> He remembered the *jantak* with its prickly thorns, and the *jingil*, even pricklier, that ran along the hedges, with violet flowers in May that were as sweet-smelling as the lilac, and the stupefying *jidu* tree, whose scented blossom was as strong and heady as a lavishly perfumed woman.

Later he developed a deeper affection for the land and a fond appreciation of its people:

> Wasn't it extraordinary that a Russian, attached with every fiber of his being to the glades and little fields of Russia, to the quiet privacy of the Central Russian countryside, who had been sent away against his will and for ever, should have become so fond of that scraggy open plain, always too hot or too windy, where a quiet, overcast day came as a respite and a rainy day was like a holiday? He felt quite resigned to living there until he died.

Although he could not yet understand their tongue, Oleg's acquaintance with half a dozen native men in the village had made him fond of their race. Beyond their unquestioning devotion to their ancient clans, beneath the surface of their outward manners, which combined genuine and beguiling emotions, he saw them as an essentially simple and open-hearted people, ready to respond in kind to sincerity and good will.

Thus, in the strange remoteness of Berlik, Solzhenitsyn was putting down fresh roots and regenerating sensitivity to life. When—or whether—this slow process would have led to a restoration of his creativity is a moot question. For his recovery reversed itself before it had significantly advanced. Even in April, Zeinegaty Syrymbetov had been struck by Solzhenitsyn's unhealthy appearance. He spoke of a "tall gaunt man with a very pale face and eyes deeply sunk in their sockets." During his first months in Berlik, Solzhenitsyn might well have hoped that his debility was a hangover from his bout with cancer and the make-do operation. But by autumn, there could be no doubt that a malignant growth was spreading through him again, this time seemingly indomitable.

XVI

Cancer

MONTHS LATER, SOLZHENITSYN ARRIVED AT an oncological hospital. "I was dying," he recorded starkly. This was in January 1954. His journey to the hospital had been arduous—the end of a long autumn of dying.

The return of the cancer was not wholly unexpected. From his arrival in Berlik, Solzhenitsyn's debility had added to the hardship of exile. "To an ill man," he wrote, "the steppe seemed too dusty, the sun too hot, the vegetable gardens too singed."

But for the first few months he had been able to function normally within the confines of the *aul*. The malignant tumor lay in his stomach, heavy but inert. Suddenly it awoke, causing a swift and drastic weakening. The tumor swelled insistently, causing Solzhenitsyn to faint frequently with pain. By the autumn of 1953, he could no longer carry on in his classroom nor with any semblance of normal life.

Berlik had a hospital: testimony to the progress of Soviet public health in this desert *aul*. But, understandably, neither specialists, equipment, nor medicines were available for effective treatment of intestinal cancer. An ordinary citizen in Solzhenitsyn's condition would have been dispatched to the nearest city with a suitable hospital as soon as arrangements could be made. But exiles were not simply sent off on the next train, even if at the brink of death. Berlik's borders enclosed Solzhenitsyn like invisible barbed wire. To be caught outside without permission would bring instant return to a camp—for twenty more years. And permission to leave the place of exile was not, to put it mildly, easily obtained.

Only the *komendant* in charge of exile affairs could grant it, and only for an objective of limited time and specific destination and purpose. If trouble ensued, if an exile failed to return or had wangled permission on insufficient grounds—a trip to a hospital, for example, that was not utterly necessary—the *komendant* was responsible. To no one's surprise, he was extremely reluctant to issue travel permits.

The nearest adequate hospital for Solzhenitsyn was in Tashkent, the capital of the neighboring Uzbek Soviet Socialist Republic. It would be a journey of several hundred miles. Not daring to take this risk upon himself, Berlik's *komendant* passed the decision to his superiors. In that place and those years, bureaucratic decisions involving the purchase of ten dozen cotton shirts could take weeks; personal requests from exiles usually took longer, in proportion to their lower priority. The officials to whom Solzhenitsyn's case was referred turned to it in the fullness of time.

(Like most former prisoners, Solzhenitsyn had consummate patience; waiting for others' decisions had been the sum and substance of camp life. But the tumor was impatient, the pain unbearable. Solzhenitsyn's description of his condition is clinical: "I was on the frontier of death, deprived of the ability to eat and sleep and poisoned by the tumor's toxin." He knew that he would cross the frontier before the officials pondered his case—unless the galloping tumor was somehow restrained. After all the last-minute deliverances in his life, the hope of another now might have seemed escapist or Messianic. Yet a strange, exceedingly slim chance lay within reach.

In the village, Solzhenitsyn had heard curious tales about a man who lived in the mountains some hundred miles from Berlik. The old man practiced folk medicine, it was said, with impressive results. Solzhenitsyn decided he must see him. Had the destination been a town, the risk would have been prohibitive; Solzhenitsyn had no "papers"—specifically, the internal passport that every ordinary Soviet citizen must carry during trips of any length. The first policeman to stop him—in his condition, a likely possibility—would deliver him to a local jail. But on a trip from one wilderness to another there was a fair chance of avoiding policemen altogether. And even though twenty years in camps was a terrible stake to play for, there seemed no alternative.

(The desperate gamble succeeded. Solzhenitsyn was not only not apprehended but markedly helped by the old man. He turned out to be a naturist homeopath with wide knowledge and experience of his mountains' herbs and roots. For Solzhenitsyn, he prescribed a root containing aconite, a highly dangerous poison which is sometimes therapeutic in extreme cases. Administered in microscopic doses at long intervals, it can ease pain and arrest tumors. Solzhenitsyn's doses kept him alive until January, when his travel papers to Tashkent were granted at last.

(Permission to travel carried with it no aid to secure the means, his next formidable task. Help from an ambulance service or medical escort was inconceivable, but Solzhenitsyn also had no priority whatever in the hectic crush that surrounded transportation facilities in those days. In this respect, the whole of the Soviet Union had something in common with Europe in the frantic months following World War II: crowds fought for space in trains, trams, and buses with desperate resolution. The nearest railway station was twenty miles from Berlik. Having made his way there, Solzhenitsyn joined the struggle for tickets. Hours of waiting in subzero temperatures were considered nothing even for a sick man if in the end they produced a place on an impossibly packed train.

In addition to the strain of coping in his condition, Solzhenitsyn was hampered by extreme poverty. Trade unions awarded sick benefits only to members of six months' prior standing, and Solzhenitsyn had joined too late. This left him without income for the duration of his illness, and dependent upon his small savings and meager loans from friends, themselves usually poor.

At last, the train arrived in Tashkent. Weak as he was, Solzhenitsyn could not go directly to the hospital. Upon arrival at a "foreign locality," exiles had to register immediately with the local *komendant;* failure to do so made them guilty of "escaping." This required Solzhenitsyn to make exhausting treks across a sprawling city: from the station to the *komendatura* to report, back to the station to fetch his things (he was too weak to carry them throughout), and from there to the hospital. He was failing fast; there was a real chance that the trip had been in vain.

Solzhenitsyn had not been alone in a big city—that is, unescorted by police agents—for more than ten years. The pain in his stomach pushed him to the brink of consciousness. The January day was sodden: a heavy winter rain lashed the streets. Without rainwear, his trips across the city left him sopping. He knew no one to approach for help. The last straw was the streetcars, bulging with bodies. "The screeching, jolting, overcrowded trams had shaken him almost to death," he would write of his semiautobiographical hero.

At the limits of endurance, Solzhenitsyn stumbled to the hospital that evening—to discover that he could not be admitted until morning. The reception of nonemergency cases had ended for the day, and, since he had arrived under his own power, he fell into this administrative category. But he could bear no more; his journey had ended, even if this meant camping on the floor. The same autobiographical character spent just this kind of first night in a hospital.

Solzhenitsyn's unauthorized intrusion provoked a flurry of protest by the nurses. But eventually they settled the exhausted man on a sofa in a corridor. It was his first night in the cancer ward which would enter world literature.

His condition was extremely grave. After the half measures in Ekibastuz and the subsequent year or more of neglect, the long wait for travel papers had severely worsened an already difficult case. This latest bureaucratic fumbling nearly cost him his life again, and he himself was certain that it had. "When I arrived that winter in Tashkent," he wrote, "I felt like a corpse. That's what I'd come here for—to die." The man who was convinced that he had the makings of an important writer whose insights mattered to the world faced extinction at the age of thirty-five, without a single completed work to prove to himself and others that his aspiration was not reverie.

⸤Yet three months later, he was to emerge from the ward almost fit, as physically sound as he would ever be again. Moreover, he was to recover his emotional well-being and spiritual confidence—to shed the camps' legacy of apprehension and feelings of inadequacy at last.⸥

Solzhenitsyn's treatment turned out to be more straightforward than could have been expected, especially in view of his protracted medical neglect and of the lost diagnosis of almost two years before—which, vital as it was now, could not be definitely reestablished. He was treated with hormones and X rays. After roughly a dozen of the latter treatments, the tormenting pains of the past months disappeared. Sleep and appetite returned at last, together with good humor.

Further treatment, however, became onerous and depressing. His appetite again disappeared in a "gut-splitting nausea" produced by the continuing course of X rays. The only relief came in an unnatural pose—stretched out with "my head hanging down." Because it played havoc with his emotions, the hormone treatment became the object of some mistrust. Still convinced he was to die soon, Solzhenitsyn wanted to do it in the relative comfort given by the first course of X-ray treatments. But to his own surprise, Solzhenitsyn's remarkable improvement resumed. "I didn't dare admit even to myself that I was recovering," he wrote. "Even in fleeting dreams I measured the span that had been added to my life not in years, but months."

⸤He would still face periodic treatment, including the use of medicines powerful enough to keep him in bed for a month at a time. But a few years later, he would be able to say that "the tumor no longer interfered" with his life, that it had "changed its nature"—that is, forfeited its malignancy. This is as much as any victim of cancer can expect.⸥

Almost twenty years later, in his middle fifties, Solzhenitsyn's health was roughly the same; the cancer was still stabilized. A Soviet journalist who visited him in 1962 (when he was forty-four) wrote that "when you look at him, you have an impression that he is in the best of health. You are misled by his mobility, energetic gestures, and by the lively expressiveness of his face. In reality, he is ill." But Solzhenitsyn not only gives an impression of a healthy person, but lives, especially works, like one—with extraordinary energy and concentration for a man of his age who has endured his hardships. The cancer is still a potential menace, but only one of many in his life. He rarely talks about it, but, when asked, replies matter-of-factly. As the same Soviet journalist observed, he treats it "as if it were alien to him, as if it were something that had nothing to do with him."

The return to this kind of equilibrium after apparently mortal pains seems to speak of more even than Solzhenitsyn's rare perseverance. Of what? What made Solzhenitsyn's treatment so uncommonly successful and durable? At this stage of medical knowledge, one cannot speak of recovery from cancer without mention of luck. The skill of the Tashkent doctors, described with profound appreciation in *Cancer Ward*, must also be presumed to have played a major role. But speculation about this mystery must include another factor, as curious as it seems crucial. One of Solzhenitsyn's closest friends has written that his tumor, although "practically terminal," was ordered by the patient to retreat—and obeyed. Solzhenitsyn himself has never denied the implication that autosuggestion was somehow involved.

Several passages of *Cancer Ward* reveal a distinct skepticism toward contemporary medical science—not toward its usefulness as such, but its claims to be the sole source of cure. All this strongly suggests that Solzhenitsyn believes that his survival was made possible by his own fierce determination not to die. The determination itself was born of a psychological and creative revival that finally materialized in the hospital. This experience was apparently so intense that it overshadowed even the cure. A new sense of purpose had seized him. And, having conquered the cancer, it propelled him into the creative tempest that transformed the anonymous exile into a new colossus of Russian literature.

XVII

Recovery

SOLZHENITSYN CALLED THE SPRING OF 1955 in the Tashkent cancer ward "the most agonizing and most beautiful of my life." The agony lay in the past, the beauty in anticipation of the future.

Camps and cancer had ravaged his appearance.

> I looked pitiful [he wrote]. My emaciated face evoked what I'd endured: creased with the camps' inescapable dark frown, covered by ashen skin deadened into leather, blighted by the slow poisons of illness and of medicines which tinged my cheeks with green. My back was slouched from the defensive habit of obeying and hiding. My ridiculous striped little jacket barely reached to my belly, my striped trousers ended above my ankles. Brown with age, the corner of my puttees hung from the tops of my stubby canvas prison boots.

He walked "uncertainly" on "unsteady legs." And breathed "cautiously so as not to provoke a stabbing pain in the chest." But this was the dark before dawn.

The trip to Tashkent did more than arrest a seemingly irresistible cancer. In Berlik, he had accepted his humble life. Although his own descriptions of exile indicate that the resignation was tinged with quiet sorrow, he was also growing fond of the remote surroundings in his short time there. He did not permit himself to look beyond the horizons of a frontier village schoolteacher. But soon after arriving in Tashkent, an inner compulsion to expand and effuse—to *create*—seized him. He remembered the ambition he had been nurturing since childhood and through the camps.

Tashkent itself was a catalyst for change. A large southern city with a mild climate, it was reminiscent of the Rostov of his youth, and far more stimulating, and in many ways more pleasant, than Berlik. In the steppe, Solzhenitsyn had rediscovered stars that had been blotted out by camp searchlights, strolls without guards, films at a local cinema. After imprisonment, it was uplifting to be an ordinary teacher in an ordinary village living in an ordinary adobe cubicle. But Tashkent offered a new level of discovery.

"For me, everything was as if forgotten or never seen before," Solzhenitsyn wrote in "The Right Hand." "Everything was interesting: even an ice-cream cart, a street-cleaning machine with water jets, women selling bunches of elongated radishes—and of course a foal that had wandered onto the young grass through a break in the wall." His hospital stood in a splendid old park. Having seen no real greenery for more than five years, he was filled with wonder at its smell and touch.

The park was inhabited by spreading oaks that threw their shade over tender Japanese acacias. And the grass of the lawns—it was succulent. I'd long forgotten that kind of grass. (In the camps, it was ordered weeded out like an enemy; in my place of exile, no variety of grass could grow.) Simply to lie face down in it, to inhale the smell of grass and sun-warmed vapors peacefully, was bliss enough.

A fragment of city bustle could also be observed from the park: a native Uzbek restaurant, a fruit kiosk, tennis players on a nearby court. And funeral processions two or three times a day, for an infelicitous stroke of town planning had put a cemetery directly across the wall from the hospital park.

But what most affected—and beckoned—him was the rediscovery of women in a city crowd. "The whole day, the gravel and asphalt paths [of the park] streamed with women, women!" he wrote; ". . . young doctors, nurses, laboratory assistants, clerks, matrons, and patients' female relations." These extraordinary creatures "passed me in white coats, austere and tender, and in bright southern dresses, frequently semitransparent; the more affluent among them twirled fashionable Chinese parasols on thin bamboo handles over their heads; the parasols were sunny-colored, blue, pink. Each woman flashing by in a moment represented the plot of an entire story: the story of the life she'd led before me—before her possible (or rather impossible) acquaintance with me."

The more Solzhenitsyn's recovery progressed, the more "despondently" he contemplated his shackles as an exile. He was no longer content to return to his desert outpost, and had no more need to hide in its remoteness. A blessing had been transformed into a burden. Observing a wider, greener, happier world, he felt ready, even yearned, to enter it. And in this other life to which he once had belonged he was not merely a teacher, but primarily a writer. It was here, at a kiosk in the park, that he spied the "tempting little notebooks"—although he was still afraid to write in them. The return of "zest for life" and appreciation of its more sophisticated pleasures simultaneously led Solzhenitsyn back to his art.

Many camp inmates had a fierce longing to tell the world what they had endured. For Solzhenitsyn as well as others, it was a principal motive for surviving. The horrors were such that it seemed no more was needed for deliverance—for universal progress—than their revelation to the world. "What should we do?" asks a Solzhenitsyn character in a camp situation that has driven him to the outer limit of despair. The reply outlines Solzhenitsyn's code: survive, remember, and recount. "What can we do? We can remember . . ."

The time for memory—and memorials—had arrived. Victims were already asking: "Where can we read about us? And when?" After his pledge given in camp, certainly to himself and perhaps to others, Solzhenitsyn had reason to feel that these questions were addressed personally to him. An aging lady in *Cancer Ward* provides another clearly autobiographical detail. She had endured camps, exile, and separation from her husband; now, as a hospital orderly, she jolts a patient with a reminder of her ordeal. Dismissed from the hospital in late spring, Solzhenitsyn returned to Berlik and turned to the responsibilities implied in his Tashkent encounters and ruminations.

In his adobe hut, he began to write. Southern Kazakhstan was still an uncongenial atmosphere for a man who wanted to be a *Russian* writer, and Solzhenitsyn had not yet fully bested his phobia of paper and pen. But he now managed to convince himself that "the wrong hands" would not again be laid on his materials. He wrote, as he put it, "in secret" and "strict solitude."

Secrecy was essential. Solzhenitsyn had not abandoned his teen-age plan for a large novel about World War I. Despite Berlik's lack of research facilities, the parts of the narrative drawing upon imagination and family lore could have been written here, and with safety. Yet he felt that his first responsibility—and need—was to deal with the experience of prison and camps. No doubt his prewar attraction to the theater helped determine the vehicle: his first completed project was a play set in a labor camp in 1945. Eventually entitled *The Love Girl and the Innocent*, the kaleidoscopic drama reflected Solzhenitsyn's own pre-Marfino months in "mixed" camps: those that contained both women and common criminals, unlike his all-male Kazakhstan camps for "politicals" only. Although the variegated cast of characters allowed for a broad panorama of camp life and although each scene generated its own excitement, the play as a whole lacks the force of Solzhenitsyn's later fiction. After its completion in 1954, another year of "normal" life, as much of it as exile afforded, was needed before he attained his full creative powers.

Above all, normal life meant free contact with ordinary people, most of which was provided by the Berlik school. His strength largely restored,

Solzhenitsyn immersed himself in teaching with his old diligence and flair. A Berlik colleague noticed that he "knew his subjects thoroughly, taught them skillfully, and, most important of all, knew how to generate an uncommonly creative working atmosphere" in his classroom. Years later, when one of his fellow teachers learned that he was a writer, she regretted his "mistake." "Teaching is his vocation," she pronounced. "He was exceptionally gifted as a teacher [and] knew how to find the key to every child's heart."

Solzhenitsyn's manner was part of the secret. His subjects were difficult, and he himself anything but a "soft" teacher; at his first examination, he failed fifteen pupils. But he soon became the favorite of many boys and girls; ten years later, one girl said, "He will always remain my ideal." A Kazakh pupil, now a teacher himself, remembered that Solzhenitsyn "never made us feel his superiority as an adult, as a man of much knowledge. It seemed to me that he enjoyed associating with us." But behind the same straightforward, wholly unpretentious manner which his soldiers had admired stood meticulous preparation and observation. Solzhenitsyn kept special notebooks in which he registered his pupils' behavior, tastes, interests, and attitudes. For a firmer understanding of their backgrounds, he often visited their homes. And his zeal was useful in a more direct way. "He would burst into the classroom like a blast of wind," a former pupil remembered. His energy infected his pupils with a distinct "excitement"; "the brain began to work feverishly—you wanted to catch the rhythm that he put before you."

Solzhenitsyn's contact with his pupils was not limited to classes. Once he became known as a first-class teacher, boys and girls sought him out for general knowledge and for arbitration and guidance. His adobe hut became their "club," although there were too many members to fit inside, and they met only in the courtyard in good weather. When a journalist visited Berlik in 1964, the former club members vividly recalled their afterschool hours with Solzhenitsyn ten years earlier, and although the journalist's summary is full of the romantic clichés virtually *de rigueur* in Soviet provincial reporting, something of the rare exchange between this teacher and his pupils comes through in his description.

All those who visited the little house in Pioneer Street in those bygone days remember endless conversation and discussion about things both simple and complicated. The wind blew in from the steppe, scented with the smell of spring grasses. Thousands of stars sparkled in the sky. One spoke of distant and unknown worlds, of the cosmos full of mysteries. Together with his pupils, Alexander Isaiyevich made a model of the firmament. When one put it over the lamp the names of constellations appeared clearly. The children raised their eyes to the sky and patiently sought out these constellations there. Must one spell out how they loved these lessons in astronomy!

The rewards that Solzhenitsyn himself derived from his teaching and extracurricular activities might alone explain his lavish expenditure of time and energy on them. His colleagues' and pupils' admiration provided indispensable reassurance that his personality and abilities had not withered. At the same time, he was encouraged by unmistakable moves toward de-Stalinization in the country as a whole. Although there had been faint hope even from the beginning that his exile would not in fact be perpetual, it was now that substantial changes were becoming evident to the attuned ear.

Apart from Beria's fall, little concrete evidence of progress could be documented. On the edge of the desert, thousands of miles from the source of decisions, Solzhenitsyn was even less privy to Kremlin secrets than the average Moscow intellectual. But he had long been an avid student of what he called the "coded instructions" of newspapers and their clues to the country's political and psychological atmosphere. In 1953 and 1954, disparaging references to "the cult of personality" proliferated in the press, together with solemn paeans to "socialist legality." Among the broad hints in this cautious criticism of Stalin was one that his victims might ultimately expect a kind of justice.

In the early spring of 1955, Solzhenitsyn returned to his cancer ward for a checkup.[1] Because Tashkent had a far wider "sample" of Soviet life than Berlik, it provided much more opportunity to test his hypotheses by direct observation. Two important political events occurred while Solzhenitsyn was in Tashkent, and their significance in the general trend toward relaxation could be gauged by listening to discussions in the hospital, where staff and patients represented a rather broad cross section. The first was the replacement of the U.S.S.R. Supreme Court, the highest court in the land—which, for a quarter of a century, had condemned hundreds of the most prominent Soviet citizens to death, confirmed the death sentences of tens of thousands of the less celebrated, and rejected millions of appeals from still-surviving prisoners everywhere in the country. Several of the most important jurists directly responsible for these crimes were dismissed in February 1955.

In that month too, Georgy Malenkov, Stalin's former private secretary and leading troubleshooter, resigned as Soviet Prime Minister. Solzhenitsyn's reaction to this news is reflected in *Cancer Ward* where replacement of the Supreme Court membership is perceived as "four muted

[1] In *Cancer Ward*, Solzhenitsyn's 1954 and 1955 visits to the Tashkent hospital are merged into one for dramatic effect, and the novel's action takes place entirely in the latter year.

Beethoven drumbeats of fate," and Malenkov's resignation is felt as if "somewhere in the lowest depths, geological strata had rumbled and stirred slightly in their bed." Solzhenitsyn described an exile reading about the events while resting, as he too did in those days, on his hospital bed. Oleg Kostoglotov seized a copy of *Pravda* from Rusanov's feet, spotted the breathtaking news instantly and read it. Then he rose from his own bed: he was unable to stay seated. Although he did not understand the article's full significance, the replacement of the Prime Minister following directly upon the changing of the entire Supreme Court was an unmistakable sign of momentous movement.

> History was on the march. Could the changes conceivably be for the worse?
> The day before yesterday he had held his leaping heart down with his hands, keeping himself from all hope and belief.
> But two days had gone by, and now—as a reminder—the same four Beethoven chords thundered into the sky as though into a microphone. . . .
> Oleg darted out of the room. He ran outside. Into the open!

No news could have been more personal or exhilarating to an exile. It tendered a promise that his restriction might be lifted, that he might be allowed to live where he wanted—even to resume the life ruptured by arrest. Moreover, ordinary people seemed to approve. Solzhenitsyn carefully observed reactions in· the hospital. Most indicated that changes devised within the Kremlin were matched at the grass roots, where whispers—and even more than whispers—showed that broadly anti-Stalinist attitudes were emerging into the open.

No public discussion was ventured of Stalin or Stalinism as such. But ordinary people had begun to criticize some of the cruder restrictions, hypocrisies, and injustices that obviously flowed directly from Stalinism's established values and practices. *Cancer Ward* depicts a doctor protesting against a colleague's monkey trial for alleged misconduct—and winning the protest! During the campaign against "anti-Soviet" conspiracies in the medical world only two years before, no such protest could conceivably have succeeded; the very attempt would have been suicide. (Nevertheless, Solzhenitsyn demonstrates that the legacy of this campaign was still distorting medical decisions in 1955.)

Other scenes record the new, freer mood. A "businessman" openly criticizes the absurdities of the Soviet distribution system, under which most of the country is deprived of tomatoes while Tashkent chokes on them. A discussion in the ward draws attention to the great material inequalities of the Soviet system. Even Moscow rumors reach the patients and become subjects for comment: talk of a mass reexamination of political sentences, of the replacement of Stalinist Victoriana by "modern" architecture and living styles, of fresh winds in literature. "This long, lanky Yevtushenko fellow crops up," announces one character. "A complete unknown, no rhyme or reason. All he has to do is wave his arms about and yell, and the girls go wild. . . ." This news is particularly convincing because it comes from a Stalinist, who disapproves.

Solzhenitsyn also describes the fear of officials implicated in Stalin's crimes, and the acute discomfort of honest men who have nevertheless come to depend on the Leader for their own sense of identity and peace of mind. It is a measure of his literary powers that a eulogy to Stalin in the thoughts of one character is more convincingly expressed than anything a genuinely Stalinist writer could produce. There is little doubt that these aspects of *Cancer Ward* portray the dramatis personae and circumstances of Solzhenitsyn's own Tashkent period with great exactness. During a discussion of the novel in November 1966, Solzhenitsyn answered attacks on its sincerity in terms of historical accuracy, stressing his attempts to register the social climate of the time with documentary precision on the basis of the characters and attitudes he had observed in the cancer ward.

The ward gave Solzhenitsyn more than a microcosm for social observation. Life there further dispelled the fear, common among former prisoners, of having become insensitive to the outside world's nuances. Solzhenitsyn saw that he had retained his basic understanding of Soviet life; that in some ways his perception had even been enhanced, not only because he understood the outlook of former inmates and exiles, but also because the jungle laws of the camp had laid bare some of the truths of human existence.

Solzhenitsyn's last days in Tashkent provided tangible foretokens of changes soon to bear directly upon his own desire to inhabit "a fertile land." In April, rumors began to circulate among exiles in the hospital that the entire exile system would soon be dismantled. The hopeful talk was given startling confirmation as he took leave of the city.

Just as he had had to register his arrival in Tashkent with the local *komendant,* he now went to record his departure. *Cancer Ward* details miraculous changes in the *komendatura*'s personnel and atmosphere. In place of rudeness and sullen suspicion, there was a "pleasant" voice that "welcomed" exiles. The hero muses that he had never heard before such a tone from the security police. The *komendant* himself assures him that "it will soon all be over—the registrations, the exile, the *komendants.*"

This episode gave Solzhenitsyn real hope of rejoining the wider world rediscovered in Tashkent. The hospital pronounced him "cured," as he put it, and, despite cancer's latent danger, there was no serious restriction on his activity. It was surely no accident that he returned to Berlik the second time with considerably broadened writing goals. Later in the year he was working on *The First Circle*, and soon thereafter began a long chronicle—which would be compressed over several years to seventy magazine pages—about a prisoner he called Ivan Denisovich. The renaissance had not only restored his creative powers, but allowed him to apply them to his most painful experiences.

Solzhenitsyn returned from Tashkent with another goal: to campaign for release from exile. However much he had come to appreciate his work and friends in Berlik, and to admire the desert flowers, he had also developed what he later called *toska*—a yearning mixed with homesickness and nostalgia—for a certain kind of unvarnished Russian peasant speech needed to sharpen his ear and stimulate his creativity. The *toska*, he found, was "dragging [him] out of Asia." He longed for a place "without the heat, with a leafy rustle of forest," where he could "disappear and lose myself in the very depths of Russia. . . ." As every Soviet citizen knew, however, this kind of longing could be fulfilled only by the most determined efforts, and only when the political atmosphere was propitious. Encouraging as the atmosphere had seemed in Tashkent, Solzhenitsyn knew that it was folly to rely on the vagaries of Kremlin politics: a sudden, secret shift could easily eradicate all the modest achievements of de-Stalinization. If Solzhenitsyn were actively to seek release from exile rather than await it as a gift, a steady campaign of petitioning, reminding, and cajoling would be required.

It became quite clear from subsequent political memoirs and other sources that de-Stalinization was hardly inevitable or assured. Strong Kremlin cliques opposed liberalization, and, at several points after Stalin's death, even as late as 1955, all gains might have been lost overnight. First Secretary Nikita Khrushchev prevailed, however, and with him, partly in the service of his personal political ends, his policy of dismantling the grosser forms of Stalinist injustice and oppression. The key moment came at the Twentieth Party Congress in February 1956. Solzhenitsyn has no doubts about its part in his own case: "In 1956, after the Twentieth Congress of the CPSU [Communist Party of the Soviet Union]," he wrote, "I was released from exile." It was, in fact, in June that his physical bondage ended, almost eleven and a half years after his arrest at the front. He was now restored to most of the rights of Soviet citizenship, though still not a free man, even in the Soviet context.

Although permitted to move about the country, he was still branded: the "counterrevolutionary" activity fixed in his record made him a kind of untouchable. "I wouldn't have been taken on even as an electrician at a decent construction project," he remarked, "whereas I felt I wanted to be a teacher." Solzhenitsyn had another nine months—of perhaps the most liberal year in Soviet history after Stalin—of knocking on doors and waiting in queues to disentangle himself of the bureaucratic snares of his sentence and win "rehabilitation"—that is, vindication of all charges. Only in 1957, he wrote, was "my sentence of 1945 recognized as invalid, and I could realize my long-standing ambition to move to Central Russia."

Releases and rehabilitations took years because millions of cases had to be processed. And despite the irreparable injustice suffered by victims and the common knowledge of what had caused it, nothing in the rehabilitation process was wholesale or automatic. Even after the Twentieth Party Congress and the branding of Stalinist secret police activities as criminal, no general pardon was granted for "politicals." Each case was treated as unique; all facts and circumstances had to be ascertained from the very beginning, quite independently from tens of thousands of precisely parallel cases. A fiction had to be maintained that each injustice had been caused by an isolated judicial error: "socialist legality" as such, together with the judicial system, remained clean.

This meant that Solzhenitsyn, like all others in his position, had to address a "petition for rehabilitation" to the Attorney-General of the U.S.S.R. The petition disputed the facts on which his sentence was grounded. Witnesses were then summoned: two friends and Reshetovskaya. As a rehabilitation document later stated, the two friends were those "to whom Solzhenitsyn was alleged to have uttered anti-Soviet fabrications. The above-mentioned persons characterized Solzhenitsyn as a Soviet patriot and denied that he had conducted anti-Soviet conversations."

The diary and letters which had been the foundation of his indictment were read with fresh eyes and it was determined, twelve years after the fact, that they contained no elements of a crime. Only after an exhaustive investigation of all the materials in the case was Solzhenitsyn fully rehabilitated. On February 6, 1957, the Supreme Court of the U.S.S.R. "ruled that the case be dismissed for lack of corpus delicti." [2]

Twenty months of strenuous effort were required to achieve this ruling —all to uphold the pretense that Soviet Russia had always been a land of justice, and that what was now being attended to were isolated aberrations. At last Solzhenitsyn was officially innocent, not an ex-convict in terms of employment regulations or any other. In the eyes of the law, his career was impeccable. He had been a student, a front-line officer, then a teacher. He need never again mention his arrest or sentence in an official document. The authorities hoped that the extirpation of wrongful conviction from records would also erase them from memories and from history.

A decade later, Solzhenitsyn's attitude toward his dozen lost years lacked self-pity. "I never thought I'd been sentenced without guilt," he said in an interview. "For I'd been expressing views which were inad-

---

[2] Solzhenitsyn's rehabilitation is often dated 1956, an error caused by a misprint in the original Russian publication of the Supreme Court's edict.

missible in those years." What bothered him then was the fate of victims sentenced for literally nothing, not even cautious criticism in private letters. Millions of innocents suffered more than he; hundreds of thousands died.

But this was in retrospect; what could he feel leaving Kazakhstan in the summer of 1956? He was almost thirty-eight. Although his promise had been evident since adolescence, his creative accomplishment had scarcely begun. What he had written was manifestly unpublishable. What he was now writing seemed equally certain never to see print. Moreover, it was a monumental project whose completion, after two bouts with cancer, could hardly be assured.

On the other hand, he was free of restrictions and preparing a pilgrimage to Central Russia, his dream of more than twenty years. There he would find conducive surroundings and time to write. The country's social developments could only encourage him to develop his chosen themes. Vladimir Dudintsev was publishing *Not by Bread Alone,* his then bold antibureaucratic novel, and Yevgeny Yevtushenko was dazzling audiences with poetry appealing for liberation from Stalinist dogma and a return to the revolution's uncorrupted idealism. After the Hungarian uprising, writers such as these would be threatened and denounced as "revisionists" intent on undermining "sacred principles." But their effect could not easily be nullified, and a substantial proportion of the Writers' Union supported the angry men of new Soviet literature—support that was reflected in some organs of the Soviet press. Even the taboo subject of concentration camps was being hinted at and mentioned—among others by the famous poet Alexander Tvardovsky, who in time would play a great role in Solzhenitsyn's career.

The gap was still wide between what Solzhenitsyn was writing and the most liberal passages approved by the censor; Soviet literary and intellectual life remained stifled. "History is too slow for our life, for our hearts," he once remarked wistfully. But there was perceptible movement in the direction of his own concepts of honesty and art, and he was born to a long tradition of patient waiting. This was not passive acceptance, as Westerners often interpret the attitude of Russian intellectuals, but a tendency to measure progress in terms of one's lifetime—or longer. A writer craving quick success would have assessed Solzhenitsyn's future to be as dim as his past had been disastrous. But on balance, his life upon leaving Kazakhstan held more promise than at any time since the outbreak of war.

Above all, he could live where and write what he liked. Recognition might come only posthumously, but he had faced death often enough not to equate achievement with acknowledgment of it during the achiever's life. His single goal was to write honestly and well—for posterity, even if this sounded high-flown. For there was no real hope of publishing what weighed on him. In the mid-1950s, the notion of publishing abroad without official permission was still quite unthinkable to Russian writers.

To compromise with his truths for the sake of publication in Russia would have obviated the very purpose of Solzhenitsyn's new life. There were no two ways: writing now meant a special kind of affirmation, involving him in literature's highest purposes. It is too much to say that his goals had been entirely forgotten by other Russian writers, but they were quite different from those which had governed the vast bulk of "open" Soviet letters for decades. Solzhenitsyn's writing was based on strikingly "revolutionary" principles.

To speak of a "new life" for Solzhenitsyn in the summer of 1956 is but slightly metaphoric. Every aspect of his prewar one seemed melted or reforged since 1941, and his old qualities of intellectual curiosity and self-discipline resided within a substantially altered man. Paradoxically, he was in some senses blessed by his ordeals. He had become much humbler than in his relatively jaunty prewar days. And unlike many intelligent, cultured men, he had a goal in life, one which would use his talents to their limits, and for which he carried all the materials and resources within him. To the prewar ambition to write was joined a body of experience worthy of epics and a maturity capable of shaping and interpreting the material. What writer could ask for more?

As if to symbolize the beginning of the new life, or the break with the old, Solzhenitsyn had a "farewell" meeting with Reshetovskaya. It took place in the summer of his release from exile, when he visited Moscow for the first time since his "expulsion" from Marfino. He was then in the legal no man's land between release from exile and full rehabilitation, in pursuit of which he traveled to the capital to consult with lawyers and petition before the special rehabilitation commission that had been established as one of the de-Stalinization reforms.

Reshetovskaya happened to be visiting Moscow too at that time, and they agreed to meet. The reunion took place in a friend's flat. There was of course much to tell each other after the ten years since her last visit to him in prison. It was a meeting not without emotion, and they parted with the understanding that fate had pulled them apart and put them on quite separate courses. For Solzhenitsyn, it must only have meant confirmation that his prewar life was not to be resurrected, and that he must begin again.

XVIII

Creation

SOLZHENITSYN LEFT KAZAKHSTAN ALONE AND free of obligations. But for restrictions applicable to all Soviet citizens,[1] the whole of the country was open to him. The choice of settlement, therefore, was his own: "I was returning at random," he wrote. "From the hot, dusty desert quite simply to Russia."

He chose Vladimir province, which lay some hundred miles northwest of the capital. This was "the very depths," as he put it, of Mother Russia, where he could absorb the sounds, smells, and landscapes, even the magic names of villages and streams. The pre-Muscovite capital of the medieval Russian state, Vladimir was one of the few Russian cities in which a substantial part of the architecture and spirit of ancient *Rus* survived. The famous Golden Gate of the city wall, the only remnant of twelfth-century Russian military art, and the Cathedral of the Dormition, one of the great works of ancient Russian architecture, were but two of the landmarks which evoked the mystical attraction of old Russia.

When Solzhenitsyn arrived in the province, many of the irreplaceable architectural masterpieces—whole monasteries together with their frescoes and stone carvings—were suffering from decades of neglect. In some ways, decay enhanced the medieval spirit. The surrounding countryside, however, needed neither enhancement nor restoration. It was here that the painter Isaac Levitan, perhaps the Constable of Russia, had done much of his most moving work, conveying the essence of the typically "Russian" landscape: quiet rivers and broad fields of rye, stands of birches, firs, and pines that were simultaneously serene and melancholy.

Having arrived in Vladimir, Solzhenitsyn requested the provincial edu-

---

[1] Soviet citizens are required to register their residence with the police, and for reasons of overpopulation and supply as well as security the registration is normally refused in Moscow, Leningrad, and other attractive major cities as well as areas on the Black and Baltic Sea coasts. Permits are issued in these "closed" locations on the basis of an essential job or influential personal contacts.

cational authorities to assign him a teacher's job in a remote and beautiful village. The first one he visited seemed ideal. It was called Vysokoye Polye (High Field), a name which Solzhenitsyn approved for its accuracy. It stood "on a rise between dales and then more rises, all dipped into the fresh dewy forest, with a pond and little dam. Just the place where I wouldn't mind living and dying."

This was the very picture of the Russian village that his mind's eye had refined over years. "For a long time," he wrote, "I sat on a tree stump in a thicket and thought . . . how I'd really love to remain here and to listen to branches rustling against the roof at night, with no noise of radios anywhere and the whole world silent."\

But practical snags attended the village's beauty. No bread was baked in High Field, "no food of any kind was sold there. The entire village hauled in sacks of provisions from the provincial center"—that is, from Vladimir. This was clearly no place for a single man intending to teach and write, who would have to attend to many of his own household chores. Solzhenitsyn was rudely reminded that Central Russia was not only Levitan landscapes but also part of the national economic system, with its limping or nonexistent facilities for distributing the essentials of life. He returned to Vladimir and requested an appointment nearer a town which offered such fruits of civilization as food shops. His new assignment was to the Kurlovsky district of the province.

The name of the second village evoked no delights, and again lived up to its promise. It was called Torfoprodukt (Peat Product), and was precisely that: a place with seemingly little purpose but peat production. The very air seems depressing in Solzhenitsyn's description of the little industrial center.

> The workers' settlement sprawled untidily among the peat bogs —monotonous shacks from the thirties, and little houses with carved façades and glass verandas, put up in the fifties. But inside these houses I could see no partitions reaching up to the ceilings, so there was no hope of renting a room with four real walls.
>
> Over the settlement hung smoke from the factory chimney. Little locomotives ran this way and that along narrow-gauge railway lines, giving out more thick smoke and piercing whistles, pulling loads of dirty brown peat in slabs and briquettes. I could safely assume that in the evening a loudspeaker would be crying its heart out over the door of the club and there would be drunks roaming the streets and, sooner or later, sticking knives in each other.

Torfoprodukt had no accommodation for visitors or newcomers, and Solzhenitsyn spent the night on a wooden bench in the railway station. He soon regretted leaving Kazakhstan at all. "This was what my dream

about a quiet corner of Russia had brought me to," he later remembered,
". . . when I could have stayed where I was and lived in an adobe hut
looking out on the desert, with a fresh breeze at night and only the sky's
starry dome overhead." But the regrets were gone in the morning.

> I couldn't sleep on the station bench, and as soon as it started get-
> ting light I went for another stroll around the settlement. This
> time I saw a tiny marketplace. Only one woman stood there at that
> early hour, selling milk, and I took a bottle and began drinking it
> on the spot.
> I was struck by the way she talked. Instead of a normal speaking
> voice she used a sweet sing-song, and her words were the ones I
> was longing to hear when I left Asia for this place.

The woman's speech itself is so rich in dialect that the flavor cannot
be conveyed in translation. To Solzhenitsyn, the peasant woman's rear-
rangement of the commonplace building bricks of language into her own
unself-conscious patterns exposed the very roots of the Russian language.
The moment he heard her, he knew that he had arrived in the one place
on earth where he would be able to graft his own literary language onto
these deep roots. The freshness of Solzhenitsyn's prose would derive from
the unique expressiveness of peasant speech, particularly from its unforced
use of the hidden resources of the language. It can be likened to Grieg's
use of folk melodies from which a richer music is developed, earthy in
substance but with subtle orchestration.

The anonymous milk seller offered more than a language lesson. She
directed Solzhenitsyn to a place to live—more congenial than Torfoprodukt, yet within walking distance of his school.

> I learned that the peat workings weren't the only thing, that
> over the railway lines there was a hill, and over the hill, a village,
> that this village was Talnovo, and it had been there ages ago,
> when the "gypsy woman" lived in the big house and the wild woods
> stood all round. And farther on there was a whole countryside full
> of villages—Chaslitsy, Ovintsy, Spudni, Shevertni, Shestimirovo,
> deeper and deeper into the woods, farther and farther from the
> railway, up toward the lakes.
> The names were like a soothing breeze to me. They held a
> promise of backwoods Russia.

After some searching, Solzhenitsyn and his guide came to the place
where he would settle for the next year or so. It was enveloped in a
primordial Russian atmosphere.

> We had come to a dammed-up stream that was short of water
> and had a little bridge over it. No other place in all the village took
> my fancy as this did: there were two or three willows, a lopsided

house, ducks swimming on the pond, geese shaking themselves as they stepped out of the water . . .

Matryona's house stood quite near by. Its row of four windows looked out on the cold backs, the two slopes of the roof were covered with shingles, and a little attic window was decorated in the old Russian style. But the shingles were rotting, the beam ends of the house and the once mighty gates had turned gray with age, and there were gaps in the little shelter over the gate.

Solzhenitsyn's landlady was an old widow whose household is described in "Matryona's Place." The story is documentary: the names of the places are real, and those of the characters altered only slightly from their models'.

> The spacious room, and especially the best part near the windows, was full of rubber plants in pots and tubs standing on stools and benches. They peopled the householder's loneliness like a speechless but living crowd. They had been allowed to run wild, and they took up all the scanty light on the north side. . . .
>
> But I had already seen that I was destined to settle in this dimly lit house with the tarnished mirror in which you couldn't see yourself, and the two garish posters (one advertising books, the other about the harvest), bought for a ruble each to brighten up the walls. . . .
>
> The village had electric light, installed back in the twenties, from Shatury. The newspapers were writing about "Lenin's little lamps," but the peasants talked wide-eyed about "tsar light."
>
> Some of the better-off people in the village might not have thought Matryona's house much of a home, but it kept us snug enough that autumn and winter. The roof still held the rain out, and the freezing winds could not blow the warmth of the stove away all at once. . . .

A cat, mice and cockroaches shared the house with the elderly woman and her lodger. The cat was sometimes successful in her lightning pounces on mice, but many escaped by keeping to channels they had burrowed between the timbers and layers of embossed, greenish wallpaper, applied "back in the good old days." While the mice scampered impudently there, cockroaches swarmed on the floors, especially in the kitchen. Switching on a light late in the evening when he went for a drink of water, the lodger saw one "rustling brown mass" on the walls and bench, as well as on the floor. But in this, the story's narrator saw life and encouragement to creativity.

> At night, when Matryona was already asleep and I was working at my table, the occasional rapid scamper of mice behind the wallpaper would be drowned in the sustained and ceaseless rustling of

cockroaches behind the screen, like the sound of the sea in the distance. But I got used to it because there was nothing evil in it, nothing dishonest. Rustling was life to them. . . . I got used to everything in Matryona's cottage.

Solzhenitsyn felt well and secure in the cottage's minimal physical comfort. A Russian friend called this sojourn "his first star-blessed days." "In an atmosphere described in 'Matryona's Place' or similar to it, he was creating his masterpiece *One Day in the Life of Ivan Denisovich*. He lived without interference and in profound peace and calm, which in our day is available only to an underground writer, lost in total obscurity."

During breaks from work, Solzhenitsyn observed the life around him. His observations often focused on his landlady—seemingly an odd choice, for, by the look of her, she was just a Russian peasant, one of tens of millions. An early love affair had been ruptured by the First World War and she had lost her husband in the Second; but if anything, this was less than the average share of national tragedy for a woman her age. She worked hard for little reward; but so did almost all of Russia's rural population. Moreover, she was far from expert in her daily work, and her standards of cleanliness were not very high. But in this woman's life and tragic death, Solzhenitsyn discovered a rare selflessness and devotion to others. Whatever the teachings of the current political ideology, he saw the moral cornerstone of the Russian people and nation in her instinctive humanity.

All this found expression in "Matryona's Place." Solzhenitsyn did not depict Matryona as typical; her unconscious virtue is in sharp contrast to her neighbors' petty selfishness. Day after day she toils at her hard chores, seeking nothing for herself beyond the requirements of existence. When she is crushed by a train at a local crossing, it is because she is helping to move the frame of a house—without having thought to question the greed which prompted the move. "She was the righteous one," Solzhenitsyn concludes, "without whom, as the proverb has it, the village could not stand. Nor the city. Nor our whole land."

Exposing ignorant petty tyranny, tragicomic poverty, and sordid piggishness, "Matryona's Place" is in some ways an unlovely picture of village life. The beautiful countryside suffers grievously at the hands of the village's more "successful," meaning rapacious, citizens. But essentially, the story is an assertion that amid the skulduggery of daily life, some people behave with true morality, effortlessly and unconsciously. These people, few and unnoticed, keep alive the promise of a better life. It is no more than a promise—only a narrow possibility—but enough for the land to endure. "Justness exists," Solzhenitsyn wrote later, "even if few people exist who feel it."

After the degradation of prisons and camps, Solzhenitsyn was anxiously scanning "outside" life to determine whether it too had been affected. He was eager to tell the world of the reassurance he found in "Matryona": flesh-and-blood proof of the nation's moral durability without which not only Russia would have been lost but his personal sacrifices, even his mission, would have been pointless. It is entirely understandable that this was his first story about Central Russia, and that all his later, larger works were built on the same moral foundation.

In the same tranquil setting, he continued to shape his memories of prison and camp life into fiction. The store of memories was vast and the body of this work correspondingly large in scale and scope. But as in the case of "Matryona's Place," Solzhenitsyn's choice of what to winnow first from his overwhelming camp experiences was also an expression of his moral commitment. Much of his camp fiction is highly autobiographical. The logical place to begin would have been with a novel like *The First Circle,* largely a chronicle of his own experiences. Having in fact started this way, Solzhenitsyn sensed a stronger imperative and set to work on something harder, but more important for him—and, he hoped, for his country.

"It's easiest to write about oneself," he once said. But he felt his first duty was not to himself nor even to his fellow intellectuals, who would be the principal characters of *The First Circle.* Much as they had suffered, much as the Russian intelligentsia had been decimated, a percentage of these people survived. Among them, writers would someday emerge to record their ordeals with greater or lesser talent. But what of the millions of nonintellectual Russians whom the purges, espionage phobias, and ruthless shifts of policy had swept into the camps like old sawdust? The simple peasants and workers who lacked skills and interest in the world of letters? Would their literary inarticulateness mean that their colossal suffering would be forgotten?

The experience of arrest and camp engulfed these people like an act of God, causing stupefaction and pain. Like islanders visited by a gigantic tidal wave, their lives were crippled by a single, inexplicable stroke. "Of all the tragedies that Russia endured," Solzhenitsyn said later, "the tragedy of the Ivan Denisoviches was the most profound." Ivan Denisovich was the Russian Everyman. Few had Matryona's moral purity, but they came from the same village background and the parallel to her was unmistakable. Their tragedy was deepest, Solzhenitsyn felt, because they least understood the political machinations that had led to their suffering, had fewer psychological (and in some cases, physical) defenses, and died in greater millions in the camps. The survivors were often physically or mentally disabled. Who would speak for this dazed, mute army?

Solzhenitsyn felt he must try. Despite his completely urban youth, he had lived among Ivan Denisoviches for seventeen years: in the Army, in camps, and, to a lesser degree, in exile. In Torfoprodukt, he was again deep in their midst. He decided to restrain the memories involving intellectuals' camp experiences and to concentrate on *One Day of Ivan Denisovich,* as the novel is called in Russian: an ordinary day of an ordinary Russian peasant in an ordinary camp. Like his models, Ivan would be semiliterate—and like them too, he would achieve no triumph greater than to survive one of his 3653 days of imprisonment.

[Solzhenitsyn wrote principally in the evenings, sometimes continuing late into the night at "Matryona's" place. In the mornings, he arose relatively late from his primitive but pleasantly warm bed: "a blanket and a sheepskin, a quilt jacket from the camps to cover the legs and a straw-stuffed sack underneath." The openhearted peasant woman cooked his breakfast and supper, usually a kind of porridge called kasha and potatoes boiled in their skins or into a soup. Black bread and the cheapest grade of lard supplemented his ordinary diet. A teacher's salary permitted more to someone with his minimal expenses, but to procure it would have required wasting time in queues or in making special arrangements with local food suppliers]

[After breakfast, Solzhenitsyn walked to school. As always, he took his teaching very seriously—distinctly more so than his predecessors in the Peat Products school. Although known for the high percentage of passes among its pupils, the school had achieved its success by a practice common in the Soviet provinces: lowering standards to enhance its position relative to other schools. "Year after year," Solzhenitsyn wrote, "the school had been deceiving parents and pupils." His own subjects, mathematics and physics, are obligatory in Soviet secondary schools. He quickly saw that he "could not go on with this deceit . . . spitting on my work and name as a teacher." This could not be said outright to the parents of unsuccessful pupils, but he evaded and otherwise resisted their pressure to observe his predecessors' traditions. With the abler pupils, he worked hard to impart a thorough knowledge of his subjects.

Teaching and writing did not wholly exhaust his time. He returned to his prewar hobby of photography and with a recently acquired camera combined the old avocation with a new one: a study of local habits and lore. Even in exile, he had taken a strong interest in the history and customs of his region. Now the interest developed into serious exploration, with particular attention to local traditions and folk art]

Torfoprodukt was set in a picturesque and deeply Russian area that contrasted sharply with its own eyesores and grime. The surrounding cluster of villages was inhabited, improbably enough, by species of primitive painters who had made their little hamlets into a kind of vast set for a folk opera. A local journalist described the scenes:

In our Meshchera section, this region is called the Palishchi cluster, and it is quite distinctive. Most of the houses here are finished in clapboard and painted with oil paint. Green and light blue are the most common shades. Blue and white borders hang gaily along carved eaves and cornices. A stranger might think he'd come to some wondrous fairyland, where almost every dwelling resembles a gingerbread house with icing. The dwellers of the Palishchi cluster are called "the daubers." This nickname was pinned on them long ago. It stems from the handicraft in which many families engage here. With a few cardboard stencils and the simplest of swabs, the daubers make bedcovers and rugs for hanging on walls; they bear pictures of deer, swans, Little Red Riding Hood and the wolf, or Russian warriors at the crossroads of a savage ancient landscape.

It was in these singular, cheerful villages that Solzhenitsyn wandered with his camera. He photographed wood carvings on the exteriors of cottages, decorations inside, old women weaving on ancient hand looms. Patiently he explored for artifacts, old ways, old words. His visual and intellectual interest was entirely genuine, but also served as a pretext to strike up conversations with the local inhabitants and immerse himself in their speech. Like their houses, it was simultaneously archetypally "Russian" and rang with highly colorful words, unusual expressions and fresh turns of phrase, a kind of distillation of elements essential for Solzhenitsyn's own approach to art.[2]

Solzhenitsyn's days settled into an unhurried but faithfully followed pattern. It was the kind of life he still enjoys best. Now the work on *One Day* proceeded steadily, with the novel as a whole and each of its sentences passing through several drafts. Solzhenitsyn outlined his sentences like an etcher, adding stroke after stroke and then reworking the material to achieve the precise effect desired. The procedure he developed would become his standard one: a deliberate operation involving both advancing to new paragraphs and returning to pages already written. Of his own working methods Solzhenitsyn has said that he "constantly feels the imprint of my mathematical training in my current literary work." Even by the standards of his own exacting personality, the attention lavished on each preposition and the placement of each comma was uncommonly meticulous. "Every line of mine takes a year to ripen," he has said.

Many take longer. After publication of his work—still many years

---

[2] Solzhenitsyn's eagerness to record peasant speech did not abate in his subsequent years of fame, continuing to be an important part of his attraction to country people and, above all, to the *muzhik*—the simple peasant. A close friend, also a writer, who shares a passion for, and professional interest in, country folk, has made many hiking trips and visits to villages with him. With less hesitation than other writers, says this friend, Solzhenitsyn will turn his back on a group of peasants with whom he is conversing to swiftly jot a striking word or phrase into his notebook.

away—he did nothing to accelerate the stubborn slowness of his pace. Tiny details would be altered and realtered until the last moment before publication—and yet again after the last moment, for lists of corrections were often dispatched to his printers. For example, the last two moralizing sentences of *Cancer Ward* were eliminated, making its conclusion more immediate and dramatic. This change, however, came too late to be included in most editions. Of *The First Circle*, he said that as he read it in print, "it was as if I were reading someone else's book. I saw all the defects immediately and I don't even want the book to be read in this shape. So I'm changing it." This was after fifteen years of work and the award of the Nobel prize, largely on the strength of these novels.

It was still a long way to all prizes, but Solzhenitsyn was now on a straight line to them. His self-confidence and ear restored, he worked away in the half-empty peasant house, listening to the cockroaches in pauses between the scratching of his pen.

More slowly than his writing, Solzhenitsyn's personal life was also changing. Close friends feel that when he was released from camp in 1953, he had a natural hope of finding a woman somewhere to share his new life. In exile, the scarcity of suitable women tempered this hope with a sober understanding: a companion would be extremely hard to find. Among other things, his life's mission would inevitably usurp much of the ease and many of the ordinary pleasures of married life.

The nature of his writings would inevitably cause additional strains. Honest exploration of the camps and their significance held no hope of publication. Solzhenitsyn would be an unpublished, unknown writer—perhaps, in a moment of domestic friction, a somewhat crankish zealot. Moreover, manuscripts would have to be concealed and a vast secret faithfully kept, circumstances which demanded uncommon understanding, patience, and trust. Beyond this, a companion for Solzhenitsyn would require intellectual gifts and a compatible cast of mind.

Solzhenitsyn knew few marriageable women well, a fact which some critics feel is reflected in his writing. Indeed, there were few women for him to know, having married at twenty-one after a lengthy courtship, and spending all but one of the ensuing eighteen years in the Army, camps, and exile. Even while hoping to remarry one day, therefore, he was resigned, his friends say, to living many years alone.

But having settled in Torfoprodukt, he was visited by the one woman who seemed to suit all his exceptional requirements and with whom he would need no time for adjustment: Reshetovskaya.

Whatever their regrets, they had understood in 1956 that their lives had been forced into very different paths. But while Solzhenitsyn worked in Torfoprodukt, memories played on them both. Since Reshetovskaya was married, her situation was the more difficult; only something extraordinary would move her to sacrifice her new family. The extraordinary stimulus appeared. During the Moscow meeting, Solzhenitsyn had recited some of his prison poems, among them verses mentioning their prewar life and shared ordeal. When she returned to Ryazan, the poems began to stir her. Reshetovskaya came to realize that she still loved Solzhenitsyn.

After an exchange of letters, she began visiting him in Torfoprodukt. Their meetings strengthened the feelings between them but distressing obstacles stood between a return to one another. Reshetovskaya's husband, the unassuming chemist, still loved her. After five years, Reshetovskaya had become deeply attached to her new family, which included the chemist's young boys. Although happy with Reshetovskaya's affection, Solzhenitsyn was disturbed by the triangle's unavoidable wounds.

Reshetovskaya's visits to Torfoprodukt continued for roughly a year. Month by month, feeling and tension intensified on all sides. The triangle had to be broken, even though one side would temporarily suffer even more. In the end, Solzhenitsyn and Reshetovskaya decided to remarry.

Their reunion after arduous years apart smacks of truth-is-stranger-than-fiction melodrama. But more than a long-belated homecoming, the remarriage was another large step toward Solzhenitsyn's reintegration into the world at large. At first through Reshetovskaya's Ryazan friends, he again began to develop a small group of trusted confidants, something he had not enjoyed since 1941. In terms of time allotted, socializing still played a small role in his life—but he again enjoyed the company of people of roughly his own background. He no longer wanted to be a kind of hermit, living in total obscurity and prepared to fashion a life, with its overtones of monasticism and self-sacrifice, that was wholly different from his prewar one.

The most tangible indication of this was his replacement of the backwater of Torfoprodukt with the kind of environment he had known as a youth—although still in Central Russia. The "promise of backwoods Russia" with which he had come to Vladimir province was superseded. With his first novel almost completed, the account of Ivan Denisovich's camp day, he joined Reshetovskaya in the city of Ryazan.

XIX

Ryazan

For nearly a decade of their second marriage, the Solzhenitsyns lived in Reshetovskaya's old flat,[1] part of an unprepossessing two-story structure shared by several families. Although not far from the center of town, it was basically a largish peasant house with an exterior of rough, dark logs, roof of dented sheet iron and a substantial courtyard where the Solzhenitsyns had a vegetable garden. Their ground-floor flat consisted of three small rooms and a kitchen. Reshetovskaya's treasured grand piano occupied nearly half the dining room, but the music it provided—often Tchaikovsky, Chopin, and other of Reshetovskaya's favorite romantic composers —compensated for the inconvenience. Reshetovskaya's retired mother and two aunts shared the flat, generating an intensely female atmosphere. The elderly women queued, cooked, washed, and cleaned for the "young people," now both in their forties, but the heavier chores of the somewhat primitive housekeeping fell to Solzhenitsyn. He split logs for the stoves and cleared the winter snow—reminders of his youthful chores in Rostov, except that Ryazan's more northerly climate made many of them harder.

"One frosty December evening I saw him going out in the yard," wrote a Soviet journalist who had observed him at home. "He was dressed in a quilted jacket and a fur hat with ear flaps, the strings of which were dangling loosely. Stunned, I thought of Ivan Denisovich." Solzhenitsyn's appearance that evening might have justified the journalist's associations with labor camps, but, for Solzhenitsyn himself, the notion would have seemed far-fetched. He liked the effort of chopping wood and shoveling snow.

Despite the Solzhenitsyns' somewhat rustic life-style, Ryazan was not an anonymous backwoods town. It was only some 115 miles southeast of Moscow—and a half a century older: first mentioned in the late eleventh

---

[1] Reshetovskaya and her second husband had divorced, after which he left the flat with his sons.

century, it was at least as important during the next few as its younger, often tougher, northern rival. By the mid-twentieth century, the Russian image of a man from Ryazan rather resembled the stereotyped Western view of Russian *muzhiks* in general. The Ryazanite was thought of as a foul-mouthed, sloppy, and perpetually perplexed in matters requiring intelligence—but this only added to the affection for his easygoing personality.

Ryazan's medieval prominence abruptly declined, and in this century it has rarely been in the limelight apart from a brief scandal during the Khrushchev era, when the first secretary of the Communist Party of Ryazan district reported a tripling of milk and butter production in one year. When the report was unmasked as a fraud, the hapless secretary shot himself, reinforcing the image of Ryazanites as rather more dashing than bright. The city returned to its accustomed relaxed pace and quiet dilapidation, taking the seasons in stride like an archetypal provincial town. It was low on every priority list and closed to all foreigners, which Solzhenitsyn would welcome for its isolated peace. With a population of some quarter million, it was known principally for light industry and as the administrative and research center of a considerable agricultural area.

In the discharge of this function, Ryazan was the seat of a regional College of Agriculture, a full-fledged institute of higher education which employed the cream of the local intelligentsia. Here Reshetovskaya taught chemistry and pursued her research in colloids. With her *kandidat* degree, she earned over three hundred rubles a month, a very handsome provincial salary.

Solzhenitsyn might easily have joined the privileged circle of provincial *kandidats* of science. Throughout his exile and self-exile, he had maintained "a sufficient horizon," as he put it, "for the work in the exact sciences." But working for a higher degree would have cut into his writing time, and he preferred the humbler job of teaching physics and mathematics in a municipal school. Day after day, for many years, he walked to work along a straight street leading to the river of his bygone honeymoon, the Oka.[2] Ryazan cathedral's once shiny onion domes would rise above him; at the end of the street, sealing it off abruptly, stood a portion of the old town's medieval Kremlin wall. Having measured time and distance to arrive several minutes before the opening bell, Solzhenitsyn proceeded briskly to his school.

He continued to teach as if it were his life's calling. Although begrudging the time to acquire a higher degree, he was unable to work with less than his inherent intensity while in the classroom. In 1963, a Soviet

[2] Roughly a hundred miles west of Ryazan, the Oka also passes Tarusa.

journalist and admirer named Victor Bukhanov praised his teaching. "It's not simply that he knows his subject," wrote Bukhanov. "The creative element in Solzhenitsyn compels him to teach with freshness and gusto which can be explained only in terms of true vocation. He keeps up with technical journals, makes extensive reports—on space flights, among other subjects—assembling facts which surprise his colleagues. His teaching constantly 'overflows' from the ordinary school curriculum."

Solzhenitsyn shunned socializing in the teachers' room and did his best to fend off his profession's bureaucratic burdens: the teachers' conferences, meetings, and planning sessions which are particularly numerous in Russia. But his thrift with time did not interfere with his teaching or rapport with his pupils. "One of Alexander Isaiyevich's pupils," Bukanov continued, "said about his teaching that 'he makes his lessons interesting. He has a good way of speaking. I never liked physics before. . . .'"

Mutual trust developed between teacher and pupils, and he was not above enlisting their help in slipping unnoticed from one of the countless teachers' meetings and hurrying home. The trust developed from Solzhenitsyn's respect for his pupils' dignity and individuality: his old ability to exercise authority without losing a sense of essential equality. And his sense of responsibility toward his pupils was as strong as his affection. After he had become famous, he would not permit journalists into the classroom lest the children be unnerved and their concentration affected. Not limiting himself to formal teaching, he supervised the school's photography club for several years, spreading enthusiasm for his favorite hobby. He also tried to inculcate some of his own values. When a boy named Sasha Dmitriyev, his favorite pupil, was asked to sum up his teacher in three words, his reply was "intelligent, scrupulous, and economical." Bukhanov quoted the boy's evidence in support of his choice of the latter quality.

"One packet of developer is dissolved in half a liter of water, while the developing tray takes three hundred grams. Alexander Isaiyevich never allows us to dissolve a whole packet in half a liter of water. He divides two packets into three parts. Each portion is just right for one third of a liter." "But couldn't you use the remaining two hundred grams of solution later?" I asked. "It'd lose its strength," Sasha remarked.

The ex-inmate's frugality still rested in Solzhenitsyn's bones. Yet rather than try to amass possessions for himself, he strove to reduce them to essentials. Unconcerned with the attendant salary reduction, he kept asking for decreases in his class hours throughout his five years of teaching in Ryazan. Originally limiting himself to fifteen hours a week—somewhat more than half the normal burden in Russian schools—he cut back to twelve hours after a year, and later still to nine. At the last stage, his earnings were some fifty rubles a month, roughly the wage of wholly unskilled laborers.

Though aware of his wife's high income, Solzhenitsyn's fellow teachers were somewhat mystified by his indifference to a living wage. One colleague concluded that he was hoarding time to write a physics textbook. "Alexander Isaiyevich is quite erudite enough for that," he commented. None of Solzhenitsyn's colleagues deduced what he was actually writing. "We suspected nothing," they said later. "He was a teacher like any other. Better than many of us. But no more than that."

Bukhanov observed a "secretiveness and polite reserve" in Solzhenitsyn, which he found "quite astounding." "He doesn't talk about his past. He voices no forecasts for the future. In general he talks very little, and only when necessary." Secretiveness about literary activity was another habit ingrained in the camps. It would never disappear, but a certain relaxation was observable over the years: from keeping only mental records in his head of the camp years to the hidden little notebooks of exile to the typing of his own longhand drafts in Torfoprodukt. In Ryazan, Solzhenitsyn no longer hid himself indoors to write. He placed a roughly carpentered table and bench under some cherry trees in the courtyard of his house and wrote there in summer, in full view of the families who shared the house. The steady tap of his typewriter also reached his neighbors from the little room of the flat that served as his studio. Many outsiders, therefore, knew that Solzhenitsyn was writing—but the subject matter was a secret shared only by a few intimate friends.

There was good reason for discretion. Solzhenitsyn was now deep in *The First Circle,* his record of Marfino and the Russian intelligentsia in imprisonment. He was also reworking—above all compressing—*One Day,* bringing each draft nearer in tenor and cadence to a peasant storyteller's tale. Nor was his old love of the theater abandoned, for he was working on at least one play in addition to the novels, as well as on several short stories and the short prose poems he calls "tinies." As the volume of work indicated, these were years of extraordinary productivity.

After Reshetovskaya, one of the most important people for Solzhenitsyn to show his work was X. Since their wartime separation, the two boyhood chums had met briefly in prison, then were taken away to serve out their separate sentences. When ten years were completed, the two men resumed their correspondence.

Like Solzhenitsyn, X was officially rehabilitated and, his intelligence undamaged, returned to his native Rostov for graduate study. His *kandidat* degree was completed, with high honors, at roughly the time of Solzhenitsyn's remarriage with Reshetovskaya, and X moved to Ryazan together with his wife and young children. But once reunited, the two men found that they now had too little in common for friendship.

The camp experience had affected them in sharply different ways. X had grown cynical about mankind in general and Russians in particular, while Solzhenitsyn, far from relinquishing the ideals of their youth, appeared to have intensified his commitment to them. X wanted to know if he was serious about dedicating himself—sacrificing himself—for what could only be lost causes in Russia. At their age, fighting a futile good fight was naïve and perhaps self-indulgent. What was important now was providing for oneself and one's family: protecting an insulated niche of private pursuits and happiness. Did they deserve less after their ordeal?

X's attitude was typical of many erstwhile idealists whom the camps transformed. Solzhenitsyn surely would have rejected it even had he had a young family of his own. As it was, however, Reshetovskaya, now in her forties, had not borne a child and probably never would. A poignant moment of *The First Circle* has Solzhenitsyn's autobiographical hero being driven through Moscow in a prison bus, from which he catches sight of a frightened little boy in a street.

> And Nerzhin, who had not thought of children for years, suddenly understood with great clarity that Stalin had stolen his and Nadya's children. Even if his sentence ended, even if they were together again, his wife would be thirty-six, or even forty. It would be too late for a child.

Strong evidence later appeared that these lines apply to Solzhenitsyn himself; he was evidently saddened by the absence of children. But as it was, their lack obviated certain real considerations—the need to ensure young children's safety as well as material security—that might otherwise have tempered his resolve. Reshetovskaya and his adult in-laws were a far less weighty responsibility.

Solzhenitsyn was not about to read his prose on street corners, but felt his duty was to write of what he knew and felt. X was increasingly appalled by what he interpreted as Solzhenitsyn's quixotism. The nature of political power in Russia was clear enough to him; certainly *he* would not risk prison again for high-minded notions of duty to truth.

The gulf between the two men was reflected in the play which Solzhenitsyn completed in Ryazan in 1960. *Candle in the Wind* is his only known work not set specifically in Russia, but in a fictional contemporary society, not recognizably Communist or capitalist. Its central problem—common, as he stresses, to industrialized societies of the twentieth century—had troubled Solzhenitsyn since his Marfino days: how can a scientist reconcile his conscience to the increasingly negative use made of scientific progress? The two protagonists are highly talented mathematicians in their early forties who have been to school and university together, and are arrested simultaneously at the front, as were Solzhenitsyn and X.

One of the friends left prison convinced that his wasted years entitled him to seize all he could from life; that material things were the sole reality and, therefore, that science's contribution to greater production placed it above moral consideration. The other man, increasingly an adversary (he is named Alex), is suspicious of science, not only because it has "served tyranny quite well" but also because it contributes to dehumanization through reorienting people from ultimate values to exclusive preoccupation with *things*. The ultimate values, as Alex comes to see them in the course of the play, are "how to live in a way so that one doesn't have remorse while dying," and how to make use of science without allowing it to extinguish human sensitivity and compassion, which are as vulnerable as the flame of a candle in the wind.

Solzhenitsyn's close friends have drawn attention to the parallels to him and X and, in emphasizing the great similarity in the background and experience of the two mathematicians, the writer posed a kind of riddle. For in youth, the hardened "careerist" had been the reflective self-doubting one, while Alex was the driving young "success story"—apparently Solzhenitsyn's view now of at least a part of himself as a Stalin scholar in Rostov. Somehow, despite nearly identical life histories, the attitudes have undergone complete reversal by the time of the play's action. Now the introspective one, Alex, struggles to involve himself in scientific activity which contributes not to dehumanization, but, through deeper understanding of the world and mankind, to conscience—the foundation of Solzhenitsyn's morality.

In real life, the controversy between Solzhenitsyn and X deteriorated into mutual recrimination; in the end—which was not long after he had arrived—the latter left Ryazan for another provincial city, where he secured a desirable scientific position, in keeping with his widely held philosophy that anyone unlucky enough to be born in Russia would do best to come to terms with it. However, X's cynicism did not take him to the lengths of providing misinformation for the crude stratagems against Solzhenitsyn that would follow in future years. In time, the bitterness between the two men abated. Both understood that their circumstances, not to speak of their personalities, were different, and that their almost identical ordeals had taught them different lessons and driven them far apart. It was a sad and paradoxical end to a long friendship.

Solzhenitsyn's disappointment over the loss of his friend was softened by his acquisition of new intellectual companions, principally from Reshetovskaya's circle. He became particularly fond of an older man who

held a high academic post in Reshetovskaya's college. A mathematician too
—and, like Solzhenitsyn, a man of universal interests who had written historical and literary studies—he is apparently the prototype for the older,
wiser scientist in *Candle in the Wind,* whose subtle reflections about
reconciling science and conscience Alex came to adopt for himself. "D.
Blagov," as he was to call himself when writing about Solzhenitsyn, was
one of the first to whom the younger man showed his manuscripts, and,
because of his intellectual sophistication and concern for conscience, his
immediate approval was important to Solzhenitsyn. His counsel continued
to be valued for years, and although Blagov is now quite elderly, their
friendship remains strong.

Sometimes with friends, sometimes alone, the Solzhenitsyns took to
exploring the countryside around Ryazan. Solzhenitsyn had retained his
fondness for unhurried bicycle trips; Reshetovskaya rode too, and in photographs of these years they resemble a demure English "outdoor" couple
enjoying their adult years. Solzhenitsyn also preserved his love for river
travel, with the Oka replacing the Don of his youth. On occasional hunts
with friends, a camera was his weapon. Such was his aversion to the instrument of his father's death that he would not take a shotgun in his
hands. The trips through the countryside inspired short prose poems, reflective tributes to Central Russia's landscapes and laments about man's
misuse of natural beauty.

He also ventured farther afield—to Leningrad, the Baltic Republics,
and even Siberia's Lake Baikal. The Leningrad trip in the summer of 1962
was unexpectedly eventful. Overwhelmed by the classical beauty of the old
imperial capital, Solzhenitsyn was also conscious of the suffering that had
gone into its construction from a remote swamp, and could not help comparing the ordeal of St. Petersburg's first peasant builders, the Ivan
Denisoviches of the eighteenth century, to that of his own generation. "The
very thought is dreadful," he wrote. "Our own disrupted, perished lives, all
the explosions of our discord, the groans of the executed and tears of their
wives—will all this be cleanly forgotten too? Will this too result in an
equally accomplished eternal beauty?" But he was as determined as ever
that the groans he had heard not be forgotten.

In Leningrad, memories of suffering were revived too by an accidental
meeting with Boris Burkovsky, a former barrackmate from his Ekibastuz
camp. During the Yalta Conference of February 1945, the then lieutenant
commander had served as liaison officer to the United States naval mission. This earned him a twenty-five-year sentence as an American spy. Now
rehabilitated, Burkovsky was in command of the *Aurora,* an old cruiser
which (at least in Bolshevik folklore) played a decisive part in the October
Revolution and was subsequently converted into a museum, permanently

moored in the Neva. Solzhenitsyn joined the steady stream of tourists boarding the landmark. Eighteen months later, Burkovsky described their meeting to a Soviet journalist.

> I climbed the ladder to the main deck to greet a new group of excursionists. It seems that first I felt, and only later saw, that one of the guests was looking at me intently: a thin man of medium height. I looked up and recognized a familiar face. We both realized simultaneously where we'd seen each other before. We took a step toward each other and spoke softly. "Boris!" "Sasha!" Then we embraced firmly and kissed. At our parting, we exchanged addresses. I've written to Solzhenitsyn twice, and he has answered.

The meeting was particularly moving for Solzhenitsyn because—in slightly altered circumstances and under the barely altered name of Lieutenant Commander Buinovsky—Burkovsky was already a character in *One Day*. Although many of the novel's characters were composites, they were based on actual persons. Suddenly, he found himself face to face with someone to whom he had devoted years of work.

It was also a comfort to stumble on an intelligent, articulate man able to confirm the accuracy of his descriptions. As a work of art, of course, a novel cannot be confirmed or denied, but must stand on its power to reveal the essential truths of its characters and situations. But Solzhenitsyn knew that the truthfulness of his novel, if published and endorsed by literary standards, would inevitably be tested in political debate too, in which case testimony that the work was not only valid as literature but also factually true would be helpful.

Preoccupation with possible controversy of this kind was wholly understandable for Solzhenitsyn that summer. For *One Day* had just been accepted, at least in principle, for publication. If (as Andrey Sinyavsky would soon argue from the dock) writing is a process consummated by publication, then in a real sense everything that happened to Solzhenitsyn before this summer was an extended preparation. He was now forty-one years old.

Twenty-one Copies

IN HIS INDEPENDENCE OF MIND AND consequent relegation to the role of heroic outcast, Solzhenitsyn's life is all of a piece. In the context of contemporary Russia, his actions, and the reactions of Soviet authorities, are a series of logical consequences. What departs from the pattern is, curiously enough, the very phenomenon of his public emergence: the glaring non sequitur of his publication in Russia. How did it happen that this personification of dissent first attracted the world through pages printed on Soviet presses and approved by Soviet censors?

The story cannot be told simply. Solzhenitsyn's publication came about under a rare configuration of political forces involving diverse factors of mood, moment, and personality. Bizarre meetings of unlikely minds, Kremlin intrigues for the highest stakes, grim and wild paradoxes—these were elements of this literary freak of nature, together with the unpredictable tastes of several Russians in crucial posts. Apart from all else, a large quantity of luck made otherwise inexplicable factors click. At the height of Solzhenitsyn's brief official fame, only months after his trip to Leningrad, a worried reader wrote of his surprise that the author hadn't been "thrown in the clink." Solzhenitsyn commented wryly that he shared the surprise.

He was, of course, the first link in the chain; but the notion that his secret writings might lead to a sequence of public events would only have seemed a grave threat to him. "I sat at home writing, year in and year out," he said of his early post-exile period. "And I gave no thought to whether [my work] might be printed, to whether my writings would be liked."

During his early years in Ryazan, Solzhenitsyn showed his manuscripts only to close friends in that town and in Moscow—what he called his "several readers." Of these, Blagov, the senior mathematician, was the first reader to appreciate the full significance of *One Day*. After an early reading of the manuscript, he joked of its explosive power. "There are now

155

three atomic bombs in the world," he told Solzhenitsyn. "The White House has one, the Kremlin the second—and you the third."

The scientist-philosopher Blagov also wrote highly original and perceptive literary criticism in his spare time: another reason why Solzhenitsyn valued his judgment. But Blagov's literary essays were unpublished in Russia, and he had no contacts with prominent literary editors. It was another friend who served as Solzhenitsyn's first intermediary to print.

The intermediary's success derived from his coincidental position as one of Solzhenitsyn's most trusted friends and, simultaneously, an astute observer of Kremlin rivalries and their literary reverberations. Without this bridge, Solzhenitsyn would probably never have been published in Russia and might be still unknown in the West. For at this time, he himself felt that the chances were remote of a censor approving his pages. "Throughout the years until 1961," Solzhenitsyn has written, "I was not only *certain* that I would never see a single line of mine in print during my lifetime, but, fearing disclosure, I didn't even dare show anything of mine except to a few of my close acquaintances."

The intermediary was one of Solzhenitsyn's time-tested friends: Lev Kopelev, his Marfino companion a dozen years before. The parting of Gleb Nerzhin and Lev Rubin in *The First Circle* conveys the depth of their attachment.

"That's how it is, old friend," Nerzhin drawled. "We've lived together less than three years, arguing day and night, giving each other a tough time. Now that I'm losing you, probably for good, I see so clearly that you're one of my very best . . . my very . . ." His voice broke. Rubin's big brown eyes, which many remembered sparkling in anger, were warm with kindness and shyness. "That's the way it's worked out," he nodded. "Let's kiss then, you old rascal." And he took Nerzhin into his black pirate's beard.

Rehabilitated after Stalin's death, Kopelev-Rubin returned to Moscow and resumed his work as a literary scholar, critic, and translator. He was still a convinced Communist in the sense of regarding capitalism as mankind's selfish past and socialism as the promise of its more civilized future. But he was no longer the passionate Stalinist idealist of *The First Circle*, struggling to reconcile his fidelity to the party with his conscience. He had come to view Stalinism as a perversion which virtually destroyed all hopes for Communism's progress.

Imprisonment had convinced Kopelev that the legacy of Stalinism could be eliminated—and a return to full-scale terror prevented—only by democratizing Soviet society. But first, many Soviet people had to learn, as he had, what Stalinism really was—and nothing could achieve this more forcefully than Solzhenitsyn's prose. As a literary critic, Kopelev recognized its elements of truly great art; in the tradition of Marxist esthetics, he believed that great art revealed its time with greater depth and a surer sense of proportion than any other medium, thereby reaching more people. Kopelev decided he must do what he could to have *One Day* published.

First, however, he had to overcome the doubts of the author himself. And a certain aversion. Distaste for "the allowed"—for the literary establishment and the many Soviet writers whose commitment to the truth stopped almost exactly at the authorities' toleration point—was often felt by Russian desk-drawer writers. Decades earlier, the poet Osip Mandelshtam reflected about this before he himself perished in a camp.

> I divide all world literature into works permitted and those written without permission. The first is scum. The second is stolen air. I want to spit in the faces of writers whose words are sanctioned in advance, I want to beat them on the head with a club. . . . I'd prohibit these writers from marrying and having children. Because children must carry on for us, must finish telling the most important things for us—whereas the fathers have been sold wholesale to the pockmarked devil for three generations forward.

This sentiment persists, and makes radical Russians today *ipso facto* suspicious of any published writing.

But for Solzhenitsyn himself, the situation was more complex. There was also an urge, almost directly counterposed to the aversion, to jettison the secrecy of his creation. In addition to the continuous strain it imposed, he felt that isolation might impede his literary growth. And he wanted reassurance from more than his "several readers" about the quality of his work. "By the age of forty-two," he wrote later, "I began to feel very oppressed by my position as a secret writer. The principal burden was the inability to test my work on readers with a developed sense of literature."

These considerations supplemented Kopelev's persuasion to show a manuscript to an editor. "The first submission to *Novy Mir* magazine of my novella, *One Day in the Life of Ivan Denisovich*, succeeded," Solzhenitsyn has written. Behind this laconic statement lies a complex and dramatic series of episodes in Soviet literary politics. Success was achieved by Kopelev's sense of timing and tactics—and that of later champions of Solzhenitsyn. But nothing would have been possible had not a fleeting confluence of political forces in the Kremlin given birth to a most unlikely alliance.

The Twenty-second Congress of the Soviet Communist Party assembled in Moscow in mid-October 1961. It was expected to be a routine talkathon about the transition to Communism, but an unexpected twist of Khrushchev's changed the country's atmosphere even more radically than the celebrated Twentieth Congress some five and a half years before. Although Stalin's personal despotism and mass terror had been condemned in 1956, the indictments of the open sessions were couched in broad, general terms. Only Khrushchev's "Secret Speech" specified some of the murderous details; but having never been published in Russia, the declamation could not be referred to before the general public. Now, at the new Congress, Khrushchev took even Central Committee members by surprise when he disclosed the substance of his charges against Stalin and Stalin's lieutenants during an address to an open session.

Suddenly, the Twenty-second Congress seemed another great leap forward. In speech after hastily written speech, citing detail after gruesome detail, members of the party Presidium jumped on the anti-Stalinist bandwagon and told the delegates and nation of gangsterish and sadistic practices at the very apex of the Stalinist regime. The head of the party clearly led the movement, and his concluding speech was memorable for its apparently genuine revulsion at the enormous, ghastly, and cold-blooded crimes that many earlier speeches had itemized. "Stalin is no longer alive," Khrushchev observed. "But ⌊we considered it necessary to debunk the shameful methods of leadership which flourished in the conditions of his personality cult. Our party is undertaking this so that such things will never happen again."

A gesture of great symbolic significance crowned this promise: Stalin's body was removed from the mausoleum in Red Square and cremated, as if to demonstrate that his dark deeds would be cauterized from Soviet society. At last the party seemed to be purging itself of its past by means of full confession, honest repentance, and a vow to strive for a humane future.⌋

Not all Russians understood the implications of these astonishing speeches, or cared to understand. Raised in a tradition of unquestioning political obedience—and therefore of profound lack of interest—the great majority perceived the revelations as too dangerous or too remote for their humble attention. But the liberal intelligentsia bubbled with excitement. At last the Twentieth Congress's promises of freer intellectual inquiry and freer *life* seemed on the verge of fulfillment. As for literature, one of the speakers outlined a bracing new program for truthful writing, reinforcing his argument with unmistakable references to the omissions and distortions of the past. He accused Soviet literature of "not telling the whole story [and of] incompleteness in portraying diverse aspects of life, its many facets, and the many problems it involves us in. Not to beat about the bush, there has been too little of life's depth and truth."

The author of these lines was not a liberal Communist who had miraculously survived Stalinism to unburden his progressive convictions at last. ⌊Fortunately for the liberal cause—and, soon, for Solzhenitsyn—his background was quite different. Alexander Tvardovsky, poet, editor, and man of letters, was born of a peasant family and gained prominence in the 1930s as the author of a long epic blessing the collectivization of agriculture in the name of his class. During the war, he composed a kind of cartoon strip in bouncy verse about the rakish adventures and indestructible good spirits of a Russian foot soldier—an effort which cheered the hard-pressed nation and won him much genuine popularity. "The Boss," as Stalin's lieutenants called him, thought it fitting that a popular poet express himself about . . . The Boss. Tvardovsky complied, producing several odes of adulation, of which the most fulsome celebrated Stalin's seventieth birthday in 1949.

Honors and offices accumulated rapidly. In 1950, the Stalin Prize poet was appointed editor of *Novy Mir*, the most prestigious Soviet literary magazine, even in those least prestigious times for Russian literature. But much of Stalinism already repelled Tvardovsky; he now felt guilty of his own role in support of it. Arrests of his friends and the ravaging of his beloved Russian countryside moved him to take grave risks: even before Stalin died, he managed to publish a grim description of Russian village life in *Novy Mir*, contrasting startlingly and dangerously with the abundance-and-joy fiction that so gratified Stalin. Perhaps because it was kept from Stalin for fear of provoking his wrath, Tvardovsky escaped attack.

Only weeks after Stalin's death, *Novy Mir* began to question the honesty of Soviet literature. Bold articles led to Tvardovsky's removal as editor, but in the hesitant advance of the campaign against the "cult of personality" he was restored to his desk, this time not only to lead the revival of Soviet literature, but also to help reform Russia's general intellectual and political atmosphere. *Novy Mir* published Ilya Ehrenburg's *The Thaw*, the novel which gave its name to a concept and an epoch, and Vladimir Dudintsev's *Not by Bread Alone*, a then startling treatment of bureaucracy's deadening effect on Soviet life. In a poem which underlined his own sense of guilt, Tvardovsky himself was the first to mention the tragedy of Stalin's political prisoners in print.

As the editor-poet's moral stature grew, he managed to sustain his political influence, exercised from his position as a candidate-member of the Central Committee. Now, at the Congress, the hour of the repentant Stalinist and moral-intellectual leader of the reformists seemed to have struck. His speech seemed to herald a momentous change in Russian life.

But no change came; the process of throttling the reformist movement began at the Congress itself. It was the work of powerful cliques in the Soviet body politic—not only men who feared for their very lives and freedom because of their direct participation in Stalin's crimes, but also an army of bureaucrats, entrenched on every level from village street to Council of Ministers. Fearful for its social and political position, this army opposed any kind of change and recognized no need to repent of anything. The veteran Presidium member Mikhail Suslov served as spokesman for these forces at the Congress, and, before its adjournment, the Central Committee "machine" hastily arranged a rebuttal to Tvardovsky from the dais. It was delivered by Vsevolod Kochetov, a writer who tirelessly campaigned for Stalinist "discipline and order" while editing *October,* a literary magazine whose notions of Communism were grounded in authoritarianism and virtually opposite to those of *Novy Mir.*

Both Tvardovsky and Kochetov were "elected" by the Congress to responsible positions—but in the nation, the latter's rigid orthodoxy everywhere prevailed. All mention of Stalin's crimes disappeared abruptly from the Soviet press. Molotov, Kaganovich, and other Stalin lieutenants remained party members despite repeated demands for their expulsion at the Congress. And liberals found the same censors suppressing free expression, the same bureaucrats stifling self-government, and the same party overlords sabotaging decentralized economic management. The Congress's promises came to nought in face of the entrenched party despotism.

At this point, Tvardovsky and other liberals thought of using literature —specifically, of publishing works that would expose the full extent of suffering under Stalin—as an explosive charge to break the Stalinist logjam. With luck, Stalinists would be discredited and their positions undermined, making possible their removal from power. The strategy was not as quixotic as it seemed, for, despite the dictatorship's total control of the printed word, liberals hoped for support at the very highest level—from the First Secretary of the Communist Party himself.

By 1961, most Westerners, including eminent Kremlinologists, believed that Khrushchev enjoyed full political power. The Soviet press, however, hinted at successful opposition to the First Secretary on half a dozen cardinal domestic issues, including his wish to settle accounts with those of Stalin's lieutenants who had opposed his own political rise. Two powerful adversaries, both with strong authoritarian convictions, had emerged at the highest level. Frol Kozlov and Mikhail Suslov represented, each in his own way, the great mass of party officials whose unsavory past and privileged position made them rigidly opposed to reform.

Khrushchev might well have shared this position; certainly his own past was unsavory enough. But the ebullient adventurer's policy was now repentance and de-Stalinization. He hoped to disgrace his adversaries as Stalinists, and, having removed them, establish himself in the kind of power Westerners—and most Russians—believed he already exercised. No one could foresee how he would use this power, but since he was seeking it by means of de-Stalinization and promises of a more humane society, high-ranking liberals were willing to help him in the hope that they would be given their freedom. Based on this *modus vivendi,* a curious alliance formed between Tvardovsky and Khrushchev—just when the former first heard of Solzhenitsyn and his work.

For Solzhenitsyn as for few other Russians, the Twenty-second Congress had a personal meaning. His long-standing perception of Stalin's evil seemed to be confirmed; the party itself appeared to have adopted the leitmotiv of his work. After the Congress, however, it became clear that an honest reckoning with Stalinism had again been thwarted. (Symbolically, Stalin's ashes were reburied, not in some obscure cemetery but at the Kremlin wall.) It was at this point that Lev Kopelev suggested that the time for *One Day*'s publication had arrived. Solzhenitsyn agreed. "I brought myself to 'come out from under,'" as he put it, "only after the Twenty-second Congress and, in particular, Tvardovsky's speech."

Kopelev's reasoning is not difficult to surmise. After the party's own confession of sadistic horrors inside the Kremlin, who could object to a far less sensational account of a good day in an ordinary labor camp? Solzhenitsyn's fears were too deep to shed quickly. "Revealing myself as I did," he has confessed, "seemed very risky to me at that time—and not without reason; it might have led to the destruction of all my manuscripts and of me personally." But together with Kopelev's prompting, Solzhenitsyn's urge to test his work and to contribute to Russia's progress prevailed over his qualms, and he consented to submit *One Day* to *Novy Mir*, through Kopelev. From the other end, Solzhenitsyn's appearance at the time of Khrushchev's need fitted Tvardovsky's plans as if by design.

Kopelev, who himself occasionally appeared in *Novy Mir*, knew of Tvardovsky's talent for publishing the unpublishable. He brought the manuscript to the Prose Department, which was headed by a middle-aged woman of long service to the magazine and Russian literature. The excitement of this editor and her colleagues can be judged by a saying first coined in *Novy Mir*'s offices: "Tell me what you think of Ivan Denisovich and I'll tell you who you are." When it reached Tvardovsky some two weeks later, the novel carried the hopes and blessings of several of the magazine's old hands. Tvardovsky stuffed it into his briefcase together with a stack of other manuscripts. He knew no more than that he was taking home two works about labor camps—one of which, as the head of the Prose Department pointed out in a note to him, had a simple peasant as protagonist.

By the time he reached *One Day* that evening, Tvardovsky had retired to bed. He turned the first pages and got up. Dressing hurriedly, he settled himself at his working desk. A few pages were enough to realize, he explained later, that it would have been disrespectful to read such a work for the first time in bed. Those few pages were enough to make clear that he had come upon a "new classic."

The following morning he arrived at his office in visible agitation. Why hadn't he been given the manuscript immediately? he rebuked his staff. How could they have withheld it for two full weeks? And who was this

Solzhenitsyn? "I didn't sleep all night," Tvardovsky said. When he next spoke to Kopelev, he chided him for not having delivered the manuscript quickly and directly to him. By that time, according to a friend of Solzhenitsyn, Tvardovsky had made it the cause of his life to publish *One Day*.

The editor felt he could take up the concentration camp theme only with a work of genuine literary excellence. Beyond this, *One Day* contained certain valuable "selling points." His strategy, and the activities of the *Novy Mir* staff in his support, are still not fully known; but he could astutely guess that Khrushchev would not only approve of the simple peasant hero politically, but also identify with him personally. This aspect appealed to Tvardovsky himself, who was concerned to record the sufferings of the great mass of workers and peasants as well as the minority intelligentsia's. A second strong point was Ivan Denisovich's "positive" attitude toward work. Like Solzhenitsyn himself, his hero's nature made him toil conscientiously in the direst of circumstances, something of potential "educative" and uplifting value generally and of special appeal for Khrushchev, with his itch to raise Soviet labor productivity.

Having chosen Solzhenitsyn, Tvardovsky and his staff set out to marshal literary support. A thorough understanding of one of the curious twists in official Soviet mentality prompted him to approach the authorities with overwhelming proof of Solzhenitsyn's extraordinary talent. Memories of the persecution of artists in tsarist Russia were kept alive in a daily flood of outraged revolutionary propaganda—with the result that there was considerable reluctance to admit that the new, socialist order suppressed proven talent too. This reluctance had been shown even in the case of Boris Pasternak, where according to official explanation, only the unworthy *Doctor Zhivago* was rejected; Pasternak's talented poetry continued to see print. Tvardovsky's plan was to gather confirmation of Solzhenitsyn's artistic merit from leading Soviet writers, at the same time letting it be known that *Novy Mir* was about to discover an extraordinary new writer. His hope was to prevent certain bureaucrats influential in the approval and rejection of works of art from smothering the novel.

Prominent writers responded quickly. The reader's reports of several senior figures, among them Samuil Marshak, Ilya Ehrenburg, and Korney Chukovsky, the grand old man of Soviet letters, provided what amounted to Solzhenitsyn's first rave reviews. Chukovsky called *One Day* a "literary miracle," indicating his amazement that from the depths of provincial Russia, the source of reams of turgid copy for decades, a work of great depth, brevity, and artistry had suddenly emerged.

News of the manuscript spread quickly as writers told their friends. Among *One Day*'s early admirers in Moscow and Leningrad was Anna Akhmatova, the empress of Russian poetry. Although her mobility was restricted in her eightieth year, she received a stream of visitors who came to pay tribute, discuss Shakespeare, or reminisce about the "Silver Age," in which she herself had had an important role. She was conscious of her position in Russian letters and of her reputation as an acid critic of all but truly great writing. From the spring of 1962, she told everyone she considered genuinely concerned with Russian literature that she had read a work which could introduce new and higher standards into the whole of Soviet art.

Thus Solzhenitsyn's name had begun to generate an artistic current before the first direct step toward publishing had been taken. Together with the writers' testimonials, this was enough for Tvardovsky to go directly to Khrushchev. Even had he not known the First Secretary personally, access would have been possible through his own membership in the Central Committee. But Tvardovsky sensed that a precipitous encounter with a startling new idea—life in a labor camp!—would probably make the elderly man recoil; and a no from Khrushchev would have routed his campaign. He chose a more promising circuitous route, through members of Khrushchev's immediate family and personal staff.

First he brought the novel and its notices to Khrushchev's son-in-law, Alexey Adzhubei, himself a competent journalist. Considered something of an intellectual by his proud father-in-law, Adzhubei acted as "the brains" of the extended Khrushchev household, as well as his personal adviser-cum-representative in foreign and cultural affairs. The very best of family connections had also secured him the editorship of *Izvestiya* three years before, at the otherwise unusual age of thirty-five. Together with Khrushchev's increasing use of Adzhubei to bypass normal bureaucratic channels, the blatant nepotism irritated many officials. Nevertheless, Adzhubei's influence in affairs of family and state was at its zenith.

Adzhubei's opinion of himself as a man of letters did not wholly lack foundation. His initiatives in enlivening *Izvestiya* were well known. Although he considered young poets like Yevtushenko and Voznesensky too experimental and too liberal, he sometimes acted as their patron and protector, no doubt in fond and somewhat inflated memory of his own writing days. And he clearly recognized the literature favored by Central Committee bureaucrats for what it was: plodding mediocrity stiffly laced with sheer stupidity. In short, he had earned, and distinctly enjoyed, a reputation as a backstage Maecenas in cultural affairs.

Tvardovsky appealed to his vanity: would he help launch a great new talent? Was it not better to go down in history beside the liberal nineteenth-century censors, rather than as a Benckendorf (a famous persecutor of Pushkin)? Having read *One Day* and the impressive file on it, Adzhubei pronounced himself deeply moved. There is no reason to doubt his sincerity. Quite apart from his own artistic appreciation and the compassion provoked by the novel, Adzhubei's political sense grasped *One Day*'s potential as an instrument in his father-in-law's grand strategy to discredit his enemies.

Adzhubei counseled caution in approaching Khrushchev. He suggested transmitting the manuscript through Vladimir Lebedev, Khrushchev's personal *chef de cabinet*. Tvardovsky and Adzhubei both counted on Lebedev's help: a former journalist, he had a genuine feeling for literature, and a plan to simultaneously support an important work and strike a blow for his chief would naturally appeal to him. Thus Solzhenitsyn's introduction to Khrushchev came in the form of a pincer operation by his son-in-law and personal lieutenant. The latter read passages from *One Day* calculated to please and move Khrushchev, while Adzhubei used his frequent visits to his in-laws to pique Khrushchev's interest. According to some sources, Adzhubei's wife, the former Rada Khrushcheva, also urged the novel's merits on her father.

Finally Khrushchev asked Lebedev to read him the full manuscript. Khrushchev himself found reading something of a strain and often had documents read to him. On this occasion Lebedev's voice, which Khrushchev admired, took on a new timbre. It was a curious scene for a pair accustomed to concentrating on reports about corn and labor productivity. The First Secretary approved.

Compassion for Ivan Denisovich, and perhaps a sense of guilt for his suffering, undoubtedly played their role. Khrushchev cried over the tale, as did his Politburo colleague Anastas Mikoyan. But a wily veteran politician such as Khrushchev would quickly have mastered his sentiment had he not divined that adroit use of the novel could bring him considerable political advantage. The portrayal of evil and of the plight of the poor peasant Ivan was so unadorned that it could not be shrugged away; yet so controlled that there could be no charge of exaggeration. Khrushchev perceived that an opponent of publication would make himself vulnerable to denunciations for supporting evil. On the other hand, anyone who approved publication could not easily oppose Khrushchev's policy of atonement and reform. In the First Secretary's calculations, the novel became something Solzhenitsyn could not have expected: a trap for Khrushchev's enemies.

Khrushchev proceeded to set it with characteristic cunning and verve. Only after his informal approval did Tvardovsky submit to him a brief on Solzhenitsyn and an official request to publish the novel. Rather than give the momentous printing order himself, however, Khrushchev chose to have the entire Presidium pronounce on the subject. Ostensibly, the Presidium was to be involved so that the final decision would seem to come from the party as a whole rather than the First Secretary alone. In fact, Khrushchev wanted his colleagues to stand up and be counted—that is, his opponents to be marked.

Solzhenitsyn's work was first set in type for *Izvestiya*'s presses, which

normally printed *Novy Mir*. Twenty-one copies of the novel, with its
literary assessments attached, were run off as trial proofs, which Tvardovsky, as editor, was empowered to authorize. Copies of this exclusive first
edition were distributed to Presidium members in the form of a classified
working paper. But if *One Day*'s sinuous route to the presses had been
wholly unpredictable, so were its chances at this point of a normal literary
birth. Nothing more was certain than that it would be a bitterly controversial issue for the Presidium.

XXI

Publication

THE EXTENT OF THE PRESIDIUM'S DISCORD over *One Day* was suggested by that body's procrastination in tabling the issue for formal discussion. Only in late summer did the members pronounce themselves acquainted with the specially printed edition and ready to discuss it.

Khrushchev's intention to publish encountered predictable objections from several of Russia's most powerful orthodox politicians. The principal opponents were Frol Kozlov and Mikhail Suslov; although rivals for position within the Politburo, they shared an antiliberal reaction to the novel. They were supported by lesser Politburo members, who also would later play a decisive part in suppressing Solzhenitsyn's work: Leonid Brezhnev, then President of the Soviet Union, and Andrey Kirilenko, whom Solzhenitsyn's friends describe as "a strong dark force." Their chief objection was to political weakness—specifically, *One Day's* inadequate treatment of prisoners remaining faithful to the party even in the camps, and of the dangers of "true enemies," such as Ukrainian nationalists, whose punishment the party continued to approve. Although no one dared object to the exposure of innocent men suffering as such, it was suggested that a more "ideologically mature" work be found, one that would portray proper "class attitudes" toward and among the prisoners. At the very least, this seemed an attempt at further procrastination in hopes that the manuscript would somehow fade away.

Khrushchev's response was a tantrum on the pattern produced during the abortive summit conference with President Eisenhower two years before and, with the aid of his shoe, at the celebrated United Nations session in 1959. His face violently flushed, his fists clenched in real or mock anger, he raged in the Kremlin no less violently—and surely more profanely— than he had in Paris and New York. "There's a Stalinist in each of you," he shouted. "There's even some Stalinism in me!"

It was the members' duty, Khrushchev argued, to themselves reject such attitudes and to help eliminate them in others. He would not tolerate further delays, but as a final concession he would give his colleagues several more days for reflection. If their answer was yes, the best Soviet writers were unanimous: nothing better than Solzhenitsyn's novel was available. If the Presidium voted no, he, a disciplined party member, would accept the decision—but the responsibility would lay on them. He left little room for doubt that one day he would remind his listeners of their profound political error, under circumstances that might be fateful for them.

Despite this, none of the members could bring himself to a definite yes when the Presidium reconsidered the matter several days later. Khrushchev chaired the meeting as usual and repeatedly called upon the participants to speak up. No one now dared object; yet no one openly supported Khrushchev. The First Secretary then resorted to his bulldozer tactics, which were second in reputation only to his tantrums. "There is an old Russian proverb," he cited. "Silence means consent." Although the Presidium's cowardly, resentful muteness was virtually opposite to the proverb's silence, the triumphant Khrushchev declared that an affirmative verdict had been registered. And what is more, he added, he himself regarded the struggle against Stalinism "not as a passing fad, but as our guiding policy line." His trap had closed neatly: not daring to oppose a decision inimical to them, Khrushchev's wary enemies nevertheless lacked the courage or perspicacity to join him, and were now exposed to charges of failing to support the popular anti-Stalinist line. Clearly outwitted, they retreated into their orthodoxy and caution.

As almost always in Soviet politics, the whole of this intrigue was acted out in the secrecy of the Kremlin. Only the loquacity of Khrushchev and his entourage provided subsequent clues to the tenseness of the Presidium maneuvering. But even if Solzhenitsyn and Tvardovsky knew few of the details, the results could only elate them. In mid-September, *One Day* was again set in type, this time by an ordinary printer used by *Novy Mir*. By this time, the novel had acquired its final title, in Russian *One Day of Ivan Denisovich*. Solzhenitsyn's own choice had been *One Day of a Prisoner*, but Tvardovsky convinced him that evocation of the character himself would be more effective than a generalization. There was still no guarantee that the work would appear: censors sometimes cut pages from magazines already bound for delivery. But the author and editor had the knowledge of Khrushchev's firm personal support—and, in addition, happy evidence of yet another shift in political and cultural affairs.

For almost a year after the Twenty-second Congress, liberals were deeply frustrated over the lack of progress toward a freer intellectual life. Even an attempt to expel from the Writers' Union members whose denunciations had caused the death or imprisonment of other members during the Stalin era had been blocked. But the man who coordinated this action, and many worse, now seemed about to lose his power.

For twenty years, this man, Dmitri Polikarpov, was one of the most powerful suppressors of Russian culture. From behind-the-scenes positions high in the party *apparat*—in 1962, he was chief of the Central Committee's Section of Arts and Letters—he helped administer the terrible postwar purge of intellectuals known as the "Zhdanovshchina," and the consequent period of cultural sterility. It was Polikarpov who organized the vicious persecution of Boris Pasternak after the writer's 1958 award of the Nobel prize. A close friend of Kochetov, Polikarpov was an implacable enemy of *Novy Mir* and its ideals. His downfall, therefore, would be a sign of great importance to the liberals—and all the more because of the circumstances which would bring it about.

According to the best-informed Muscovites of the time, Khrushchev finally came to read *Doctor Zhivago,* no doubt in an attempt to understand his new literary allies. The novel left him furious—not at its author, but toward the organizers of his persecution. Khrushchev found the book less anti-Soviet than apolitical—and, in any case, too abstruse to appeal to more than a sliver of intellectuals. The men who had created the embarrassing international scandal and made Pasternak a martyr, Khrushchev is reported to have said, clearly cared nothing for the country's prestige. Polikarpov was officially reprimanded and Khrushchev determined to liquidate his section, which busied itself with suppressing unorthodoxy in all branches of the arts. It was to be replaced by an "ideological commission" with a much smaller staff, depriving it of the means to exercise massive preliminary censorship.

This news spread swiftly and joyfully through the Soviet artistic world. The 1962–63 theatrical season opened to an onslaught against local Polikarpovs in every artistic union, publishing house, editorial office, concert agency, and exhibition committee. Once again, hope flourished for free and honest art. Desk-drawer manuscripts flooded editorial offices and Russia's first exhibition of mildly modernistic painting in more than thirty years was hastily organized in the capital's most prestigious gallery on Manezh Square, drawing on works long hidden by museum curators, private collectors, and the painters themselves. An astute American observer of those golden autumn days compared the mood with Poland's in the famous spring of 1956, "although not the autumn, when the outbreak actually occurred."

In this heady atmosphere, typescripts of *One Day* began to circulate widely. Although the novel's existence had become generally known over the spring and summer, only a handful of leading writers and politicians had read it. Now many prominent figures in the cultural world managed to secure a copy. "Despite the strictest rules requiring the handling of manuscripts in editorial offices as classified material," wrote Blagov, "people kept unceremoniously stealing *One Day* from Tvardovsky's safe, retyping it, and giving thousands of others the chance to read it." Thus even before the novel's publication, "honest writers had had time to praise [Solzhenitsyn] and to bow to him as to a new luminary."

Blagov's assessment of the still unpublished writer's effect is surely sound, though perhaps he was coy about *Novy Mir's* security arrangements. If, after several long months of secrecy, purloining the manuscript suddenly became easy, it could well have been by intention: the wider Solzhenitsyn's circle of admirers, the more difficult would be retraction of permission to publish. Moreover, this helped to swell the liberals' confidence and to worry the conservatives—which also lessened the chances of a last-minute suppression of the novel. "People really believed," said the American observer, "that after Khrushchev's authorization of this revolutionary item, almost anything short of a personal attack on him or on Communism as such could get by."

Publication was scheduled for the November *Novy Mir*. Whether by coincidence or design, it was to coincide with a new plenum of the Central Committee. Rumors (later proven accurate) circulated that Khrushchev intended to open the entire question of Stalinist mentality in officialdom and the refusal to relax its reactionary grip on every area of national life. He would demand that party workers unable to adapt to the new style of leadership—designed to replace bureaucratic controls with initiative by experts in various fields—be replaced. As for the arts, Polikarpov's section would be formally disbanded and Zhdanov's stultifying edicts, which it had so long and zealously administered, formally repealed. At the same time, Khrushchev gave the liberals even more cause for optimism. In a discussion with a small group of select writers, the First Secretary revealed his personal determination to keep Stalin in his grave. "Some people are waiting for me to croak in order to resuscitate Stalin and his methods," he said, as reported to a French correspondent. "This is why, before I die, I want to destroy Stalin and destroy those people, so as to make it impossible to put the clock back."[1]

These concessions could be considered recompense for the considerable help that Khrushchev was given by the arts in his preparation for the plenum. In mid-October, a large-scale campaign was launched in which artists, from cartoonists to composers, were enlisted to discredit Stalin and Stalinists. The highlight was Yevtushenko's celebrated "Stalin's Heirs." "We have carried Stalin from the mausoleum," wrote the young poet, "but how

[1] Michel Tatu, *Power in the Kremlin* (Collins, 1969; Viking, 1970), p. 306.

do we banish Stalin from Stalin's heirs?" The poem reflected Khrushchev's line precisely, and it is not surprising that he ordered its publication in *Pravda*.

Thus *One Day* was hardly an isolated event in the autumn of 1962, and not even the first account of life in Stalin's labor camps. The November issue of *Novy Mir* was given its final "signing for printing" on November 3, with the censor's authorization, the issue went to bed for its normal printing of a hundred thousand copies. Three days later, *Izvestiya* published a short story on the same theme, though with markedly different treatment. The author, a previously unknown former inmate named Georgy Shelest, set his story in a camp with conditions harsher than those of *One Day*—yet blandly stated that the patriotism, optimism, and enthusiasm of its good Soviet inmates were barely affected. While Solzhenitsyn had deeply and painfully explored the effect of the camps on a wide range of recognizable people, Shelest offered stereotyped characterizations of positive heroes selflessly devoted to the party, and negative rascals who deserved imprisonment, if in more humane conditions. The Shelest story set a pattern for the literature acceptable to the Kozlov-Suslov bureaucrats and politicians—until they succeeded in suppressing even that.[2]

But this aspect of Shelest's story—its covert attack on Solzhenitsyn's work—was then apparent to only a handful of Russians. At this point, all of cultural Moscow was waiting for the appearance of *Novy Mir* several weeks later. The first copies of the issue were delivered to subscribers and news kiosks on November 17. This was the crest of the 1962 liberal wave, and, when it subsided, even before the end of the month, little of lasting value except for *One Day* had been washed ashore.

[2] It is not clear why the story was published in Adzhubei's *Izvestiya*. Adzhubei might have wished to show himself objective and open to all points of view or it might have been a result of some other politico-editorial intrigue.

XXII

Reaction

THE BESIEGING OF BOOK COUNTERS BY agitated crowds is not an uncommon sight in Russia; a hundred thousand copies of a new collection of verse can vanish in hours. But Russians' reaction to the November issue of *Novy Mir* was extraordinary even in this context. On the morning of the magazine's distribution, Muscovites dashed to kiosks to strip their supplies in minutes. Queues scattered as fast as they were formed; men and women ran to the next counter and the next, faces flushed with an anticipation that no novel, however great, can produce unless it provokes hopes far beyond the ordinary concerns of literature. In this case, the first page was enough to feed—and sharpen—a hunger for new truths at last replacing old fears.

The crush to procure a copy was intensified by knowledge of *Novy Mir's* limited circulation and of the chronic paper shortage which kept it restricted. Kiosk operators pasted signs in their windows to ease their harassment: "*Novy Mir* number 11 [November] is not on sale." This was often insufficient, as burdened salesmen complained. "First I'd answer that the magazine wasn't available," related one. "Then, just for my own interest, I started to count how many people came to my kiosk to ask [for the magazine]. . . . I counted and counted . . . and finally gave up when I reached twelve hundred."

Among the intelligentsia—elderly professors and editors as well as young students—there was little talk of anything else that morning. The lucky owners of copies made lists of who had next reading rights; one engineer had ten people in line for his before he'd reached the tenth page. Friends rang friends of friends; copies were read by three and four people together. A young librarian in the Lenin Library read in five-minute snatches from a copy that her superior had borrowed for a few hours from *her* former superior in the periodicals room. No one seemed to mind that normal work in the library was ignored.

171

Six weeks later, the excitement had only slightly abated. A breathless reader informed Solzhenitsyn that her turn to read the novel had come on New Year's Eve. She had only the one night—in the virtual absence of official Christmas, New Year's is Russia's most important holiday—but devoted it happily to the magazine instead of to her family. Another woman had also secured the book on December 31 for one night—a feat made possible because she herself had served time in the camps and had friends in the local library. Professors and senior surgeons impatiently waited their turns while she, "a simple nurse," enjoyed precedence.

The excitement was not limited to Moscow as a man from Kharkov indicated in describing the situation there to Solzhenitsyn. "I've seen every kind of queue in Kharkov. When they were showing a Tarzan film, for butter, for women's drawers, for chicken giblets, for horsemeat sausage.[1] But I can't remember such a long queue as the one that cropped up in the library for your novel. I waited for six months on the list—all for nothing. I accidentally got hold of a copy for forty-eight hours."

In early January of 1963, a cheap mass edition of the novel was printed in three quarters of a million copies. It still did not satisfy the demand. This edition's retail price was twelve kopeks, but a provincial reader informed Solzhenitsyn that he had paid four rubles for his copy on the black market, a premium of over three thousand percent.

The nationwide agitation was fanned not only by Russia's well-known word-of-mouth communication but also by the clear indication in the press that something highly unusual was afoot. A rush of reviews in literary and popular newspapers, both central and provincial, was as unusual for the swiftness of its reaction as for its volume. *Izvestiya* was first, on November 18—a deserved scoop for Adzhubei's staff. Speed and space were not, however, matched by quality of thought or prose. *Izvestiya*'s title—"About the Past for the Sake of the Future"—was as significant as anything in the text, for subsequent headlines were to be variations on the same theme. "That This May Never Be Repeated," "As It Was, So It Will Never Be Again," "For the Sake of the Future" . . . the banality of these titles can be explained not only in terms of Soviet newspaper style in general, but also by a Central Committee "line," whose general content was unmistakable from the headlines alone. Two heavily belabored themes ran through all articles: the party's new triumph in righting past wrongs, and the Soviet people's fundamental loyalty to the Soviet system, notwithstanding any accidental bygone misfortunes. "Despite everything," an *Izvestiya* reviewer revealed, "Solzhenitsyn's heroes in their overwhelming majority remained what they had been before the camps: true Soviet people. The party has designated writers its helpers. It seems to me that in his novel,

---

[1] The cheapest variety, usually attracting the longest queues.

Solzhenitsyn has shown himself to be the party's genuine helper in the sacred and essential cause of the struggle against the cult of personality and its consequences."

Triteness, then, was not the reviews' most disappointing quality—not even the cant with which Solzhenitsyn's purpose was twisted. Worse was the unmistakable hypocrisy of some of the reviewers. The author of the article with the most grandiloquent title, "For the Sake of the Truth, for the Sake of Justice"—and in *Pravda,* the country's most authoritative newspaper—was none other than Vladimir Ermilov, one of the most active denunciators, and therefore exterminators, of Russian writers during the "cult."

While spreading the news that a tale about concentration camps was now available, these reviews were more likely to inspire skepticism than enthusiasm among the readers Solzhenitsyn hoped to reach. Erstwhile prisoners were especially mistrustful, as Solzhenitsyn himself later observed.

When former prisoners learned from the unisonous trumpet calls of all newspapers that some kind of novel about the camps had appeared, and that newspapermen were vying with each other in its praise, they decided unanimously: "More crap. They've got together again on a cock-and-bull story for this business." That our newspapers, considering their usual lack of proportion, should suddenly be head over heels in praise of the truth—well, that was rather too much to imagine. Some people wouldn't even touch [the novel].

Several reviews, however, were both sincere and thoughtful. The central message of Solzhenitsyn's supporters was distinctly different: that with one stroke, *One Day* had wrought a fundamental change in Soviet literature, and this, in turn, would spark an equally radical change in Soviet life. Tvardovsky proclaimed the rebirth of genuinely free Russian literature. "This grim tale," he wrote in *Novy Mir,* "is yet another indication that today there are no areas or phenomena of life to be excluded from the Soviet artist's scope or kept inaccessible to truthful portrayal. The artist's own ability is all that matters."

One of the most perceptive reviews ran in *Literary Gazette,* the paper of the Writers' Union. The reviewer, a minor novelist and short-story writer named Grigory Baklanov, greeted the sudden appearance of a masterpiece among the daily flood of books.

Such a work influences what is being written and what will be written. . . . After this, it becomes wholly obvious that one cannot go on writing as before. Not that everyone must fling himself immediately into treating the same theme . . . but that a new level of discourse with the reader has been attained, and on this level what might have satisfied him but recently has become simply uninteresting and outdated.

The "new level of discourse" which Baklanov perceived was better defined by some of Solzhenitsyn's readers than by any reviews. They spoke of the novel having transported them almost physically into the camps to feel "such pain that it seemed my heart might stop." "It may be painful and bitter," wrote another reader, "but as long as it's the truth." A former inmate informed Solzhenitsyn that "now I read and weep, but when I was serving my ten years in Ukhta, tears wouldn't come."

What these nonliterary readers were fumbling to express cannot, in fact, be understood without literary analysis. For it was not any element of exposé in the description of Ivan Denisovich's camp that caused the pain and induced the catharsis, but Solzhenitsyn's art, and the permission for it to appear, prompting hopes that the hypocrisy had finally ended. Unlike most of the press, which pretended that Solzhenitsyn had revealed something shockingly new, almost no "ordinary" reader spoke of having his eyes opened, as opposed to his heart pierced. Most Russians knew about labor camps in some detail; only One Day's artistic power can explain its grip on them.

Surprisingly few critics and scholars have attempted to define this aspect, the literary quality, of Solzhenitsyn's work. Among the few, Solzhenitsyn's friend Blagov wrote the most perceptive analysis, a year after One Day's publication.

In pursuit of his goal Solzhenitsyn had to write not memoirs, not an analysis or exposé, but a poem, with a rhythmic text and structure—or, more precisely, a *folk legend* . . . and this is what he did in writing One Day. In this legend, the concentration camp and its evil have been set in a rhythmic pattern—an inner structural and spiritual rhythm which, with the help of a kind of resonance or induction, penetrates the inner being of, for example, a rehabilitated prisoner, warming him to the core. As if they were microwaves, these rhythms break up the stone which lies in that inner being and turn it to dust to be carried away by spiritual breezes, restoring life functions to the frozen parts of the soul—and, in particular, returning the capacity for tears and laughter. . . . For those who feel Solzhenitsyn's works deeply, their rhythms replace personal passage, both physical and moral, through the hell of the camps, thus ensuring that this hell shall not return.

In other words, it was the purifying effect of Solzhenitsyn's art that caused the intense reaction.

To say that One Day performed a kind of collective catharsis on the Russian people—that portion of them willing to examine their country's psyche—is obvious hyperbole. Yet as Blagov pointed out, there was an element of liberation through releasing of hidden horrors. Stalin's mass liquidations were like

> a dreadful event in a person's past which had descended into his subconscious to dwell there, forming a kind of hidden, self-enclosed province in his psyche of which this person is not aware, which he has "forgotten," but which is nevertheless a cause of sickness. And when this person is made to recollect, when the self-enclosed formation in the psyche is "lanced," dredged up, and brought into his consciousness, this may lead to a cure.

For all its quasi-Freudian terminology, this is a penetrating analysis of Solzhenitsyn's deepest effect on Russians, and was one reason why, as a Soviet critic pointed out, *One Day* was in great demand even among people who normally do not read novels. One such intermittent reader told the critic that "I don't know whether [the novel] is written well or badly. It seems to me that it couldn't have been written in any other way." Nor is the frame of reference purely Freudian, of course; that confession can relieve shame and guilt is an old Christian insight. With its lack of codified morality, the Russian Orthodox Church in particular placed great emphasis on purgation through confession, a concept that became integral to Russian attitudes over centuries. In bringing Raskolnikov to the understanding that peace of mind could come only through full public confession of his crime, Dostoyevsky demonstrated his insight into the Russian psyche. In its own time, *One Day* performed a similar function for the nation.

As a document of labor-camp conditions, the novel was received by some ex-prisoners as less than the whole truth. Although every word rang true, much was omitted. "You describe a relatively bearable camp without the harsher living and disciplinary conditions," wrote a former inmate to Solzhenitsyn. "You can't get an answer to this question from your novel: why did so many people not return from the camps?" Solzhenitsyn agreed. In a commentary to letters he'd received, he called *One Day* a "first account, still curtailed and muffled," and the reaction to it but "a measure of what will come when the full truth bursts forth."

What burst forth immediately, however, were angry accusations from predictable segments of Soviet society over the publication of even this curtailed and muffled story. Critical letters to Solzhenitsyn indicated that the Kozlov-Suslov stand had considerable spontaneous support among ordinary Soviet citizens. Former camp guards and officials could not have been expected to react otherwise, but their outrage showed how far they were from recognition of their responsibilities.

From former warders, Solzhenitsyn received no hint of defensiveness or repentance, but only angry complaints that his "sorry effort" threatened essential supports of the cherished social order. "The main astonishing feature of this novel, if I may be so bold as to call it that," wrote one man, "is how the author debases our soldiers and guards." "Soldiers who guard work gangs on their way to work fulfill such a difficult and responsible duty!" responded another. "This novel insults soldiers, sergeants, and officers of the Ministry for the Preservation of Public Order," offered a third. A female employee of a camp appealed to Solzhenitsyn's sense of pity— for the warders! "They're human beings, for goodness' sake. Doing their job then, just as they do it now." [2] (Despite its distortion of priorities, this kind of appeal might have helped prompt Solzhenitsyn to portray a camp guard in a later novel with a deep understanding of his position.)

Other readers with no apparent involvement with prisoners or camps felt offended for their country, whose shortcomings—if they in fact existed —should not be paraded before the world. "One tries to cover up a blemish on one's body," wrote an irate woman, "not exhibit it for display." Other readers sensed an unwarranted insult to the country's new socialist order, of which they felt themselves a proud part. "We've paid too dearly for Soviet rule," commented an irritated man, "to allow its workings to be debased." Still others were offended by the insult to the march of history, as understood from Marxist-Leninist teachings. "History's never had need of the past. Still less does the history of socialist culture need it." Many were offended by Ivan Denisovich's shortcomings as a positive hero in the socialist-realist mold. "I don't want that kind of hero—all stomach and no brains."

The collection of approving and grateful letters is long, and many, especially from former prisoners who wept while reading about themselves, are extremely moving. Former inmates of many camps wrote of the uncanny feeling of having their hearts opened to their own ordeals, with no shadow out of place nor any shadow of misjudgment or misinterpretation. But the list of denunciatory letters is also long, and, despite the unintended humor of many, each is a reminder of how deeply rooted was the opposition to any disturbance of Soviet society, however grave and glaring its errors. It was an opposition based more than anything on a certain social position, often very slight, and a certain personality—that is, a combination of privileges to protect, visceral antagonism to change, and anxiety about inferiors challenging their "betters." The tragedy in Russia of people with

---

[2] "Doing their job now," however, apparently affected the offspring of some penal officials, if not the officials themselves. "I've got two daughters of school age, you see," complained a KGB major a few years later to people in the camp where he worked. "They read that *Ivan Denisovich* and took it into their heads that now they can criticize their father. It's questions, reproaches, tears every evening. First I tried to reason with them, but then the only thing to do was toss the magazine into the stove. And that finished that."

an inherent esteem for authority and instinct for "keeping things in their proper place" was that this led them to apologize for terror.

Solzhenitsyn's rank-and-file opponent was sketched by Nadezhda Mandelshtam, the widow of the great poet, from her memory of teaching in a provincial city. The student she cites is the daughter of an official who was retired after the anti-Stalinist revelations of the Twentieth Congress—but the girl herself has had no experience of, not to say guilt for, the terror.

> "The ends don't justify the means," said a student in my class. "And I say they do," said a handsome young girl severely. She lived in a fine flat and enjoyed all the privileges a provincial city can provide its most honored citizens. Special hospitals, rest homes, and shops closed to and hidden from the general public. . . . Of the entire class, only she knew what she wanted. And she alone had read Solzhenitsyn—and came out firmly against the publication of such books. She cared only for the fourth chapter (of Stalin's extremely oversimplified, all-encompassing treatise purporting to give the final explanation of all social and historical phenomena and order). [She] hoped that the past could return.[3]

The attitude exemplified by the handsome girl would become the principal source of support for Solzhenitsyn's continuing persecution.

In the West, *One Day's* introduction took the form of front-page news, followed by editorial-page speculation about the event's political significance. The invariable point was that the novel represented confirmation from Soviet sources of the existence of labor camps; the inevitable question was whether this foreshadowed a Kremlin upheaval and radical reform. Understandably enough, the interest of most Westerners was primarily political, prompted by their concern with the Soviet Union as a great power. If the regime were indeed mellowing, this could lessen anxiety—and, in the end, taxes—from Helsinki to Hawaii.

Understandably too, the interest of most publishers was financial. But the Soviet Union's refusal to join international copyright conventions transformed a scramble to translate into a wild free-for-all. Like everything else published in Russia, *One Day* was unprotected and up for grabs, just as the Soviet Union takes what it wants of Western publications, without permission or compulsion to pay royalties. The result was predictable: publishers and translators worked more like Monte Carlo pit crews than with the decorum usually associated with literary endeavors. At least three translations into English were printed. The first was prepared in Moscow by Ralph Parker, a former British journalist who "chose freedom under

[3] Nadezhda Mandelshtam, *Hope Against Hope.*

Stalin," as he put it, in the late 1940s. He turned Solzhenitsyn's sharp, distinctive prose into a thin porridge and countenanced an abundance of distortions, dampenings, and outright omissions, often of the most piercing images. His text is still in print.

Of the other two English translations, one, prepared by a Russian émigré in America, was correct in the literal sense, but vapid. The other, the work of two Oxford dons, Max Hayward and Ronald Hingley, was both accurate and readable, if not entirely polished. With the notable exceptions of France and Sweden, this unhappy exercise was repeated in a dozen Western countries and surpassed in Germany. In that country, home of a large corps of excellent translators from Russian, no fewer than two translations were published from the English, and the sole translation from Russian itself was performed by a team of four translators working simultaneously on the seventy-page manuscript. When Solzhenitsyn eventually learned of the fate of his cherished words at the hands of eager and often unscrupulous publishers, he complained vigorously, publicly, and repeatedly. *One Day*'s treatment made him deeply suspicious of the very idea of publication in the West.

Flaws in translation helped delay appreciation of Solzhenitsyn's literary powers in many Western countries. But nothing could lessen the novel's impact on a particular group: politicians and intellectuals who had long been emotionally involved with the issue of Soviet concentration camps. Especially in the countries with large Communist Parties, such as Italy and France, attempts to document the existence of Stalin's millions of political prisoners—and to deny their existence—had provoked bitter political and legal clashes throughout the postwar years. The deepest passions involving the great questions of socialism, truth, and mankind's future were aroused.

For a committed socialist, impatient for humanity's progress from capitalism, to admit the existence of these horrors in the first country of socialism caused great conflict and pain; for a committed humanist, equally concerned about the fate of Soviet prisoners as human beings, to deny the strong circumstantial evidence caused anguish. But it was more than a conflict between sincere socialists and sincere humanists: the cold war had put this issue, as all others involving Russia, in an intellectually false perspective, and some extremely bitter people on both sides were making use of this issue to club opponents in the name of mankind. The argument of many Western superpatriots—that people who challenged the fundamentals of capitalist society were in effect leading the free world toward Soviet concentration camps—was, pathetically, accepted by a substantial portion of the challengers themselves. For as rigidly as McCarthyites who accused them of subversion, prominent leftists branded the very mention of Soviet labor camps as a slander of socialism in the service of American imperialism. The arguments of both sides, sadly, contained elements of truth—and both ignored the overwhelming reality of the suffering itself in the camps.

Men of great intellect might have had inner doubts about this logic, but many succumbed to it in the end. Jean-Paul Sartre was perhaps the most disturbing example. Early in the 1950s he was asked whether one should recognize and fight the evil of Soviet concentration camps if their existence were proved. One should not, he answered, *"pour ne désespérer Billancourt"*—so as not to discourage the people of this grim, working-class Paris suburb. No one questioned Sartre's humanitarian intention, but his attitude in fact reflected the morality of perpetrators of cruelty.

For many, the chanting of political slogans masked an otherwise thundering moral compromise, and the few strains of protest that rose above the din provoked intense bitterness from both groups of conformists. The clearest voice belonged to David Rousset in France, where the controversy was also most vicious. The inventor of the concept of *univers concentrationnaire* was a socialist writer—but in 1949, when he began to publish overwhelming evidence of the nature of Stalin's camps (including several near Solzhenitsyn's), outraged Communists and sympathizers denounced him as a crude falsifier. Legal action followed in the French courts, during which the fierce determination to deny the facts was demonstrated by the testimony of one of Rousset's principal assailants, the personal aide to the Secretary General of the Communist Party. If camps did in fact exist, this man was asked, would he then condemn them? "If you ask me," he responded, "whether I would condemn my mother were she a murderer, I would answer: 'Monsieur, my mother is my mother and will not be a murderer.'"

Thus, as prisoner III-232 struggled to survive in Ivan Denisovich's camp, French intellectuals were denying not only the existence of such camps but the possibility of their existence. This issue, a kind of Dreyfus case in reverse—the extreme left was fighting here for obfuscation instead of truth—was one of the most emotional in postwar French intellectual history.

After *One Day*'s appearance in Russia, the extreme left's *volte-face* was swift; Rousset's former attackers did not attempt to eat their words so much as to deny they had spoken them. One of the most violent now took it upon himself to write the preface of the French edition of *One Day*. Though some French Communists were reluctant or insincere, though many hated to abandon the blind reliance on Russia as the socialist Motherland, Solzhenitsyn's devastating impact left them little choice.

France's example was repeated elsewhere. *One Day* was not the first lesson in the left's painful accommodation to the realities of the Soviet Union, upon which they had projected so many of their own aspirations for a better life; but Solzhenitsyn's ability to make even foreign readers shiver with vicarious fears and frosts of camp life made it one of the sharpest. The shock helped several major Communist Parties, including the French and Italian, to work themselves loose from deep psychological dependence upon the Soviet party, and European Communists' reaction to Czechoslovakia in 1968—so different from Hungary twelve years before, especially in the willingness to make common cause with Eastern European and Russian liberals—is in some measure the work of Solzhenitsyn's art.

Even had Solzhenitsyn been apprised of the political impact of his work abroad, even had he foreseen his continuing effect in Europe and elsewhere, the provincial teacher would not have been likely at this time to grasp either the full significance or the complexity of his influence. His welcome by some Marxist literary critics would have puzzled him no less. The doyen of this group, the octogenarian Hungarian Georg Lukács, spoke of Solzhenitsyn's work as the clearest harbinger of a renaissance of genuine socialist-realist literature. In Russia, socialist realism represented then, as it does now, literature directed by edict; Lukács hoped it would return to the searching honesty that Marxist ideals had inspired in the 1920s. "If socialist literature again remembers its calling, if it again perceives its artistic responsibility toward the great problems of our time, this will unchain powerful forces within it." More than anyone, Solzhenitsyn encouraged this hope.

XXIII

Limelight

HALF A DOZEN INHABITANTS OF RYAZAN EARNED their living as authors, and belonged to the local branch of the Writers' Union. None of the six enjoyed a reputation in the neighboring district centers of Kaluga or Tula, not to speak of Budapest, Paris, or even Moscow. When Ryazan's literati had occasion to walk (or drive, for authors of even local prominence were among Russia's minute motoring elite) in Solzhenitsyn's rather backstreet neighborhood, they had no reason to suspect that a new perception of "the great problems of our time" was being worked out inside a nondescript cabin in Kasimov Lane.

Outwardly, there was nothing about Solzhenitsyn himself that autumn to suggest anything other than a provincial schoolteacher. His movements, manner, and somewhat seedy clothes all implied the opposite not only of international fame but even of modest professional achievement. The marks of his ordeal had all but disappeared from his face; perhaps only observant Russians could guess that certain furrows about the mouth had been cut by years of hunger. Still, Solzhenitsyn's appearance in a street or crowd suggested even greater anonymity than that of most Russians in impersonal situations. His face was a blank mask, as if his first priority were to be unnoticed. But protected as he was by Ryazan's provincialism and his own rigid control of his time, he was nevertheless quickly searched out by the limelight.

It reached the town first in the form of extraordinary instructions from Moscow to enlist Solzhenitsyn in the Writers' Union. Normally, a first-book author is admitted to the union only after a cumbersome process of application, recommendations, and due consideration by his local branch. In Solzhenitsyn's case, the local writers were reduced to office boys: the secretary of the Ryazan branch was directed from Moscow to deliver application forms to Solzhenitsyn and urge their quick completion for dispatch directly to the capital. It was there that the secretariat of the Russian Republic's union as a whole admitted Solzhenitsyn post haste.

After the halcyon days had passed, Solzhenitsyn would recall the circumvention of all bureaucratic procedures, stages, and delays. The secretariat, he said, "was in such a hurry to admit me that it gave me no time to submit recommendations, and didn't allow me to be taken by the local Ryazan branch, but accepted me itself and sent me a telegram of congratulations." The Ryazan literary elite lost even the subsidiary honor of presenting Solzhenitsyn with his membership card. For this occasion, the chairman of the Russian Republic's union hastened to Ryazan to discharge the function personally. He was Leonid Sobolev, a writer-bureaucrat known previously as an implacable enemy of the thaw. But knowledge of Khrushchev's personal interest convinced him to subordinate his personal feelings about *One Day* to a bureaucrat's zeal in executing his chief's predilections.

Solzhenitsyn accepted the membership card—but little else. To an author of his instant fame and with his "big hand," as the Russians say, in the Kremlin, the attendant privileges might have been numerous. A move to Moscow, the dream of most provincial writers, was not only possible, but repeatedly urged upon him. He would have had a fine flat there in a relatively luxurious building, together with the wherewithal—entrance to restricted restaurants and restricted films; a dacha in a restricted area— to enjoy the Soviet version of life at the top. But the temptations of Moscow's minuscule café society and artistic elite more repelled than attracted him, and he stubbornly refused to leave Ryazan. "I was afraid of losing my concentration," he explained. At this point, his devotion to work seemed somewhat exaggerated, not only to illustrious Moscow colleagues, but even to Reshetovskaya. Determined to maintain an environment conducive to writing, he rejected all changes which did not advance his aim.

For the first flashes of fame only sharpened his sense of mission. Even more than before, he channeled his time and energy to its service.

The single major change he effected was to forgo teaching. Serving out the school term, he taught his last class on December 28, and became a full-time author—the final consummation of his childhood "unconscious notion . . . that I had to become a writer." During his final month, he taught with his accustomed dedication, and would not submit to lionization by his colleagues in the staff room. In school, he continued to treat his writing as a wholly private affair; but people now understood why he had been indifferent to earning more than the barest living as a teacher—and what had lured him home directly from school so consistently throughout the years. He rushed to his room, observed a journalist that autumn, "as if hurrying to the main purpose of his life."

It was not his fifty-ruble salary that kept him at the job that final month, but responsibility to his pupils and school. *One Day* had made him rich enough for several untroubled years—longer than otherwise because of his attitude toward money. The respect for each precious ruble nurtured in the camps had not disappeared. A visitor noticed that he calculated his expenses in advance with his usual precision, and adhered to his estimate. What interested him was the number of working days his royalties would buy. And throughout future years, he would stretch his small savings—to six years in the case of *One Day's* royalties— keeping his expenditure at the "basic level of my teaching days," never spending more on himself than he would have had to pay a secretary.

Apart from withdrawing from teaching and acquiring a car,[1] Solzhenitsyn refused to change his life-style. Although a more modern flat would have been his for the asking, he remained in his old quarters, chopping firewood as before. Above all, he protected himself resolutely against fame's intrusions and encumbrances—which displeased Reshetovskaya. Her outgoing, lively personality led her to a natural interest in some of the public aspects of Solzhenitsyn's success: his fame, the opportunities to meet new and interesting people, "how the world was reacting to her husband," as mutual friends explained. After years of sharing his obscurity and helping to support him in every sense, she could not fully understand his determination to maintain old habits in such radically changed circumstances. Victor Bukhanov, the journalist who managed to see Solzhenitsyn at this time, spoke of his "recluse-like existence" and "almost ascetic way of life."

Bukhanov was the only journalist who overcame Solzhenitsyn's resistance enough to gather sufficient material for a short article on Solzhenitsyn's thoughts and personal life. Solzhenitsyn made himself wholly unavailable to other reporters, Soviet and foreign. The *Teachers' Gazette* was understandably eager to run a scoop on the new celebrity in the ranks of the profession, but Solzhenitsyn sent their man packing. And for all his fine literary connections, Bukhanov obtained his rather scanty material thanks only to his remarkable tenacity. Nevertheless, a substantial portion of his article explained why the full story remained untold.

He does not hide his lack of partiality toward reporters. He dis-

---

[1] He bought his modest Moskvich in a hard-currency shop and christened it "Denisik" (as Ivan Denisovich might have tenderly called his son if he had christened him after his own father). Solzhenitsyn paid for this car with royalties from the Swedish edition of *One Day*, which were passed to him by the Swedish embassy in Moscow. This was the only foreign income he received from *One Day*. Those Western publishers who did pay him royalties did so through Mezhkniga, the Soviet agency, and Solzhenitsyn never saw a penny. In late 1965 he declined to extend his three-year contract with Mezhkniga, informing its officials that they "had not acted properly in defense of my interests as an author."

likes the craving of readers to "find out and digest everything as quickly as possible." Apparently, his basic inclination toward deep analysis rebels against any kind of superficiality. It's difficult for a journalist to talk to Solzhenitsyn. His unfailingly polite and firm "no's" drive one to gloomy despair. I spoke to him in Moscow and met him in Ryazan for four consecutive days, almost against his will. Solzhenitsyn captivated me with his mind and moved me with his charm, but I've had enough—this was my last attempt to talk to him on assignment from editors. Personally, I'm convinced that Solzhenitsyn will never talk about his working habits, how many pages he fills with text in a week, what projects he's nurturing and what brand of paper he prefers. "You'll learn about all of that after my funeral," he told me without a trace of humor in his voice. Stubbornly, I would say fiercely, he defends his right to say nothing about his work. "The channel from a writer to his reader is only his books," he repeated his conviction for the nth time. . . .

Apart from a distaste for superficiality, Solzhenitsyn obviously resented journalists for their usurpation of time budgeted for work. Bukhanov observed that the writer not only loved work, but the word itself, which he pronounced with longing mixed with occasional mild abuse of the increasing number of distracting "admirers" and pilgrims. "I want to work in peace and quiet," Solzhenitsyn insisted with a certain nostalgia for the classical age of the Russian novel and, in the comparison, a hint of self-assurance.

Take the writers of the previous century. They just lived and worked. . . . Nobody hung on their backs for stories and scoops. People simply read them. And they were pretty good writers, weren't they?

As usual, Solzhenitsyn was engaged in several projects simultaneously; the most ambitious was *The First Circle*, which he had started in 1955, even before *One Day*. He was now deep in writing and rewriting, advancing to new ground in his method, and repeatedly reworking earlier pages. He was also composing short stories and his closely guarded poetry. On the heels of *One Day's* reception, two stories had been set in print for *Novy Mir*, and Solzhenitsyn was extremely meticulous with the galleys. He did not know, of course, that he would have few further chances to correct his work in Soviet print—but he would not have been surprised to hear it.

Apart from resenting changes that would commandeer his time, Solzhenitsyn saw other reasons, unpublishable in the Soviet press, to shun fame. Beyond permitting Kopelev to submit *One Day*, he himself had done nothing to promote his own emergence as a public author. His desire for and fear of publication seemed to have canceled each other out, and he also hesitated to interfere because, as he told friends, he did not fully understand the interplay of personality and political intrigue that had made possible *One Day*'s publication. Some four years later, when Khrushchevian liberalism had been all but extinguished in the government, he hinted at a suspicion that the explanation lay in a miscalculation by the then-deposed Nikita Sergeyevich. "I've been living off the mistake of Russia's last dictator," he told a visitor half jokingly.

He might have overemphasized the purely accidental element in publication. Even without his imprisonment, long provincial isolation had made him less knowledgeable about the inner workings of Soviet politics than men like Tvardovsky and Kopelev—and therefore more pessimistic. Russians removed from sources of information and political gossip, the narrow pinpoints of insight into behind-the-scenes intrigues, are likely to picture the regime much more as the gray monolith of unanimous agreement projected by the radio and press. During the euphoric autumn of 1962, Khrushchev's promise of de-Stalinization "not as a passing fad but as our guiding policy line" had actually come very close to realization; and had it been realized, Russia's subsequent history would have been significantly changed. Like many intellectuals who had suffered, Solzhenitsyn was deeply skeptical of good omens and promising "openings." In the end, however, his pessimism turned out to be justified.

For within a week of *One Day*'s appearance, the tide of de-Stalinization had turned; soon its ebb would follow. While the enthusiastic reviews were appearing in the press, the Central Committee plenum for which Khrushchev had been so assiduously preparing convened. As the First Secretary knew, the underlying issue was momentous—enough to justify expansion of the plenum to include the entire party elite: leading officials of the party *apparat* came from all over the country to join the Central Committee members. But Khrushchev was wrong about the outcome and, since he had already in effect been defeated, probably mistaken in his strategy.

His tactics at the plenum were to carry on as before in pursuit of his own vision of reform. Khrushchev was as vehement as ever in denouncing Stalinism and cutting about the man himself. "Stalin did not believe in the masses. He was a member of a workers' party but did not respect workers. Of people who came from a working-class background, he would say contemptuously: 'That one's crawled out of some grease pot. Where does he think he's poking his pose?' "

But the First Secretary's thunder resounded no further than the walls of the Kremlin hall. Of his obviously tempestuous speech on November

23, only the sentences quoted above found their way—indirectly—into the Soviet press; [2] the rest was suppressed, even in the stenographic record of the plenum, which noted only that a speech had been made. The suppression was possible because Khrushchev had been bested by the Kozlov-Suslov forces. "The great majority of my colleagues," he later admitted to a Western journalist, "disagreed with me."

To Western journalists too, his entourage leaked the gist of the suppressed speech. It dealt at length with the arts, with specific honor paid to Solzhenitsyn in an appeal for pressing on with de-Stalinization despite bitter opposition from part of the Politburo. But as the First Secretary hinted to an ambassador several days later, his policy of permitting greater freedom of expression—which if nothing else was required by the new level of the Soviet economy—had been overruled.

Several factors brought about Khrushchev's defeat; it is enough to say here that the First Secretary was too weak to overcome the conservative political-bureaucratic party establishment which, in its panic over the stirring of liberalism and threat of change, had dug in furiously. And Khrushchev's own position had been undermined by the gamble of his Cuban missiles, which frightened large segments of Soviet society, wounded the national pride, and added damaging weight to the arguments against his "adventurism," whether in the Caribbean or in domestic cultural affairs.

The First Secretary saw his weaknesses and plotted his game. His first consideration, as always, was to protect himself. To the Stalinists, one of the most alarming prospects had been the unleashing of liberal intellectuals. As a quick move to reestablish his orthodox party name, Khrushchev ended his short-lived alliance with liberal Communists. With this, the strategy of using literature to discredit Stalinists lost its *raison d'être* and was unceremoniously jettisoned. Light on his political feet, Khrushchev did not so much shuffle back from his previous position as execute a deft about-face. At the exhibition of mildly modernist paintings that had been specially mounted in the prestigious Manezh Hall, he gave himself up to one of his rages—but this time for reasons nearly opposite those which had prompted his Presidium outburst several months earlier. He castigated the intellectuals who, in their moral depravity, had produced such monstrosities as abstractionist brush strokes ("as if a child had done his business on the canvas"). "Gentlemen," he said to the liberal intelligentsia at large (snidely likening them to the old bourgeoisie by not calling them "Comrades"), "we are declaring war on you." Within hours,

---

[2] In a *Novy Mir* article about Solzhenitsyn published in January 1964. It is probable that had the censor understood the implications of quoting from a speech that was not only unpublished but unreferred to elsewhere, he would have deleted the passage.

a vast, incessant campaign was in motion throughout the public media for the restoration of socialist realism, first in painting and then in all branches of the arts. The exhibition had served as a neat pretext for Khrushchev to proclaim the termination of his short venture as a patron of liberal artists and to reassert himself as the guardian of ideological purity.

Until now, Solzhenitsyn's name, protected by Khrushchev, had been sacrosanct. The harshest criticism of *One Day* had been to ignore it, which only one major newspaper managed to do. Now in a matter of days the Stalinists would present their accounts to Solzhenitsyn. The first depreciation of the novel appeared on December 8. For all its praise of Solzhenitsyn's talent, the review was essentially a restatement of the Kozlov-Suslov charge of ideological weakness and lack of proper class attitudes. Solzhenitsyn's immunity from public criticism had lasted three weeks.

The hopes for a liberal renaissance were now dim indeed, but many intellectuals clung to them. After all, only a few weeks ago a young poet had expressed their aspiration that "time is on our side, on the side of my friends and myself." It was hard to relinquish the surge of optimism that had been gaining momentum throughout the autumn. At first most liberals told themselves that there had been some sort of misunderstanding: Khrushchev's outburst at the exhibition had been an unfortunate accident, caused by his volatile personality, not by a change in policy. In a clever little stratagem by academic portraitists of Stalin and Stalin's image of Russia, the First Secretary had been calculatedly shown several modern paintings he could not be expected to understand. The simple man reacted in his artless way, exploding with bewilderment and anger. So went the liberals' wishful thinking. If only all this could be explained to Khrushchev, he would see there was no evil in what he had been shown and would continue to uphold his expressed support of greater artistic freedom.

The reality was quite different. Perhaps Khrushchev was genuinely outraged by the paintings shown him, as he had been moved when listening to *One Day* a few months before. His inner feelings are not open to analysis—and are largely irrelevant in any case, since they were subordinated to political maneuvering: his use of the exhibition as he had used *One Day*, if on an opposite tack. Concerned as they were with the implications for intellectual and artistic expression, most liberals could not bring themselves to recognize this.

On December 17, two weeks after his visit to Manezh, Khrushchev held a reception for the celebrities of Soviet arts and letters. It took place in a mansion used for official entertaining near Khrushchev's residence on Lenin Hills, overlooking Moscow. Khrushchev's purpose was to make his new position on cultural policy absolutely clear to the intellectual community: bridled himself, he wanted to rein in the runaway aspirations that he had set loose. Despite the strident new campaign for orthodoxy in the visual arts, despite the quotation of Khrushchev's first favorable mention of Stalin for years several days before in the press, the intellectuals were understandably confused. Could the line have switched again? So swiftly? So sharply? Even men who had read all the ominous signs since the November plenum did not fully understand what had happened and why—or how far Khrushchev would go at this confrontation. No artist could be sure of what might be said or done to him, or of how far his own work might be judged to have deviated from still fuzzy standards.

The dress at the reception reflected the prevailing unease. Many guests seemed to wear their thoughts—and fears—of how the meeting would end. Some arrived in old Stalin-style tunics, prompting one participant to remark to himself that *their* expectations were easy enough to interpret. Other guests came in their best dark suits and starched white collars, appropriate to a diplomatic banquet. Still others felt that a demonstration of humility was appropriate, and dressed unobtrusively in business suits. The phenomenon of "clothes reflect the expectation" was observed by a painter sitting by himself and analyzing character with professional interest and resigned amusement. Then he noticed a man enter whose dress defied interpretation.

He seemed to have been plucked straight from the audience of a small-town opera house. The first impression was of the singular gray lumpiness of Russians in a crowd. The artist registered that he was a tallish man with a slight stoop, probably in his forties—but of what vocation? Something in the very datedness of his clothes made it obvious that they were the provincial's Sunday best. His suit hung on him as if chewed by a cow, in the words of the Russian cliché; his shoes had the blunt crudeness of the previous decade's mass production. This man's costume was so quaint that it could only be real. Obviously, he had no intention of producing one impression or another—but how had he gotten a pass to this select reception?

At that moment, Khrushchev was surrounded by a small knot of his guests. When he noticed the man who appeared to have wandered in, he broke off his conversation. "Comrades," he announced, "Solzhenitsyn is among us."

The First Secretary beamed, lifted his arms, and began to clap in his characteristic fashion: an obvious invitation for public participation. *One Day* had surely not appealed to everyone at the reception, for the guests included rigid conservatives and the same academic painters who had plotted the Manezh incident. Nevertheless, everyone quickly followed Khrushchev's lead, producing what Soviet press reports of public speeches call "stormy applause." The artist who had been observing the guests' apparel now peered intently around him, eager for a glimpse of the mysterious unknown who had caused such a sensation. It was only when everyone had seated himself again and the man with the cheap suit and crude shoes remained standing that he understood.

Studying his "subject," the artist was now puzzled by the man's expression. Solzhenitsyn's face indicated no visible reaction to the honor he'd been given; not only was there no smile, but a faint sternness could be read into the set of his mouth and the blankness of his eyes. It was an odd response to what ordinarily would have been a patent moment of triumph.

By this time, Solzhenitsyn's "prisoner's mask" had no doubt become integral to the underground writer's personality; it was not his nature to display emotions to strangers. But there was good reason to be especially cautious with the strangers gathered here. Some four hundred of Russia's most successful men and women had acclaimed him, under the baton of the First Secretary himself. Solzhenitsyn knew that the seemingly unanimous applause concealed deep divisions, but he would not commit himself until he had learned his way in the maze of cabals and alliances at the summit—until he could judge how the honor proffered him would affect his mission in the long run. One day, he would emerge as a consummate political tactician, but only after years of orientation and concentrated application.

As the applause for him died down, Solzhenitsyn remained impassive. But the vacant mask concealed a welter of emotions, and in the privacy of his work room, Solzhenitsyn committed them to paper. His bewildered and grateful surprise over his fame, his confirmed sense of mission and the relief of abandoning the secrecy of his work all found expression . . . in a prayer.

It was not a literary device but a wholly personal address to God. For Solzhenitsyn had become a believer. He guards his religious beliefs as one of the most private aspects of his carefully protected personal life, and it is not known, for example, when he acquired them. Although he often attended church services in his early childhood and spoke, as a fully established writer, of their impression on him—"singular in freshness and purity, which no personal suffering and no intellectual theories were able later to erase"—there is no evidence that religion played any part in his university or army years. On the contrary, it appears that he left Marfino in 1949 a philosophical skeptic, and that he was unreligious at least up to his release from the camps. Perhaps he disguised his feelings as he and his mother had buried his father's tsarist medals. In any case, he has clearly defined faith's appeal for him: a psychological need for a steady presence of powerful good to which a man can relate, thus feeling that he is, in his words, at least "a tiny fragment of the universal spirit." Such a presence can help a person see both great suffering and the petty cares of daily life in perspective.

> For people have always been self-seeking and often fallen short of the good. But the peals of eventide would float over village field and forest. It was a reminder that petty earthly pursuits must be put aside and an hour of thoughts be given over to the eternal things. This pealing . . . raised man so that he would not sink to four legs.

In other words, religion's attraction lay in its relating the self to a higher entity as a part of the whole, thereby preventing exclusive preoccupation with the part.

But deep faith and love of God are not born of reason alone, and it is not known, apparently even to Solzhenitsyn's close friends, what factors besides the rational ones brought about his conversion. Nevertheless, his 1962 prayer, written soon after his rise to fame, is evidence enough of the intensity of his faith.

> How easy it is for me to live with Thee, Lord! How easy to believe in Thee! When my thoughts pull back in puzzlement or go soft, when the brightest people see no farther than this evening and know not what to do tomorrow, Thou sendest down to me clear confidence that Thou art, and wilt make sure that not all the ways of the good are closed.
>
> On this ridge of earthly fame, I look back in wonder at the road which I would never have been able to divine alone—that wondrous path through hopelessness to this ridge from which I too have been able to radiate among men a reflection of Thy rays. And Thou wilt grant me to continue reflecting them as long as need be. And that which I cannot complete will mean that Thou hast allotted it to others.|

Solzhenitsyn did not permit his ardent faith to distort his literary observations of social reality. Believers receive no more sympathy than other sufferers in his works, and, in keeping with the facts of Soviet life, almost all of his protagonists are either indifferent to religion or but mildly curious. But by this time, and almost certainly years earlier, Solzhenitsyn's self-imposed duty to survive and record the experiences of camps had developed into a sense of mission to which he gave more than human purpose. Even most of Solzhenitsyn's fondest political supporters who applauded his mercurial rise to "the high ridge of earthly fame" on that December day would have been astonished to know this. During the following decade, interest in Christianity was to grow among Russian intellectuals searching beyond political philosophy for ultimate values;

but in 1962, a scientist-writer of the highest objectivity would have provoked only incomprehension had he proclaimed his faith in God.

Predictably, the meeting which had begun with the acclaim of Solzhenitsyn went badly—although not disastrously—for the liberals. When the gathering was called to a kind of order, the principal speaker was Leonid Ilyichev, whom Khrushchev had recently appointed chairman of the Central Committee's new Ideological Commission [3]—in other words, the country's director general of ideological affairs, responsible for instilling and upholding approved political-social-moral attitudes throughout the Soviet population. A bland bureaucrat, Ilyichev had spent his entire working life in ideological affairs; his allegiance was to his superiors, whatever their policy. He began by chiding those intellectuals who, in the excitement of the autumn, had challenged the right of party officials to make the daily decisions of cultural affairs: what books shall be published, symphonies performed, and paintings exhibited. The party, he made clear, had no intention of relinquishing these functions to the artists themselves. As Ilyichev cited evidence of just such impermissible challenges and quoted intellectuals' petitions, Khrushchev interrupted to demand sharper condemnation of deviates. The two politicians kept up this curious fugue for ten hours—after which even the most sanguine optimists surely understood that Khrushchev no longer encouraged greater creative freedom. Despite this, disaster was avoided. Ilyichev limited himself to relatively polite warnings—artists must restore "party-mindedness" as an underlying theme of their works—and although Khrushchev added spice, he did not so much as hint at sanctions.

Even without Solzhenitsyn's avid interest in the varieties of human character, this rare opportunity for close observation of the rulers was fascinating. The ten hours of Ilyichev's theme and Khrushchev's developments provided little more in content than a skillful reading of the proceedings—as published several days later, pruned of some of the sharper tones and repeats—would have provided. But in the informal exchanges among the meeting's participants, Solzhenitsyn had his first direct insight into the atmosphere of the upper reaches.

In these exchanges, several guests bravely contradicted Khrushchev in defense of modern art. Yevtushenko's repartee was boldest, sharpest, and

[3] Khrushchev had intended this commission to replace Polikarpov's reactionary Section of Arts and Letters. But the conservatives managed to save both Polikarpov and the instrument of his repressive zeal, which continued to function side by side with the new commission. Thus the cultural bureaucracy was inflated by compromise instead of diminished. The two bodies worked cheek by jowl until Khrushchev's fall, when the commission was abolished and the old section reigned supreme, as it does now.

wittiest—a direct rebuttal to the First Secretary that caused a collective gasp.[4] The participants then burst into applause—in which Khrushchev soon joined. Despite the leaders' stern words, therefore, the atmosphere at the top seemed astonishingly more permissive than the provincial writer could have imagined—or anyone else lacking this unique first-hand view, for Yevtushenko's retort of course went unmentioned in the press.

Solzhenitsyn also had his first direct glimpse of Kremlin intrigue: hints of factions forming and threats implied—such as revelations of the Stalinist skeletons in many liberalizers' closets, including those of Tvardovsky and Khrushchev themselves. Although the meeting was ostensibly dedicated to throttling creative artists, literary rivalries revealed themselves in pursuit of social goals and political alliances: indispensable instruction for the future public protester and author of *The First Circle*, with its portrayal of Soviet politics at the summit.

Moreover, Solzhenitsyn found that he himself had been deeply involved in the grim game of literary politics, and in a way which could only have been repugnant to him: the party had made of him an unwilling alibi. For as the suppression of liberals took its steadily accelerating course, his work remained in high official favor, widely brandished as proof of the party's honesty, humanity, and profound sincerity. Having purged itself of the consequences of Stalin's personality cult—according to the propagandists' refrain—the party could now face all legitimate criticism, even Solzhenitsyn's. It was only unfounded criticism that it rejected; only "slurs and blackening" it had a duty to suppress. The line first emerged as Solzhenitsyn himself listened, in Ilyichev's speech:

> Our party endorses the healthy, life-affirming critical trend in the art of socialist realism. Artistically and politically powerful works that truthfully and boldly expose the arbitrariness that prevailed [under Stalin] . . . have been published recéntly with the approval of the party's Central Committee. It is enough to mention A. Solzhenitsyn's novel *One Day in the Life of Ivan Denisovich*.

To Ilyichev, who had opposed the novel's publication from the first, these were hard words to utter; but there was nothing new in a politician reversing his tastes for the sake of his career. The line he issued here was to remain in force for several months. Disingenuous as it was in many cases, the press and cultural bureaucracy would continue to proclaim respect for Solzhenitsyn, but only in the service of a full-scale campaign for orthodoxy. Solzhenitsyn was used as a prop in a grand political production: someone to distract the public's attention from other writers and

---

[4] When Khrushchev, referring to the abstractionist painters cited the Russian proverb that only the grave straightens out a hunchback, Yevtushenko answered immediately that "we have come a long way since the time [of Stalinism] when only the grave straightened out hunchbacks."

artists who, soon after Khrushchev's reception, were threatened and harassed. Voznesensky and Victor Nekrasov were among the most prominent targets, both for recent works considered politically or morally dangerous. Solzhenitsyn said nothing in their defense—no liberal did at this stage—or even in objection to the use made of his name. He was not yet thinking in terms of protest.

In fact, he said nothing in public at all about the interpretation of *One Day* and the short stories that followed during that winter in *Novy Mir*. He neither supported his admirers nor contradicted his detractors, neither approved of the use of his name for purposes he subscribed to nor disapproved of the obvious misuse. The misuse in this case—the Khrushchev-Ilyichev line formulated during that December reception—was abandoned in late spring, when the need for it died. It was to be followed by other lines, incidents, and episodes. Solzhenitsyn maintained his silence in every case, throughout some four and a half years of increasing controversy and sharpening attack—until certain acts of the authorities threatened what most mattered to him: his existence as a writer.

XXIV

Skirmishes

FROM HIS ENCOUNTER WITH RUSSIA's famous and infamous, Solzhenitsyn returned to his last physics classes in Ryazan. The term ended, and he returned to Moscow for a very different gathering: a New Year's Eve party at a theater called the Sovremennik. The Sovremennik (the Contemporary) occupied a special place, suggested by its name, among Moscow's three score theaters. Although not avant garde—no such theater enlivened the capital at that time—it was the city's youngest and liveliest company, which sought to vitalize an overwhelmingly stale theatrical atmosphere by restoring life to Stanislavsky's fossilized "method." Although not free of overdramatic acting, it was Moscow's most creative company in terms of new ideas and techniques. This gave it a distinct role in the movement for artistic emancipation, of which Solzhenitsyn had quickly become the spearhead.

The party was attended by the lions of Moscow's young bohemia: writers, painters, and designers as well as theatrical and cinema figures. The young generation's artistic elite had changed in the twenty-odd years since he had known theater people connected with Zavadsky's studio in Rostov, yet he felt quite at ease with them. Guests gathered around him in curiosity, admiration, and a sense of fraternity. Although the names and faces of cinema actors and other celebrities were famous, Solzhenitsyn was the evening's brightest star.

It was his "festive emergence," as Bukhanov called it, and Solzhenitsyn clearly enjoyed himself. His easy and occasionally booming laughter prompted an observer who had been struck by his recluselike existence in Ryazan to remark that the evening belied the notion of his "onesidedness." More than this, the party laid the foundations of several enduring friendships, and these confirmed Solzhenitsyn's belief that the Sovremennik's concern for reviving forthright realistic art was akin to his own. Like all Russian theaters, the Sovremennik was a repertory company and therefore a kind of informal club as well as a place of work. Solzhenitsyn became a member of the club and remains one to this day. When in Moscow, it is one of the places he visits for communion with kindred spirits. His actor and director friends always welcome him, even during periods when the authorities, deeply angered by Solzhenitsyn himself, could only be displeased with those who befriend him.

Solzhenitsyn had been introduced to the Sovremennik by Tvardovsky in late autumn after the editor had learned several completed plays, including *The Love Girl and the Innocent,* were among his manuscripts. Solzhenitsyn's old love for the theater still led him to sacrifice an uncharacteristic amount of writing time to the organizing and arranging required for staging the drama. His ambitions as a playwright ran a close second to those as a novelist, and after the success of *One Day,* producing *Love Girl* became his most important short-term goal. It was arranged that Solzhenitsyn himself would read the script to the assembled actors and directors. Years later, one of Russia's leading actors agreed to describe the encounter on the condition that he remain anonymous.

> Soon after the awing experience of *One Day,* Tvardovsky told the members of the theater that Solzhenitsyn would shortly be coming to visit us. Naturally, we held our breath: what would this mysterious new colossus be like? We waited. And pulled back in surprise when he actually appeared, because it was a very curious man who stood before us. He looked like a dental technician or a bookkeeper. His suit was made of rather good wool but extremely old, with old-fashioned trousers as wide as the shoes—which no one in Moscow circles had worn for years. And his hat was incredibly crumpled, as if his physics pupils had played football with it in the school yard. . . .
>
> There was nothing at all remarkable about his face except, perhaps, for the dominating impression of bad teeth. But as for his character, we got a hint of it immediately, as he was led around and introduced to everyone. He did not treat this as a formal ritual, but as an important human act. He stopped and listened to each name very carefully, asking that those he didn't fully understand be repeated. Then he mused on each man's name while looking at him, until the sound had sunk home. From this first act, it was clear that this was not a man of outward appearances, but of deep substance.

Solzhenitsyn sat down and read the title of the play: *Olen i Shalashovka.* Many of his sophisticated listeners did not understand. *Olen* is "deer" in Russian, but what might *shalashovka* mean? In fact, both were camp slang: *olen,* in Solzhenitsyn's own explanation, "means a trusting simpleton, an inexperienced novice," and *shalashovka,* a female prisoner who evades the struggle for survival by being a kind of courtesan to wardens, administrators, and well-fixed prisoners. The English title no more than suggests the implications of these two kinds of characters and the contrasts between them. In Solzhenitsyn's play, the "innocent" is an Army officer who has been delivered to the camp fresh from the front on charges of anti-Soviet agitation. The "love girl" is the twenty-two-year-old daughter of a farmer dispossessed during collectivization. The love of the two prisoners holds together a series of "slice-of-life" episodes from their camp, in which a chain of events is depicted that bears on their relationship, both directly and indirectly.

Solzhenitsyn read the script in a room of the theater. From professional habit, the leading actor who had been surprised by his appearance listened carefully to Solzhenitsyn's inflection and timbre as well as for a possible part for himself.

> He read rather badly, like a somewhat hammy provincial actor. True, he was extremely intense, assiduous, even zealous in his "performance"—but he sometimes forgot to change voices when changing characters, so that the "love girl" would come out exactly like the camp commandant—that kind of "minor" error. The reading was every bit as curious as his appearance.

Clearly, Solzhenitsyn had not entirely abandoned his acting ambitions; clearly he had had little opportunity to develop the talent that impressed Zavadsky a quarter of a century before. But, the actor continued,

> It was the inner voice—the content and the implications—that mattered. And this moved us. This transfixed us. We were professional people and accustomed to drama—but we cried openly after the first act. Solzhenitsyn examined us carefully. "When I read this to former inmates I know," he said, "they didn't cry. They laughed."

The contrasting reactions which Solzhenitsyn observed were a measure of the play's dramatic powers. To former prisoners who had lived through everything, the scene of drunken self-deception that ends the first act would indeed be hugely amusing. To other audiences, especially Russian ones, the nightmarish atmosphere in which the comedy is set would bring uncontrollable tears.

Solzhenitsyn said little after reading the play. Still somewhat intimidated by the "reader," [1] the company found it "magnificent." Even at a distance of eight years, the anonymous leading actor sighed nostalgically for it. "Lord, how we loved that play. How we wanted to do it!"

Solzhenitsyn's instructions for the sets and staging were meticulous.

---

[1] Conversation with Solzhenitsyn was at first slightly strained by his reputation. In awe of him, the members of the company whispered, "Let the man with the wide trousers talk"—and did not appreciate his genuine interest in *their* comments until later meetings.

The public was to be as deeply immersed as possible into the concentration-camp atmosphere. Spectators were to watch the action behind barbed wire strung along the orchestra pit, as if they had been brought to the fence of a camp. Guards were to march through the audience, barking orders to clear the way. Some reports maintain that it was the effect of this frightening realism on tense Russian nerves that aborted the play's premiere. At a preview for a select audience—according to these reports —several people became hysterical and many wept. As a result, the administrators of the theater, or its censors, decided that Russians could not yet face so graphic a portrayal of the recent past.

Another version—offered by several Sovremennik personnel, among others—has it that the company itself decided not to stage the play after preliminary run-throughs with the author. This was done, it is said, for tactical reasons and even with Solzhenitsyn's agreement, the aim being to prevent him from being labeled a "singer of a single melody," the concentration-camp theme. This version seems to be contradicted by Solzhenitsyn's publication at this very time of short stories unconnected with concentration camps—and by his accusation in 1967 that the play, which the Sovremennik had accepted five years before, "has not so far been cleared for production." Whatever form the ban took, its effect on Solzhenitsyn, in addition to keen disappointment, was to reinforce his reluctance to involve himself in arranging and organizing—or "pushing," in the Russian image. Shunning literary "business," he now devoted all his energies to writing, especially to *Cancer Ward*, which he began in 1963.

As Solzhenitsyn worked quietly, a series of skirmishes raged about him. The controversy he provoked in 1963 was many-faceted, diffuse, and above all verbose, but after a full year of the outpouring, Blagov felt called upon to write a literary analysis of Solzhenitsyn because "writers, literary critics, and specialists . . . seem to have their mouths full of dirty water which prevents them from speaking." Blagov's underground study, with its image of Solzhenitsyn's "microwaves" breaking up the stone in the inner being of the Soviet people, is the only known Soviet examination of *One Day*'s artistic power—and it was never published in Russia. Otherwise, the vast body of Soviet commentary about Solzhenitsyn is intended to score political points. Whether in the service of conservatism or of liberalism, these points shed considerable light on Soviet social and political conflicts—but reveal almost nothing about Solzhenitsyn's esthetic individuality. They could just as easily have been made about a very different writer dealing with his subjects. In their very political point-scoring, however, the polemics demonstrated yet again the power of his art. In attempting either to dismiss Solzhenitsyn or to make use of him, both conservatives and liberals illuminated *One Day*'s most significant qualities, if only by default. The arguments clearly indicated intensifying pressures on the writer.

The grand design of the "anti" campaign was unveiled in January 1963 by Lydia Fomenko, a leading conservative critic. She represented Solzhenitsyn as a good portrayer but a poor thinker, a man incapable of "embracing the conflicting social phenomena of his time." He did not understand that, despite "monstrous crimes" during Stalin's era, "the nation's inexhaustible creative power was accomplishing the great historic task" of building socialism and national might. Although "perhaps" lacking Solzhenitsyn's artistry, other writers who had been in the camps demonstrated a broader comprehension of Soviet life. They portrayed people who, whatever their suffering, "organically could not cease to be Communists."

By holding up the Shelest story (run in *Izvestiya*) as an example of the comprehension Solzhenitsyn lacked, Fomenko implied that the "anti" campaign in fact preceded *One Day*'s publication. Shelest had indeed described prisoners who "organically could not cease to be Communists" —as did Solzhenitsyn—but also suggested that these prisoners alone deserved sympathy; most of the others had been convicted with cause. In other words, Solzhenitsyn made clear that guiltless Communists *also* suffered, while Shelest implied that the innocent victims were *only* Communists.

Shelest's approach was developed and deployed throughout the year through the publication of suitable fiction as well as in literary criticism. Even in Russia it is now widely believed that Solzhenitsyn's was the only major tale of the camps officially published in the Soviet Union. In fact, several novels and memoirs appeared in 1963 whose descriptions of brutality often exceeded Solzhenitsyn's in bluntness. In March, for example, Boris Dyakov, a writer previously known for his works of homage to Soviet labor heroes, published a memoir of his time in camp in which guards are described as being offered regular bonuses for the murder of sick and weak prisoners, who were then reported "attempting to escape." Nothing in Solzhenitsyn's work matches the cruelty revealed by this and other of Dyakov's accusations. Yet conservative critics flourished his memoirs as an example to Solzhenitsyn. Their logic was simple: in Dyakov's interpretation, the party's fundamental policies had been correct and these errors, however savage, were no more than bureaucratic lapses in the judicial and penal systems. Even if the repression of "class enemies" had gotten out of hand in scale and execution, the important point was that the Soviet system *had* been threatened by dangerous, internal class enemies whose throttling *was* necessary. Solzhenitsyn's "poor thinking" had revealed itself in the absence of this heinous species of inmate in Ivan Denisovich's camp. And in the implied moral statement which underlies all of *One Day:* whatever crimes a handful of the prisoners had actually committed, those visited on them in return were so monstrous that the men had been turned into martyrs.

Of course the conservatives were enraged by much more than Solzhenitsyn's failure to "rise to the philosophy of the times," as Fomenko phrased it. If his representation of the camps was accurate, the men who had engineered the policy of class repression—in other words, many of the party's present leaders—were guilty of mass crimes. On Dyakov's evidence, by contrast, the maximum charge could only be negligence in supervision—and even this no longer held since the party had repented openly and sincerely, an act which, in the Russian national psychology, goes far toward dissolving the guilt itself.

Throughout Khrushchev's remaining eighteen months in power, *One Day* was subject to criticism in the Fomenko vein. It was expressed by implication, juxtaposition, and damning with faint praise; and usually accompanied by generous acknowledgment of Solzhenitsyn's talent. Only provincial newspapers unlikely to be brought to Khrushchev's attention permitted themselves to call Ivan Denisovich "a lackey ready to toady to anyone for a piece of sausage or pinch of tobacco." Mere authors and critics could not openly challenge a decision of the First Secretary. Moreover, most authors did not want to challenge it; at this point, *One Day* still enjoyed a clear preponderance of support.

And there was no lack of rebuttals to the Fomenko-Shelest thrust. Of these an article in *Novy Mir* was the most substantial. Its author was Vladimir Lakshin, Tvardovsky's right hand in the editorial offices as well as the chief of the department of literary criticism. A penetrating literary critic with encyclopedic knowledge of Russian literature, an implacable and witty campaigner against hack Soviet writing, Lakshin had done yeoman's work the previous year helping Tvardovsky enlist influential supporters for the manuscript of *One Day.* By making obvious points absolutely clear—Solzhenitsyn's careful avoidance of the most brutal horrors of the camps; his selection of a "good" day for Ivan Denisovich— he demolished the conservatives' "blackening" charges; by stressing the conditions of the camps in those years, he highlighted the hypocrisy of holier-than-thou detractors who found Ivan Denisovich unworthy of sympathy because he had stolen an odd bowl of soup from the kitchen and ousted a weaker prisoner from a mess-hall bench. But even Lakshin's defense of Solzhenitsyn was not free of cant in the liberal cause. He exaggerated Ivan Denisovich's enthusiasm for work, one of the novel's "selling points" to Khrushchev, to the point of calling it "perhaps" the prisoner's most valuable human quality. It was indeed a valuable asset in a political defense of the story; but much as he was addicted to hard work himself, Solzhenitsyn would scarcely agree that this was his protagonist's most important quality. Thus even Lakshin's polemics failed to illuminate Solzhenitsyn's esthetic individuality, although his article had the integrity to mention that some people might be troubled by the omission.

The criticism of *One Day* continued largely as "stealthy pin-pricks," in Lakshin's phrase. But Solzhenitsyn's three short stories—two published by *Novy Mir* in January 1963, and the third in July—were an entirely different kind of target. These works had no blessing from Khrushchev or the party Presidium, and their appearance was the signal for an open season on Solzhenitsyn.

The antiliberal wave that followed the November plenum was still rising when "Matryona's Place" and "An Incident at Krechetovka Station" were published in January. Khrushchev thus gave no further support to Solzhenitsyn beyond reaffirming the value of *One Day*. Nothing prevented the "anti's" from venting their full dislike of Solzhenitsyn—and, indeed, the first reaction to the two new stories was predominantly hostile. "Matryona's Place" was the essential statement of Solzhenitsyn's ethical credo of selfless generosity and love for one's neighbors. A Western critic pointed out that although the story—the old woman dying through others' greed for her roach-ridden hovel—clearly reflects the tenor of contemporary life, Solzhenitsyn's condemnation "applies as much or even more to Western as to Soviet society." For Matryona's virtues are "the very opposite of the selfishness, greedy materialism, and lust for possessions of modern capitalist societies." But such subtleties were not for Soviet critics of 1963. They saw in the story only an offensive description of village poverty and of Matryona's harrying by local authorities.

It is hard to imagine an ethical point more explicitly made and more perversely missed. Apparently confused by Solzhenitsyn's use of names of real villages, one journalist objected that rich collective farms could be found near Matryona's village—a spurious argument even in criticism of a newspaper article. Another attack, in the magazine *October* (edited by Kochetev), was unusually vicious. "The fundamental principles of our society, consecrated to serving the interests of the working people, appear [in the story] as a hostile, oppressive force," wrote its critic, implying that Solzhenitsyn intended to subvert the very foundations of the Soviet system—and foreshadowing future charges of "anti-Sovietism."

To give it its due, however, *October* was one of the few publications which even bothered to criticize Solzhenitsyn's second story. The very subject matter of "An Incident at Krechetovka Station"—secret police treatment of Soviet citizens during the war—prompted most publications to ignore the work completely. Its theme was subtle: one naïve but honest man denounces another to the NKVD as a spy and is tortured by his conscience for the rest of his life. In attitude and outlook, the protagonist is based on the positive hero of typical "socialist-realist" literature; and, in fact, he is a fundamentally benign and likable man. But Solzhenitsyn shows how isolated and "dark," in the Russian expression, his society's restrictions have made him.

Interlaced with these restrictions as the cause of the tragedy is the sense of alienation that pervaded Soviet society at that time, arising, in turn, from the senseless suspicion in which Soviet citizens were steeped. Although both denouncer and denounced belonged to the intelligentsia, propaganda campaigns about vigilance and spies had so estranged them that words no longer kept the same meaning: an innocent expression by one was a danger signal to the other. But *October* overlooked all of this; in its interpretation, the tale sought to demonstrate—since the two men's essential virtue came to nothing—that goodness and honesty were but a "house of cards" and that brutality alone carries weight. It was as if these crude and deliberate misunderstandings of Solzhenitsyn's stories were meant to prove the very theme of "An Incident."

Distortions of this kind were enough to provoke a writer of far less precision and moral purpose than Solzhenitsyn. Happily, however, this first bout of critical mutilation was brief. In April 1963 the grand anti-liberal counterattack launched in November began to decelerate unmistakably. It was no mature reconsideration of the campaign's purpose—control of the arts by party officials [2]—that brought this about, but more accidental factors. Kozlov suffered a severe heart attack in April, which incapacitated him for work. By this time, Khrushchev had gone far toward reestablishing his position as defender of the faith. Brakes were sharply applied to the crusade for orthodoxy, giving Solzhenitsyn several months of respite.

The first indication of improvement came in an editorial by Tvardovsky in *Novy Mir* (the delayed April issue, approved by the censors in early May). The editor lauded the Central Committee for the breadth of its literary viewpoint, demonstrated most clearly by its approval of *One Day*. The editorial went on to reinterpret the entire Kozlov-Suslov crusade as narrowly as possible, as if it had been directed only against a handful of abstract painters and an insignificant selection of poetry and prose. In case anyone believed that this editorial was Tvardovsky's private initiative, *Pravda* published an interview with him in early May, in which the same points were repeated and developed for the entire country.

Once again, the attitude toward Solzhenitsyn served as the hallmark for the change; once again, his role was wholly passive. From someone

---

[2] Party control of art was a matter for serious discussion. One interested person complained that the real trouble lay in the outmoded conditions under which writers work: they sit alone in their rooms, working away on goodness knows what without supervision. His recommendation was to install party supervisors who would examine the manuscripts in the process of their production, correcting the imperfections—on the basis of the necessary pattern—as the work progressed.

to distract attention while other writers were hounded, he was again made into the yardstick against which Soviet literature was to be measured. "In my opinion," Tvardovsky was quoted as saying, "*One Day* is one of those literary phenomena whose appearance makes it impossible to discuss any literary problem or literary fact without measurement against it."

Shortly after, the Central Committee's June plenum convened—to deal, as had been announced, especially with the party's ideological tasks. At one point, the intellectuals' hope for miraculous liberation at the November plenum had swung to the conservatives hoping to strangulate them totally—a reflection of the volatile mentality formed in the years when Stalin gave and took at will. But the politics of 1963 were less violently manipulable; more like a cow chewing ideological cud than a wolf hunting class enemies, the Central Committee limited itself to proclaiming eternal Marxist-Leninist verities, leaving liberals and conservatives to control their accustomed territory. As before *One Day,* the conservatives ran the party machinery and most publishing enterprises while the liberals had a foothold in several literary magazines and other cultural institutions. In the cold war of ideas, both sides had been sobered and learned caution. The war of movement, carrying hopes of a clinching victory, had become a war of position, with Solzhenitsyn one of the key redoubts.

In the return to familiar battlegrounds, Tvardovsky began to measure not only Soviet writers by Solzhenitsyn's talent, but world literature too. An international symposium of writers that met in Leningrad in August offered a suitable forum. The principal conflict at the symposium was between representatives of the *nouveau roman* proclaiming the extinction of the traditional novel and opposing writers, including the entire Soviet delegation, who defended realism as a living, even dominant, literary form. In support of the latter position, Tvardovsky drew on the evidence of Solzhenitsyn. "No new literary event can be judged unless in juxtaposition with this artist," he declared. Although the antinovelists were not to be convinced, all references to Solzhenitsyn's work evoked warm appreciation of its talent and social significance. By this time, Jean-Paul Sartre had joined Tvardovsky, implicitly abandoning his earlier opposition to fiction which might shatter illusions on the Left Bank and in working-class suburbs. Sartre offered "Matryona's Place," with its Tolstoyan penetration into the core of human morality, as a model for genuine socialist literature.

When informed of the issues at the symposium, Solzhenitsyn reacted less to the praise of his work than to what he considered the discussion's speciousness. On the issue of whether the traditional novel was alive or dead, his answer was a disparaging cliché—loosely translated, "the proof of the pudding is in the eating." The position of the antinovelists was strong, he remarked, only because the traditional novelists, Russians especially, undermined their own case by producing feeble novels.

Several years later, he elaborated on his antimodernist position.

From the West, they tell us that the novel is dead—and we wave our hands about and prepare speeches: no, it hasn't died. But the point is not to prepare speeches but to publish the kind of novels that would make them squint as if from a dazzling light. Then the *nouveau roman* will pipe down and the "neo-avant gardists" will be petrified.

Since Solzhenitsyn himself often regrets his considerable ignorance of twentieth-century Western literature, to say nothing of trends as recent as the *nouveau roman,* this hostility revealed the depth of his determination to remain a "nineteenth-century man" in artistic tastes. In the visual arts too, his strongly stated preference is for the naturalistic genres favored by the nineteenth-century Russian masters. His disapproval of cubist painting and of the notion that color photography has made naturalists redundant was expressed in a short story:

Experts teach us that in oils, everything needn't be painted just as is. That color photography exists for this. That instead of things themselves, the spirit of things should be conveyed in crooked lines and combinations of triangles and squares. But I'm perplexed: what color photograph can select the faces necessary to make the points desired? . . .

His censure was severe, even though, of course, many artists before him had reacted similarly to uncongenial trends: Tolstoy the moralist denied the value of Shakespeare the sensualist. In any case, Solzhenitsyn was deeply entrenched in his realistic ways, and his unequivocal opinions were not based on *One Day* alone. Although only his closest friends knew it, he had now almost completed *The First Circle* and was well into *Cancer Ward.*

Despite spasmodic criticism, the year following publication was the pinnacle of Solzhenitsyn's domestic success. Of the several tokens of official esteem, perhaps the most whimsical was an invitation to appear before the Military Collegium of the U.S.S.R. Supreme Court—the very body which had confirmed his sentence in 1945 and issued his rehabilitation twelve years later. Now moved by the part they had played in Solzhenitsyn's triumph, the justices wanted to complete their satisfaction by listening to him read from his work. So-called meetings with readers are a common feature in the life of established Soviet authors, but a command performance on this level is, to say the least, rare. And to crown the strangeness of the occasion, this was the first court that the convict-author ever faced; all legal phases of his case had been dealt with without his presence.

This and other demonstrations of official sympathy did not leave Solzhenitsyn untouched, and his attempt to bridge the gap with officialdom while holding to his principles was reflected in his writing of this period. The July issue of *Novy Mir* contained "For the Good of the Cause," his third short story. Each of Solzhenitsyn's previous publications had provoked a quantum intensification of controversy. Irrespective of all political vagaries, the new story caused an even sharper skirmish.

"For the Good of the Cause" is one of his weaker published works. Trite characterization of positive and negative heroes by physical features, introduction of superfluous characters for the sole purpose of exposition, unnatural-sounding word forms which fail to be expressive—these flaws make it seem that the story was written with uncharacteristic haste. This suspicion is enhanced by the extreme topicality of some of the themes: a party worker, for example, exhibits precisely the kind of yearning—to become a qualified specialist in some "productive" occupation—that Khrushchev tried to promote.

The story takes place in a technical college of a town much like Ryazan, where a similar incident is said to have happened in Reshetovskaya's institute. At the last moment, a building constructed for the college—partly by volunteer labor of enthusiastic students—is requisitioned for higher state needs. The justification is in terms of the good of the cause; the reality, that the decision served the careers of several local officials.

On this slender plot hang some of the greatest issues in contemporary Russia: moral, political, and even economic. For though it is artistically weak for Solzhenitsyn, the story burgeons with social content. As with *One Day*, he brought into the open many thoughts and moods that had been weighing down Russia in diffused forms.

These moral, political, and economic issues, all the thoughts and moods, reveal themselves through the requisitioning of the college building, as ordered by the First Secretary of the provincial party committee. Stories which revolve around a decision by this crucial political figure are abundant in Soviet literature—but in Solzhenitsyn's tale he does not intervene at the last moment to restore justice, as is virtually *de rigueur* in socialist realism. He is himself the source of injustice. Solzhenitsyn's First Secretary rules his province like a minor Stalin.

> As Stalin's word was once in Moscow, so is Knorozov's still now in this province: it was never reversed, never rescinded. And although there had been no Stalin for some time, there was Knorozov. . . . He could not imagine a different kind of leadership.

"Lenin died, but his cause lives on!" is one of the most frequently seen and heard of all Soviet slogans. The essence of Solzhenitsyn's tale can be grasped by replacing Lenin with Stalin.

To Russians, the story's impact is immediate and acute because of their instinctive reaction to the institution of the provincial First Secretary. One can imagine his role in every Russian province only by making, say, the governors of American states autocratic rulers who, operating both in their own interests and on orders from Washington, make all important decisions about the state's economic and social life as well as its political arrangements. One of Russia's heaviest burdens is the legacy Stalin left in the form of these "stiff, punctilious men" with iron masks for faces. Naturally enough, men of Knorozov's mentality, genuine "heirs of Stalin" in Yevtushenko's sense, gravitate to dominant positions within the party and implement the "party rule" that is but an abstraction in Western textbooks.

The reaction of Solzhenitsyn's characters to Knorozov's power reflected the social realities and hopes of the time. Some community leaders admired the First Secretary for the verve of his leadership. But conscious opposition had begun to manifest itself: students considering a strike; an idealist teacher suggesting that human and civic interests may sometimes have to be protected against the party and state. For the first time in Solzhenitsyn's work, a call appeared for the *glasnost*—openness and candor in public affairs—that was to become central to his entire campaign for democracy in Russia. Indeed, the story contains the first sketches of ideas which emerged three or four years later in Russia's small but extremely significant protest "movement."

Ideas of protest were embryonic here. Another means of dissolving the power of the Knorozovs—through flexible, understanding men within the party, whom Khrushchev liked to promote as representing his "new style" of leadership—turned out to be abortive. This and other elements of the story (such as ardent appeals to Lenin and Communist ideals) marked Solzhenitsyn's closest rapprochement with authority in his career as a published writer. Insofar as Khrushchev was anti-Knorozov, Solzhenitsyn was willing to help, to the point of writing this story, perhaps for the good of the de-Stalinization cause, with less than his full artistic powers.

But no inclusion of Communist ideals protected Solzhenitsyn from the wrath of orthodox critics. Delighted to register the absence of Solzhenitsyn's usual "plasticity and authenticity" of characterization, they pounced on the author, above all for having portrayed the triumph of injustice in Soviet society. No one claimed that Knorozov was just, but with seeming good will and tortuous hypocrisy it was argued that Solzhenitsyn was "unmodern" for suggesting that such a man could wield so much power. "Unmodern" meant that Solzhenitsyn imagined Stalinists playing roles from which they'd already departed in contemporary Soviet society. It was again emphasized that only "knowledge and deep understanding" of political laws—that is, support of the party's outlook—would allow Solzhenitsyn's talent to mature into greatness.

After the first negative verdict, weeks passed before space in the press was reluctantly yielded to support of Solzhenitsyn. The author of one article quickly took up the real issues behind the "tone of quiet good will" of the attacks. Certain people in authority, he said, were opposed to de-Stalinization; certain people liked to use the state's interest as camouflage while feathering their own nests. "For the Good of the Cause" exposed their tactics, methods, and philosophy.

Elsewhere, the attack on Solzhenitsyn was anything but quiet. Kochetov's *October* flailed the story as a distortion of Soviet reality—after all, the state builds dozens of technical colleges every year—and the magazine's blend of naïveté and viciousness was spiced by Kochetov's thinly veiled attack on the man who had unleashed Solzhenitsyn on the Soviet reader: Khrushchev himself, a cunning operator, he hints, whose adventures border on class treason. Kochetov's innuendo about Khrushchev a full year before his fall was so astonishing and dangerous that it was passed over in silence, and the main skirmish was confined to bitter political-literary politeness. In the end, literary considerations all but disappeared and everything boiled down to a crucial question: Are Knorozovs running the country or not?

Almost immediately after the defense of Solzhenitsyn appeared, critical fire was returned in these terms. With staunch editorial support, a prominent newspaper published a letter from a Leningrad party worker declaring that the atmosphere which Solzhenitsyn had described could not, in the author's opinion, exist anywhere in the country. *Novy Mir* answered with a selection of letters from Old Bolsheviks, lathe operators, and a university lecturer, all of whom testified that Knorozovs did indeed flourish and thanked Solzhenitsyn for having exposed them. The newspaper which had lent its editorial support to the "Knorozovs-are-no-longer-a-problem" forces sorrowfully regretted that *Novy Mir* had chosen to publish only letters in praise of its authors. *Novy Mir* then exposed conscious fraud behind this hypocritical sorrow: Tvardovsky's editorial board revealed that twelve letters it had received in support of Solzhenitsyn were but carbon copies of letters that had been sent—and never published—to the very newspaper which had accused it of slanting its selection. *Novy Mir* pressed home its argument in figures. In all, it had received fifty-eight letters about "For the Good of the Cause." Fifty-five were wholly positive. Two disapproved of Solzhenitsyn's prose style. Only one criticized the story itself—but in unprintable language. *Novy Mir* could not have run it in its columns, but were "ready at any moment to show it to the editors" of the antagonistic newspaper.

The controversy between Solzhenitsyn's supporters and his detractors had its encouraging side as well as its humorous aspects. Narrowly confined and cautiously worded as the arguments were, the underlying issues were the real stuff of politics in other countries—for which, in Russia, literature often served as the only vehicle for discussion. Solzhenitsyn had opened previously closed issues and expressed latent social and moral aspirations; and, as *Novy Mir* indicated, his initiative had stimulated others to think and even to express themselves. After Russia's decades of numbness, fifty-five letters meant as many awakened readers, willing to risk the anger of their own local Knorozovs.

By late 1963, within a year of the healing shock of *One Day*, Solzhenitsyn had become the focus of the most important literary-political controversy in the country. *One Day* had dealt with the recent past, but two of the three short stories touched on acute contemporary issues—primarily moral in "Matryona's Place," primarily political in "For the Good of the Cause"—and therefore the most sensitive nerves in contemporary Russia. From his seclusion in Ryazan, Solzhenitsyn followed the skirmishes that he had provoked with interest. He was excellently informed by his own reading and reports from his friends of opinions at home and also knew far more about his echo abroad than did the average Soviet citizen, partly by frequent listening to the Russian-language broadcasts of foreign radio stations. "He followed everything and knew everything about all the arguments involving him," said a close friend. "At least everything he could possibly learn in his circumstances."

Still Solzhenitsyn took no public part whatever in the skirmishes. He would not write, act, speak out, or involve himself in any matter before weighing the ramifications to his own demanding satisfaction.

XXV

Nomination

IN DEFENDING SOLZHENITSYN AS A "Soviet" writer, most liberals tried to make him comfortable to the conventional ear by removing the more ringing notes and passages. Their soft-pedaling not only blunted his political significance but distorted his artistic voice. In all his works until now, this voice had carried an unmistakable overtone of tragedy, reflecting the Russian people's powerlessness to accomplish significant changes in their hard lives. But official optimism made tragedy—that is, situations from which there was no successful, if not triumphant, outcome—unacceptable in the portrayal of life under the Soviet social system. This being so, many liberals tried to demonstrate that Solzhenitsyn's tragedies were not really that.

In early January 1964, for example, *Izvestiya* ran a feature which repeated the elements of "For the Good of the Cause" almost detail for detail—but the story had a *happy* ending because "in Smolensk [the setting of the controversy over a school building reported in the article] no diehard Knorozov turned up." Five days later, the same newspaper informed its readers that Lieutenant Commander Burkovsky (who, as Buinovsky in *One Day*, seemed destined to perish in a punishment cell after a furious but futile protest about camp conditions) was not dead at all, but flourishing in Leningrad and faithful to the party. The intention of these unusual articles was clear: to indicate that Solzhenitsyn did not portray genuine social tragedies, but merely isolated instances of injustice which, in Soviet literature no less than in Hollywood, resolved themselves happily in the end.

The caution that the liberals had acquired in the previous year was still very much operative, though manifesting itself in literary criticism more than in fiction. *Novy Mir* continued to publish sharp—in the Soviet context, even radical—prose and poetry; but liberal critics did not so much uncover as disguise its genuine significance. At the same time, conserva-

tive critics fell upon these works—and, in their loathing, came closer to
revealing their full implications than liberals in their protective love. Thus
the *October* critic who castigated Solzhenitsyn for having glorified Matryona's religiously rooted righteousness (with its passive acceptance of evil,
which, however, did not interfere with her own goodness—all in unmistakable contrast to the Soviet social ethic) was far closer to the story's
true meaning than the efforts of a liberal novelist to interpret the story
as an "unmasking" of righteousness.

Another conservative critic wrote in perceptive anger that Ivan Denisovich was far from the keen, active fighter that "life itself and the whole
history of Soviet literature" had shown as typical of the Soviet people, but
was far closer in spirit to the traditional Russian *muzhik*, formed by the
old fatalistic, patriarchal way of life. This reflected Solzhenitsyn's portrait
much more clearly than all the liberals' attempts to paint Ivan Denisovich
as a truly "Soviet" man in unusual circumstances. And in defending "For
the Good of the Cause" on the ground that it portrayed a good party
worker of the "new type" as well as Knorozov, liberals simply ignored that,
in the story, the expression of these very qualities leads to a party worker's
loss of influence.

The paradox was sharp: despite their affection for Solzhenitsyn—or
perhaps because of it—liberals were often less accurate in interpretation
than neo-Stalinists. It was not the first time that good men had resorted
to masking their thoughts for the sake of good causes. Kind warders in
the camps often passed themselves off as brutes.

The tactic of "defense by dilution" was most notably employed in
support of Solzhenitsyn's candidacy for the Lenin Prize. During the first
four months of 1964, engagement around this bastion was the most extensive battleground of the literary-political cold war.

Awarded annually at that time, the Lenin Prize for literature was a
seal of approval from the highest authority. Together with a substantial
monetary award, the title of laureate gave its bearer and his supporters
proof of their "Sovietness," and was as important for determining the drift
of literature in the immediate future as for its sign of the judgment reached
on the recent past. If Solzhenitsyn were to win the prize, it would be considerably more difficult to declare him a "mistake," whatever the course
of Soviet politics; Tvardovsky's ambition to make genuine realism the
standard of Soviet literature would be a long step closer to realization. It
was *Novy Mir* that nominated Solzhenitsyn, as the announcement of the
various candidates informed the public in the last days of 1963.

The news of Solzhenitsyn's nomination generated strong enthusiasm
among many scholars, scientists, and technicians, in addition to literary
liberals. For if such an author could be slid into the cartridge belt of

Soviet literature, opportunities not only for other writers but for historians, sociologists, even economists, to deliver their own vision of truth would be significantly improved. The Lenin Prize would be effective ammunition: "I'm only doing for my subject what Solzhenitsyn did for his." This hope played a significant part in the excitement of the next four months.

Although his candidacy seemed at first to have thin support—apart from *Novy Mir,* whose interest was obvious, the only official organization to support it was the Central State Archive of Literature and Art—the sheer dominance of, and continuing excitement about, *One Day* forced it forward. The nomination brought a deluge of mail, four times greater than the previous year, to newspapers and the selection committee, and, at their meetings about the prize, writers seemed reluctant to discuss other subjects. Articles began appearing in the press that seemed to catch this spirit too. It was not surprising that Lakshin, writing his extensive essay in *Novy Mir* about the entire background of Ivan Denisovich as a social phenomenon,[1] defended Solzhenitsyn vigorously—indeed, divided the whole of thinking Russia into Ivan's friends and enemies. Nor was the more cautious support of Adzhubei's *Izvestiya* unexpected. In late January, however, these publications were joined by nothing less than *Pravda,* the party's highest organ. Its editor, a Khrushchev appointee, commissioned Samuil Marshak, a highly popular poet who had won the Lenin Prize the year before, to write an article supporting Solzhenitsyn's candidacy. Marshak was one of the weighty literary experts whom Tvardovsky had enlisted to impress Khrushchev when *One Day* was still a manuscript, and his *Pravda* article was an extremely forceful recommendation of the novel.

By February, a genuine draft for Solzhenitsyn seemed to be developing. With some two and a half months remaining, the neo-Stalinists became alarmed enough to attack Solzhenitsyn in a new way. Dropping the pretense of amity, they treated him for the first time as a conscious foe.

One of the principal assailants was Dmitri Eremin, a leading party official in the Writers' Union known for his angry sallies against the first stirrings of freer literature after Khrushchev's "Secret Speech." At an important meeting of Russian writers convened to discuss the prize, Eremin, again illustrating the paradox of Solzhenitsyn's attackers revealing essential qualities of his art, declared that it would be a grave mistake to award a Lenin Prize to an author whose philosophy departed so fundamentally from Leninism and its "active fighting spirit." Solzhenitsyn was in fact far closer to Tolstoyan philosophy, with its "worship of passive sanctity and meekness of simple, ordinary people." Polite as he was, Eremin's meaning was unmistakable, and his impudence—the implication that First Secretary Khrushchev had sponsored a philosophy widely disparate from

---

[1] See p. 199.

Leninism—caused early speculation about possible support for him in high party circles. The speculation was to grow with each attack, and the selection committee's final days would show that it was far from idle.

⌊Meanwhile, the committee began its first weeding in early February. Two weeks later, an unusually long interval, it was announced that seven of the nineteen submitted works had been selected for the second round. Six of the seven books, by liberal as well as conservative authors, ranged from mediocre to mildly talented. The seventh was *One Day*, discussion of which had clearly caused the committee's unusual lingering over the first round.⌋

The announcement that Solzhenitsyn's novel was still in the running provoked an even more impudent attack, which, although phrased in excruciating evasions, advanced the charge against the author. In place of relatively lofty arguments about philosophical deviation from Leninism he was now identified in terms of tangible, immediate political danger to people who had "lived as adults" under Stalin—that is, those in Soviet society who had ridden high under Stalin and were still doing so these ten years later. Solzhenitsyn's attacker, in other words, was saying that repentant Stalinists who supported Solzhenitsyn—such as Khrushchev himself—were digging their own graves. The broadcasting of Solzhenitsyn's voice through the land might make the whole edifice of dictatorship weaken and crumble.

This cynical but brave warning came—on the very next day after the second tour announcement—in the form of an editorial article in the *Literary Gazette*, the newspaper of the Writers' Union. It was the same newspaper which had perpetrated the petty letter-counting fraud in its polemic with *Novy Mir* two months before. The *Literary Gazette* was one of the most important strongholds seized by neo-Stalinists in their offensive during the previous winter. It was now run with a strong, skilled hand by its new editor, Alexander Chakovsky, whose opposition to Solzhenitsyn was heightened—although it needed no direct personal interest of this sort—by the coincidence that he himself was one of the seven remaining candidates for the prize. Quite apart from this, the editor, a highly intelligent and articulate conservative, was emerging as one of Solzhenitsyn's most determined and enduring foes. Like Inspector Javert dogging Jean Valjean, Chakovsky would continue to hound Solzhenitsyn. He behaved as if Victor Hugo's saying—"Literary freedom is the daughter of political freedom"—were his guiding principle, but applied in reverse of Hugo's intention.

Thus by late February, the support for Solzhenitsyn had provoked a hard core of opposition, no less determined for its unwillingness to speak in clear language. The opposition was strong enough to prompt concern in *Izvestiya* about the outcome of the third and final ballot—which, being secret, lent itself to what the newspaper called "extraneous considerations"; that is, to outside pressures. *Izvestiya* warned that if the open discussions and first two ballots gave clear preference to a certain work of art, the selection committee would have to account to the Soviet public—a favorite Khrushchev menace—in the "abnormal" circumstance of that work failing to win the final vote.

Arguments and innuendos proliferated. Had he chosen, Solzhenitsyn could easily have undermined the conservatives' case. A single article from him containing the faintest nod in the direction of the party leadership would have enhanced his advocates' position enormously. He could have made such a gesture while maintaining his position; indeed, accomplished it simply by noting the party's role in dismantling Stalin's cult. But to resort to the double-talk of literary politics would have offended the writer's dignity. Khrushchev too did nothing—nothing public, at least—to help his protégé's candidacy, although a few words in a speech indicating continuing allegiance to the writer might well have swung the balance irrevocably. But in these last months of his waning power, the First Secretary was often out of Moscow and had become increasingly passive.

In March, the conservatives intensified their counterattack. A shift in position by *Pravda* signified that urgent maneuvering was taking place behind the façade of noninterference at the highest level. The party newspaper first withdrew its support of Solzhenitsyn and declared itself neutral; then, shortly before the April vote, indicated that in the opinion of most Soviet people, *One Day* was not, after all, worthy of a Lenin Prize.

But despite changes in the official organs of public opinion, that opinion itself was still strongly pro-Solzhenitsyn. So strongly, in fact, and in such unusual volume that when the selection committee met for the final vote in mid-April, *One Day* was still the favorite nomination. It was only now, at the last minute, that the directors of backstage intrigues against Solzhenitsyn were forced to step out from the wings. The selection committee was composed of essentially cautious, senior literary establishment figures and representatives of several important "social" organizations such as trade unions and the Young Communist League. Tvardovsky was the most active of the small liberal contingent, and it was he who made the presentation in support of *One Day*. His speech in elaboration of the novel's merits was uncharacteristically blunt and, perhaps remembering *Izvestiya*'s warning in February of accountability to public opinion, many of the members appeared to be persuaded. No one could predict the final ballot with certainty, but according to one excellently informed observer *One Day* had "the strongest chances," and seemed on the verge of sanctification with Lenin's name. Then a man named Sergey Pavlov rose to speak.

Pavlov addressed the committee as the First Secretary of the Young

Communist League, a position of vast influence. Beyond this, he was known to enjoy the most intimate relationship with Vladimir Semichastny, the Chairman of the KGB: when Semichastny himself was leader of the Young Communists (from which he was directly promoted to head the security police) Pavlov had been his right-hand man. The views on Soviet culture of these extremely powerful young statesmen were unambiguous: in his time, Semichastny had called Pasternak "worse than a swine," and only a year before he now rose to speak, Pavlov, in a reference to Yevtushenko and his circle, had appealed for a skimming of the "dirty scum" from the clean waters of Soviet literature. These men were almost caricatures of the younger generation of Stalinists in power: Yevtushenko later described them as yearning to "knead poets' souls like wax" into their own image.

Pavlov did not limit himself to a discussion of *One Day*'s artistic merits, or even to the political issue of whether or not its truths were "Leninist." It was Solzhenitsyn's honor which he attacked. Comrades, he said, possible new evidence has just come to light. There has not been time to investigate it thoroughly; therefore, I am not saying that the following reports are true—but it is my duty to give a signal now. It appears that the author of *One Day* may have concealed an important aspect of his past. Much sorrow has been lavished on him as a victim of Stalin's purges, but according to information now available, he in fact served his sentence for nothing but a common crime. And furthermore, he was never rehabilitated. Over and above this, he was a prisoner of the Germans during the war, and you all know what that might mean.[2] These reports are as yet unverified, but you can well imagine the terrible scandal if they turn out to be true—about a Lenin Prize laureate.

Coming from a man whose relationship with the head of the KGB was common knowledge—as was the KGB's reputation as an investigating agency of people's backgrounds—this warning could not be dismissed, even by the skeptical. Tvardovsky leapt to his feet shouting that he knew Solzhenitsyn's record not from hearsay but from documents. But he did not have copies of Solzhenitsyn's documents with him, naturally enough, and there was no time to produce them: the selection committee was working to a deadline, since the awards were always announced on April 22, Lenin's birthday. Since the committee was unwilling to accept Tvardovsky's word on such a potentially damaging matter, it was immediately clear that Solzhenitsyn would not win the prize. Several days later, when Tvardovsky did produce documents showing that Pavlov's "information" was false on every point, the Young Communist chief apologized willingly; but his work had been done. The prize had gone to an undistinguished

[2] This was a clear hint that Solzhenitsyn might have collaborated.

novel by a Ukrainian writer. Still loyal to Solzhenitsyn, Adzhubei reacted by publishing not the customary article of praise, but an excerpt from the winning novel which served to display its mediocrity.

For liberals, it was a defeat that went well beyond the loss of the prize's potential political and psychological benefits. They retired from this engagement clearly weakened; their banner had been stained by Pavlov's innuendo. The announcement of the prize was handled in its usual way, as if there had been no excited public debate; together with the rest of the committee's proceedings, Pavlov's speech remained secret. Nevertheless, word quickly circulated through Moscow's intelligentsia.

By nature a man who jealously guards his good name, Solzhenitsyn was enraged by Pavlov's character assassination. "There are great men," said one of Solzhenitsyn's closest friends, "who don't care about their reputation; Alexander Isaiyevich is not one of them. He finds it very hard to forgive those who cast the slightest shadow on the morality of his behavior." Of course Pavlov had not merely cast a shadow, but tried to sully some of Solzhenitsyn's proudest years as a front-line officer.

Solzhenitsyn's fury was accompanied by a new wave of misgivings over having played any public role at all in a Russia still dominated by Stalinist political instincts. And indeed, the fiasco of the Lenin Prize nomination was the beginning of a new time of troubles. If, during the halcyon days of 1962, he had felt that his years of caution after leaving camp had been excessive, now event after event made him regret his temporarily dropped guard. Solzhenitsyn once stated that he valued his inner calm even more than the immediate fate of his works. From this point and for many years, Pavlovs and Chakovskys would take pains to disturb this inner calm regularly.

Solzhenitsyn at the age of 21

1943: First Lieutenant

Solzhenitsyn in the late 1950s

1955: in his cottage in Kok-Terek
1959: writing "Matryona's Place"

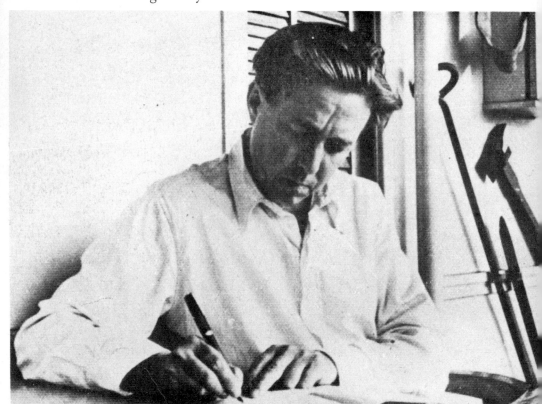

1965: Moscow

Ryazan: the new apartment building on Yablochky Street
where Solzhenitsyn moved in 1966

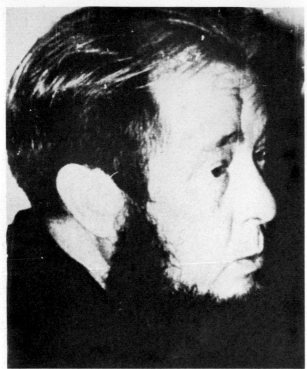

1968 or 1969
(more precise date not known)

1968: Obninsk

Fiftieth birthday

With Kornei Chukovsky, "granny" of Soviet letters

1968: "The Three Musketeers of Sharashka—Twenty Years On." In the *First Circle* the three were portrayed as (left to right): Lev Rubin, Gleb Nerzhin, Dmitry Sologdin.

1972: Solzhenitsyn with his new family, Natalya   Svetlova
and Yermolai

XXVI

Interdictions

SOLZHENITSYN AND TVARDOVSKY RECOGNIZED that the failure to win the Lenin Prize was not only that, but also an opening for attacks by powerful neo-Stalinists. Tvardovsky was confident that their offensive would be temporary, that the slanders would backfire against their initiators, and that more anti-Stalinist literature would be published in the end, including new works by Solzhenitsyn. Solzhenitsyn was far more skeptical about his future. Yet neither man—no one in Russia, for that matter—believed that he would not publish again in Russia—which, except for two slight works, would be the case. During the coming years, Solzhenitsyn was to encounter proliferating bans, escalating slander, frustration after frustration in attempts to publish and, finally, police harassment.

Tvardovsky's enduring confidence was based on resumed support from Khrushchev. A visit by the editor-poet to the First Secretary at his Black Sea villa was given wide publicity. At the same time, *Izvestiya* published Tvardovsky's sharply satirical poem about the Soviet bureaucracy—a work that had circulated for a decade in typescript and been published abroad, but until then suppressed by the censors. In the same month that Solzhenitsyn's nomination was rejected, *Novy Mir* ran an editorial mentioning Khrushchev's "precious support" for its anti-Stalinist policy, in the face of "unconcealed hostility" by certain nameless people. After allusions and implications, this was the first explicit statement of Khrushchev's role in the publication of anti-Stalinist literature. Clearly, Tvardovsky would not have made this personal reference, so unusual in Soviet politics, had he thought it might displease the First Secretary. And Khrushchev's support allowed Tvardovsky to regard the Lenin Prize failure as merely an unpleasant reversal in a generally forward trend.

In November 1963, *Novy Mir* quietly announced that "a new story by A. Solzhenitsyn" would be published in the following year. The first seven months of 1964 passed with no further mention of story or author. In

August, UPI reported from Moscow that the story would appear very soon —in the July issue of *Novy Mir*. (As often, exhausting maneuverings to outwit the censors—not only on Solzhenitsyn's account—delayed the magazine's appearance.) Reporting that the decision to publish had been taken after a backstage debate in literary circles, the news agency summarized the plot, which centered on the reawakening of viciousness in former guard dogs of a labor camp closed after Stalin's death. However, this story, which subsequently appeared in *samizdat* and was believed by many to be Solzhenitsyn's, was in fact by another author. *Novy Mir*'s July issue appeared in late August—with nothing by Solzhenitsyn, and his promised story is still unpublished. Whoever had given Tvardovsky permission was overruled, even at the cost of international embarrassment over a clear demonstration of literary suppression.

This first outright suppression of a Solzhenitsyn work was a bitter disappointment to Tvardovsky. Clearly Khrushchev's "precious support" no longer worked its former magic. But a single defeat would not force the hardened editor into a general retreat. That summer, Lakshin summed up *Novy Mir*'s attitude to a visiting Yugoslav journalist. "Each time we find ourselves under attack," said Lakshin, "we publish something even sharper instead of defending ourselves." These were the tactics now adopted in Solzhenitsyn's case, with his new novel serving as the vehicle. For at this time, *The First Circle*—which was indeed something sharper—had been virtually completed.

As for Solzhenitsyn himself, the ban could only have rekindled his old fears, and his behavior in the preliminary stages of *The First Circle* affair confirms this impression. Despite his great trust in Tvardovsky, despite the editor's proven devotion, Solzhenitsyn was unwilling to send a manuscript of the novel to *Novy Mir* before a contract for publication was signed. Understanding his caution, Tvardovsky himself traveled to Ryazan in late summer or early autumn. His first reading of the novel gave him a kind of double shock. He was overwhelmed by its artistic and moral power— its deeply moving exploration of the depths and ramifications of Russia's multiple tragedies—yet the exploration was far more extensive than he had imagined. Stalinism's deepest historical roots were uncovered and its injustices, even the most petty, fixed as if on film. Stalin had been previously portrayed in Soviet literature as unmercifully cruel, but now Solzhenitsyn showed him as also pathetically vainglorious and pitiably isolated. This made his spell over his lieutenants—the country's present rulers— even less excusable, and was bound to anger them.

Unlike *One Day*, with its devotion to honest toil on the part of some prisoners, nothing in *The First Circle* softened the devastating impact on the official eye and ear. The naïveté of Western "friends of the Soviet Union," previously a sacrosanct subject, was mercilessly satirized. In describing the present ("For the Good of the Cause") Solzhenitsyn had demonstrated that he was not implacably opposed to the party—more precisely, to the liberal faction's aspirations. But no such concession obtained in his description of the past. The novel's sole "selling point" was the respect of several of its positive characters for Lenin—indeed, the inspiration they found in him. According to friends of Solzhenitsyn, Tvardovsky told him that he was too radical. "You can't forgive Soviet rule anything," the editor sighed. Nevertheless, he felt *The First Circle* was a truly great novel and promised to take up the hard fight for its publication.

Soon after the editor returned to Moscow, *Novy Mir* signed a contract for the novel. Even if the manuscript were to fall into "the wrong hands" now, it could not easily be branded "anti-Soviet" (the basis for a criminal charge) without an implication that *Novy Mir* was an accomplice. Solzhenitsyn sent copies of the manuscript to Moscow, but the first stage of the campaign for publication, the unavoidable assembling of commendations by literary luminaries, had hardly begun when Soviet politics took a drastic new turn.

In October 1964, Khrushchev was deposed. Solzhenitsyn's pangs over his lessened chances for publication were accompanied by an almost affectionate contempt for the former First Secretary himself. "The Tsar's throne," he told a friend, "has been vacated by Little Fool Ivan, maybe the first and last of the line." Little Fool Ivan is a stock figure of Russian folklore, a naïve, bungling peasant who often precipitates disasters but, thanks to his hidden strength and straightforwardness, conquers evil and marries the fair princess in the end. Despite this humorous detachment, however, his patron's overthrow caused Solzhenitsyn considerable apprehension. Khrushchev's successors, the group who became known as the collective leadership under First Secretary Leonid Brezhnev and Prime Minister Alexey Kosygin, did not immediately reveal themselves as rigid disciplinarians, determined to stifle all change. On the contrary, they tried at first to win the confidence of all social groups, including the liberal intelligentsia's. But Solzhenitsyn recognized the rulers as Stalin-trained bureaucrats, among whom it was too much to hope—at the very least, in terms of mathematical probability—that another Little Fool Ivan would predominate. The First Secretary's personal opposition to *One Day* was also widely known. When Solzhenitsyn met Tvardovsky shortly after Khrushchev's fall, a mutual friend sensed a deep unease in the writer. "Solzhenitsyn was worried like nobody else about Khrushchev's overthrow," the friend remarked. "Tvardovsky kept reassuring him that nothing terrible had happened. But Solzhenitsyn's eyes were full of anxiety and depression."

Despite Tvardovsky's reassurances, he himself realized that, at best, the fight for *The First Circle* would be much more arduous without Khrushchev. Later in October, *Novy Mir* announced works scheduled for publication in 1965. This time, nothing was promised from Solzhenitsyn, but readers were told that he was "working on a big new novel." The implication was that the magazine would like to publish it, but no assurances could be made.

By midsummer of the following year, Tvardovsky's campaign for publication had reached a critical stage. In late July, he and the author were invited to discuss *The First Circle* and other literary matters in the office of Pyotr Demichev, the Secretary of the Central Committee in charge of Ideological Affairs. Demichev promised nothing, though behaved with courtesy and apparent goodwill. But the civilized treatment of Solzhenitsyn at this level—he was still, after all, a respected Soviet writer—was in grotesque contrast to the petty abuse visited upon him in his daily life, persecution of which officials of Demichev's level could not be unaware, if they had not actually devised it.

Solzhenitsyn's persecution had begun with Sergey Pavlov's sinister "error" before the Lenin Prize committee and gradually, if irregularly, gained momentum throughout the following year. Like Pavlov's insinuation and apology, not a word of it reached the press in any form, but it was no less real, and in a certain way more exasperating, for that. As Solzhenitsyn worked in Ryazan—by this time, he was polishing the final drafts of *Cancer Ward*—reports filtered back to him of persistent, swelling slanders against his background and intentions. The rumors were varied, in some cases imaginative. Solzhenitsyn later charged that they were set in motion "at closed briefings and meetings by people occupying official posts." Some had it, in the Pavlov vein, that he had served time as a common criminal. Others described him as having surrendered voluntarily to the Germans—even serving the German cause. Still others maintained that he "committed treason" in some other unspecified way. In March 1965, the First Secretary of the Moscow Communist Party, a figure of great importance, denounced *One Day* as "ideologically and artistically debatable" (i.e., "too wrong to justify debate"). It was the first public attack on this work by a member of the party leadership. At approximately this time, Solzhenitsyn heard that some libraries had received instructions to withdraw *One Day* from circulation. The instructions were followed: in some cases, the book was removed to the "special fund" to which access is granted only by permit.

Throughout the year, the writer and his work were increasingly harassed. Relatively low-level and unaccompanied by publicity, the persecution was unknown to the outside world and difficult for Russians themselves to document—indeed, to measure in terms of extent and intensity. Solzhenitsyn himself learned of it only because his admirers and well-wishers, distressed by the rumors and inexplicable unavailability of

One Day, took the time to pass on their evidence to him. If the world press somehow got wind of the story at this point, it could be explained away by references to excessive zeal by a minor official of one or another locality. Solzhenitsyn, however, strongly suspected that the planning had been done at a higher level.

From his perspective, at the center of intense surveillance, he needed no telling that the personal side of his harassment, at least, could not have been seen to without thorough high-level organization. Sergey Pavlov's background and attitudes had left little doubt that his attack on Solzhenitsyn was in some way inspired by the KGB. By now, Solzhenitsyn had no doubt whatever of that agency's interest in him. Years later, he protested bitterly against "the inspection of all my correspondence, the confiscation of half of it, the search of my correspondents' houses and their official and administrative persecution, the spying around my house, the shadowing of visitors, the tapping of telephone conversations, the drilling of holes in ceilings, the placing of recording apparatus" in his residences . . . Solzhenitsyn here was describing the full panoply of KGB measures employed against him throughout the following years. But it was after the Lenin Prize episode that he first discovered the degree of their interest in him.

A fair measure of both the extent of Solzhenitsyn's harrying and the official duplicity about it was revealed during his protracted efforts to move his household during the greater part of 1965. A record of these efforts was kept by Dr. Zhores Medvedev, a geneticist of international standing and good friend of Solzhenitsyn, whose own persecution by the authorities five years later would provoke one of Solzhenitsyn's most angry challenges of KGB methods. The story began when the opportunity arose for Solzhenitsyn and Reshetovskaya to move from Ryazan to more desirable quarters in another town. They had long sought another location within Ryazan itself, for along with its charms, their ground-floor flat in the log house was cramped and damp. "But the local authorities," Medvedev wrote, "irritated by 'For the Good of the Cause' with its description of the Ryazan episode, had long refused the writer the opportunity to improve his working conditions."

Early in 1965, Solzhenitsyn had a reunion with Professor Timofeyev-Resovsky. The scientist who had organized Solzhenitsyn's 1945 lecture on atomic physics in Butyrka prison now held a high post in a medical research institute in the town of Obninsk. Primarily a cluster of scientific institutes set in unspoiled countryside—a much smaller version of the new "science cities"—Obninsk lies near the main Moscow-Kiev road, roughly 80 miles southwest of the capital city. During Solzhenitsyn's reunion with Timofeyev-Resovsky there, the professor mentioned that his institute had an opening for a senior research chemist which Reshetovskaya might fill. The job would be a significant professional advancement for her, and for Solzhenitsyn Obninsk was attractive on three accounts: it was quiet, boasted a large intellectual community employed in the town's research institutes, and would cut the traveling time of his "errand" trips to Moscow.

Reshetovskaya entered the competition for the research post. As was customary, the decision was made by the institute's Learned Council in secret ballot—in which Reshetovskaya, whose association with Solzhenitsyn was known by only one scientist, won eighteen of twenty ballots on the basis of her credentials. "Essentially, there were virtually no serious competitors for her post," wrote Medvedev (who was also a member of the institute and worked under Timofeyev-Resovsky).

The Solzhenitsyns prepared to move. As they embarked on the first of many bureaucratic formalities, the Obninsk authorities realized who the husband was, whom Natalya Reshetovskaya was planning to bring to the town with her, and they fell into panic. "Until then," comments Medvedev, "the small town was all peace and quiet. Neither the city party committee nor the Young Communist organization nor other urban agencies had known any perturbations." Pressure to stop the Solzhenitsyns from moving was generated locally; higher authorities—especially the "urban agency" —had good reason to be responsive to it. "Evidently the system of surveillance of the writer had been well worked out in Ryazan. Now it would have to be dismantled and set up elsewhere. In Ryazan, the writer was isolated to a certain degree, whereas in Obninsk he would find himself in a circle of scientists, and they might ferment."

In late July, Medvedev was told in confidence that Reshetovskaya's candidacy would not be sent to Moscow for official approval. To prevent her resigning from her post in Ryazan, he quickly informed the Solzhenitsyns. It was just at this time that the writer and Tvardovsky visited Demichev—to whom, after their discussion of literary matters, Solzhenitsyn told the story in outline. Demichev's reaction was outrage. He "assured the writer that he would put a stop to the lawlessness and on the spot, in the writer's presence, telephoned on a direct official line to the First Secretary" of the region in which Obninsk lies. Demichev gave strict orders that the First Secretary personally ensure that everything possible be done to welcome the Solzhenitsyns in Obninsk, starting with the assignment to them of a fine flat. The next day, the kingpin of the district indeed scurried about Obninsk to supervise preparations for the couple's imminent arrival. Assurances were given to Reshetovskaya that the job was hers, and justice not only seemed done but was seen to be done. With this security, and on the suggestion of the Obninsk institute's director, Reshetovskaya did resign from her job in Ryazan.

But "for some reason," as Medvedev puts it, Moscow's confirmation of her new appointment was not forthcoming. And after more delay, not only did *she* find herself unemployed; so did all sixty senior scientists who had won competitions for the other vacancies in Obninsk. The Learned Council's entire selection (unusually large that year) was declared null and void —and the composition of the council itself altered before the entire process was begun again. All this subterfuge, together with the accompanying dislocation to the lives of more than sixty families and disruption of scientific work, was felt necessary in order to exclude Solzhenitsyn from Obninsk without allowing anyone to prove why. Had it done nothing more than impugn the honesty of an important institute's Learned Council, this episode would have been remarkable.

But the arsenal of foul play was far from exhausted. Despite the reshuffling of the council, Reshetovskaya stood an excellent chance of winning the post in the second competition. To prevent this, a set of even more breathtaking ruses was employed. The voting slips for Reshetovskaya's post—and her post alone—were not prepared on time, causing postponement of the vote on her case because it was unthinkable without the required slips of paper. The postponement was in violation of the rules of competition. While the vote was still pending, the Presidium of the Academy of Medical Sciences of the U.S.S.R. (to which the Obninsk institute was subordinate) convened in Moscow to allow the august body to debate a single question: to permit or not to permit Reshetovskaya to stand again for the post. Finally a pretext was found: in the absence of the head of the institute laboratory, who was eager to employ Reshetovskaya, it was argued in speech after speech that a senior chemist who had worked in agricultural research could not fill a chemistry post in medical research. However, the institute's director disagreed, and Reshetovskaya remained in the running. Concerted efforts to recruit a stronger candidate proved unsuccessful. Finally, the same Presidium of the Academy of Medical Sciences "suddenly revised the institute's personnel table, canceling the vacant chemistry post." Actually, the position was not eliminated but transferred to a clinic subordinate to the Ministry of Health. Since ministerial posts are filled by appointment rather than competition, Reshetovskaya could now be excluded without further trouble—or explanation or interference from stubborn Obninsk scientists. Just one final step was required: interdepartmental shifts of posts must be authorized by the U.S.S.R. Council of Ministers, the highest governmental body in the land. This meant making a chemistry job an affair of state—but, as Medvedev comments dryly, "it was a special case."

This is an abbreviated account of why Solzhenitsyn did not move to Obninsk at this time; the full saga involves a degree of casuistry, equivocation, callousness, and derangement—let alone sheer waste of valuable scientific and governmental time—that even Soviet citizens find difficult to follow. The central element throughout, from the "failure" to produce voting slips to the marshaling of eminent medical voices in support of ludicrous arguments, was a kind of Byzantine duplicity, ameliorated only by characteristic clumsiness and bureaucratic inefficiency. In the end, it remained unclear whether Demichev had taken an active part in the deception, as Medvedev strongly suggests, or whether his good intentions were simply overruled. In either case, by the time the affair dragged to its sorry end in late autumn, Demichev's motives had become a matter of relative unimportance. For before this, Solzhenitsyn had been faced with far graver difficulties than ministerial ruses to prevent him from moving. Earlier in the autumn, his worst fears at the moment of his literary surfacing three years before seemed about to be realized, for the KGB now had made a direct intrusion into Soviet literary affairs, including his own. The campaign of security-police repression which has lasted until today was launched only weeks after Solzhenitsyn's meeting with Demichev.

Tvardovsky's campaign to publish *The First Circle* dragged on into September. By this time, neither he nor Solzhenitsyn had any great hope of success, but the editor continued to draw on all his cunning and finesse in literary-political tactics. He cultivated personal relationships where he could, including one with Alexey Kosygin, the new Prime Minister. Solzhenitsyn was kept fully informed.

Early in September, the writer went to the *Novy Mir* office during one of his regular "business" trips to Moscow. There he collected three copies of the massive *The First Circle* which he had earlier supplied to the editors. He put them into a small suitcase and left the editorial office; Medvedev reports that he required them for "a certain amount of rewriting," and Solzhenitsyn later confirmed that the editors had proposed some changes. To avoid carrying the rather heavy suitcase with him on his errands in the sprawling capital, he took it to the flat of D. Blagov, his "first reader" and trusted Ryazan friend. Now retired, Blagov had left Ryazan and settled in Moscow. On September 11, officers of the KGB appeared at Blagov's flat with a search warrant and confiscated the three copies of *The First Circle*, together with other materials belonging to both men.

The underhandedness of this operation was underlined by the explanation of what had provoked the search. Improbable as it sounded even then, the KGB stated that it had nothing to do with Solzhenitsyn directly but was merely part of an investigation to determine Blagov's identity, inasmuch as his article about Solzhenitsyn had been found criminally "anti-Soviet." The KGB later embroidered their story, claiming that a foreign tourist had been apprehended trying to smuggle Blagov's article abroad. Convinced that the contents of his suitcase had prompted the raid, Solzhenitsyn bluntly branded the KGB stories "a lie." "My place of safekeeping," he said angrily, "was discovered by ordinary, everyday street-shadowing, tapping of telephone conversations, and bugging of rooms."

The secret police stuck to Solzhenitsyn like cobwebs. His friends assume that someone in the *Novy Mir* office, perhaps even one of the typists who had seen him pack the manuscripts into his suitcase, alerted the KGB as soon as he left the door, after which he was followed to Blagov's flat. The tightness of their surveillance was probably animated by their reaction to *The First Circle*, which, as a matter of official procedure, would have been read by a rather high-level security-police officer in the months when the manuscript lay with *Novy Mir*. In the novel's description of meticulous, automatonlike NKVD officers of 1949, such a reader could not help recognizing his own contemporary KGB colleagues, if not himself. The novel's security-police lieutenants and majors had moved up to colonels and generals in the intervening years.

In the same hour of that September 11, the KGB raided the flat of a young Moscow engineer, Blagov's closest friend. He too had been keeping some of Solzhenitsyn's papers—among other items the one and only copy of "The Feast of the Victors." Although the typescript of the bitter verse drama was unsigned, its authorship was soon established. The single work publicly branded as "anti-Soviet" (as opposed to merely slanderous or ideologically immature), this was to become the authorities' most powerful weapon against Solzhenitsyn. Theoretically, the threat of prosecution for it still hangs over his head.

These forays, together with the subsequent summoning to Lubyanka and questioning of several of Solzhenitsyn's friends who might have read *The First Circle* manuscript, brought the writer's alarm to its highest pitch. "It seemed to me an unforgivable mistake," he has written, "that I had uncovered my work prematurely, and so wouldn't be able to bring it to completion." The dismay over the threatened frustration of his mission would remain with him for many months, but his first reaction was an understandable guilt about having exposed his friends, especially the aging Blagov, to possible danger. According to a story widespread in Moscow literary circles, Solzhenitsyn felt so strongly about this that he hurried to the KGB to demand a hearing. It was granted, and Solzhenitsyn told the officers that Blagov knew nothing about the contents of the suitcase. If the novel contained elements of a crime, he argued, it was he who should be "investigated," and, if not, the manuscript should be quickly returned. The KGB reply is not known, but in response to later inquiries from the Writers' Union the agency stated that the confiscation was a "security measure" intended, in Solzhenitsyn's own interests, to prevent his manuscript from reaching the West and being exploited by profit-hungry publishers.

That the KGB had waited for the manuscript to leave the *Novy Mir* office before seizing it indicated their unwillingness to risk challenging Tvardovsky directly. However, nothing more was heard about publishing *The First Circle* in the Soviet Union, and it can be assumed that the editor now understood that further efforts could only be futile.

Far from worrying about possible danger to themselves, Solzhenitsyn's friends were proud to have helped him and were more concerned about *his* safety and the fate of his work. For it is a well-established NKVD-KGB pattern to attack an important target first through his friends, undermining the victim's morale and generating a public impression that he has been moving in unsavory circles.

The situation looked even grimmer when it became clear that the KGB had not acted against Solzhenitsyn and his friends alone. The day after the raid on Blagov and the young engineer, Andrey Sinyavsky and Yuli Daniel were arrested. Their subsequent trial and harsh sentences were to become a turning point in the history of the Russian intelligentsia—a kind of focus for hitherto dormant dissidence and embryonic protest. Although the case of Sinyavsky and Daniel was distinctly different from that of Solzhenitsyn—they had authorized pseudonymous publication abroad of works they knew were unpublishable in Russia—their arrest indicated that the KGB had been given license to use police methods against relatively well-known dissidents. Until Khrushchev's fall, only complete unknowns had been subjected to this treatment.

Solzhenitsyn himself has spoken of the KGB's "horrified" reaction to the descriptions of labor camps among his confiscated materials, "as if these writings carried the imprint of the condemned." Had this been the Stalin era, he said, "nothing could have been simpler": he would have disappeared, and no one would have asked a question. But the situation now, after the Twentieth and Twenty-second Party Congresses, did not allow such simple solutions.

The investigation of Blagov and his young friend lasted several months. At one point it seemed that the KGB would have them charged with conspiracy to spread anti-Soviet propaganda and that Solzhenitsyn might be added to the "plot" as the author of the seditious materials. In February 1966, Sinyavsky and Daniel were sentenced to long terms in labor colonies. Petitions and objections by part of the intellectual community against both the principle of prosecuting literature and the blatantly repressive trial represented the first public, organized protest since Stalin's consolidation of power some thirty-five years before. Solzhenitsyn's friends believe that this saved the writer and his "group" from prosecution. For, with all the sympathy for Ivan Denisovich, its perpetrators had to ask themselves what the reaction of the nascent public opinion would be if the fate of relative unknowns had caused such indignation. A few weeks after the Sinyavsky-

Daniel trial the investigation against Solzhenitsyn's friends was quietly abandoned, and he understood that he was in no immediate physical danger.

Even before Solzhenitsyn realized he had this partial security, he responded to the KGB's raids on his friends with an outburst of fury. Despite years of living with lawlessness, he had always been extremely assertive about what he considered his unalienable rights as a human being and a citizen. Even as a prisoner, he had been known for his thorough knowledge and vociferous assertion of the most paltry benefit due the inmates.

Nothing infuriated Solzhenitsyn more than the kind of manifest violation of his rights which he saw in the confiscation of his archive. It contained poems, sketches, and early projects as well as highly personal material relating to his past. He quickly formulated a series of protests, the first since his prison days. He wrote to Demichev, to the Central Committee, then to Secretary Brezhnev personally, demanding the return of his papers. At this point, he was careful to keep his communications within "proper channels." Despite the formal abandonment of the investigations —that is, the dissolution of the thin legal pretext for the theft of Solzhenitsyn's papers—the material was not returned and the Central Committee did not reply. Solzhenitsyn persisted, struggling doggedly, for over eighteen months, to assert his rights through established bureaucratic procedures.

Although the Central Committee did not respond to Solzhenitsyn, it can be deduced that they were impervious neither to the contents of his protests nor to the power of their language. If the communications came to be published abroad, they would be a resounding slap to Soviet prestige. This is probably what prompted another fling at duplicity. In odd contrast to what Solzhenitsyn could only regard as sinister harassment, the writer now began to receive unsolicited assurances that he would continue to publish and to play a role in Soviet literature. For more than two years, not a word of his had appeared in print. But in the late autumn of 1965, the *Literary Gazette*, still under the editorship of Solzhenitsyn's obdurate enemy, Alexander Chakovsky, asked the near-outcast, whose work and friends were still being investigated for anti-Soviet tendencies, to participate in a debate on the development of the Russian language. Solzhenitsyn agreed, and his contribution appeared in early November.

The 1500-word article summarized Solzhenitsyn's experience of working with language. He had long treated the "craft" aspect of writing with particular attention, of which the careful listening to and recording of peasant speech was only the first phase. For sharpening the expressiveness of language, he suggested two basic approaches. The first was essentially morphological, and grounded in the vast potential of the Russian language for building new words from existing elements. Solzhenitsyn felt that this potential—which is almost impossible to explain in terms of other languages [1]—was barely being tapped, and made clear suggestions for how this might be done, using word elements instinctively understood by Russians. His own prose makes striking use of this inventive expressiveness—and inevitably loses this part of it in translation. Solzhenitsyn's second approach pertained to syntax. Ever since Peter the Great's Westernizing reforms, he argued, the Russian language had been emasculated by foreign influences. He appealed for a restoration of intrinsically Russian structures, the kind exemplified in proverbs, with their concise substance. This "special liveliness which calls to us from practically every Russian proverb"—Solzhenitsyn begged that attention be paid to the lessons it offered—is again characteristic of his own prose, producing an intonation which cannot be mistaken for any other author's. Throughout the article, Solzhenitsyn quoted his favorite Dahl, whose dictionary he used to read in the camps. And he ended with a plea to save the language, by diligent work on every sentence, from the steady drain of its vigor and unique qualities, a process greatly advanced by the spread of bureaucratic and newspaper malformations.

The *Literary Gazette* article was Solzhenitsyn's first and, as it turned out, only published contribution to literary theory. That autumn too, he was promised that a collection of his short stories would appear the following year, and that he would be invited to append a short autobiographical statement which would dissipate the rumors and slanders about his background. An even more encouraging development took place in January 1966: *Novy Mir* published a new short story. More a travel sketch than a work of fiction, "Zakhar the Pouch" sharply criticized the neglect of a monument commemorating a great Russian victory over the Tartars six hundred years before. By implication, this was a rebuke to the authorities, but in a permissible tone of disquieted patriotism. The story honored Zakhar, the old battlefield's miserably poor watchman, as a selfless caretaker of the landmarks of Russian history and an instinctive preserver of the Slavic idea in its struggle with Asia. And it hinted—most seasonably, since Russia was now quarreling bitterly with China—that danger did not come exclusively from the West.

The story's preoccupation with Russia's survival foreshadowed dominant themes of later work, especially the "principal project" of his life, which he had conceived before the war and would return to several years from now. And although hardly a major work, "Zakhar the Pouch" became a landmark of its own kind in Solzhenitsyn's life. The slender, intensely patriotic story represented his last appearance in print inside Russia.

---

[1] An English example might be coining a word such as "dethrall," whose meaning would be clear to most readers even when not used in context. Rich in prefixes and suffixes, the Russian language lends itself easily to this kind of creativity.

Stalemate

The publication of two of Solzhenitsyn's works within three months initially made it seem plausible that he was being restored to official acceptance. Promises of future publication seemed to confirm this, and went beyond the agreed book of short stories. In early 1966, the first part of *Cancer Ward* had been polished to its final draft, and, in contrast to the manifest problems caused by *The First Circle,* it was intimated to the author that there was no reason why this much less political novel should not be read sympathetically. The reassurance was made despite the KGB's continued refusal to return Solzhenitsyn's confiscated manuscripts and papers. For their own reasons, probably two principal ones, the authorities sought to nourish a public notion of Solzhenitsyn's professional well-being and a private optimism within Solzhenitsyn himself.

The first reason was connected with the relentless exertions of Khrushchev's successors, once they felt strong enough, to suppress radical dissent in Soviet society and restrain the influence of establishment liberals. The authorities' response to the protests against the Sinyavsky-Daniel trial was on two planes: while harassing the petitioners, they simultaneously sought to reassure the rank-and-file intelligentsia that the punishment of a few "anti-Soviet" writers did not signify a generally restrictive trend. If admirers could be convinced that Solzhenitsyn, the focus of Russian liberalism, was to remain prominent in Russian life, this would be telling reassurance. This was another attempt, as in the winter of 1962–63, to use Solzhenitsyn as a decoy during a period of political and cultural freeze.

The authorities' second aim was to lessen the risk that Solzhenitsyn himself would speak out publicly with personal or general grievances. It was reckoned that while he had a fair chance of publishing his fiction he was unlikely to jeopardize it by promulgating protests.

During the following months, this strategy seemed to work. Talk of Solzhenitsyn's imminent publication had a certain pacifying effect, and, while the author awaited the appearance of his short stories and the passage of *Cancer Ward* through the narrows of the literary bureaucracy, he maintained his uneasy public silence. It was not, however, a total hush: from Ryazan, he wrote to Tvardovsky and the Secretariat of the Writers' Union, inquiring about the progress of his manuscripts. Lack of any apparent progress, together with *Cancer Ward's* curious wanderings, caused him increasing impatience.

Although it was not a propitious time for literary innovation, *Cancer Ward* was not only less disturbing politically than *The First Circle* but also touched fewer socially sensitive issues than *One Day* or "For the Good of the Cause." Essentially a kind of Russian *Magic Mountain*, as Lukács has pointed out, the novel delineates intricate relationships among the staff and patients of a hospital, clearly based on the one in Tashkent where Solzhenitsyn was saved in 1954. Rather than with social institutions, Solzhenitsyn was preoccupied with the personality of his characters as revealed in the interplay among themselves and with their disease and the times. Each character is portrayed internally, through his own view of himself and his affliction, and externally, through the perception of the other characters. Fundamentally, the fictional cancer hospital is like its real equivalents anywhere, and the censors could hardly take exception to the description of this setting, as opposed to Ekibastuz and Marfino.

Moreover, *Cancer Ward's* principal narrative thread is essentially private: the approach toward death and slow recovery of its central character, the semiautobiographical Oleg Kostoglotov (who, however, is distinctly less autobiographical than *The First Circle's* Gleb Nerzhin). Kostoglotov's return to life is twofold: as a recently released camp inmate as well as a cancer patient. From the official point of view, this was surely an acceptable, if not welcome, subject. Nor could the most eager censor object to the delicately erotic account of Kostoglotov's rediscovery of women after his long separation from them as a prisoner.

Torn from their routines to fight death, patients find that they must reexamine their lives, and in some cases reorder their values. But in the first part of the novel at least, the final values at which the patients arrive range from officially praiseworthy to ideologically exceptionable, but not wholly taboo. A young, obviously incurable geologist, for example, "compresses months into days and years into weeks" to work out his cherished hypothesis about the location of minerals—the kind of personal drive which is officially encouraged. Just this side of the impermissible, a tough "lone wolf" discovers—too late—that only a sense of belonging through love can bring him genuine fulfillment. Party ideologists disapproved of this (essentially Tolstoyan) attitude, but it had been encountered often enough in previous Soviet literature.

In general, the first half of the novel (as opposed to *Cancer Ward II*, which was not yet completed) embodied only one challenge to the system —albeit in an extremely vulnerable area. Pavel Rusanov, a middle-aged, middle-level bureaucrat and former NKVD informer, suffers as painfully as any other patient in the ward, and is unable wholly to suppress twinges of conscience about his past. Yet he is shown, subtly and with great force, to subordinate all moral considerations to a determination to preserve his privileged social position as a member of the political machine. Even when drug-induced hallucinations conjure up victims of his denunciations in the 1930s, he cheats on his conscience to avoid a confrontation with truth. Since Rusanov's background is typical of Soviet bureaucrats', censors could be expected to raise substantial objections to several aspects of his role and personality. Otherwise, social criticism in this first half of the novel was almost incidental, occurring only when the characters encounter, in the course of their lives, the harshness, absurdities, and privations of Soviet society under Stalin and immediately after. By 1966, the worst of these hardships and cruelties belonged to the past.

Solzhenitsyn submitted *Cancer Ward I* to *Novy Mir*. Tvardovsky recognized it as a kind of encyclopedia of contemporary Russian personalities and attitudes. He was especially impressed with the portrayal of the characters both as their "normal" personalities and in the torturous process of self-discovery induced by grave illness. Tvardovsky devoted several months in mid-1966 to the usual preliminary "arrangements," now made more difficult because of the harsher political and cultural climate in general and Solzhenitsyn's particular troubles over *The First Circle*. Then the first of a series of odd events took place: as Solzhenitsyn put it, *Novy Mir* "turned down" the novel.

Neither the circumstances nor the reasons are known. Although Tvardovsky had not been included in the new Central Committee formed in March 1966, he was still too powerful politically to be ordered outright to reject a manuscript. And since less than a year later he was to rededicate himself to an ardent campaign for publication, it is unlikely that he suddenly cooled toward the novel's artistic merits. With hindsight, it seems likely that Tvardovsky succumbed to "advice" of some sort. Perhaps it was the notion, occasionally put about in establishment literary circles at the time, that he was doing neither Solzhenitsyn nor Soviet literature a service by "monopolizing" him, prompting gossip that the writer had somehow become his personal cause. The warning was probably conceived as part of a larger strategy of delay: unwilling to reject *Cancer Ward* outright, the authorities found it expedient, as they often do, to postpone, prevaricate, and obfuscate in the hope that the problem might somehow evaporate. It did not: Solzhenitsyn persisted. Whatever Tvardovsky's confidential explanation to him of the rejection, *Novy Mir's* singular decision could not be expected to have assuaged his apprehensions over having "surfaced."

But he had decided that his inner fears should not influence his outward stance.

Solzhenitsyn proceeded by submitting the manuscript to a Leningrad literary magazine and a Russian-language periodical in Kazakhstan. The latter's circulation was a mere fifteen thousand, of which all but a handful of copies were sold in the home republics, thousands of miles from Moscow. This speaks of Solzhenitsyn's eagerness to publish, however humble the medium. Moreover, there seemed to be a special selling point for editors in Kazakhstan, namely the locality of the novel's rather lyric scenes, which were set in the republic. Solzhenitsyn's evocation of the smells and sensations of the steppe was bound to warm Kazakh hearts. The selling point might have been even stronger in Uzbekistan, since the cancer hospital is evidently set in Tashkent, its capital, but that city was known for the unusual severity of its censorship, while Alma-Ata, the Kazakh capital, was then publishing (and continues to publish) significant fiction, even about purely Russian themes, that could not pass the censors in Moscow and Leningrad.[1]

While the manuscript was being read in Leningrad and Alma-Ata, it was proposed that the Writers' Union subject it to a formal discussion and debate. This was not an uncommon practice: discussions of works soon to be published are regularly organized by the relevant section of the union. In some cases, the overriding purpose is to caution an unconventional author; in others, to draw attention to an unusually worthy work. In almost every case, the very organizing of such a discussion indicates that the work is of uncommon interest, and the discussion itself, since it takes place among professional colleagues and behind closed doors, is far more outspoken than anything in the press.

The examination of *Cancer Ward* was organized by the Prose Association of the Moscow branch of the union. As customary, attendance was restricted to members. Obviously, they had had to read the manuscript before discussing it. This required its dissemination to a largish group of Solzhenitsyn's colleagues—a highly unusual step if, as now seems clear, the ultimate decision makers had no intention to publish from the first. Desperate to delay what they correctly foresaw as Solzhenitsyn's explosion in the event of a final rejection, the authorities chose the lesser evil and allowed a selected group of writers to acquaint themselves with the text, even in the certain knowledge that it would elicit glowing admiration. Nevertheless, careful precautions were taken against further dissemination

---

[1] Solzhenitsyn was also struck by the name of the Kazakh magazine's editor: Ivan Shukhov—an amusing parallel to his own Ivan Denisovich Shukhov, especially considering the rareness of the name. In a letter to the editor, Solzhenitsyn asked where (since his own Ivan Denisovich was barely literate) he'd acquired his literary education after being released from camp.

by making the manuscript available only in the office of the Writers' Union. (One of the participants in the discussion claims that it had to be signed for and could only be read in a special room.) Moreover, the authorities' hesitation over their own temporary expedient was all but headlined by repeated postponement of the discussion. The chosen date was canceled and advanced three times in three months and it was only in mid-November that Moscow prose writers presented their cards of invitation at an auditorium in the Central Literary Club.

Not even all of the discussion's organizers, let alone the invited writers, knew of their political superiors' real intentions. Arkady Belinkov, a prominent Moscow critic who attended the affair shortly before defecting to the West, spoke of a genuine desire for publication even by a certain segment of politicians—men, however, who had been steadily losing power as the new Brezhnev leadership stifled liberals. "The meeting was convened," Belinkov wrote, "only after everything had become unfavorable and alarming. Which was precisely why it was called. The chiefs didn't want to print *Cancer Ward*—but not all of them didn't. And those who did want it—people with no power or who'd lost it—consoled themselves with the hope that if a so-called responsible and representative assembly should come out for printing, the Central Committee would listen. Well, if not listen, perhaps at least hear."

The assembly indeed approved of publication. Solzhenitsyn arrived at the auditorium to find fifty-two of his fellow writers in the audience, of whom twenty-four rose to speak during the course of the prolonged, late-afternoon session. Not one of the speakers was substantively negative.

The principal address was by A. Borshchagovsky, one of Russia's most prominent liberal critics. He compared Solzhenitsyn to Tolstoy in the depth of his characterization, and to Saltykov-Shchedrin (the Russian Swift) in the incisiveness of his satire—comments which set the tone for the subsequent discussion. *Cancer Ward* was brought into its clearest focus by Venyamin Kaverin, an extremely gifted writer of the 1920s whose genius was later mangled in conflict between his artistic conscience and the requirements of survival as a writer under Stalinism. Kaverin set Solzhenitsyn in the context of Russian literature as a whole, assigning him first place among a new wave of writers who would restore its brilliance and originality. "This literature will enjoy world success," he said, "if only steps are not taken to prevent it."

According to Kaverin, above and beyond Solzhenitsyn's "amazing sense of harmony" and ability to bring his experiences to life, he was endowed with two special "precious traits" for his work in restoring Russian literature: an "internal freedom" and a "mighty striving for truth." Kaverin's own frustrated talent gave his definition of internal freedom special significance and poignancy. "We older generation of writers," he said, "hid ourselves from ourselves for many years, entangling ourselves in contradictions. This was a natural result of two decades of Stalin. Solzhenitsyn and the best makers of the new literature are free from all this. They have renounced all goals and purposes except the desire to tell the truth." *Cancer Ward*, Kaverin summarized, was a book of "vast conscience," precisely the quality which had inspired the best of Russian literature. Four years later, the Nobel Prize Committee was to define Solzhenitsyn's contribution to Russian and world literature in very similar terms.

While Kaverin's attitude might have been predicted, the support for publication by several uncompromising Stalinists was surprising. In at least one case, this support had overtones of the grotesque. At the Sinyavsky-Daniel trial nine months earlier, the KGB's literary spokesman had been Zoya Kedrina, a critic who condemned the defendants in the name of "public opinion." Now, at the discussion, this authentic secret police informer took the floor to express loathing of Solzhenitsyn's fictional informer Rusanov! The attitude of people like Kedrina no doubt helped convince everyone present that *Cancer Ward* would appear after all. The speakers' only urging in this connection was that the event take place soon. Again in hindsight, Kedrina's remarks now appear more like camouflage than an old conservative's panic, for which Solzhenitsyn's supporters took it at the time. Despite the political climate, liberals at the discussion were convinced that there was no stopping *Cancer Ward* now.[2] Two years later, at Yale University, Belinkov poured scorn on the optimism of that day. "On November 17, 1966," he wrote sarcastically, "it was abundantly clear that a new era was on the way—that it was close by, at the very door or perhaps behind the curtain."

Optimistic or not, Solzhenitsyn was plainly pleased by the discussion, his first professional encounter with a substantial gathering of his colleagues. It had not been free of criticism; many of the speakers took issue with one or another aspect of the novel. But Solzhenitsyn was gratified by its level. The character of Rusanov drew most of the objections: one young critic suggested that the old bureaucrat was not human enough because Solzhenitsyn had "driven everything human" under his skin instead of drawing it 'out. Several of Solzhenitsyn's admirers agreed—and, in his own remarks to the assembly, Solzhenitsyn himself confessed that

---

[2] The general climate was indeed bleak, but the publication of a few formerly suppressed works, notably by Osip Mandelshtam and Mikhail Bulgakov, was just enough to lift liberals from deep depression after the Sinyavsky-Daniel trial. Besides, there had been a hope earlier that year that literary suppression might be lessened. Censorship had become so severe that even the Party Committee of the Moscow Writers' Union drew the Central Committee's attention to the "inexplicable power" that it had arrogated to itself, and Demichev, the Ideological Secretary, promised that "we'll straighten it out." They did not.

Rusanov was "not quite right." "I dare not argue with so many critics," he said.

His acknowledgment of professional criticism—even more, his desire for it—was no polite cant. Several months later, in circumstances wholly free of any pressure, Solzhenitsyn remarked that a writer's only legitimate demand from society was the objective assessment and criticism which were indispensable for literary development. Only in exceptional cases—such as this very assembly—did Soviet society give him this help. Indeed, it is likely that the meeting itself brought him to his full appreciation of the role of constructive criticism. For he admitted now that his isolation, which had long been partially self-imposed, had had certain adverse effects on his work. "It turns out," he said, "that in single-handed combat with paper, when readers were few, one's demands upon oneself were inevitably slackened." He emphasized that none of the speeches had given him the slightest offense. On the contrary; since he was in the predicament of "writing book after book which remained unpublished," discussion such as this gave him his only opportunity for needed professional reaction and criticism.

At the conclusion of his remarks as at the beginning, his gratitude welled up, and he stressed that his colleagues' attention had moved him. His emotion seemed to run over into the final minutes of the meeting, when it was decided to send a transcript of the discussion to both magazines which were considering *Cancer Ward I*. A writer proposed that *Moskva*, the magazine of the Moscow Writers' Union, print the novel "at home," as it were. As the meeting was adjourned, Bella Akhmadulina, the impulsive young poet who had gushed eager optimism in 1962, rushed to the dais. "What a wonderful man!" she shouted. "Let's pray to God to grant Alexander Solzhenitsyn good health!"

The euphoria was short-lived. The winter of 1966–67 brought not the expected triumphant publication, but swelling frustration and danger. Only in the peripheral matter of housing did the authorities' vaunted goodwill materialize into tangible action. While critical literary issues hung in the balance, Solzhenitsyn was at last allocated new quarters in Ryazan, perhaps in the hope—which would reflect the level on which most officials measured human needs—that a better flat would better the writer's attitude. The flat was indeed an improvement: rather spacious by Soviet standards, although far humbler than those of leading establishment writers and of the political elite. With Reshetovskaya, his mother-in-law, and the two aunts, Solzhenitsyn moved to a three-room apartment in a large stone block of flats off a central street, a three-story building in the hulking style of the 1950s. A friend who visited him shortly after the move noticed that the new building, characteristically, was already shabby, and that Solzhenitsyn's ground-floor flat was reached by "a dirty corridor smelling of a burst drainpipe."

Solzhenitsyn was satisfied with the new quarters and his separate study —but with little else. Despite the enthusiasm and buoyant hopes of the November discussion, *Cancer Ward I* was rejected both in Leningrad and in Alma-Ata. Solzhenitsyn then submitted extracts of the novel to five other Soviet literary newspapers and magazines and received no offers from any of them. In January, a chapter was published—but in a Slovak translation in Czechoslovakia, where harbingers of the "Prague Spring" had already appeared.

Curious as this might seem, there was nothing extraordinary about it. Even before the Prague Spring, Soviet manuscripts not published at home —even manuscripts rejected by the censors, which *Cancer Ward* was not —often appeared in Czechoslovak magazines. In this case, a Slovak journalist wrote to Solzhenitsyn, asking for an unpublished work of prose. The author posted a chapter of *Cancer Ward* to Bratislava, where it was published not in a literary magazine, but in Slovakia's *Pravda,* the most prominent possible place. The Bratislava journalist who made the arrangements would soon be involved in publication of the entire novel abroad, a far more complicated and dangerous affair.

As magazine after magazine rejected the novel, publication of some of Solzhenitsyn's other writings placed him in danger. Since they fell into the pattern of a singular form of Soviet governmental pirating, these publications were further evidence that the writer's harassment had been organized at the highest level. Under a special Soviet system, a selection of Russian and foreign books considered important for the few but unfit for the public is produced in small "closed" editions for officials and trusted scholars on a "need-to-know" basis. As with classified materials in other countries, each reader must sign for his numbered copy. Among the system's select public, Solzhenitsyn became the major attraction of the 1966–67 winter season. The texts for his special editions had been run off from the manuscripts confiscated by the KGB from Blagov and his young friend. Solzhenitsyn was not so much as informed of their publication.

Two works circulated widely in the exclusive "market": *The First Circle* and, far more alarmingly, the "anti-Soviet" "Feast of the Victors," which, despite Solzhenitsyn's repeated renunciations of the fifteen-year-old epic poem, was touted as his latest work. In addition, acid slander, heightened with new fantasies, was spread by word of mouth to a widening public. Supplementing earlier vague accusations that Solzhenitsyn had been a common criminal and a traitor, it was bluntly put about that he had "served the Germans" and—in one version—even worked for the Gestapo.

Whether by design or by accident, the authorities had trampled on Solzhenitsyn's most sensitive nerve. Beyond an acute concern for his good name, he had the innocent prisoner's fierce resentment of anything remotely suggestive of guilt for a true offense. Even more than the misuse of his writings, the slander infuriated Solzhenitsyn and he answered with a salvo of protests to the press and the Writers' Union board—still through the proper channels. In vain: "The board did not even respond," he later wrote. "Not a single newspaper printed or published my answer to the slanders."

The deliberate silence was not surprising; publication of Solzhenitsyn's protests could be authorized only in the highest places, and by this time an ominous development had occurred there. In October 1966, the neo-Stalinists emerged as an identifiable, coherent, and, in a certain sense, open pressure group.

The occasion was a closed, though not hypersecret, meeting of leading party ideologists. Several called for a reappraisal of Stalin because, as their spokesman put it, his name was associated with the great victories of the Soviet people in the 1930s and 1940s, and "we are proud to be Stalinists." These men and their cothinkers, who included figures such as General Yepishev, deputy minister of state security during the last wave of Stalin's terror in 1952–53, never managed to seize power; if they had, Solzhenitsyn probably would have been silenced once and for all. Nevertheless, they occupied offices just below the highest level—Yepishev, for example, was (and is) in charge of political instruction and reliability for the Soviet armed forces—and from these positions, with a new, self-confident assertiveness, they pulled powerfully on Soviet politics. According to a liberal poet they were "dangling on the clock of history and fiercely clutching the hands, trying to yank them back." In the Brezhnev-Kosygin regime's long, slow slide backward that would take them to police persecution of liberals, the invasion of Czechoslovakia, and destructive inflexibility in virtually all aspects of domestic affairs, the outspoken oath of allegiance to Stalin in October 1966 was a critical moment.

Liberal literary magazines were high among the targets of the Stalinists, who demanded the suppression of such subversive influences on the Soviet people's morale. Yepishev went so far as to boast openly of his solution to the problem within his own realm: forbidding military personnel from subscribing to *Novy Mir* and other undesirable publications. Although Tvardovsky had no intention of succumbing to the intense pressure on *Novy Mir* by altering his editorial policy and rejecting "sensitive" manuscripts, he could not now take up Solzhenitsyn's personal grievances as he had two years earlier when exposing the public-opinion fraud.

Weeks later, when the spirit of the October meeting of ideologists became known to the politically aware, it convinced them that the Sinyav-sky-Daniel trial had not been an aberration; even optimistic liberals understood the need for caution. Solzhenitsyn's political sensitivity told him that he could no longer reasonably expect the public media to state his position. By the spring of 1967, there had been no effort to scotch even the outrageous rumors of his collaboration with the Germans. As earlier—in his labor camps and when threatened by cancer—he decided that only Solzhenitsyn could defend the interests of Solzhenitsyn, and the time had come to seize the initiative. After almost five years of observing the operation of literary politics, he felt he had the necessary tactical skill.

XXVIII

Protest

IN THE SPRING OF 1967, SOLZHENITSYN FELT that the time was approaching to make a public assertion, if necessary unassisted, of the rights of Russian writers. His own rights had been violated systematically, and his attempts to defend them by conventional means had proved futile. He had every reason to believe that years earlier a ban had been ordered on his work regardless of its content. He prepared himself, therefore, for an entirely different stance vis-à-vis the authorities.

His preparations were expedited by chance, and, as often in Russian life—more often than in more open societies—by an appreciative reaction abroad. After the excitement caused by the publication of the *Cancer Ward* chapter in Czechoslovakia, the journalist to whom Solzhenitsyn had posted the ten pages was sent to Russia to interview the author. The journalist was also a translator of Russian literature into Slovak, and his sponsor for this trip was Czechoslovakia's most progressive literary magazine. Pavel Ličko arrived in Moscow in March 1967, and made his request for the interview through the Writers' Union.

No stranger to Soviet bureaucracy, Ličko was not put off by the union's barrage of "no's." He was told that it was impossible to see Solzhenitsyn because the writer was "busy, or ill, or almost dying—and in any case he did not like visitors." Nor could he make the three-hour trip to confirm this sometimes alarming news, for Ryazan is closed to all foreigners, even citizens of socialist countries. After amply observing all the proprieties of working through official channels, Ličko ventured to telegraph Solzhenitsyn directly. A reply received the same day invited him to visit the author at home, and provided detailed traveling instructions.

Solzhenitsyn's response foreshadowed his new strategy. He had already heard from mutual Moscow friends that Ličko was a reliable, responsible, and likable man, but until recently this would have meant little; he would have refused to see the visiting Slovak, as he had declined to see all other journalists throughout the years of his fame. And although this in no way impeded his literary endeavors—he still believed that during a writer's lifetime the public need know nothing more about him than what his work revealed—it was a decided disadvantage to someone who had resolved to play a public role. A protest from a shadowy figure inevitably carries less weight and perhaps even less conviction than the same statement from a widely known personality. In fact, Solzhenitsyn might even have considered whether his years of rigid refusal to expose himself in the public media were not, in retrospect, a tactical mistake. Had the whole of Russia become "personally" acquainted with him in 1962 and 1963 through substantial television and press coverage, the campaign of slander against him would have been infinitely more difficult to pursue. Now he had come to the point of seeking—too late—a platform to refute the slanders.

Ličko's telegram, therefore, came at an opportune moment, as the promptness of the reply demonstrated. Ličko himself was delighted even though his trip was still far from assured. "I needed a special visa for Ryazan," he has written. "But I'd never have gotten it through the Writers' Union despite Solzhenitsyn's invitation." Ličko turned to another channel: his association with Soviet veterans. Without mentioning the real purpose of his trip, he asked the Soviet veterans' organization, with which he had old contacts,[1] to help him obtain a visa for Ryazan. The document was readily issued to the trusted old war comrade.

"But even this proved insufficient," Ličko continued. Obviously, the KGB had intercepted Solzhenitsyn's telegram of invitation, and, although they preferred not to disclose this by withdrawing Ličko's Ryazan visa, they set about strewing nails in his path.

> First, some officials on the train tried to tell me that the bridges to Ryazan had broken down, that the train wasn't going there, and that I should leave it in an unknown town an hour and a half out of Moscow. Then I was dumped about ten miles from Ryazan, at a small station in an open plain. It seemed to have no name. After a while, I found a taxi driver and noticed that he had a labor camp number surrounded with a crown of barbed wire tattooed on his wrist. I told him that I'd come to see Solzhenitsyn. He didn't ask the address. He just took me there, refusing to talk on the way, in total silence. And he refused to accept the fare.

After this, Ličko was not surprised to hear Solzhenitsyn referred to as "the Field Marshal," meaning the spiritual leader of the army of former prisoners.

Ličko spent the better part of the day with Solzhenitsyn, and the two

---

[1] Ličko had fought in Slovak resistance, was appointed liaison officer to the approaching Red Army, and was then made an officer in the Soviet military intelligence.

resumed their conversation several days later in Moscow. In Ryazan, Solzhenitsyn was already well established in his new flat, which was "crammed with books and sheets of music and full of old but tasteful furniture, including [Reshetovskaya's steadfast] grand piano." The journalist's first impression of the writer himself was of "a very tall, bearded man —very athletic-looking." As the hours passed, the picture he formed was quite different from that of people who had known him as the haggard ex-prisoner and gray, self-effacing schoolteacher. Ličko made note of Solzhenitsyn's brisk self-confidence and the "efficient, no-nonsense manner of an American corporation executive. . . . He dresses fashionably, moves like a sportsman, and walks in broad strides." However, the writer's fundamental character traits remained unchanged. Ličko was struck by Solzhenitsyn's "computer brain [which] gives birth to sentences molded in mathematically precise words and uttered with machine-gun speed." And although Ličko was fed by his host, "this was the only time in Russia that I was refused a second glass of vodka." Solzhenitsyn still preferred sober discussion to primed merrymaking.

The talk centered on Solzhenitsyn's life and attitude toward literature. In the latter subject, Ličko found the writer very "Russian." "Good literature arises out of pain," Solzhenitsyn said. "Eastern Europe, in which I include Russia, has lived through violent cataclysms, and therefore I look on its literary future with great hope." Western Europe, by contrast, had enjoyed too much prosperity and tranquillity to stimulate great literature. Solzhenitsyn regretted, as he does often to friends, that he had had no time in life to read widely in Western fiction. Nevertheless, he had a feeling "that a great part of their literature is rather petty."

Literature arising out of suffering is indeed characteristic of Russia, as were the corollary convictions expressed to Ličko that "literature is based on getting to the depths of social phenomena," and that the writer's principal task is "not to overlook a single mistake in the social development of his country." He went on to expound his views on literature's role at some length, and later approved Ličko's summary.

Because he observes the world with an artist's eye and because of his intuition, many social developments reveal themselves to a writer earlier than to others, and from an unconventional aspect. This is what comprises his talent. And from his talent springs his duty. He must inform society of what he has seen, especially about everything that is unhealthy and cause for anxiety. . . . Russian literature has always addressed itself to those who suffer. Sometimes the opinion is offered in our country that one should write about what is coming tomorrow, touching up where necessary. But this is falsification—and justifies lies. This kind of literature is cosmetics.

This attitude was in sharp contrast to Stalinist theory—and not only theory, for a vast corpus of Soviet literature since the early 1930s has devoted itself to picturing the virtues of the new society's brilliant future, described as if they already existed. As one writer put it graphically, the Soviet literary mirror should reflect the beautiful new highways planned for tomorrow rather than the pitted, muddy roads on which the Russian people must still—if very temporarily—slog along. However, opposition to this interpretation of socialist realism was widespread among non-Stalinists, and Solzhenitsyn's criticism, sharp as it was, still lay well within the bounds of, say, *Novy Mir*'s own philosophy. In fact, on the very March day when Solzhenitsyn and Ličko were conversing, Tvardovsky was propagating the same view to the Secretariat of the Writers' Union. It was during one of his innumerable, fruitless attempts to persuade the members to approve publication of *Cancer Ward*, a consummate realization of non-cosmetic, warts-and-all realism.

However, Solzhenitsyn's views on a writer's primary allegiance were far more controversial—even heretical. "A writer's mission should be considered not only in terms of his duty to society, but also from the standpoint of his most important obligation: to each individual." This was a ringing dissent not from the goals of Marxism itself, but from one of the most fundamental axioms of the collectivist philosophy which permeated Soviet society and dominated its literature. Even Tvardovsky did not share this view. But Solzhenitsyn's commitment to it was unequivocal.

> An individual's life is not always the same as society's. The collective does not always assist the individual. Each person has an abundance of problems which the collective cannot resolve. A person is a physiological and spiritual being before he becomes a member of his society. A writer's duty to the individual is no less than to society.

After almost four decades of relentless exaltation of the tribe, this assertion was as much a shock and challenge as avant garde painting to the academicians.

As unremarkable as Solzhenitsyn's concern for the individual would have seemed in the West, his theory of the novel, which flowed directly from it, contained an originality of approach in any country. His concentration on the individual—each individual who entered his stories—led to a formula which excluded the notion of a principal hero. "The author of a novel with a main hero," he told Ličko, "involuntarily devotes more space and attention to him." But in Solzhenitsyn's view,

> each person becomes the main character when the action involves him in particular. This way, the author can be responsible even for

dozens of heroes. He gives preference to none of them. He must understand and make valid every character he has created.

In other words, each character should be fully explored in his own world, rather than serving primarily as a prop to a central set of heroes or plot. He called this the "polyphonic novel," a little-known term originally coined by a Russian critic in description of Dostoyevsky's fiction. The great bulk of Solzhenitsyn's own fiction—*Cancer Ward, The First Circle,* and the World War I novel that would come later—followed this pattern. Although Solzhenitsyn did not invent it—one thinks of Dos Passos as well as of Dostoyevsky—he was the only major living novelist to practice "polyphony" at that time, and his revival of the difficult and seldom-used method was largely responsible for the great sweep and universality of his work.

The conversation between Ličko and Solzhenitsyn lasted some six hours. Solzhenitsyn's unusual generosity with his time was probably prompted by more than his liking for the bluff and engagingly frank former partisan with the wry wit and soldierly openness—and by more than his eagerness to recount something about his life and ideas. For the writer had just completed the second part of *Cancer Ward,* and even he might have felt entitled to a short break.

Two weeks after Pavel Ličko visited Ryazan, the first substantial description of Solzhenitsyn's life and views appeared in Bratislava's progressive literary magazine. It was soon reprinted elsewhere in Eastern Europe. This was the chance to explain his life that Solzhenitsyn had sought at home, and, had Ličko's article been published in Russia too, the forthcoming clash might have been avoided. But not only did the deliberate silence about him continue; it was also indicated, through the editor of Ličko's magazine, that the Soviet authorities were annoyed by the interview and article.

It was now clear that Russia's leaders were intent not merely on doing nothing to "rehabilitate" Solzhenitsyn, but also on hindering his own efforts toward this end. Since the previous year, for example, Solzhenitsyn had been giving public readings of his works before small audiences in Ryazan and elsewhere. As part of his "going public" in the absence of a platform or vehicle to refute his vilification, he devoted considerable time to this activity, previously considered a distraction almost as unnecessary as interviews with journalists.

"Meeting with the readers" is an important aspect of *kultmass* (culture-for-the-masses) work, in the bureaucratic vernacular that Solzhenitsyn so abhors. Ordinarily, arrangements are made through the Writers' Union and the authors appear in the auditoriums of factories, offices, and other "collectives." In Solzhenitsyn's case, the readings could hardly be organized through the union, in view of its abetting of the slanders, but were set up with representatives of the collectives themselves, who had sought him out as readers had been doing ever since the appearance of *One Day*. As Solzhenitsyn's initial avoidance of these invitations gave way to a realization of their potential as his only contact, however limited, with the public, he plunged into the activity with his usual gusto, appearing evening after evening. But the authorities soon responded by quashing the performances. In November 1966, for example, nine of eleven scheduled readings were canceled "at the last moment," as Solzhenitsyn later charged. Measures were also taken to muffle any mechanical transmission of Solzhenitsyn's voice for the current or later generations. "Thus," wrote Solzhenitsyn, "the [party] secretary of the Frunze District of Moscow summoned the director of the Academy of Sciences' Institute of Russian Language and forbade the recording of my voice on tape in that institute."

Nevertheless, Solzhenitsyn continued to make arrangements for readings and some actually transpired, no doubt because of insufficient vigilance by local party officials in one or another area. In Moscow, for example, Solzhenitsyn appeared in at least three educational institutes during the winter and spring of Ličko's visit, the probable explanation being that his strong appeal among educated readers made party secretaries in these institutions unsuccessful in preventing his appearances there.

A member of one of these audiences in early 1967 has described Solzhenitsyn's stage manner. Predictably, the first impression was of energy, intensity, and dedication. But unlike the actor of the Sovremennik Theater in 1963, this witness was enthralled by Solzhenitsyn's delivery. Perhaps the explanation of the contrasting evaluations lies less in the witnesses' disparate perceptions than in changes with Solzhenitsyn himself: in the five years since he had read *The Love Girl and the Innocent* before the assembled actors, his self-confidence had developed significantly with the cumulative experience of speaking before both hostile and admiring audiences. In any case, Solzhenitsyn transfixed this audience in particular for more than three hours, reading excerpts from *Cancer Ward* and *The First Circle*, and answered questions passed up from his listeners.

It spoke of Solzhenitsyn's new mood of independence that he chose to read from his unpublished—and now seemingly unpublishable—novels. A final incident spoke also of the authorities' determination to stop him. In late May, Solzhenitsyn was scheduled to "meet the readers" of a restricted military institute. On the day of the reading, the institute's party secretary pinned a sign to the auditorium door announcing that Solzhenitsyn was ill and the evening canceled. But a large part of the audience was not taken in by this familiar tactic, and, when Solzhenitsyn arrived in apparent good health, the secretary was unable to overcome the clamor for the reading to be held. Solzhenitsyn then read excerpts from the unpublished novels and his most recent writing, a work of nonfiction appealing passionately for a restoration of Russian literature's independence and dignity. The military officers cheered and Solzhenitsyn took careful note of their reactions. By this time he was emerging into open protest and direct confrontation with the authorities. However, this was the last public platform from which he could read his own works or present his case for liberating Russian literature.

By mid-spring, Solzhenitsyn understood that there was no hope whatever of defending himself through accepted channels and, for the first time, entered the realm of public protest. It was a difficult decision. To protest openly was, of course, to flaunt the Soviet tradition of petitioning for justice by formal application to higher authority. Even the essentially public protests against the Sinyavsky-Daniel trial the previous year— themselves a new departure—had been carefully masked as requests addressed to the proper officials. Nevertheless, Solzhenitsyn felt that the mood, at least among writers, was ripe for a less prevaricating attitude toward authority.

The increasingly restrictive censorship under Brezhnev and Kosygin had caused a "traffic jam," as Tvardovsky put it, of manuscripts delayed in processing. Even works by veteran writers, even an important study of Lenin, were affected. Tvardovsky described the cultural atmosphere in terms of "dumb silence, gloomy bewilderment, vagueness, and inert temporizing." But the editor's comments were made almost a year later; at this point not only had no one publicly defined the writers' prevailing mood, but the government's retrenchment itself had barely been stated in words. Sensing this, Solzhenitsyn calculated that maximum support for his views would be won by presenting them openly to literary public opinion rather than by continuing to pen seemly letters to titled officials.

The battlefield almost selected itself. The Fourth Congress of Soviet Writers, by statute the profession's most representative assembly, was scheduled to convene in late May 1967. Some 6600 registered Soviet writers chose approximately one tenth of their number to represent them at the Kremlin hall where the Soviet "parliament" also sits. The Ryazan branch of the Writers' Union did not choose Solzhenitsyn as its delegate, but, like any member in good standing, he was entitled to address the Congress in writing about professional concerns.

He composed a statement to the congress—short by Russian standards, and extremely concise, even by Solzhenitsyn's own—defining critical, literary, and social issues. Diligently and patiently, he himself typed out some 250 copies on his shaky old machine and inscribed each by hand to delegates and literary institutions. These were mailed to the addressees on May 16. Solzhenitsyn was unwilling to involve anyone, even a typist, in the potential risk.

The boldness of his statement lay in the directness of its tone, which omitted all customary verbal bows to the authorities, and in the gravity of the issues raised: not stopping at traditional limits, Solzhenitsyn went to the ultimate source of literature's impediments in Soviet society, and, above all, to prescriptions for cure. The document's thrust was established in its first sentence. "I ask the congress," wrote Solzhenitsyn, "to discuss the no longer endurable oppression to which censorship has subjected our literature from decade to decade, and which the Writers' Union cannot tolerate in the future." Censorship, he said, was "not provided for by the Constitution, and is therefore illegal." [1]

Solzhenitsyn went on to document forty years of literary persecution, emphasizing the suppression of writers of the 1920s who, in calling attention to Stalin's "peculiar traits," had tried to avert the national tragedy. Many banned writers, these and others, were published only posthumously, when they could no longer embarrass the establishment. Thus "Pushkin's words are coming true: 'It is only the dead whom they can love.'" [2]

But more than crippling talented writers, censorship lowered the quality of literature in general. "Many members of the union, even delegates to this congress, know that they themselves have not stood up against the pressures of censorship but made concessions in the structure and design of their books, changing chapters, pages, paragraphs, and sentences, providing faded titles—all for the sole sake of seeing the works in print, with the resulting irreparable distortion." This is what deprived Russian literature of the "leading position in the world" that it had enjoyed in the late nineteenth century and of the "experimental brilliance" of the 1920s. And perhaps censorship's most pernicious effect was the "grasping" of this "forever vacillating, perishable institution . . . to appropriate the mission of imperishable time: sorting worthy books from the unworthy."

Solzhenitsyn's remedy was as drastic as his diagnosis. "I move that the congress adopt as its platform, and strive for, the abolition of all censorship of literary works, overt and covert."

Sharp criticism of the operation of Soviet institutions—all except the party leadership—is tolerable to the more liberal leaders. But for a non-official to demand the complete abolition of an institution is almost incomprehensible to the official mind. It is stunningly indecent, as if a stranger demanded access to a couple's marriage bed.

Solzhenitsyn's second proposal was equally radical: that the Writers' Union become what it was in theory, a defender of "members who are subjected to slander and unjust persecution." This presupposed that the Union put its members' interests first, adopting an independent stance when necessary. To a party which obsessively guarded its self-proclaimed "right" to make every last decision in the land—which had gone so far as to write into the Constitution its domination of every institution— this proposal too was sacrilegious. Not since the 1930s had so much as a chess club enjoyed the autonomy that Solzhenitsyn now urged the delegates to proclaim. The union's history of subordination, he said, had led to "sorrowful" results: the surrender of more than six hundred wholly innocent writers to execution and imprisonment. Solzhenitsyn called upon the delegates to elect a new leadership which would have "no historical need" to share responsibility for this tragic past.]

[Solzhenitsyn's third proposal concerned his own case, but he asked the congress to deal with it only if it satisfied his earlier demands—that is, within the framework of a new, genuine Writers' Union. He sought redress on eight issues, from confiscation of his manuscripts to prohibition of his public readings. Items on the list concerned the slanders upon his honor and the ban on his work. Suppression had gone so far, he said, that the mere giving of one's own manuscripts to be read and copied—something which "old Russian scribes were permitted five centuries ago"—had come under the sanction of criminal law.

Solzhenitsyn concluded with an extraordinary challenge.

> Thus has my work been permanently muffled, locked away, and defamed. With such gross violations of my rights as an author and in other respects, will the Fourth Congress undertake to defend me or will it not? It seems to me that this choice is not without importance for the literary future of some of the delegates as well.
>
> I am confident, of course, knowing that I shall fulfill my tasks as a writer in any circumstances, and from my grave even more successfully and incontestably than while I live. No one can bar truth's course, and for its progress I am prepared to accept even death. But perhaps repeated lessons will teach us, at last, not to arrest a writer's pen during his lifetime. Not once has this embellished our history.

The whole of the statement was a mere 1500 words. With it, Solzhenitsyn emerged as the central figure of Russian protest, as he had taken his place in Russian literature with the succinct *One Day*. His public persona was now complete.]

XXIX

Repercussions

SOLZHENITSYN'S SENSATIONAL DECLARATION produced the predictable shock waves. By Soviet standards—in the absence of press coverage—the reaction was remarkably swift. The first recorded written support came three days after Solzhenitsyn had mailed the statement, even before whispers about it could swell to their natural volume. This first acclamatory letter, with an appeal for an end to political control of the arts, was dated May 19, three days before the congress convened.

By opening day, a stream of supporting letters and telegrams, most calling for an open discussion of Solzhenitsyn's declaration, was flowing to the presidium of the congress from the literary community's left wing. Solzhenitsyn's boldness had rekindled some of the solidarity and determination generated during the Sinyavsky-Daniel case; and together with an underlying despair over the country's political slide backward, there was also a hope that honest discussion might somehow put things right. Everything hinged on recognition by the congress of Solzhenitsyn's letter as a proper document to be included in its records.

But hope diminished on the first working day. A long account read to the congress, a kind of State of Soviet Literature Message summarizing literary events since the previous congress in 1959, failed to mention Solzhenitsyn's name even in a purely artistic connection. This prompted the most remarkable supporting letter of all, a statement signed by eighty-four writers, including half a dozen of world reputation. Many of the signatories were not delegates, and simply gathering the endorsements of this highly individualist lot was a minor feat. But the apparent refusal to take up Solzhenitsyn's issues had caused severe indignation, and the letter sharply condemned the presidium for its stubborn deafness. The writers declared that it was their "civic duty" to draw attention to this for the sake of Soviet literature, with its mission as "the nation's conscience."

Thus Solzhenitsyn's appeal pierced the dam, as he had calculated. One writer protested against "cruelty to works of art which [is] incompatible with our fundamental laws and unthinkable in any normal community." Many other writers objected to censorship, and in describing its effects—in films, painting, and sculpture as well as their own medium—the letters ranged from black anger to black humor. A well-known novelist, for example, cited the case of a film on which he had recently worked. "Unfortunately," the shooting was completed just when Khrushchev was deposed, so "all scenes in which corn appeared were cut." But most examples were more appalling than amusing, and it was a source of special grief to several of Solzhenitsyn's supporters that the arbitrary and willful censorship had reached its zenith in this, the fiftieth jubilee year of Soviet rule.

In all, more than a hundred writers declared their solidarity with all or part of Solzhenitsyn's demands. Even those who felt that Solzhenitsyn wanted too much too soon asked that certain minimal conditions be quickly satisfied. A minimum demand in censorship, for example, was the elimination of at least its "ugly covert" aspects. Since the very existence of censorship was nowhere publicly recognized, writers were unable to meet with its practitioners. Communication was made only through specially selected members of the editorial boards of magazines and publishing houses. Now several writers asked for the right to meet censors and to appeal to their superiors about expunged material.

Many more writers sympathized with the content of Solzhenitsyn's letter, but objected to its form—that is, the startling appeal to the literary community over the heads of its superintendents. Tvardovsky was among those who felt that, despite the "incontrovertible force" of Solzhenitsyn's arguments—not a single one of his points could be faulted—he ought to have used the proper channels. "I'd have signed with both hands," he said, "yet I neither wrote nor signed any documents in connection with 'the letter,' believing that all questions bearing on it should be resolved by the normal method of collective discussion in the [Writers' Union] Secretariat."

Discussions in the seclusion of the Writers' Union Secretariat indeed erupted during the following months—and turned out to be as scandalous as earlier phases of Solzhenitsyn's persecution. At the congress itself, however, nothing was heard. Throughout the working sessions, signed appeals for a public reading of Solzhenitsyn's declaration continued to be dispatched to the presidium; but still in vain. The organizers not only refused the reading, but managed to stifle almost all mention of Solzhenitsyn's demands. A liberal Czech writer who was in Moscow at the time observed that the leaders of the Writers' Union were as infuriated by Solzhenitsyn's manifesto as liberal writers had been stirred. They reacted "with equal severity" to Solzhenitsyn's attack on them and, "in tune with official denunciations, declared [the letter] to be prejudiced, untrue, and libelous."

Above all, literary officials were offended. The chairman of the U.S.S.R. Writers' Union later talked of Solzhenitsyn's appeal as "a slap in the face, as if we were depraved sinners, not representatives of the creative intelligentsia." Since personal injury would not do as an explanation for their attitude, the anger toward Solzhenitsyn was couched in high revolutionary-patriotic terms—he was criticized for having spoiled the harmony of the celebrations after a half century of solid Soviet achievements.

Stifling discussion required considerable exertion. Intense pressure was put on the speakers before they mounted the platform, and only "reliable" writers and editors were chosen to speak. Even discounting the effects of Brezhnev-Kosygin's deliberalization, a comparison of the Fourth Congress's speakers with the Third's indicates that practically all known and suspected liberals had been denied "clearance." Tvardovsky's failure to speak —he was still editor of the country's most important literary magazine and a secretary of the union—was a conspicuous example. Only twice was the *cordon sanitaire* seriously threatened, although never breached. The first offender could not have been suspected beforehand.

On the third day of the congress, Oles Gonchar stepped to the dais. This writer's credentials were impeccable: he was a deputy to the Supreme Soviet, member of the Central Committee of the Ukrainian Communist Party, and chairman of the Ukrainian Writers' Union, the country's second largest. And since it had been his characteristically mediocre novel which had won the 1964 Lenin Prize for Literature in preference to *One Day*, no one expected him to champion Solzhenitsyn's case or cause. Yet his speech provided the first brief echo of one of the letter's themes. Discussing the plight of a Moscow writer who was not being published despite his patriotism, military record, talent, and seriousness of purpose, Gonchar expressed "pain" and "solidarity." "The strictest, most finicky editor," he appealed, "and even the invisible man grasping his red pencil, must understand that only a primitive mind, a bureaucrat trembling to hold on to his desk, a careerist, a cast-iron dogmatist, is interested in cramping the thoughts of the Soviet artist and shortening the range of Soviet literature. Whereas the working man—our people and our party—can only benefit from giving more scope to the writer's creativity." The roar of applause which interrupted the speech testified loudly to the anticensorship sentiment.[1]

Gonchar's oblique two-paragraph defense whetted, but hardly gratified, the liberals' craving. The presidium remained impervious to all appeals,

[1] Gonchar's motivation is unknown, but the very fact of his "kneeling rebellion," as the Russians say, is a measure of how far gloom had spread among writers. The Ukrainian writer-politician was not forgotten or forgiven by the authorities. His next work after this speech encountered its own difficulties in publication, and Gonchar himself was gradually stripped of his official positions.

maintaining what one delegate called an "enigmatic silence, as if [Solzhe-
nitsyn's] important document simply doesn't exist." The congress plodded
on, its twice-daily speech-making sessions producing a torrent of words
which under the circumstances seemed like so much regurgitated porridge
to Solzhenitsyn's supporters. To have ignored his works was one thing; to
submerge the heads of six hundred writers in platitudes about socialist
realism and the virtues of Soviet art while fundamental questions stalked
the hall drove the bewilderment and frustration to much higher levels.
An element of surrealism was added to the unreality when Mikhail
Sholokhov, Russia's only living Nobel Prize author—and relentless enemy
of literary "deviates"—complimented the congress late on its fourth day
for the sensible orderliness of its proceedings. Everything had gone,
purred Sholokhov ironically from the platform, "as with respectable folk:
quiet, peaceful, calm, without sharp speeches and without excessive
trouble or agitation." The calculated, blank-faced ignoring of momentous
and electrifying issues clearly pleased Sholokhov.

On the fifth day, Solzhenitsyn was finally mentioned by name. In the
course of a defiant speech, a Leningrad writer named Vera Ketlinskaya
spoke out against censorship and in support of Solzhenitsyn's other major
demand, that the Writers' Union should genuinely defend its members
and their works. Ketlinskaya used the word "Stalinism," taboo even in the
most enthusiastic days of de-Stalinization, and her defense of Solzhenitsyn's
ideas was in the context of a general condemnation of the halting of
de-Stalinization. One can like Solzhenitsyn or not, the elderly lady asserted,
but one must not pretend, as previous speakers had, that the phenomenon
simply doesn't exist. It was a fighting speech which indicated that, despite
the organizers' control and the opposition to Solzhenitsyn by a large body
of run-of-the-mill writers themselves, not all liberal voices could be
entirely stifled. Long, stormy applause greeted Ketlinskaya's plea.

But acclamation on the floor left the presidium unmoved, all the more
so because an onslaught on Solzhenitsyn's views also won long applause.
Alexander Chakovsky, Solzhenitsyn's Inspector Javert, spoke soon after
Ketlinskaya, condemning the writers who sought greater freedom as "ir-
responsible," since their kind of literature might easily undermine readers'
"faith" and lead to the disintegration of Soviet society. It is impossible to
measure the support of the two camps numerically, but Chakovsky's had
the overwhelming advantage of occupying the chair and controlling the
floor.

Gonchar and Ketlinskaya were buried under an avalanche of a quarter
of a million bland words.[2] Despite more and more strident urgings "not to

---

[2] Konstantin Simonov, a prominent novelist who had also had recent troubles with
the censorship, appealed forthrightly for an end to the rewriting of history to con-
form to the changing party line, but his personal concern with historical distortion
was not directly connected to support of Solzhenitsyn's demands.

hide away" Solzhenitsyn's letter, the liberals felt genuine anguish as the congress approached its close. Their yearning for an honest review of the issues was intensified by the disclosure of Solzhenitsyn's personal tribulations. His publishing difficulties were generally known in the profession before the congress, and were not startlingly exceptional; but the letter provided a first glimpse of the KGB's molestation of him and his work. This was exceptional and hair-raising, for even writers too young to remember knew what police raids on literature had led to in the past. The combination of general and particular grievances lifted several writers, in their messages to the presidium, to impassioned eloquence in Solzhenitsyn's defense.

The last speeches were scheduled for the fifth day of the congress. Now even the hardiest optimists understood that the vague rumors of a fair hearing of the issues had been put about only to deflate the protestors' pressure. In the clarity of rage, Georgy Vladimov, a young novelist and author of the suppressed guard dog story, wrote to the presidium:

> I have had the good fortune to read almost all that [Solzhenitsyn] has written. He is the writer whom my Russia now needs most of all, who is destined to make her illustrious in the world and to answer all the aching questions which the tragedy we have suffered has lodged in us. . . . I mean no insult to the congress, but nine tenths of its delegates will probably not succeed in carrying their names across the threshold of this century. Alexander Solzhenitsyn, the pride of Russian literature, will take his name further.

Vladimov tossed his own bitter challenge to the delegates.

> So I should like to ask the plenipotentiary congress: are we a nation of rats, squealers, and informers or are we a great people who have given the world an incomparable constellation of geniuses? Solzhenitsyn will fulfill his tasks . . . but we—what about us? Did we defend him against raids and confiscation? Did we see to it that his works were published? Did we pull away the sticky, smelly hand of slander from his face? Did we at least give him an articulate reply when he sought answers in our editorial offices and boards? At that time, we were listening to greetings from Mr. Dürrenmatt and Mrs. Hellman.[3] Well, that's a task of sorts too, like solidarity with struggling Vietnam and suffering Greece. But time will pass and we'll be asked: What did we do for ourselves and for our neighbors who lived and worked in such hardship? . . .
>
> I move that the congress debate this letter in open session, adopt a new and unequivocal resolution about it, and present this resolution to the government of the country.

---

[3] Friedrich Dürrenmatt and Lillian Hellman, Swiss and American playwrights who were invited guests to the congress.

Like all previous appeals in this vein, Vladimov's was wholly ignored. Twenty months later, obviously after bitter clashes over the editing of the historical record, the "stenographic transcript" of the congress was ready for printing. To it were appended page after page of greetings and congratulations from soldiers, factory workers, collective farmers, and other citizens. By contrast, all messages to the assembly from Solzhenitsyn and his supporters went unmentioned and became unstatements for the Soviet public.

Suppressed at home, Solzhenitsyn's declaration quickly left the country on the persons of foreign intellectuals visiting Moscow and Russian writers traveling abroad. Russians brought some of the first copies to Czechoslovakia, the country where Solzhenitsyn's ideas had the most intense topical interest. It was still seven months before the emergence of Dubček and the Prague Spring, but the Stalinist regime there was weakening. By coincidence, the Fourth Congress of Czechoslovak writers opened in June 1967, a month after the Fourth Soviet Congress closed. Far more than in Moscow, the writers assembled in Prague were determined and united, almost to a man, to unshackle themselves from intolerable controls. The mood was most succinctly expressed by the Slovak national poet Laco Novomesky, a lifelong Communist, who declared from the dais that the time had come to liberate literature from the onerous controls of the party, and the party from the debasing task of controlling literature. Bold demand followed ringing appeal, among them that writers be better informed. Why should it be necessary, one speaker asked, to learn of important literary events like Solzhenitsyn's letter from the Western press?

The delegates applauded. Declarations of solidarity with Solzhenitsyn were pronounced. A leading writer offered to read Solzhenitsyn's letter, of which he had a Czech translation in his pocket. The proposal was put to a vote; one lone delegate voted no, and two abstained. And at this moment, one of the critical turning points in the genesis of the entire Prague Spring arrived. As the first sentences of Solzhenitsyn's letter were being read from the platform, Jiři Hendrych, the regime's second most powerful politician, rose from his seat. Increasingly "seething," as an observer put it, over the ringing calls for free literature, he "boiled over" at the public reading of Solzhenitsyn's manifesto. Storming from the hall, he paused just long enough to threaten the Writers' Union with doom: "You have lost everything, absolutely everything."

Hendrych's rage was provoked not by Solzhenitsyn's text alone, but also by the implications of its use at the congress. For one thing, he dreaded the Kremlin's fury over this public reading. And by appealing to the authority of a Soviet writer, the Czechoslovak delegates seemed to be laughing in the face of ritual tributes to the "elder brother" of socialist countries. Instead of evoking the Soviet example, as was done virtually every day by every newspaper, to justify the strengthening of state power and suppression of free art, the writers had now ventured to cite a Russian in defense of liberation! The specter of international liberal solidarity was beginning to haunt the socialist camp.

After Hendrych had quit the hall, "there was nothing left for me to do," explained the writer who had produced Solzhenitsyn's declaration, "but to read the remaining five pages of the letter clearly and loudly." He did—and the emotional tension and its release were so strong that he himself left the hall while the applause to Solzhenitsyn was ringing. Overcome by dizziness, he had to grip the bannister on his way to the bar. After a stiff Russian vodka, he spent the remainder of the day "as if in a fog," aware only that an "unprecedented crisis" was upon the nation.

As it happened, not the writers but Hendrych lost absolutely everything. His exit from the congress marked the first organizational rupture between the Czechoslovak regime and an important social institution. A chain of events following from this break led to the collapse of the old government, Hendrych and all, in January 1968. Solzhenitsyn's manifesto —the force of his words and inspiring clarity of his moral position— pushed the Czechoslovak writers over the brink and contributed to the emergence, by way of a conflict between the party's Old Guard and society, of Dubček's Socialism with a Human Face.

There was far more than an accidental, or even tactical, link between Solzhenitsyn's stance and Czechoslovakia's future development. The socialism of the Prague Spring, with its commitment to replace dictatorial controls and bureaucratic manipulation with genuine concern for human needs, was close to Solzhenitsyn's own vision of ethical socialism, a vision that was most clearly delineated in the second part of *Cancer Ward*, completed only months before the two writers' congresses. In that novel, one of Solzhenitsyn's most tragic characters begs a listener not to blame socialism for the "cruel years" and to remember that capitalism is ethically doomed and has no place in mankind's future except when restricted to very narrow limits. He pleads for more civilized human relationships, transcending both Stalinism's brutality and capitalism's "greedy appetites" —a society in which every activity, from the upbringing of children to the use of leisure time, would be based on laws and principles deriving directly from, "*and only from*," an inner ethic. All questions of what should or should not be undertaken would be decided by measuring their value in terms of ethical demands.

Scientific research? Only when not at the cost of ethics—and first of all, those of the researchers themselves. The same for foreign policy! The same for any question about frontiers: we mustn't think how much richer or stronger one or another step will make us or how it will raise our prestige, but only of one thing: how ethical it is.

This, says Solzhenitsyn's character, is what ethical socialism ought to be. Moreover, society must teach people to strive not for happiness but for mutual affection. For although a beast gnawing its prey can experience the former, only man is capable of mutual affection, "the highest given to human beings." The statements in *Cancer Ward* offer some of the clearest glimpses of Solzhenitsyn's ultimate political morality, the impetus for the letter. Although the time for these ideas had arrived in Czechoslovakia, Russia's sheer size, diversity, and historical tradition of isolation and backwardness worked powerfully against their quick acceptance there. Not only were the Soviet regime's defenses less vulnerable, but its stubborn, introverted conservatism enjoyed far more popular support, if only passive. Even among the writers, only a portion—albeit Russia's most talented—supported the declaration that won virtually unanimous approval in Prague.

The weakness of Russian liberalism vis-à-vis the regime's defenses was reflected in Western reporting of the Czechoslovak and Soviet congresses. The writers' declaration of independence in Prague was instantly and fully reported, whereas nothing of the drama of the Soviet congress—not even a hint of the Solzhenitsyn "movement"—reached Western reporters in Moscow until after the fact. At that embryonic stage in its development, Soviet protest was still enveloped by Russia's deep, pervading isolation. Had it not been for the publication of Solzhenitsyn's text itself in late May in Paris, the congress might still seem to have gone, as Western correspondents informed the world at the time, according to the "prepared script" of the Writers' Union. Now the news was a front-page story. Although the phenomenon of protest in Russia had been known since the Sinyavsky-Daniel trial some sixteen months before, few readers thought of it as anything more than a quixotic pursuit by some "fringe" intellectuals. It was the Paris publication of the letter that made the world aware of a much broader and more deeply rooted dissent.

For the dissenters themselves, Western publicity was important both for the partial protection it provided them and for the spreading of news of "the movement" inside Russia, by way of radio broadcasts on foreign stations. And the stand of the Prague congress was indeed heartening news. But these benefits hardly compensated for the failure to open debate within Russia about what Solzhenitsyn later called "the fate of our great literature . . . which has now lost its [world] position." As in the 1956–57 "thaw" and the 1962 liberal offensive, the authorities had again contained a tentative liberal movement—this time, even before it reached the public media.

Yet in the long run, the letter did affect Russia's literary climate. As *One Day* had made some writers sense that they could not go on writing as before, this declaration spread a feeling that it was wrong to tolerate outrages as before. One liberal writer described this conviction:

> When I first read this astounding letter, it occurred to me that Russian literature itself had gazed back over the path it had traveled, pondering and measuring all it had had to endure, counting its bereavements and losses, remembering the persecuted . . . taking stock of the damage done to the country's spiritual wealth by the persecution of writers, and pronouncing with Solzhenitsyn's voice: Enough! No more! Life must be different!

With this effect on the psychological atmosphere of literary circles, the letter had much to do with the defiance of a portion of Soviet writers in the following years.

But in the period directly following the congress, the principal feeling of those whom the letter had stirred was a deep sense of defeat. The intense urgings for a new beginning by Solzhenitsyn's supporters turned to bitter resignation tinged with shame over their own impotence. Now letters of protest went not to the congress presidium but to a higher authority. An elderly poet, much decorated with Stalin Prizes—for which he later expressed deep repentance—wrote to Pyotr Demichev, the Central Committee's Secretary for Ideological Affairs. "If a Soviet writer felt compelled to address his brothers in literature with a letter such as Solzhenitsyn's," stated Pavel Antokolsky, "this means that we are all responsible before him and before our own readers. If he cannot tell his own truth to his readers, then I, this old writer, am stripped of the right to look my readers in the eye."

XXX

Rupture

SOLZHENITSYN'S STINGING CRITICISM MIGHT HAVE been expected to bring an immediate and total end to his relations with the literary establishment. More than this, outsiders would have been justified in speculating about his arrest. But this was not how the current rulers operated. There was machinery for physical repression, serving as a permanent threat to potential victims, but the dictatorship's aging warders lacked the nerve to apply unmasked lawlessness; personal experience had taught them that once unleashed, terror might eventually knock at their own doors.

Least of all did the authorities care to arrest a celebrity, for above all, the senescent professional revolutionaries feared the disturbance to their stolid rule of a new *cause célèbre*. If the Sinyavsky-Daniel affair had sparked such protest in Russia and abroad, similar tactics were clearly unsuited to the much better known Solzhenitsyn. On the contrary, the authorities were now intent upon "tranquilizing public opinion," as Solzhenitsyn put it. Once again, therefore, officials sought him out, bearing hopefully tempting gifts.

Solzhenitsyn had demanded that the congress take up his personal case only after the inauguration of sweeping general reforms. Resisting all political and social changes, the establishment reversed these priorities. Now the odd spectacle materialized of officials swallowing their pride and making solicitous noises at Solzhenitsyn. Their intention was to dull his sense of outrage and assure his supporters of their good will.

After the congress, Solzhenitsyn could have little illusion about favors proffered by officials. Moreover, he is not a patient man in this sense; he dislikes procrastination, does not suffer empty arguments gladly, and detests wasting time. Nevertheless, he mustered his patience for the new round of promises. He was determined to demonstrate that, while standing on his principles, he would not open himself to charges of aloofness or unreasonableness.

Two weeks after the congress, a newly elected secretariat of the Writers' Union (almost entirely the same veteran bureaucrats) invited Solzhenitsyn to call upon them in Moscow. When Solzhenitsyn did, in mid-June, the union officials fairly oozed politesse and high-minded sympathy for his personal and publishing problems. The slanders about him and his war record appeared to cause them positive indignation; no less than four secretaries assured Solzhenitsyn that the union considered it its duty to arrange a public refutation. They also promised to "examine the question" of publication in general and, at the very least, to resolve the deadlock of *Cancer Ward*.

[Solzhenitsyn stressed the urgency of the latter matter. After years of not being published, he had let a relatively wide circle of friends read manuscripts of *Cancer Ward, The First Circle*, and several short stories. The friends made copies for their friends—a process for which the term *samizdat*, roughly "do-it-yourself publishing," was coined. By the summer of 1967, *samizdat* was almost a cottage industry, and Solzhenitsyn its most wanted author. (The price for a blurred carbon copy of one of his novels reached some eighty rubles, the average monthly wage of a semiskilled worker.) [1] Solzhenitsyn told the secretaries that with hundreds of copies of *Cancer Ward* in circulation, it was impossible to prevent the novel's "leaking" to the West. To avoid the embarrassment of its appearing there first, publication in Russia ought to be hurried.

The meeting ended in apparent reasonableness. Solzhenitsyn was promised that even if the full text of the letter were not published—but there was a fair chance it would be—the issues he had raised would be publicly discussed in one form or another. If nothing else the secretariat's comments on the letter would be published shortly. The text had already been prepared.

A reply to Solzhenitsyn had indeed been prepared which, judging from later references, was clearly conciliatory. But three months passed without its release. Nor was there public discussion of any of Solzhenitsyn's issues. During this interval, only one positive development took place: despite *Novy Mir*'s previous procrastination, Tvardovsky made known his readiness to publish *Cancer Ward* immediately. By this time, Solzhenitsyn was well into a new novel about labor camps, but the uncertainty about *Cancer Ward* continued to distract and distress him. With *The First Circle*, the decision had at least been clear-cut; and there was a certain logic in an increasingly rigid leadership banning a book which stirred painful

---

[1] A Western correspondent in Moscow described a copy of *The First Circle* which came to him, through Russian friends, in the form of two extremely bulky volumes of photographed text. "To every page were glued four photographs of typewritten pages, just large enough to be readable. The typing was bad. So were the gluing and photography. Some of the pages were hardly legible. Quotations in foreign languages had simply been left out by the typist."

memories of a shameful past. But as Solzhenitsyn said, *Cancer Ward* had fallen into "an odd equipoise—neither a direct ban nor direct permission." Apparently no one in authority was willing to order an unequivocal suppression, perhaps for fear of being identified as a protector of the denouncer Rusanov. On the other hand, recognizing themselves in the novel, present-day Rusanovs did not want others to perceive them as the author had. The procrastination and endless hedging irritated Solzhenitsyn and offended his mathematician's penchant for simple, elegant solutions. At the very least, he was determined to make the Rusanovs stand up and be seen.

Other incidents, episodes, and rumors intensified his anger that summer, among them gossip that his archive was about to be returned and that *Cancer Ward* and the collection of short stories would definitely be approved. In the Western press, the rumors appeared as facts, and some of Solzhenitsyn's supporters repeated them in good faith, even with pride over their contributions to these achievements. The plan to sedate public opinion was apparently succeeding internationally as well as domestically —without helping Solzhenitsyn in any way, for nothing in the authorities' attitude matched the rumored good news.

On the contrary, defenses against Solzhenitsyn were hastily reinforced. As word spread to the general public of the letter—and the passionate commitment to it by some of the country's most respected writers— new explanations of the writers' lapses were required for "the masses." To this end slander, far from being publicly refuted, was enriched with what Solzhenitsyn later called "new and fantastic nonsense." In confidence, party ideological instructors informed "activists" and participants in indoctrination seminars that Solzhenitsyn had fled the country—in some versions to Britain and in others to the United Arab Republic.[2] This extraordinary charge was a kind of updating of allegations about Solzhenitsyn's wartime disloyalty; again an attempt had been made to equate his dissent with treason.

Was this done out of fear of Solzhenitsyn or, primarily, uncontrollable resentment and wrath? As a calculated program to discredit him, undermining his influence on Russian readers, or as an expression of frustration and

---

[2] Solzhenitsyn was to draw attention to this fantasy more than once. In the absence of any rational reason for the ideologist's choice of the U.A.R., one can only assume that it had something to do with the recent Six-day War. Throughout Eastern Europe and Russia, liberal sympathy for Israel was considerable, and resentment over Arab irresponsibility and weakness so widespread that hints of it were even reflected in the otherwise rabidly pro-Arab Soviet press. Thus—if this guess is not fantasy too—the United Arab Republic might have been chosen in the hope of discrediting Solzhenitsyn in two ways: by linking him to the enemies of Israel (making him disagreeable to many Russian liberals) while these same Arabs were resented by many Russians of all social strata as crushingly expensive allies and a miserable investment.

spleen about a man and a talent somewhere felt superior and uncrushable? In any case, the "cancer of slander," as Solzhenitsyn called it, was spread far and wide. Five years later, he elaborated on the methods. Since 1966, he explained, lecturers in the country's network of party and public indoctrination—which provided for a schedule of lectures in every institution in the land, from military units to state farms—had been ordered to talk about him in closed meetings for insiders only. The themes were that Solzhenitsyn's imprisonment had been for a serious offense, that his rehabilitation was unjustified and that his works were "criminal." Since the lecturers themselves had "never in their lives" read his works—their superiors would not risk it—they simply followed orders to say what they were told. The "nonsense" they sowed was soon to include talk "at the lowest gutter level" of his family life, and they liked to "play around" with his patronymic Isaiyevich to hint that he had Jewish blood, adding, as if incidentally, that his real name was "Solzhenitser" or "Solzhenitsker," which sound Jewish to the Russian ear.

Solzhenitsyn stressed that it was not market women but "paid propagandists" who disseminated such information, in keeping with the tendency in Russia "to try to bait people not with arguments, but with the most primitive labels, the coarsest names, and also the simplest-designed, as they say, to arouse the fury of the masses." In the 1920s, he said, the label was "counterrevolutionary"; in the 1930s, "enemy of the people." Since the 1940s, it had been "traitor to the country"—the charge which always caught the attention of audiences in the indoctrination meetings, and which obviously stung Solzhenitsyn most sharply. "You should have seen how they leafed through my military record, how they tried to establish that I might have been a prisoner of war for at least a day or two, like Ivan Denisovich—that would have been a real find!" [3] A gullible public, he said, can be made to believe any lie, and for years, Russians were told that he had voluntarily surrendered to the Germans—or better still, surrendered an entire battery. This was embellished by tales of his having served as a policeman for the Germans in occupied territory, having fought in the Vlasov army and, best of all, having worked directly for the Gestapo.

For a man so committed to honor and with such instincts to take action in his own defense, the impossibility of answering the charges was severely galling. Even could he travel to all the cities involved, he would not have been admitted to closed auditoriums. Besides, there were "thousands of these lectures. There is nobody to complain. This slander takes hold of people's minds." Moreover, the entire campaign took place without any official recognition of it, under a tranquil and happy surface. "On the

---

[3] Like many others, Ivan Denisovich was in a labor camp only because he had been a German prisoner of war—in his case, for only a few days.

outside, it's a peaceful paradise and no defamation whatever, while irre-futable slander is poured all over the country." Although still in an early stage now, in mid-1967, the campaign had become an inescapable presence in Solzhenitsyn's life and would continue "to this day," as he stressed in 1972.

The organizers of the new campaign also undertook to blunt any re-newed curiosity about the writer. Although he had not published a word in eighteen months and nothing of substantial volume in four full years, word-of-mouth news of the letter drew public attention to him again. Far from issuing his promised new books, therefore, the authorities suppressed his old works, largely by hastening the removal of *One Day*—and, now, the November 1962 issue of *Novy Mir*—from normal library circulation.

Throughout the summer, Solzhenitsyn made no response. His restraint was almost certainly planned to give the union's secretaries time to fulfill their promises. But in mid-September, three months to the day after his meeting with the secretariat, Solzhenitsyn wrote to the union. In urgent tones he described his current situation and insisted that "my novel be published forthwith." In reply, he was invited to a second meeting at the secretariat.

Solzhenitsyn arrived at one o'clock on September 22—to an atmosphere sharply different from that of the June meeting. Some thirty of the union's forty-two secretaries were present, and watched over by a representative of the Central Committee's Cultural Department (Polikarpov's old agency). From the first, Solzhenitsyn was berated in tones of bitter acrimony and injured innocence. "Solzhenitsyn's second letter cut me to the quick," said the chairman of the meeting. "I feel it was an insult to the members of our organization."

The chairman was Konstantin Fedin, a man whose path had already crossed Solzhenitsyn's several times. Fedin was associated with *Znamya* when the twenty-year-old mathematician-writer submitted his works un-successfully to that magazine before the war. In 1962, however, Fedin's praise of *One Day* was one of Tvardovsky's most valued endorsements in the campaign for publication. His opinion was made weighty by more than his august pillar-of-the-establishment position or archetypally "Cheko-vian" appearance. Fedin also enjoyed a considerable literary reputation, based on the great subtlety and intelligence of his prose in the 1920s. His disintegration, like that of so many other writers, began in the following decade. Although there is no evidence that he was arrested or physically mistreated during the terror, by the 1950s he had become little more than an instrument of the authorities. He served as both a "fixer" in delicate cultural matters, working, for example, to pull Boris Pasternak and other old literary acquaintances into line, and as a model for others—the "good" writer who, although not a party member, accepted every party decision with an understanding nod. But he could also act admirably when the atmosphere seemed propitious, as in his edifying support of *One Day's* publication. An old Moscow saying had it that if the moral core were pared from a Russian intellectual, what remained would be Fedin—stoop, gold-rimmed glasses, civilized patter, and all, and decorated with his sympathetic smile.

That September, Fedin was seventy-five years old and seriously ill. But the secretariat's meeting was important enough to pull him from his sick bed; though probably less important to him than to the animators of the pathetic but sinister intellectual zombie. For he had been assigned the key job: not his customarily discreet backstage manipulation, but crude, conspicuous hacking. No doubt this would diminish his future effectiveness as the old-friend-of-the-talented—if the ailing elder had a future at all. But cost was secondary where Solzhenitsyn was concerned. The heaviest talent had to be mobilized, and Fedin had the added edge of being chairman of the Writers' Union, its nominal head. Besides, he had taken no discernible part in the anti-Solzhenitsyn campaign; on the contrary, he could be presented as a principled supporter who had been let down by an unruly, unreasonable protégé.

Throughout the five and a half hours of the meeting, the rigid secretaries repeatedly pelted Solzhenitsyn with a dominant question: What was his attitude toward the use of the letter by bourgeois propaganda? Why hadn't he "dissociated himself" from such use? (They were referring to the letter's publication in *Le Monde* and elsewhere, and to the subsequent excitement it generated throughout the West.) Early in the meeting, Chairman Fedin advised Solzhenitsyn to reply but, riled by the chairman's aggressive-cum-offended opening remarks a few minutes earlier, the writer exploded at the bossy suggestion. He was, he said, "no schoolboy to jump up each time he's asked a question." He would speak when his turn came.

Disregarding this flare of temper, as if Solzhenitsyn were in fact a naughty schoolboy, the secretaries continued to question him. When the writer again refused to submit, the meeting almost disintegrated. Angry murmurs swelled: Solzhenitsyn was snubbing his senior colleagues and should admit it outright. No doubt realizing that his entire cause might be jeopardized if he could be explained away as a man of capricious temperament, Solzhenitsyn regained his self-control and submitted to his questioners, even at some cost to his dignity.

Solzhenitsyn declared himself willing to state his attitude toward "bourgeois propaganda" but insisted that the secretariat first "clear the way" for this by publishing the letter together with its own comments, and by undertaking to redress his grievances. Fedin would make no such guarantees—no promise whatever until, as he repeated, Solzhenitsyn "protested against the dirty use of his name by our enemies in the West. . . . Then we shall see."

Solzhenitsyn answered with two arguments. First, he could not understand why a response to the West should take precedence over settling his own affairs at home. "The word 'abroad,'" he said, "is being used here with great significance and great emphasis, as if it were some important office whose opinion is highly valued. I find this odd . . . I don't understand this great sensitivity toward the outside world rather than to our own country with its living public opinion." [4] The second argument complemented the first. Even if he were to set aside his view of the correct priorities, how could he express himself on foreign reaction to a document of which Russian readers were ignorant? Unless the letter were printed alongside, what sense could Russians make of his statement about it?

Solzhenitsyn soon saw that this logic could not dent the secretaries' serried indignation. Nevertheless, he deliberately spoke as if to a group of his intellectual peers, men open to persuasion and free to form independent judgment. His purpose in this also became quickly clear: he had obviously determined to use the assembly to put on record his views on a variety of subjects, if only to the leadership of the Writers' Union. Careful to avoid a recurrence of the temper which had nearly scuttled this intention, he spoke at length several times, sometimes making statements that showed signs, even granted his great precision in extemporaneous speech, of advance preparation.

He took the opportunity to renounce "Feast of the Victors" yet again. The poem, he said, reflected the "impasse" of his position as a "nameless prisoner" of 1949, and "bore no relationship whatever" to his current work. Solzhenitsyn deplored attempts, at this meeting and elsewhere, to use the epic as a kind of prism for analyzing his present position. Aggressively, he challenged the ethics of discussing a work stolen from an author's hiding place, whose reproduction and even reading the author had taken pains to prevent. Before the thirty-odd influential witnesses, he repeated the full story of the confiscation of his archives and subsequent, fruitless petitioning; and told of the increasingly insulting slanders.

And he did not limit himself to self-defense. Speaking as if he genuinely believed that the wild misinterpretations of *Cancer Ward* had resulted from genuine misunderstandings, he ventured an explanation of the novel. How could it be claimed, he asked, that the cancer was symbolic of some national disease when his aim—and achievement—was to portray the illness as he personally had known it? How could the work be called

---

[4] This argument was later echoed by Tvardovsky. In the final phase of the fight to publish *Cancer Ward*, he wrote angrily that "a document one or two pages long has become for us writers more important than a six-hundred-page novel."

"antihumanist" when "quite the contrary, it shows the overcoming of death by life, of the past through the future"? [5] He even favored the secretaries with the best explanation he is known to have produced of his broader concept of the writer as an explorer of "the secrets of man's heart and conscience." Solzhenitsyn could hardly help realize that these appeals to civilized literary understanding would be fruitless. But he could not have known what proportion of his audience had accepted instructions and was totally deaf to him. He could not know that Fedin's ultimatum to him—renounce Western "exploitation" of the letter as a precondition for everything—had been approved by the secretariat during the two hours that it met, in confidence, before Solzhenitsyn joined it. Nor that these two hours had been devoted to rehearsing the scenario, including who would say what to Solzhenitsyn. After this drill, none of the secretaries individually could have entered into honest discussion, not to speak of negotiations, with the writer. In this sense, the meeting was a mockery.

Why, then, was it called at all? Surely not in the hope that Solzhenitsyn would surrender. But any one of three motives might have prompted it. The confrontation provided an opportunity, first, to put the position of the parties on neat bureaucratic record and, second, for the literary officials to vent their long-suppressed anger against the "defamer." Beyond this, it may have been an attempt to intimidate Solzhenitsyn's supporters through an impressive display of official displeasure.

The display was indeed impressive. Alexey Surkov spoke on the general topic of Solzhenitsyn's work, and expressed the secretariat's position with characteristic force. An orthodox poet, Surkov had been chairman of the Writers' Union during the Pasternak affair, in which capacity he had bedeviled Pasternak as Chakovsky now harried Solzhenitsyn.[6] Comparing the two cases, the former chairman concluded that "Solzhenitsyn's works are more dangerous for us than Pasternak's: Pasternak was a man remote from life, while Solzhenitsyn has a lively, militant, socially conscious nature. He is a socially aware person."

Other speakers were equally hostile but further from the point. With more Pavlovian conditioning than logic, a Belorussian writer named Petrus Brovka reproached Solzhenitsyn for basing his work on his personal experience instead of on what he was told. "Many people in Belorussia served time in the camps," Brovka admitted, and mentioned one local writer who had not complained even after twenty years. But unlike Solzhenitsyn, "these people understood that the responsibility for these in-

---

[5] There is in fact one passage in *Cancer Ward* where the hero thinks, "A man dies from a tumor, so how can a country survive with growths like labor camps and exiles?" but this is no more than a passing thought in a long and complex description of cancer as such.

[6] It was Surkov who had been dispatched to Italy in 1957 with the delicate mission of foiling the publication of *Doctor Zhivago*.

justices does not belong to the people, the party, or Soviet rule." More puzzling was a kind of why-do-you-lynch-blacks interrogatory put by a Ukrainian playwright. "Do you realize that there are thermonuclear weapons in the world," he asked Solzhenitsyn, "and that, despite all our efforts for peace, the United States may use them?" The playwright did not explain how Solzhenitsyn's surrender would disarm American imperialism. The examinee commented indirectly on the level of this discussion by remarking that he would not now be surprised if he were declared "a supporter of the geocentric system or [the man] who sent Giordano Bruno to the stake." The tragedy implied by Solzhenitsyn was that men capable of using these hopelessly specious arguments had the power to dispose of his work.

The meeting was formally devoted to the question of whether or not to publish *Cancer Ward*, and, in their discussion of it, several simple men unwittingly revealed their own literary philosophy. "I read *Cancer Ward* with great displeasure," proclaimed one provincial writer. "All its characters are former prisoners. It's a murky story without a single word of warmth in it. It makes you sick just to read it. . . . Why does the author see only the dark side? Why don't I write darkly? I always strive to write only about joys. . . . I'd have thought it courageous if Solzhenitsyn were to renounce *Cancer Ward*. Then I'd embrace him like a brother."

More sophisticated opponents argued for suppression not in terms of personal predilection, but from the lofty standpoint of *raison d'état*. Surkov and Brovka went to the extreme of comparing *Cancer Ward* to Svetlana Alliluyeva's memoirs, generally accepted as treasonable. Solzhenitsyn's novel, they said, was more dangerous: Svetlana's "notes" were "female prattle," while he was "an acknowledged talent."

Most of the secretaries supported the attack; the letter had so angered the Soviet leadership that no official dared defend it. Even Tvardovsky suggested that Solzhenitsyn be "strictly warned" for his "inadmissible, unacceptable" deed of addressing the public over the heads of officialdom. But despite all this, discipline was slighty bent. Even several of the establishment writers present realized that total suppression of an author sensed to occupy first place among his contemporaries was wrong for Soviet literature. Several maintained, therefore, that *Cancer Ward* was a separate matter from Solzhenitsyn's insubordination, and should be considered on its own merits. Resisting pressure, these few secretaries—who had earlier condemned other activities of Solzhenitsyn—cautiously submitted that they saw no reason not to publish *Cancer Ward*; and three men appealed outright for a positive decision.

Tvardovsky was the most forthright. Having paid lip service to the letter's condemnation, he proceeded to defend Solzhenitsyn from the slanders and tried to move the meeting toward neutrality to the author.

Undaunted by *Cancer Ward*'s buffeting, he declared that *Novy Mir*'s editorial board saw no objections to running the novel. "We'd like only to receive the secretariat's approval," he said. "Or at least [a statement] that the secretariat doesn't object." The editor knew full well that most secretaries objected strongly, but was trying to commit them to an official decision which he could then appeal directly to the party, the "Supreme Court" for these matters. But Fedin, who had obviously been instructed to apply maximum pressure on Solzhenitsyn and Tvardovsky without offering this procedural opening, did not permit Tvardovsky's suggestion to become a formal motion.

The meeting adjourned amid calls to Solzhenitsyn, shrugging in mock horror, to "renounce his role as the leader of the political opposition in our country." The five and a half hours had shown Solzhenitsyn and the secretariat to be virtually irreconcilable. But a complete break was still avoided: the writer was unwilling to relinquish even the smallest opportunity of being published in his own country, and the union was equally reluctant to lose the slightest chance of converting, or at least silencing, its formidable adversary. Parted, the two sides returned to a waiting game.

During the following weeks, vague promises were once more fluttered before Solzhenitsyn and Tvardovsky—while the anti-Solzhenitsyn campaign fell to a more ominous level. In early October, the writer was again publicly attacked, this time before an audience of employees of Leningrad publishing institutions. The speaker in this instance was no low-level party propagandist but Mikhail Zimyanin, the editor-in-chief of *Pravda* and chairman of the U.S.S.R. Union of Journalists. Again casting doubt on Solzhenitsyn's innocence of his labor-camp charges and repeating that he had been a German prisoner of war, Zimyanin called the writer a "mentally abnormal man, a schizophrenic" for whom the camps were "the only subject . . . an *idée fixe*." Since insane asylums were already being used to dispose of dissidents, this was not only a smear on Solzhenitsyn's past but an unmistakable threat to his future.

The gist of Zimyanin's remarks was promptly reported to Solzhenitsyn, but he continued to confine himself to work in Ryazan, and the next formal move was made by his adversaries. Two months after the September meeting, the secretariat wrote to ask his decision after reflecting on "the attitude of literary public opinion" as expressed in the September "discussion." Solzhenitsyn quickly replied, summarizing new slanders and old grievances, and inquiring whether the secretariat would undertake to help him. His clear implication was that unless the secretariat demonstrated at least willingness, he would do nothing. His minimal condition for further "negotiation" was discussion of *Cancer Ward II* by the union.

No tangible help was forthcoming, but the secretariat still wanted to appear reasonable. It was suggested that if Solzhenitsyn felt unable to speak out about Western exploitation of the letter, he should do so in a confidential communication to the secretariat; with this on record, publication might again be arranged. This "compromise" was unacceptable to Solzhenitsyn: it would have him appear to the world as a "fighter for freedom," while privately denouncing some of the consequences of his own actions—and, in the process, exposing himself broadly to blackmail by the union. Both sides seemed frozen into immutable positions—until Tvardovsky again broke the ice.

After the September discussion, the editor chose not to submit to the majority of the secretariat nor to temporize further but, in the absence of an explicit ban, to publish *Cancer Ward*. It was a calculated gamble. Tvardovsky hoped that the embarrassment of a portion of the decision makers in issuing an unequivocal interdiction—that is, in joining the neo-Stalinists—would outweigh the discomfiture of the objectors, who, in the event of publication, would seem inconsequential fools. The chance was small, but the only one remaining, and for the sake of *Cancer Ward* Tvardovsky was willing to brave the severe displeasure he would incur in either case. Later that autumn, he and Solzhenitsyn prepared a new draft of the novel, incorporating slight changes that the editor wanted.[7] *Cancer Ward I* was scheduled for serialization in its entirety in *Novy Mir* during the first months of 1968, with the first installment of eight chapters to appear in the January issue. When they were set in type in December, twilight seemed to be descending at last on the era of procrastination.

The final confrontation about the novel came early in January. Since *Novy Mir* was formally the organ of the Writers' Union, the secretariat was empowered to determine its content. Normally, the editor took full responsibility for all editorial decisions; but in the case of *Cancer Ward*, Tvardovsky was called in by Fedin and two high aides. The editor said that he wanted nothing more than to put the decision in the hands of his magazine's editorial board, thus absolving the secretariat from any responsibility if the decision were positive. Although the three secretaries present were hardly champions of literary freedom and each had harshly attacked Solzhenitsyn in September, Tvardovsky sensed that two of them might support this idea, probably out of embarrassment and eagerness to divest themselves of the onus of rejecting the manuscript. Fedin, the third secretary, was also ill at ease; Tvardovsky described his tone as "petulant," "embarrassed," and "discontented with himself and all of us." Whatever his misgivings, however, the aging writer rigidly rejected the notion that

---

[7] For example, Tvardovsky prevailed upon Solzhenitsyn to delete a disrespectful reference to Ilya Ehrenburg, whose accommodation to Stalinism perturbed him although Ehrenburg became one of the first liberals after Stalin died. This was the kind of compromise that Solzhenitsyn accepted.

Novy Mir should determine *Cancer Ward*'s fate. The novel must be "held up," he declared, until its author had done his duty by renouncing Western reaction to the letter. Despite the attempted implication that the novel was not being rejected as such and that the author himself was responsible for its "delay," this was a clear refusal by the Union's chairman.

Fedin's behavior attracted more than one protest. Tvardovsky wrote to him politely, as if still appealing to reason. But Venyamin Kaverin, Fedin's friend of almost a half century (and the man who had so clearly defined Solzhenitsyn's importance in November 1966), dispensed with courtesy. Addressing Fedin in the intimate form, he enumerated the chairman's sins against Russian literature and described the swelling disgust that his part in the *Cancer Ward* affair had provoked. "A writer who throws a noose around another writer's neck is a figure who will endure in the history of literature, independently of what he himself has written, and in full dependence upon what the other has written. While perhaps not suspecting it, you are becoming the focus of hostility, indignation, and discontent in literary circles."

Kaverin may have been indirectly addressing someone far higher placed than his old friend: it was widely rumored at the time that Fedin's counsellor was Leonid Brezhnev, Secretary General of the Communist Party. At a meeting in the autumn of 1967, according to this story, the two men agreed upon a *de facto* ban on all Solzhenitsyn's works and devised tactics to implement their decision. According to the rumors, moreover, Brezhnev's personal hostility—reinforced by his humiliation in being among the losers in the Politburo battle against *One Day* in 1962—was ultimately responsible for the doggedness of Solzhenitsyn's persecution.

But why did Fedin (who had been on Khrushchev's winning side in that battle) make himself Brezhnev's eager instrument? To resist the pressure to do so would probably have cost only his chairmanship of the union, not a great sacrifice for a man of his standing. Even Kaverin, after some fifty years of friendship, was at a loss to understand why, on the brink of his grave, Fedin tarnished his name forever with his vengeful persecution of a talented colleague. Kaverin concluded his letter with an appeal to Fedin to "find the strength and courage to rescind [your] decision." Ignoring the growing hostility, however, in January [8] Fedin ordered the destruction of *Cancer Ward*'s type, thus precluding the novel's formal submission to censorship and extinguishing all chances of publication under the existing regime.

Now even vague promises to Solzhenitsyn ceased—while all mention of him disappeared from print. For some time, a partial ban on his name had been in effect, based on informal instructions to editors. This caused

[8] By this time, galley proofs were ready, and Solzhenitsyn had worked on correcting them.

the expunging of his name from a translated Japanese article in a literary magazine, for example, and even from a petition by writers to halt the pollution of Lake Baikal. But whereas committed editors could defy this informal interdiction, it now became a formal, therefore ineluctable, censorship instruction. It was communicated to Tvardovsky in January when an editor of a publishing house was bold enough to telephone him with the information that, in accordance with a directive from higher authority, he was about to delete Solzhenitsyn's name from a collection of his, Tvardovsky's, articles. Tvardovsky flatly refused and the volume did not appear. But despite Tvardovsky, the "unpersoning" of Solzhenitsyn continued: he was not only deprived of any part in current Soviet literature, but also in its official past.[9] After years of slashing and withdrawing, slandering and prevaricating, the rupture between the writer and the political and literary establishments was complete, and it remained only to formalize the condition.

[9] During the following years, the name "Solzhenitsyn" was deleted from all published records of Soviet literature: textbooks, academic compilations, and monographs. Several of the examples, including an academic history of Soviet literature published in 1971, give evidence of expunging, rewriting, and substituting of pages which can only be described as Orwellian. "The idea," Solzhenitsyn explained later, "was that not a line would be written about me, no one would ever mention my name, even to curse it, and after a few years I would be forgotten. And then [they would] take [me] away." It was foiled by *samizdat* and the spreading of his books through the country and abroad. "There was no way to keep me quiet."

XXXI

Intrigues

SOLZHENITSYN'S CASE BOTH REFLECTED AND reinforced a stifling general political atmosphere. During early 1968, influential neo-Stalinist factions were ever more active and successful in the country as a whole. In January, several intellectuals were sentenced harshly for publishing "underground" manuscripts, including a record of the Sinyavsky-Daniel affair. The courts found them guilty of disseminating anti-Soviet propaganda with subversive intent. As intent was extremely difficult to prove in these cases, the authorities' willingness to resort to this statute after the prosecution's blatant weakness in the Sinyavsky-Daniel trial was an ominous development for Solzhenitsyn. With thousands of copies of *The First Circle* and *Cancer Ward* circulating in *samizdat*, he too was imperiled if the authorities were willing to use the vague charge of "anti-Soviet agitation" against him.

On the other hand, the January trial elicited the strongest resistance yet from the liberal intelligentsia. More than seven hundred men and women, predominantly writers and scientists in good standing, signed petitions protesting against violations of law and procedure, among them the effective conduct of the trial *in camera*. *Podpisant* ("signer") was the word coined to describe this new figure in social life. They knew they had much to lose; and in fact within the first month alone over a hundred lost their jobs, and almost all party members among them were expelled. This sacrifice for defendants almost unknown before their trial was evidence of an awakened devotion in Russia to genuine legality. It was now clear that criminal prosecution of Solzhenitsyn would provoke a storm of petitions, perhaps even street demonstrations or strikes. And while any such opposition could be crushed within days, this would cost the regime dearly in terms of the intelligentsia's willingness to keep contributing its much-needed professional skills. As one writer put it, "We can't conquer despotism, but we can hinder it—keep it from doing all it's ready, willing, and able to do." This "potential for interference" by a significant percentage of the best-educated Russians was Solzhenitsyn's strongest shield against police repression.

The hope that he would one day communicate his knowledge and experience to the world had lived with him for decades, and been one of his strongest sources of support during his hardest trials. Twenty years earlier, before any of his known work existed, this hope was expressed in lines composed in his head as a prisoner, and quoted in Blagov's essay.

My work! Year after year you'll mature with me,
Year in, year out, you'll tramp dusty convict roads.
The day will break when you'll warm more blood than only mine,
When not only I will be seized by your shivers. ⟩ Solzhenitsin.

The prediction, which at the time could have been taken for an anonymous unfortunate's attempt to sustain himself with dreams of glory, was now on the verge of fulfillment throughout the world.

Early in 1968, a new set of circumstances arose which involved both more threats and more promise. It was set in motion by the publication of *Cancer Ward* and *The First Circle* abroad, and the ensuing furor. The process subjected the author to evident dangers, but when these had passed he was left with a distinctly enhanced sense of security, both from direct police repression and from his gnawing anxiety about interference with his writing—even, perhaps, from a surviving element of uncertainty about his artistic and intellectual authority.

This was the larger significance of the events of 1968. In its realization, however, Solzhenitsyn had to deal with much that was petty, nagging, and alarming. For as *Cancer Ward* and *The First Circle* thrust him toward the summit of his international fame, publication of the novels seemed to signal his further downfall in Russia. Most frustrating for a man accustomed to exercising the most carefully calculated control over his own affairs was that he had virtually nothing to do with it—and, for a time, feared that his works might be manipulated in his own worst interests. Like a nuclear physicist who has contributed a critical new equation, he was powerless to dictate the use to which his work was put.

By coincidence, the process began but weeks after the destruction of *Cancer Ward*'s type in Moscow. As Solzhenitsyn had warned, *samizdat* copies of the manuscript found their way abroad, and in February 1968 a Milan publishing house, Il Saggiatore, issued the first foreign edition of the novel, although still in the Russian language.[1] Published as an anony-

---

[1] Foreign publishers rushed the texts of *samizdat* novels into print in Russian, not because there was a wide readership in that language in Western countries, but because the publishers naïvely hoped to establish copyright thereby. However, the legal position is that works of authors residing in the Soviet Union are protected by

mous work [2] and with a text often garbled into mumbo-jumbo, its stunning sloppiness enraged Solzhenitsyn when a copy reached him several months later. It was a cruelly disappointing début—the first edition anywhere—of his most polished full-length novel. However, much more serious trouble threatened him during the following month.

On March 29, a magazine called *Grani* cabled Tvardovsky from Frankfurt that it was preparing to run extracts of *Cancer Ward* immediately. *Grani* itself was published by an émigré organization called the National Labor Union: "NTS," according to its Russian initials. Originally influenced by Mussolini's Fascism, the NTS collaborated with the Nazis during the war in the hope of overthrowing Soviet rule. Having largely broken this association during the last year of the war, the organization evolved a more democratic program and won support from several intelligence services, in time principally American, eager to take advantage of its precious personal contacts with Russians on their native soil during Stalin's last years. Later, these contacts helped make *Grani* one of the principal Western outlets for Russian "underground" texts.

Grani's great contribution was its dissemination of a large body of valuable material that would otherwise have remained unpublished. Its danger to Russian nonconformists lay in its present intelligence connections and collaborationist past, which the regime seized upon in its ceaseless effort to equate dissent with treason. Moreover, for its own purposes—the replacement of virtually all the social arrangements initiated by the revolution with its own all-embracing ideological concept—the NTS saw fit to exploit almost any activity that might shake Soviet rule, from intellectual dissidence to hooliganism. In this respect, Solzhenitsyn was a

---

copyright only when published first in a country recognizing the copyright conventions—and with the express consent of the authors or their representatives. The Soviet Union is the only major European country which does not recognize the copyright conventions, and its authors are wholly unprotected: once their works appear, either in Russia itself or elsewhere in the world without the conditions outlined above, they may legally be republished by anyone, in the original or in translation.

While many Russian writers are profoundly displeased by this situation, Solzhenitsyn is one of the few to have insisted, repeatedly, on its being changed, calling upon the Soviet government to join the conventions, so that Soviet auhors can "receive a reliable means of protecting their works from illegal editions abroad and from shameless commercial scrambles for translation."

The Soviet government's motives in refusing to join the conventions seem to be purely mercenary: the country translates considerably more books into its languages and publishes them in far larger editions than the rest of the world does with Soviet books. Thus the signing of a convention would cause a trade deficit and loss of hard currency.

[2] In Italian law, an anonymous work is presumed to have been written in the country of publication. Il Saggiatore, therefore, might have hoped to establish copyright for itself of the "nameless" novel.

tempting ideological prize for the NTS; nor was the organization insensitive to commercial considerations. Almost four years before, *Grani* had managed to publish some of his "microstories" within weeks of their first circulating in Moscow. In the absence of copyright restrictions, the NTS had a perfect right to do this—but not to claim its own copyright for these stories and to sell their (nonexistent) translation rights, as its publishing house later did. In 1966, the same house issued a collection of Solzhenitsyn's short stories, still arrogating to itself copyright for the "microstories" —and, on its jacket, presenting the author as anti-Communist in the sense of its own total rejection of everything Soviet.[3]

Grani's cable to Tvardovsky in late March 1968 justified the immediate publication of *Cancer Ward* on the ground that the KGB, acting through an intermediary named Victor Louis, had sent a new copy of the novel to the West (beyond the one the magazine claimed to have possessed for some time) with the intention of "blocking" its appearance in *Novy Mir*. A Soviet citizen who is widely believed to work as a "fixer" for the KGB (but perhaps, more importantly, for the Politburo itself), Victor Louis was a logical choice for this accusation; he had brought more than one manuscript to the West, among them a version of Svetlana Alliluyeva's memoirs, accompanied by her private photographs. In contrast to previous and subsequent occasions, however, Louis explicitly denied this NTS accusation, and the organization has never revealed when and to whom Louis passed the manuscript in question.

Contrary to prevailing Western opinion, moreover, the NTS implication that publication of the novel abroad would preclude its appearance in Russia was dubious. A long poem of Tvardovsky's, for example—one of several cases—had been published in *Izvestiya* and *Novy Mir* after first appearing in an émigré publication, and Pasternak's play *The Blind Beauty* was to travel a similar route in 1969. In short, *Grani* appeared to be cloaking a potentially profitable and prestige-building operation in the guise of foiling a KGB scheme. A copy of *Cancer Ward* had probably come into the magazine's possession and, quite simply, it wanted a way to justify publishing it. Meanwhile, more publishers were entering the competition. Simultaneously with the NTS, the YMCA Press in Paris, a more neutral émigré house, acquired another manuscript and, before publishing it in Russian, sold American translation rights for a large sum.

The edition of the novel which eventually predominated in most countries was based on yet another manuscript, this one given by the author

---

[3] "The construction of Communist society does not concern Solzhenitsyn," the blurb began. This was a blunt untruth since "For the Good of the Cause," which this very volume included, deals precisely with the humane, as opposed to the ruthlessly bureaucratic, approach to establishing a Communist society.

to the Slovak journalist Pavel Ličko shortly after their six-hour interview the previous March. For many reasons, some more and some less obvious, a full account of Ličko's role cannot now be told.[4] In outline, it is a story of differing interpretations about what Solzhenitsyn intended him to do with the manuscript. That the two men did not meet again after March 1967—despite Ličko's trip to Moscow a year later specifically to see the writer about the manuscript—made even more tenuous communications that were already strained by censorship, distance, and the need for caution. In any case, Ličko sat on his manuscript for a full year, and, only after there was no hope whatever for publication in Russia, entered into a contract for it with the publisher, the Bodley Head of London. He believed that Solzhenitsyn's instructions gave him authority to do this, although Solzhenitsyn's position is that Ličko's discretion to arrange its publication extended only to Czechoslovakia. (Publication there could cause the author no real harm since even from the Soviet standpoint there was nothing illegal in the appearance in a socialist country of a work not yet published, or even already suppressed, at home.)

Ličko's decision caused Solzhenitsyn anxiety and irritation at the time, although the former could not have foreseen the principal cause. To prevent other publishers issuing a welter of editions—by this time Il Saggiatore had put out its horrendously garbled text, and houses in other countries were preparing translations on the basis of various manuscripts—the Bodley Head felt it necessary to claim exclusive rights in court. Although the proceedings were held *in camera* to protect Solzhenitsyn, documents about his conversations with Ličko were leaked to the press by people involved in the action to whom they were shown in confidence. When it reached Moscow, gossip based on this—and on Ličko's own incautious talk—was enough to alarm Solzhenitsyn that Ličko's statements might be used against him. But in the end, the Bodley Head edition brought some order into the melee. Proper royalties were paid for Solzhenitsyn's eventual use, and the writer's legal representative confirmed

---

[4] Imprisoned in Bratislava during September 1970, and sentenced to eighteen months on charges that his liberal activities had damaged Czechoslovakia's interests abroad and politically perverted its youth at home. Ličko was simultaneously accused by Western journals and Soviet specialists of having acted against Solzhenitsyn's interests, and perhaps even for the KGB. Most of the Western innuendoes about the ex-Communist (he resigned from the party after the Soviet invasion of Czechoslovakia) are founded on distorted information about his life, from the time he was a prominent fighter in Slovakia's anti-Nazi resistance movement to his dismissal, on the Novotny regime's orders, from a job with Czechoslovakia's most progressive cultural magazine after publication there of his Solzhenitsyn interview and restoration to responsible positions immediately upon Dubček's emergence. Although Solzhenitsyn himself was for a time extremely irritated with what he considered Ličko's recklessness in the *Cancer Ward* affair, he dismisses the notion that Ličko acted in the KGB's interests, or intentionally against his own.

the arrangements which Ličko had initiated and saw to it that his next novel, which appeared in 1971, went to the Bodley Head and those houses in Germany, the United States, and other countries with which arrangements had been started through Ličko—even when these firms were far from the highest bidders.

Solzhenitsyn's alarm in the spring and summer of 1968 was caused principally by a fear that he had lost control over an important aspect of his affairs; the fear, in turn, was caused largely by an unavoidable ignorance of the reputations of the competing Western publishers and which of them might be friends, enemies, or simply eager businessmen. Nor could he know which manuscript had come to which publisher in what condition. Contrary to prevailing opinion abroad, publication in the West was not of itself a prerequisite for prosecuting Soviet writers: both before and after 1968, several prominent *samizdat* writers were tried not for passing manuscripts for reproduction abroad, but solely for dissemination within the Soviet Union. *Samizdat* circulation was quite enough for Solzhenitsyn's conviction, but if the authorities wanted to concoct charges against him and he could be linked to foreign publication, the prosecution would have strengthened its case.

On the other hand, if anything was clear in the complex tangle—and the fifteen years of post-Stalin Soviet literature, in cases as disparate as those of Pasternak, Yevtushenko, and Joseph Brodsky—it was that, whatever their "offense" and status, writers with international reputations were persecuted less severely than those who were not known abroad. Thus Solzhenitsyn's world fame was his second shield—a stout reinforcement to the protection provided by the Russian public's potential to erupt if he were persecuted. And it was *Cancer Ward*, together with *The First Circle*, which followed almost immediately, that generated the bulk of Solzhenitsyn's international literary fame. Partly because of the "rush," as Solzhenitsyn lamented, that had "spoiled" translations of *One Day*, partly because the Western reader approached the novel with less knowledge and a different esthetic perception, the Russian appreciation of that first novel as a work of art eternalizing an already familiar story did not spread to the West and establish Solzhenitsyn as a major literary power. *One Day* struck the West largely as a revelation, and led most readers there to regard its author primarily as a witness of a particular situation—articulate, observant, and highly sensitive, but not necessarily able to deal with the larger problems of the general human condition, beyond the distinctive ones of the *univers concentrationnaire*. True, he was not only a superb witness but, as the letter to the congress demonstrated, an uncommonly brave man in denouncing the outrages against Soviet literature—but in the world's eyes, this was not yet the courage of genius. It was only with

the first excerpts of *Cancer Ward* published in a Western language that
his world reputation soared.[5]

Solzhenitsyn's reaction upon hearing of this first translation—apparently he still knew nothing about the Saggiatore Russian edition—was to
fix responsibility as firmly as possible for *Cancer Ward's* appearance
abroad. In a letter to the union secretariat in mid-April he placed the
blame entirely on that agency, pointing out that a wasted year had passed
since he had warned of this very probability and that "the inevitable had
happened." He apprised the secretariat that he would now circulate the
record of his exchanges with them: his letters and his own transcripts of
their various meetings. His purpose was to "inform our literary public" and
establish the secretariat's position and responsibility. But much as he
regretted that *Cancer Ward's* first publication had been outside Russia,
he did not at this point protest against the publication as such.

Two days after he wrote to the Secretariat, Solzhenitsyn learned about
the projected *Grani* publication. Several days after this, he was informed
of copyright litigation between Alberto Mondadori, the owner of Il Saggiatore, and the Bodley Head. He decided that it was time to make his
position as clear as the circumstances allowed.

NTS was the simpler problem. Solzhenitsyn immediately sensed something "nebulous and provocative" about *Grani's* cable to Tvardovsky. Protesting explicitly about the magazine's planned publication and Victor
Louis' alleged role in it, he called upon the Writers' Union to help him trace
the itinerary of the manuscript involved. The union secretariat did nothing,
while *Grani* ignored Solzhenitsyn's explicit plea and proceeded to publish
its extracts. And again, the NTS went on to market translation rights, although this time without success.

The litigation between Il Saggiatore and the Bodley Head was more
puzzling to Solzhenitsyn. His statement expressed surprise that such a
dispute should be conducted "while the author is alive!" Exclamation mark
and all, this seemed a clear hint that anyone wishing to acquire the copyright of a work should address himself to the author. But at that time,
the thought of bypassing official channels to contact a Soviet citizen directly struck publishers—those who cared, at least—as impracticable and
foolhardy. Would this not imperil the author? It would indeed, but perhaps not so gravely as imagined by Westerners with an impression of
KGB omniscience and omnipotence. Experience with Soviet writers later
in the 1960s indicated that contacts between them and Western representatives would not lead to arrests, even if the contacts were uncovered and the
authors were of lesser stature than Solzhenitsyn. In Solzhenitsyn's case in

---

[5] The reaction was immediate even though this first translation was a double one.
The original Russian had been rendered into Slovak by Pavel Ličko's wife, and from
that language into English.

particular, the risks of seeking direct communication might well have been smaller than acting on the basis of informed guesswork and statements by third parties. But the conditioning of Stalinism, as strong in the West as among many Russians themselves, precluded this. Having lived with danger all his life, Solzhenitsyn could hardly be expected to understand that fear—for their own safety too—deterred publishers from sending someone to Russia to ask his permission.

Since no one had asked him for the rights to *Cancer Ward,* the writer could declare in good conscience that "no foreign publisher has received from me either the manuscript of this novel or authorization to publish it." Therefore, continued the statement, he "did not recognize as legitimate any publication, past or future, without my permission. Or anyone's publication rights." But since the statement stopped short of a direct and explicit protest against publication as such,[6] the Bodley Head and other Western publishers who believed they had authorization from Ličko took it upon themselves to proceed even after reading it.

Moreover, Solzhenitsyn's April statement was unknown to the West for roughly two months. Its suppression during that critical period was seen to by the same authorities who four months earlier had been obsessed with the notion that Solzhenitsyn "dissociate himself" from Western use of the letter. Now that Solzhenitsyn was protesting against *Cancer Ward's* publication by an anti-Soviet organization and dissociating himself from all other Western editions and pretensions, Soviet officials stifled his voice while it might have been effective.

In vain, Solzhenitsyn insisted that the Soviet press publish his statement without delay. When the *Literary Gazette* took no action on the copy it was sent, another copy was mailed to *Le Monde,* through whose columns Solzhenitsyn first learned of the Saggiatore-Bodley Head dispute. The registered letter was never sent on, even though postal censorship is illegal in Soviet law. Luckily, a distinguished Italian expert on Soviet literature, the liberal Communist Vittorio Strada, was then in Moscow, and agreed to take a copy with him for publication in *L'Unità,* the organ of the Italian Communist Party. Strada's copy was confiscated by Soviet customs officers. Solzhenitsyn protested against this arbitrary act and entered into a heated and complicated wrangle with the customs service—which, inexplicably, he won in the end. The confiscated copy was released and appeared in *L'Unità* in June, the first indication to the West of Solzhenitsyn's attitudes toward his publication there. But by this time, *Cancer*

---

[6] A clear distinction was made between publication by *Grani,* against which Solzhenitsyn did protest explicitly, and by other houses—which, although Solzhenitsyn would not recognize as legitimate at this stage, he did not condemn. The word "prohibit" was used, again with apparently calculated distinction, only in relation to any possible staging or screening of the novel.

Ward I was already in the bookshops in Italian, and distribution in the world market had begun.

During the interval between Solzhenitsyn's statement and its appearance, more of his work leaked abroad. Early in May, *The First Circle* appeared in Western Europe in the form of a photocopy of a Russian typescript. Solzhenitsyn could not help knowing that, were he to be tried, the far sharper political content of this novel would make better pickings for the prosecution. Nevertheless, *The First Circle* caused him much less immediate worry, probably because only one major publisher had a copy of the manuscript that spring.[7]

The manuscript appears to have reached the West on microfilm, after which it was sold by an American house—claiming "world copyright" for itself—to European publishers of high reputation. But perhaps suspecting that the copyright was invalid and fearing the appearance of a competing manuscript, the American house rushed its translation with extremely unfortunate results: in addition to countless errors and infelicities, some fifteen percent of the text simply disappeared, perhaps because the translator hadn't the time or knowledge to decipher Solzhenitsyn's subtle syntax and coined words not to be found in dictionaries. Moreover, at least one major European publisher rushed its translation, in turn, not from Russian but from this emasculated American rendition. It is a measure of Solzhenitsyn's talent that the novel enjoyed a huge critical and popular success despite the injury to some of its most impressive elements: the originality and expressiveness of its language and the precision of its imagery. But despite this success, it is unsurprising that the publishers of *The First Circle* were not involved when Solzhenitsyn made arrangements for his next novel to appear abroad.

Almost a month after *L'Unità*, the *Literary Gazette* at last published Solzhenitsyn's April statement. His two hundred words—the last to be printed under his signature in Russia—were accompanied by some 4500 words of editorial. Editor-in-chief Alexander Chakovsky used the opportunity to brand all protesters as accomplices in bourgeois propaganda, and he virtually dismissed Solzhenitsyn as a Soviet writer. "It has become clear once and for all," he declared, "that A. Solzhenitsyn is wholly satisfied with the role assigned him by our ideological adversaries." Calling attention to Solzhenitsyn's inadequate protest against the use of his name and work in the West, the article failed to mention his explicit condemnation of *Grani*'s enterprise.

Although such petty dissimulation was nothing new to Solzhenitsyn, other aspects of the article excited his anger and apprehension. Far from

---

[7] The copy was of a version edited and somewhat toned down for *Novy Mir*. The novel as written has never been published.

denouncing the slanders as the union secretariat had promised, the union's organ now slyly corroborated them by "putting in doubt," as Solzhenitsyn himself later pointed out, "the rightfulness of my rehabilitation through a tricky evasive phrase about my 'having served my punishment.' It did not elaborate, leaving the impression that my sentence was deserved." The article did mention Solzhenitsyn's rehabilitation, but in a way which left unclear whether it or his punishment was justified. And even more suggestive was the word *mnogoopytny* ("practiced") used to describe Solzhenitsyn himself. Although its literal meaning is "much experienced," the ironic and pejorative adjective is restricted to people of doubtful reputation.

But there was nothing subtle, linguistically or otherwise, about Chakovsky's threats. In an unmistakable parallel to the wording of the Criminal Code, the article called *The First Circle* "a work containing malicious slander of our social order." (*Cancer Ward,* by contrast, was merely said to "require substantial ideological revision.") For the first time since he was published in 1962, a threat of prosecution was publicly poised over Solzhenitsyn.

Yet even now, Chakovsky could not help a grudging concession to Solzhenitsyn's "literary capabilities." This involuntary tribute to his talent was the beginning of a curious new line. Previously, dissident writers had been represented as bereft of artistic merit—a canon, with slight amendment, invoked even against Boris Pasternak. Pasternak is a good poet, Soviet officials had chorused in a pretense at literary discrimination; but *Doctor Zhivago* is a weak novel. By now, the application of any variant of this line to Solzhenitsyn's prose would have produced only ridicule. *Faute de mieux,* a new official category of artist was conceived to cover the "gifted writer" who is nevertheless "ideologically immature."

In other words, Solzhenitsyn had forced the first public acknowledgment that conformity was an indispensable attribute of a Soviet writer. It was now demonstrated beyond all doubt that no pressure he might exert on the authorities nor support he might enlist from his fellow writers would bring about his publication in Russia.

XXXII

Expulsion

UNDERSTANDING HIS INABILITY TO CONTROL the destiny of his manuscripts either in Russia or abroad, Solzhenitsyn reverted to his former total preoccupation with writing and avoidance of "literary business." But before plunging into work, he made some significant changes in his personal life. First, he moved from Ryazan. His new residence was in the forests southwest of Moscow, near the village of Rozhdestvo (Nativity), but the location was known more simply as "the eighty-third kilometer" (from Moscow). Although he and Reshetovskaya selected the location and completed the arrangements together, their relationship was deteriorating rapidly.

The strains on the couple that accompanied Solzhenitsyn's sudden fame in late 1962 had intensified during the following five years. Working entirely at home now, the writer was theoretically more available to Reshetovskaya, yet being together only underscored the differences in their interests and outlook. Solzhenitsyn's refusal to accept the role of a celebrated writer remained firm, and his intense devotion to work—the steady twelve-hour days from which almost everything else was resolutely excluded—also had not changed.

Respect for Solzhenitsyn's extreme sensitivity about his private life forbids the disclosure even of the few facts of their estrangement that have become known. At this point, it can only be said that some friends of the couple see a parallel between their troubles and those of the Tolstoys: like Tolstoy's wife, Solzhenitsyn's could not cope with marriage to a titan. Reshetovskaya's feelings made Solzhenitsyn's free time, often measured in minutes rather than hours a day, sometimes unhappy, and also disturbed his work. "One great passion, once settled within a person," Solzhenitsyn had reflected in *The First Circle*, "cruelly displaces everything else. There is no room in a man for two passions."

The decision to separate from Reshetovskaya did not come easily to

Solzhenitsyn. Although they had not been married in church, he went so far as to take advice from a morally authoritative Moscow priest. They continued to share company until at least the following summer, but their relationship was drawing to a close. More intimate factors were also involved, but, after the drama of their interwoven lives, the disappointment of such an end needs no comment.

Solzhenitsyn's new quarters at the eighty-third kilometer, however, were extremely conducive to work, and therefore much to his liking. In the unspoiled woods southwest of Moscow, he had bought several years earlier a little clapboard summer bungalow that Russians call a "Finnish cottage." The price was some 2000 rubles, a tenth of what the dachas of many lesser writers cost, and the accommodation—a single room on the ground floor, a single room above it, and a garage he later built himself— were correspondingly humble. But Solzhenitsyn was very fond of it for its solitude and silence.

["A small stream runs beside the house," wrote a visitor, "and a beautiful view opens onto forest and field. Nearby stands an abandoned church like those he had described so sympathetically in his short stories." The bungalow stood near a main road into Moscow and the same small town of Obninsk, with its secluded research institutes and handsome settings, where the Solzhenitsyns had intended to move three years before, when Reshetovskaya's job was eliminated by the Council of Ministers. The town contained two old friends with whom Solzhenitsyn met occasionally: the biologist Nikolai Timofeyev-Resovsky, whom he had known since his prison days, lived there, and had introduced the writer to a younger colleague, Zhores Medvedev, who was struggling to free Soviet science from bureaucratic shackles.] Medvedev and Solzhenitsyn had been close since 1964; one of the intellectual foundations of their friendship was an absorbing interest in human and civil rights—the substance of their actual application, as opposed to their paper existence[Neither could guess how the KGB would try to exploit their loyalty to each other some two years later. The writer's little bungalow had an added advantage of being only ninety minutes by road from the center of Moscow, and beyond the reach of inquisitive foreign correspondents (who are restricted from traveling more than forty kilometers from the capital without permission). In his forest retreat, Solzhenitsyn plunged into writing with even more than his customary zeal. Among other things he was almost certainly engaged in some of the voluminous research for his fictional treatment of Russia's disintegration during World War I. Solzhenitsyn interrupted his work only to potter briefly about the house for repairs, walks in the woods, and an

---

[1] It was Medvedev who provided the most detailed account of the Solzhenitsyns' abortive move to Obninsk in 1965. See p. 219.

occasional tea with an invited friend on the forest lawn near his house. The tea and food were served on a rough-hewn table obviously made by a peasant carpenter.

As for his political behavior, Solzhenitsyn displayed a new caution. He signed no protest against the persecution of dissidents or the invasion of Czechoslovakia; in fact, he made no public statement of any kind. As before, he refused to see foreign journalists and visiting Western intellectuals.

Despite his renewed efforts to avoid publicity, Solzhenitsyn was forgotten by neither his international nor his Russian public. In 1968, the *Literary Gazette* conducted a poll about the most admired Soviet writers of recent years. On the basis of some ten thousand replies, it was established that despite his long "dry" years and, more recently, the unavailability of his work in libraries, Solzhenitsyn was in second place among prose writers whom readers most wanted to see published in the newspaper—and this in a country where reading is an avid activity and vital source of guidance. Not surprisingly, Chakovsky's newspaper suppressed this tribute. On December 11, Solzhenitsyn turned fifty, and this occasion provided more evidence of his enduring popularity despite his blacklisting. It is a tradition of the Writers' Union to commemorate the "round date" birthdays of its members in one of its two weekly publications—if only, in the case of less significant writers, by means of a few lines of celebration and good wishes. Solzhenitsyn's fiftieth birthday was accorded no such mention nor any other public token of esteem within Russia, nor was his personal history known to a wide public. Nevertheless, he received hundreds of congratulations from throughout the Soviet Union.

Hundreds were also sent from abroad, but only a small percentage delivered, a circumstance that helped prompt Solzhenitsyn to protest against postal service "banditry" roughly a year later. The congratulations had touched and encouraged him, and he was indignant that he could not acknowledge all the good wishes, even through the courtesy of a traditional notice of thanks in a newspaper. He replied personally to many admirers, but writing to them all would have taken weeks of treasured working time. He put himself on record, therefore, in a letter to the *Literary Gazette*.

To the editorial board of the *Literary Gazette*
Copy to the magazine *Novy Mir*

I know that your paper will not publish a single line of mine without attributing a distorted, erroneous meaning to it. But there is no way I can answer the many people who have sent me their greetings except through your newspaper.

Deeply moved, I thank the readers and writers who sent greetings and best wishes on my fiftieth birthday. I promise them never to be unfaithful to the truth. My sole dream is to prove myself worthy of the hopes of the Russian reading public.

Ryazan, December 12, 1968

Indeed, not a line of this letter was published in the Soviet Union. The union's unmistakably deliberate disregard of Solzhenitsyn's birthday suggested to some of his friends that trouble was coming from that organization. Its behavior toward him, an officially enrolled writer, was unprecedented; by every outward indication, it was treating Solzhenitsyn as if he were no longer a member. That some colleagues desired just this was already clear. More than a year before, zealous provincial writers had urged his expulsion from the union, but were told that such a move "should not be hurried." The threat, however, was in the air, and it was perhaps in an attempt to deal with it that Solzhenitsyn tried to have his change of residence officially recognized. He went personally to Moscow to ask V. Ilyin, a secretary of the union—not a writer but a bureaucrat—for a formal transfer to its Moscow branch. Any attempt to expel Solzhenitsyn from that branch, the Soviet Union's largest, with strong liberal influence, would provoke determined, perhaps insurmountable, opposition, as well as instant worldwide publicity. When his request for transfer was refused, however, Solzhenitsyn accepted the decision without protest.

In short, he had again retrenched. He knew that the authorities had not lost interest in him. The KGB intensified their surveillance of his bungalow, adding the services of a photographer. Attempts to blacken his name now achieved the bizarre. Rumors began to circulate in Moscow that Solzhenitsyn was drinking heavily and publicly in expensive restaurants. Eyewitnesses swore to their friends that they had seen him behaving violently, swearing obscenely, cursing the Jews, and stating that he was Russia's greatest writer, Alexander Solzhenitsyn. The accounts were accurate—except that the man in the restaurants was not Solzhenitsyn. He did resemble Solzhenitsyn in stature and appearance, and when the writer's friends finally cornered him he turned out to be a certified lunatic. The friends were convinced, however, that the pseudo-Solzhenitsyn, who has since disappeared, was directed by "remote control." Despite such onslaughts Solzhenitsyn hoped that, knowing his potential to cause international embarrassment and internal conflict, the authorities might leave him alone, at least temporarily.

But in marked contrast to his own silence at the eighty-third kilometer, it was during these months that his name as a novelist began to resound through the world. Translations of *Cancer Ward* and *The First Circle* had begun to appear in all major languages, making "Solzhenitsyn" an instantly recognizable name. This heightened the world's interest in works by Soviet underground writers—and, more disturbingly from the official point of view, underground works by "aboveground" writers—which were now appearing regularly in London, Frankfurt, New York, or Paris. The new word *tamizdat* entered the Russian language. It means literally "publishing over there"—"over there" implying "in the West"—and rhymes wittily with *samizdat,* the "do-it-yourself" publishing.

Tamizdat authors could not be punished legally without proof that they were responsible for publication abroad. In many cases they had merely given their uncensored works to friends to read. The friends reproduced them by typewriter and distributed copies to *their* trusted friends. Eventually one of the copies left Russia in the luggage of a visiting foreigner. In Soviet law, none of these actions constitutes a crime unless it can be proved that the published work had been written, in the words of the criminal code, "for the purpose of subverting or weakening Soviet authority." In practice, proving anti-Soviet intent had been an almost impossible task for all works so far published in the West, as the Sinyavsky-Daniel trial showed. So long as there was no return to Stalin's terror—to which the law was virtually no restraint—there could be no legal punishment without a legally defined crime.

Moreover, the party had long been reluctant to harass well-known writers significantly. Petty harassment was often practiced on liberals who had annoyed the regime: reprisals such as withholding exit visas for foreign travel and delaying the printing of an offender's books because of a "paper shortage." But no liberal, as opposed to a radical underground dissenter, had been deprived of his livelihood, exiled, or beaten up, the party fearing that repression of this kind might dangerously widen the circle of protesters.

The growth of *tamizdat* provoked predictable reactions in the KGB and the party. The latter was infuriated because works such as *The First Circle* shattered its image abroad, and, rebroadcast into Russia by foreign radio stations, encouraged Russians to challenge the regime's self-proclaimed sanctity. The KGB were disturbed by their partial loss of control, not only over what was circulating in manuscript form inside Russia, but also over what was leaving the country. Short of examining every suitcase and pocket everywhere along Russia's vast frontiers, their only recourse was to frighten writers into not allowing their manuscripts to circulate.

As the most prominent *tamizdat* author, Solzhenitsyn was the KGB's prime target, and much evidence suggests that the campaign against him was planned as a first step in a new KGB drive to suppress underground publishing in general. Intimidation and punishment of writers were to be the principal means, Solzhenitsyn the principal example.

The first quasi-public move against him was made in October, at a meeting of the Communist Party organization within the Moscow branch of the Writers' Union. The party secretary, a writer of thrillers named Arkady Vasilyev, denounced members whose works had been published abroad without permission from Soviet authorities as having violated the union's statutes. Such authors should be expelled, he said, whether or not they were responsible for the foreign publications. The union's statutes obligated members to write in the spirit of socialist realism—which "illegal" works appearing abroad contravened; otherwise bourgeois houses would not have published them.

Vasilyev was known as the KGB's leading literary consultant. In the mid-1960s, when the security police were trying to crack the identities of Sinyavsky and Daniel—whose novels and essays were then appearing pseudonymously in the West—Vasilyev advised the KGB on the case (lifting a scene from a Sinyavsky novel to insert into his own film script in the process). At the Sinyavsky-Daniel trial, he joined the prosecution as a so-called public accuser supposedly representing the interests of Russian writers. His own literary work extolling the heroism and virtues of superpatriotic Soviet security agents clearly indicated access to KGB archives—including, for example, highly classified information on Soviet espionage activities in Germany during World War II.

Vasilyev's speech did not mention Solzhenitsyn by name. The attack took the form of an appeal to the party to recommend expulsion from the union of two of Solzhenitsyn's friends and prominent public supporters: Lev Kopelev and the novelist and essayist Lydia Chukovskaya, both of whom had written pamphlets defending Solzhenitsyn that circulated widely in the underground and were published in the West under their own names. Vasilyev encountered strong opposition, and the meeting adjourned without approving his recommendation. But his prominence in this opening maneuver against Solzhenitsyn convinced Moscow liberals that the KGB, as opposed to some other branch of authority, was directing the campaign. This second attack on Solzhenitsyn's friends, four years after the confiscation of the manuscript in Blagov's flat, was so standard a KGB technique that it was hard not to see its hand in the operation. This, indeed, may have accounted for its ineffectiveness, for even some of Solzhenitsyn's most implacable enemies resented KGB interference in literary affairs.

The attempt to frighten writers into submission by expelling Solzhenitsyn's friends having failed in Moscow, the authorities mounted a frontal attack on the principal target himself in Ryazan. The town's six writers (Solzhenitsyn was the seventh) were mobilized for the action. On the afternoon of November 3, these men, all unknown beyond the city limits, were called to a meeting to banish their world-famous colleague. Although they had been deprived of the honor of accepting Solzhenitsyn's membership into the union in 1962, they were now assigned the duty of expelling him.

Solzhenitsyn himself made a partial transcript of this meeting. It shows that in addition to six of the seven Ryazan writers, other participants were Alexander Kozhevnikov, the local party secretary in charge of propaganda, and Franz Taurin, a writer of adventure stories and secretary of the parent Russian Republic's Writers' Union, who had come specially from the capital. Taurin opened the meeting with a general political summary. Anatoly Kuznetsov's defection to Britain, he declared, and an increasing flow abroad of unpublished works by Soviet writers made it necessary to strengthen writers' political education and intensify vigilance against the West's anti-Soviet ideological warfare. Solzhenitsyn's work, he continued, served the West as ammunition for this war, and the author's refusal to repudiate this use was intolerable. Since Solzhenitsyn was a member of the Ryazan writers' organization, it was up to the local writers gathered at this meeting to examine his case.

Unlike Solzhenitsyn—who emphasized that he had not been informed that his case was to be discussed—the local writers had been fully briefed on the meeting's aims and strategy, even before Taurin's statement of purpose. They had their orders and knew they would follow them—but at least two of the men were abashed by the prospect. The inner turmoil visited upon even the least talented creative artist was suggested by the behavior of Ernest Safonov, the secretary of the Ryazan union, who went to extraordinary lengths to avoid both the responsibility for Solzhenitsyn's expulsion and the wrath of the authorities which would have befallen him for failure to cooperate.

On the morning of the meeting, Safonov was taken to the hospital with what he described as symptoms of acute appendicitis. Having cut him open, the surgeon found no disorder—but he could hardly be delivered from the operating table to the conference room in time for the meeting. Immediately after the operation, he was visited in the hospital by no less a personage than Kozhevnikov, the chief of the Department of Agitation and Propaganda of Ryazan's Communist Party Committee. Kozhevnikov demanded that Safonov ratify Solzhenitsyn's expulsion. Safonov refused. Only a month later did he succumb to relentless pressure and approve the action.

Safonov's recalcitrance that morning, and his sacrifice to the knife, burdened the authorities with the added inconvenience of delivering a certain Nikolay Rodin to Ryazan from the neighboring town of Kasimov. And the unfortunate Rodin was genuinely ill. A highly reliable Soviet underground periodical called *Chronicle of Current Events* described the scene.

Having received his orders from Ryazan, the secretary of Kasimov's [Communist Party organization] forced Rodin to enter a car belonging to the party committee and leave [for Ryazan]. But Rodin soon returned, saying that he might die on the way. The secretary of the party committee made him set off again. "There are four hospitals along the way," [he told Rodin,] "in Gus Zheleznyi, Tuma, Spas-Klepiki, and Solotcha. Just step inside and see the doctors."

This is the kind of pressure—against a distinguished local comrade—to which the authorities resorted to ensure a "legal and proper" vote against Solzhenitsyn. For a Writers' Union statute required a quorum of five for taking decisions of this nature.

The minimum five writers thus corralled for the meeting were all members not only of the Writers' Union, but also of the party. An hour before the opening of the union meeting the five were convened as an informal party council in the presence of the secretary for propaganda of the Ryazan party, the same Kozhevnikov. As the official who supervised all cultural, ideological, and public-media activities in the area, reporting directly to the corresponding department of the Central Committee in Moscow, he had the duty of double-checking the writers' mood—that is, of ensuring personally that no "deviation" would occur during the official session to follow.

The union meeting itself confirmed that he had reason to worry, if not about the vote, at least about some of the speeches that preceded it. After the party "caucus," the same five writers, having been joined by Solzhenitsyn, duly convened themselves as an official meeting of the Ryazan Writers' Union branch. After Taurin's general introduction, the attack against Solzhenitsyn was led by Vasily Matushkin, an author of factory and collective-farm novels who had personally delivered the union's application forms to Solzhenitsyn seven years before. He alleged that Solzhenitsyn "has not taken part in our work, helped young authors, or attended our meetings, and has isolated himself from us. . . . We're not familiar with his latest works, but they're directed against everything that we ourselves are writing. The West is using his name to sling mud at our country, which is sacred to us."

Three writers supported Matushkin. But the fourth, Yevgeny Markin, hesitated. He suggested that the praise-censure pendulum had swung too often and was troubled by the lurching from one extreme to the other. "If we expel Solzhenitsyn today but may have to readmit him later," he concluded, "I want nothing to do with this business."

In the end, Markin did vote against Solzhenitsyn. Later, it became known that he had been persuaded before the meeting by the offer of a new flat. (He hinted broadly at his extremely cramped living conditions during the meeting itself.) During the next few days, according to Ryazan residents, he roamed wildly drunk through the town, repenting loudly, cursing himself and bemoaning his weakness. Two years later he published some poems which many interpreted as condemning himself and other members of the establishment intelligentsia for acting against their consciences in the Solzhenitsyn affair.

Another colorful participant on the discussion was an editor of the local publishing house, who observed that Solzhenitsyn had "blackened everything" because he himself was "all black inside." Solzhenitsyn was then allotted ten minutes to defend himself. Rejecting the accusations, he said that the union had not sent him any young writers to help, and had refused to discuss his own novels with him despite his repeated requests. That *he* had refused to consult with *them* was sheer untruth. If he had occasionally missed meetings, it was because he no longer lived in Ryazan, and had requested transfer to the Moscow branch.

He then described aspects of his harassment by the KGB and the suppression of his work in Russia. The chairman interrupted him in midsentence, but then consented to several extra minutes for Solzhenitsyn to conclude. Solzhenitsyn summed up the respective positions of the Writers' Union and himself:

> It has come to this: how we act is unimportant—but only what people will say about our actions. And so that they will say nothing derogatory, we must remain silent about everything happening around us. Abominations should indeed cause shame—but when they are committed, not afterward described. . . .
>
> The swing of a pendulum has been mentioned here. It does not concern me alone. . . . Stalin's crimes cannot be concealed indefinitely. These crimes were committed against millions of people and must be exposed. Think for a moment: what is the moral effect of concealment on our young people? It only perverts new millions. Our contemporary youth is not stupid, they understand perfectly. We have suffered crimes against millions and they have been ignored, as if everything were fine and dandy. What, then, stops any of *us* from committing injustices? This too can be fine and dandy.
>
> I shall not retract a single line of my letter to the Writers' Congress [of May 1967]. I then said: "I am confident that I shall fulfill my tasks as a writer in any circumstances, and from the grave more successfully and incontestably than while I live. No one can bar truth's course; and, for its progress, I am prepared to accept even death." Yes, I *am* prepared to die—not merely to be expelled from the Writers' Union. . . . Go ahead and vote. You are the majority. But remember: the history of literature will be interested in our meeting today.

Solzhenitsyn was expelled by five votes to one. The vote against the motion was his own. The resolution cited "antisocial behavior . . . radically in conflict with the aims and purposes of the U.S.S.R. Writers' Union." (In Soviet parlance, "antisocial behavior" is an extremely broad charge equally applicable to an intellectual dissident, a black marketeer, or a compulsive exhibitionist.) The expulsion order was read from a pretyped draft. The meeting ended after ninety minutes.

The dragon had been slain. But did the Ryazan "musketeers of literature," as Solzhenitsyn called them, lose their nerve at the sight of the corpse? The next day, their behavior was curious. Solzhenitsyn told his Moscow friends about his half-expected expulsion; they in turn informed Western correspondents. But the incredulous and skeptical among the reporters who rang Ryazan for confirmation could make no sense of the stutterings of the official who answered at the local Writers' Union. The callers persisted, and the response shifted: several hours later the union office began issuing half-hearted denials of the expulsion, explaining that no final decision had been taken.

Ryazan's vacillation could easily have been caused by the failure of someone in Moscow to brief provincial officials on how to deal with the formidable, frightening intrusion of the Western press. Lapses of this sort are not uncommon in the Soviet bureaucracy. But it is odd that when the briefing did come, as indicated by Ryazan's changed response to the correspondents' calls, it was to stall rather than to confirm. It seemed that time was needed now for a review of the situation on the highest party levels in Moscow. It would not be the first time that the full implications of an affair were driven home to the Kremlin only by Western reaction.

In any case, Ryazan affected ignorance. Official confirmation would not be issued for a full six days, but responsibility for it now shifted to Moscow. On November 6, the secretariat of the Russian Republic's Writers' Union met in Moscow to review the expulsion. Solzhenitsyn was informed of the meeting by telephone in Ryazan, where he was staying, temporarily, in his old flat. The call came two hours before the session was scheduled to begin. When Solzhenitsyn pointed out that Ryazan was 115 miles from Moscow and the train trip took three and a half hours, he was told . . . to take a taxi.[2] He never got to the meeting.

Neither did one member of the secretariat, who was unable to perform as required. Although slightly indisposed on the eve of the secretariat's sitting, a sometimes opportunist, sometimes liberal writer named Nikolai

---

[2] The remark was more absurd than insolent in Russian conditions. In Ryazan, no taxi could be found for a trip of this length except after many hours of searching and "fixing." And even at night, with no traffic, 115 miles on the Moscow–Ryazan road could not take less than three hours.

Rybakov spent the night in debate with himself and members of his family, some of whom begged him to obey his conscience and vote no. Rybakov teetered, but the most he could venture was not to attend the meeting citing illness. Braver writers did appear, and expressed a minority opposition to the Ryazan decision. Danil Granin, a popular novelist and long-standing supporter of Solzhenitsyn, and Victor Rozov, the script writer for *The Cranes Are Flying*, are said to have defended Solzhenitsyn and abstained from voting. Nevertheless, the expulsion was confirmed by majority vote.

Even after this decision, no announcement of Solzhenitsyn's expulsion was made for a further five days. The October Revolution holidays can account for some delay, but the prolonged silence suggested continuing internal conflict about the final disposition of the case.

On the evening of November 11, the last fruitless debate on the case took place at the command headquarters of Soviet literature: the Sector of Literature of the Communist Party's Central Committee. Its bureaucrats sided with the Ryazan "musketeers," hardly a surprising development since it was they who had originally instructed the Ryazan branch. The following morning, the announcement of Solzhenitsyn's expulsion was published in a Moscow paper, confirming the Ryazan decision to the world.

Since the Ryazan resolution was meant solely for circulation within the Writers' Union—only Solzhenitsyn himself made it public as part of his documentation—it could be as unspecific and threatening as required to intimidate other writers, whose apprehensions might be easily aroused by memories of a time when similar resolutions often led to the offenders' physical destruction. The Moscow announcement, by contrast, had been drafted for world public opinion, and presumed to present a concrete case. It justified the expulsion in terms of Solzhenitsyn's failure "to publicly express his attitude" toward "a campaign of slander against our country" connected with his name and works. "In fact," the announcement continued, "he helped increase the volume of the anti-Soviet uproar through certain of his actions and statements." No specific instances were cited. Thus the sole explanation of the disbarment was "what will Mrs. Grundy say?" and, moreover, a foreign Mrs. Grundy.

Solzhenitsyn answered his expulsion with an open letter to the Writers' Union dated November 12. Just as the suppression of his work led him to raise the whole problem of the rights of artists in Soviet society, his expulsion now moved him to examine the country's modes of decision making. He assailed the union's dishonesty, from petty deception to substantive lies, and demanded the elimination of Russia's inordinate secrecy in the running of social life. He used the word *glasnost*, roughly "openness and candor in public affairs," to evoke the rallying call of Russian liberals a century before. The word imparts a distinctly Russian concept, born in opposition to the secretiveness and evasiveness of the mid-nineteenth-century tsarist autocracy. In the development of Russian political life before the revolution, it acquired the intellectual and emotional impact of "democracy" for Americans and "rule of law" for Britons. Long out of fashion after the revolution, *glasnost* was now revived by Solzhenitsyn, with his instinct for the right concept at the right moment, and the right word to evoke it. The full implications of the term became clear in the context of his letter, a ringing manifesto of "the other Russia"—of all that is not represented by banal socialist-realist, onward-and-upward literature.

Shamelessly trampling on your own statutes, you have expelled me *in absentia*. As if rushing to a fire, you did not even summon me by telegram, giving me the four hours I needed to make my way from Ryazan to be present. You have shown openly that the decision preceded the "discussion." Was it easier for you to invent new charges without me? Were you worried that you would have to give me ten minutes to answer? I am compelled to substitute this letter for those minutes.

Wipe your watchfaces—your watches are behind the times! Lift your costly, heavy curtains—you don't even suspect that day is dawning outside! This is no longer the mute, gloomy, hopeless era when you expelled Akhmatova [3] with the same servility. Nor even that timid, chilly day when, baying, you expelled Pasternak. Was that disgrace too small for you? You want to enlarge upon it? But the hour is near when each of you will seek to scratch out your signature from beneath today's resolution.

The blind leading the blind! You fail even to notice that you are wandering in a direction opposite to the one you've proclaimed. In this time of crisis for our gravely ill society, you are incapable of offering anything constructive, anything good—only your hatred and vigilance, only your "grab him and don't let go!" [4]

Your flabby articles flop around, your vacuity listlessly rattles —but you have no reasons, only voting and bureaucratic procedures.

Solzhenitsyn went on to defend Lydia Chukovskaya and Lev Kopelev against attacks in the Writers' Union and elsewhere for having violated the rules of "privileged secrets" and artistic decisions by "the *hierarchy*."

---

[3] The last classic poet of Russia was one of the principal targets of the Zhdanov-Stalin postwar persecution of writers.

[4] A reference to a Chekhov character representing a semiliterate, angry-citizen type whose notion of self-fulfillment was to seize any citizen suspected of causing disorder and not to relax his grip until the police arrived.

Referring to one of Lenin's key promises of 1917—that "the masses would know about and discuss everything *openly*"—he contrasted present bureaucrats and their methods.

> "The enemies will overhear"—that's your excuse; eternal and permanent "enemies" are a convenient underpinning for your positions and your existence. As if there were no enemies when immediate openness was promised. And what would you do without "enemies"? You couldn't even exist without "enemies"; *hatred* has become your sterile atmosphere, a hatred conceding nothing to the racial variety. But this way a sense of mankind's unity and wholeness is lost, and its extinction accelerated. If the polar ice were to melt tomorrow and make us all a drowning mankind—whose nose would you rub into the "class struggle" then? I do not even speak of the time when the few surviving bipeds will roam our radioactive earth, dying.
>
> After all, it is time to remember that what we belong to first of all is mankind. And mankind has emerged from the animal world through *thought* and *speech*. And in the nature of things, these must be free. And if we chain them, we will return to animals.
>
> *Glasnost*, honest and total *glasnost*—this is the first requisite for any society's health, including ours. And whoever doesn't want *glasnost* for our land is indifferent to his country; he thinks only of his own advantage. Whoever doesn't want *glasnost* for his country doesn't wish to rid it from its sickness, but drive it inward, to fester there.

The confrontation between Solzhenitsyn and the authorities was again wholly open. He had not sought the conflict, but answered persecution with a challenge to the very essentials of the dictatorship's procedures. Once again, what Boris Pasternak had called "the unarmed power of naked truth" was pitted against the entire might of the state.

XXXIII

Commotion

LIKE BORIS PASTERNAK, SOLZHENITSYN HAD BEEN demoted from Soviet writer to literary renegade. But several days after Solzhenitsyn's expulsion from the Writers' Union, events occurred in Moscow which would have amazed Pasternak. When the author of *Doctor Zhivago* was expelled from the Writers' Union a decade earlier, the bravest of his literary colleagues did no more than grumble or express private sympathy. Now, with the dramatic growth in self-confidence of at least a portion of the intelligentsia, public protest materialized and developed into the embryo of a movement. First, a group of twelve well-known writers passed a resolution demanding Solzhenitsyn's immediate reinstatement into the union. A second group of five then called at the union's headquarters to request the immediate convening of an emergency congress.

By late November, some seventy union members had protested, including Yevgeny Yevtushenko, the then roving ambassador of Soviet literature. Alexander Tvardovsky, still editor of the embattled *Novy Mir*, called for an urgent meeting of the U.S.S.R. (as opposed to the Russian Republic's) Writers' Union board and secretariat to reconsider Solzhenitsyn's expulsion. Tvardovsky was a member of both of these governing bodies, and the union's constitution empowered them to overrule the decisions of the Russian Republic's secretariat, the highest organ which had so far dealt with the case. Both national bodies have a strong liberal minority, which was no doubt why Tvardovsky's request was denied.

At least three hundred additional intellectuals signed protests during the following weeks. Most went to the Writers' Union, but some were addressed to the highest organs of the Communist Party and Soviet government. A good number of Solzhenitsyn's friends among leading scientists spoke up in his defense. Another source of protest was the radical dissidents of the new "underground." Thirty-nine of them, including many prominent in the democratic "movement," signed a protest dated December 19, 1969. "The expulsion of Alexander Solzhenitsyn," they wrote, "is a disgrace not for the man expelled. It is a disgrace for the history of our literature. And above all, for our writers—who, silently or explicitly, approved the action. . . . We regard Solzhenitsyn's expulsion as another drastic manifestation of Stalinism, a reprisal against a writer who personifies the mind and conscience of our nation." This was the most forthright recognition of Solzhenitsyn's inspiration to "the other Russia."

The world reaction to Solzhenitsyn's expulsion would also have astonished Pasternak. After the latter's Nobel Prize ordeal in 1958, the response of many intellectuals was cast in a rigid cold war mold. Non- and anti-Communist writers protested against the abuse heaped upon Pasternak; but official Western Communist organizations, publications, and writers either supported the Soviet campaign of vilification or remained silent. Years later, it became known that the silence of several prominent Communists—Louis Aragon, Frank Hardy, and others—was uneasy or tortured. But throughout the intimidation of their distinguished Russian colleague and until well after his death in 1960, they kept their misgivings to themselves, in service to their notions of the larger Communist cause.

In Solzhenitsyn's case, strong protests from Western organizations were not surprising. The PEN Club cabled that it was "appalled and shocked," prompting a rude retort from the Soviets to stop interfering in "the internal affairs of the Writers' Union of the U.S.S.R." An international group of literary intellectuals including Arthur Miller, Günter Grass, and Jean-Paul Sartre "rejected the conception that an artist's refusal to humbly accept state censorship is in any sense criminal in a civilized society, or that publications by foreigners of his books is grounds for persecuting him." One of Bertrand Russell's last acts was to protest against Solzhenitsyn's expulsion in a personal letter to Kosygin.

The outpouring of remonstration from intellectuals of this stature was important, both as a source of moral support for Solzhenitsyn and as a record of civilized world objection to his persecution. But it was the protests by foreign, especially Western, Communists that carried particular weight in Moscow. Dissatisfaction by prominent Communists could not easily be brushed aside as "enemy propaganda." To ignore it would cost Moscow considerable authority with the increasingly restive Western Communist Parties.

The most striking change from 1958 lay precisely in the quick salvo of protests from foreign Communists. One of the strongest was a statement by the French National Writers' Committee, which is predominantly Communist. The committee argued that, contrary to Soviet contentions, it was not Solzhenitsyn's work that harmed the Communist cause and the Soviet Union, but his persecution. Their statement described the expulsion as "a monumental mistake which not only harms the Soviet Union, but also helps confirm the view of socialism propagated by its enemies."

Perhaps the most telling statement came from the Italian Communist Party, both the strongest and the most "liberal" in the West, through its official cultural weekly *Rinascita*. "Without sharing all of Solzhenitsyn's concepts," the magazine declared, "the true left cannot fail to recognize the moral value of his work from the socialist point of view."

Not all foreign Communists supported Solzhenitsyn. The Communist Party of the United States, for example, exceeded even Russian neo-Stalinists in vilifying him. In Britain, the *Morning Star* was opened to both defenders and detractors of the writer. Some correspondents, principally party intellectuals, wrote of their "dismay" over the writer's "shameful harrying," but others thoroughly disagreed. "I support one hundred percent the Soviet Writers' Union," wrote L. Hickox of Wellingborough, "which has, after prolonged discussion, decided it must expel Solzhenitsyn. In my view, people like writers who are in a position to influence not only a handful of people (as might an ordinary worker) but even millions, *have* to be controlled by the properly constituted authority." This blatant apology for dictatorship (as distinct from the traditional Soviet formula about a writer being free while his heart belonged to the party) clarified, and therefore slightly helped, Solzhenitsyn's case: it was obvious that other leading comrades felt what Hickox wrote. In the Western countries where they took place, the arguments of the Hickoxes and their opponents were largely academic and changed little. But in Russia itself they helped widen a critical fissure.

For there the expulsion and subsequent protests led to an open clash between an embittered intelligentsia that had changed markedly—and was, many hoped, on its way to regaining the Russian intelligentsia's traditional independence—and an authority which had hardly changed at all, in the sense that it retained its Stalinist inflexibility, if not ruthlessness. Among the intelligentsia, this confrontation provoked a wider and more intense resentment than even the suppression of Solzhenitsyn's letter some two and a half years earlier.

Naturally the authorities tried to mobilize support for their position among cultural figures. But only one literary luminary was recruited in the union's defense. Predictably, it was Mikhail Sholokhov, once a novelist of great talent who had written nothing significant for almost thirty years and had become one of the most outspoken enemies of "troublemakers," young and old. Like a celebrated character of Soviet folklore, he could say about himself that he had never (at least since the early 1930s) deviated from the party line—because he deviated *with* it. Tvardovsky recalled that in 1963, when Solzhenitsyn was Khrushchev's favorite, Sholokhov spoke of

One Day "with warm approval," and asked the editor "to give the author a hug for him." But the party line had changed.

In November 1969, Sholokhov used the platform of a congress of collective farmers for "literary reflections" calculated to appeal to his audience. Solzhenitsyn was not mentioned by name, but the reference to him was unmistakable. "You [collective farmers] have done away with pests," said Sholokhov, "but unfortunately we still have Colorado beetles—those who eat Soviet grain but want to serve Western bourgeois masters and send their works through secret channels. Soviet men of letters want to get rid of them." The Moscow correspondent of the *Morning Star* commented dryly that this speech "can only be interpreted as an endorsement by Sholokhov of [Solzhenitsyn's] criticism and expulsion."

In contrast to the farmers' congress, two high-level conferences of writers and other intellectuals convening in Moscow within a month of Solzhenitsyn's expulsion, especially for the purpose of publicizing the writer's inequities, failed to produce derogatory statements about him by anyone of importance in the Soviet cultural world. Perhaps their most significant aspect was the prominent role played by the poet and playwright Sergey Mikhalkov, another well-known KGB spokesman in literary affairs. Mikhalkov, who had openly boasted to his friends of his close links with the security police, was then chief of the Moscow branch of the Writers' Union. In this capacity, he supervised one of the two meetings devoted to discrediting Solzhenitsyn, to whom he referred as "a talented enemy of socialism." Since to be an enemy of socialism or of the Soviet system is punishable under Article 70 of the Russian criminal code, Solzhenitsyn would be brought to trial if Mikhalkov's views became official.

Another attempt to implicate Solzhenitsyn in antistate crimes was made in late November by the *Literary Gazette*. According to Chakovsky's newspaper, *The Times* of London had recently reported that "anti-Soviet centers abroad have been making use of Solzhenitsyn's works for straight financing of various subversive organizations." What *The Times* had reported on November 20 was that the president of Praeger, an American publishing house, had paid royalties for their edition of *One Day* to a committee which organized escapes from Eastern Europe. This ostensibly crude and tactless gesture by a firm often reported by the American press to have connections with the CIA was conceived and consummated without Solzhenitsyn's faintest knowledge—and in respect to a work in the public domain which could be exploited without legal obligation to pay royalties to anyone. Not surprisingly, however, the *Literary Gazette*'s story implied that Solzhenitsyn had been involved in the transaction.

Liberal Russians with access to high government officials have reported that after his *glasnost* letter with its direct challenge to methods of rule, the possibility of Solzhenitsyn's arrest was "close and real." But Solzhenitsyn's potential as a lightning rod for national and international protest continued to protect him, and instead of prosecution, the authorities resorted to yet another device designed to undermine his standing in Russia. A not very subtle hinting campaign was inaugurated in semiofficial newspapers, such as the Writers' Union's, with the innuendoes playing about a central theme: Solzhenitsyn should leave Russia, and was perhaps even willing to do so. The strategy here seemed obvious: if Solzhenitsyn were to emigrate, he and his supporters might then be associated with defection, and therefore treason. Actually, Solzhenitsyn had repeatedly told both his friends and his enemies that he would never leave Russia ("Brezhnev will run first," he is rumored to have said), and this was public knowledge in literary circles. Nevertheless, the *Literary Gazette*'s prompting in late November was unmistakable.

> "Grab him and don't let go . . ."—that, according to Solzhenitsyn, is the attitude of the Writers' Union to men of letters. But why "grab and don't let go"? No one has considered adopting this policy—even if Solzhenitsyn would care to betake himself to those places where his anti-Soviet works and letters are always welcomed with such delight.

If this hint were somehow not clear enough, editor Alexander Chakovsky told a visiting foreigner that Solzhenitsyn should indeed emigrate, since he was "incompatible" with Soviet society. Soviet journalists and cultural figures went so far as to argue the merit of emigration from the standpoint of Solzhenitsyn's own interests. He should leave Russia, they said, to find peace and quiet for his writing, much of which they admired. The political controversies he provoked only interfered. Years later, this was confirmed by Solzhenitsyn himself, who spoke of "open hints that I should get out of the country to justify the charge of 'traitor to his country.'"

The eagerness to push Solzhenitsyn out of Russia suggests that some high officials had developed serious misgivings about the Solzhenitsyn "line." They had begun to realize that Vasilyev, Mikhalkov, their KGB backers, and the ultra-orthodox overseers of cultural affairs had little control of the Solzhenitsyn phenomenon. For years, they had bridled maverick writers with well-developed carrot-and-stick techniques, but these did not seem equal to Solzhenitsyn's bold and challenging, yet meticulously legalistic, tactics. In other words, these high officials were apprensive that Solzhenitsyn had generated an opposition stronger than the Kremlin cared to cope with. Instead of ridding society of him, the expulsion was making Solzhenitsyn an involuntary focal point of organized protest.

Disposing of the focal point of opposition by induced emigration seemed a desirable solution to some high officials. They could hardly have forgotten that sweeping liberalizations in Hungary, Poland, and Czechoslovakia all began as protest movements within their respective Writers' Unions.

XXXIV

Dispositions

A MONTH AFTER SOLZHENITSYN'S EXPULSION, Vyacheslav Molotov was asked how Stalin would have dealt with him. Molotov could guess as well as any living man, having been one of Stalin's closest associates for decades. His answer came without hesitation: "Solzhenitsyn would have been shot."

Facile comparisons to the Stalin era can be misleading. For if there were now no threat of execution, the converse—that Solzhenitsyn was in no physical peril whatever—did not follow, as well-informed Russians observed. What alarmed Solzhenitsyn's friends most about the expulsion were references to him as an "enemy of socialism" who had "passed into the enemy camp." Coming from known members of the KGB, this posed a clear and present danger. It was again time for sensible caution.

At this time, Solzhenitsyn decided to leave Ryazan's provincial obscurity. Liberal Muscovites speak of malevolent campaigning in the city by party zealots and ugly gestures by toughs: as long ago as 1968, these sources contend, local anti-Solzhenitsyn sentiment had been whipped up by professional propagandists speaking in factory and institute auditoriums, and threats of violence even appeared in his mailbox. A nastily hostile atmosphere was hardly the most worrying situation Solzhenitsyn had faced since 1940, but since he was making a domestic break—leaving the flat he shared with Reshetovskaya—he felt it best to move from Ryazan entirely. Essentially a summer place, the "Finnish cottage" near Obninsk was extremely uncomfortable after November. Solzhenitsyn needed new quarters.

Deciding to move in Russia is one thing; implementing the decision quite another. Even if accommodation is found at short notice, obtaining police permission for residence, in certain areas even temporary residence, is often more difficult. To ignore the regulation and simply move to new quarters on one's own is no solution, since failure to apply to the police within three days may deliver the offender to a year's imprisonment.

Many of Solzhenitsyn's Moscow friends would have been honored to welcome him in their homes, but without official protection—a champion in the higher bureaucracy—he had no hope of procuring the coveted police stamp for residence in the capital. The problem of where to settle was solved by the celebrated cellist Mstislav Rostropovich, who invited Solzhenitsyn to live in his country house in the village of Zhukovka, seventeen miles west of Moscow.

Zhukovka was no ordinary village. Before the revolution, successful professional and commercial families much favored it for their summer retreats, and soon after 1917 Russia's new rulers requisitioned the properties for their personal use. The families of Soviet officials now spent weekends here—among them Svetlana Alliluyeva, who has described (in *Twenty Letters to a Friend*) her childhood summers in the idyllic countryside.

A handful of leading artists, Rostropovich among them, shared with high officials the rare privilege of a large dacha, usually in a coveted "beauty spot" near a large city. As with the sites of government dachas everywhere, Zhukovka's privileged residents enforced zoning regulations to ensure that its natural delights remained unspoiled, despite its proximity to Moscow. Its groves of pine and birch evoked the spirit of Central Russia so important to Solzhenitsyn.

But the writer hardly relished the prospect of taking up new quarters; at the very least, it upset his tight working schedule for the World War I novel. Besides, as demonstrated by his fondness even for his place of exile, he is involuntarily attached to the place where he happens to live. Nevertheless, this move was necessary for his own safety, and Rotropovich's dacha in particular offered him many advantages. Although set in the forest, a level of security was guaranteed because someone was always present—if no one else, a full-time maid—to deter sneak searches.[1] The living quarters were adequate; an annex to the garage would make a serviceable writing studio. The Zhukovka police had no reasonable pretext to deny one of its most prominent residents a permit to accommodate a friend. (Several pretexts could easily be produced in Moscow, such as a generalized prohibition against establishing residence in the capital or insufficiency of "living space," allegedly for medical reasons, in city apartments.) Zhukovka was only a half hour's run from central Moscow in the aging Moskvich. But most of all, the pervading rural tranquillity was wholly congenial to Solzhenitsyn.

The significance of Rostropovich's offer to Solzhenitsyn was appreciated only by people thoroughly familiar with the workings of Soviet society;

---

[1] Rostropovich's wife, the well-known soprano Galina Vishnevskaya, led a busy professional life of her own. The need for precautions against KGB searches would be brutally demonstrated in August 1971.

outsiders could hardly suspect the pressures on him not to make it and, for his part, the element of self-sacrifice required to resist them. At forty-three, Rostropovich was at the height of his powers as a performing musician and recognized as one of the world's most accomplished artists. Having reached maturity as a cellist a decade before, he also performed as a symphonic conductor and director of opera. From Tokyo to London, his fame was peerless.

In Russia, his achievements brought more than professional esteem: Soviet artists of his rare merit live near the top of their society, possessed of material luxuries undreamed of by most citizens. In addition, Rostropovich enjoyed perhaps the most coveted privilege of all: a passport for foreign travel that allowed him to come and go virtually at will. The Ministry of Culture and the KGB had to approve his trips abroad, of course. But both organizations had come to look favorably on his professional invitations, not least because of the enhancement of the regime's prestige by his concerts, and the contribution of hard currency to the state's coffers, which represented anywhere from fifty to ninety per cent of the income from his foreign concerts.

It is widely assumed that a charmed circle of Russians exist who, because of their supreme talents and international stature, are immune to the grosser forms of pressure from the dictatorship. This "untorturable class of Soviet citizens," as Graham Greene has called it, would number no more than a few dozen celebrities, and clearly includes Rostropovich. The Soviet government, the argument goes, would not dare interfere with these artists' careers—if not from respect for world culture, at least from fear of adverse publicity and damage to their own prestige. It is a reasonable theory, but its application to the contemporary Soviet Union is incomplete. Prima ballerinas with even greater Western reputations than Rostropovich's are duly punished for behavior offensive to the dictatorship: for stepping out of their places as performers or creators, for example, for signing liberal petitions or refusing to sign statements supporting Soviet foreign policy. The punishment includes cancellation of foreign performances, assignment to provincial tours within Russia, and other forms of direct interference with their careers.

Rostropovich was of course fully aware of this; he harbored no illusions about being "untorturable." Yet he put his career in jeopardy to help a fellow artist and friend, illustrating the loyalty Solzhenitsyn inspired among people who yearned for freedom and honesty in Russia. As it happened, the relationship between the writer and musician was not of long standing. Their first meeting had taken place some two years before this, when Rostropovich gave a concert in Ryazan. He had read Solzhenitsyn's novels and, of course, knew his reputation in Moscow's intellectual circles. After the concert, he appeared at Solzhenitsyn's flat—Solzhenitsyn had never seen him before—and introduced himself. By the end of the evening, a foundation for intimacy had been established.

For all his privileges, perhaps even because of them, Rostropovich was pained by Solzhenitsyn's persecution. His indignation was made explicit almost a year later in a stirring open letter to several Soviet newspapers which, although none of them published it, was publicized in the West. He was dismayed at the expulsion of a *writer* from the *Writers'* Union "at the very time when he was working strenuously on a novel about the year 1914." He knew and admired Solzhenitsyn's work, he wrote, and was convinced that "everyone must have the right to think independently and without fear and to express his opinions about what he knows [and] has personally thought about." And he felt certain that "through his suffering," Solzhenitsyn had won the right "to write the truth as he saw it."

Rostropovich explained that his convictions had come after bearing witness for over twenty years to blows inflicted upon Soviet music. Even such towering musicians as Shostakovich and Prokofiev had been harassed by "people totally incompetent in the field," yet possessing "the final word." His support for Solzhenitsyn, he continued, was an expression of his disgust at the power such people wielded "to discredit our art in the eyes of our people." Thus, in addition to personal sentiments, Rostropovich's support for Solzhenitsyn emanated from a belief that Russia must have freedom of expression, and that its greatest living writer had the first claim on it. Rostropovich shared this belief with many artists and intellectuals, but few had yet shown the courage of their convictions.

He was not spared retribution for his stand. Almost as soon as Solzhenitsyn's move to Zhukovka became known, pressures to turn him out were exerted on the cellist. By the spring of 1970, they were applied by a high official in the Ministry of Culture, who warned Rostropovich that he might have to cancel appearances at several foreign music festivals. Rumors of Rostropovich's acid reaction cheered Moscow intellectuals. "I'll be glad to miss the festivals. I'm tired of traveling anyway. Why don't you go and play in my place?"

All this lay in the near future, together with graver consequences for Rostropovich. As for Solzhenitsyn himself, having made the move to the cellist's house he was eager to return to work. But new problems disturbed his concentration. Although the new quarters diminished worries about his physical security, difficulties arising from the publication of his works in the West became acute. What troubled him now was "The Feast of the Victors." That winter, the old verse epic turned up in Germany. In one way or another, the KGB was responsible, its agents having stolen the only copy from the Moscow flat of Solzhenitsyn's friend. From that moment, the repudiated work continued to haunt Solzhenitsyn, who feared that publication of the twenty-year-old verses, written by a bitter and anonymous camp inmate, might serve as the basis of a criminal charge. That he had every reason for concern was again shown early the following year, when editor Alexander Chakovsky told one of Solzhenitsyn's English translators that much as the Soviet authorities disapproved of Solzhenitsyn's other works, only "The Feast" was "anti-Soviet" as defined by the Soviet criminal code.

Solzhenitsyn's fears were fulfilled at the beginning of December 1969. Apparently unaware of the implications, the respected Hamburg weekly *Die Zeit* published an excerpt of a verse epic under the title "Prussian Nights." It described the murder by Soviet soldiers of a German girl who they suspected was engaged to an S.S. soldier.

An informed guess at that time suggested that "Prussian Nights" was intimately related to "The Feast," if not a word-for-word excerpt. Solzhenitsyn's Moscow friends subsequently confirmed this, adding details of the KGB's role in what they call a "maneuver of mystification." Although "Prussian Nights," they say, was not a literal reproduction of a section of "The Feast," it had much in common with the larger epic. Obviously, the KGB version—for Solzhenitsyn's friends are convinced that this was indeed a calculated provocation—was compiled from "The Feast" after a careful study of its confiscated manuscript. Less obvious is why the KGB tampered with the epic rather than circulating an exact copy. Perhaps they feared the potential artistic impact of the original. In any case, the appearance of "Prussian Nights" was yet another threat—and all the graver in light of *Die Zeit*'s announcement that a translation of the entire work was being prepared for serialization.

Solzhenitsyn considered protesting to the newspaper, but knew that making his position clear would cost lengthy explanations and perhaps polemics—even if his mail got through. He had little time to act, and scant inclination to sacrifice energy jealously guarded for his new novel. But there was a possible alternative. He had long pondered how to defend his interests abroad, and engaged a Zürich lawyer to represent his interests there, an unprecedented action for a private Soviet citizen. This remained unpublicized until the "Prussian Nights" episode, in which the lawyer took his first major action.

Solzhenitsyn's choice was Dr. Fritz Heeb. In some ways the very picture of a Swiss lawyer, the soft-spoken, polite, and hard-bargaining Dr. Heeb is also a left-wing Social Democrat, which is rather unusual for someone of his profession in his country. Solzhenitsyn has called the combination "extremely felicitous." He gave his representative a signed power of attorney to "protect his rights outside the Soviet Union." In keeping with professional ethics, Dr. Heeb considers his relations with his client confidential, and declines to discuss the circumstances of his appointment. But it is known that he has close connections with "liberals" whose ideas are akin to Dubček's "socialism with a human face," and a supposition that the appointment came through these channels can be reasonably made.

As for Solzhenitsyn's introduction to Heeb himself, the writer's friends feel it is not yet time to disclose the details. But the precise circumstances of Dr. Heeb's appointment are less important than its results, which were very quickly beneficial to Solzhenitsyn. In December, Heeb protested against the publication of "Prussian Nights" to *Die Zeit,* whereupon the weekly promptly canceled its plans for further serialization.

In March 1970, Dr. Heeb issued a statement as "Alexander Solzhenitsyn's authorized attorney" which fully explained for the first time his client's attitude toward publication in the West. Heeb began by emphasizing that Solzhenitsyn had "repeatedly attempted to publish his work in his own country so that it could be read by his compatriots. . . . To this end, but without success, he repeatedly turned to the Soviet Writers' Union for support." Solzhenitsyn had also tried to enlist the union's help in protecting his author's rights abroad, but, "as a consequence of his expulsion from the Writers' Union, he lost all prospect of such assistance . . . [and] entrusted his Swiss attorney with the protection of his rights outside the U.S.S.R.."

In other words, the statement stressed that Solzhenitsyn's initiative had resulted from intolerable Soviet inaction: he organized his own self-defense only because the competent Soviet authorities had refused to fulfill their obligations, leaving him easy prey to the Western publishers willing to exploit the situation.

Heeb's appearance did not mean that Solzhenitsyn had retracted his objections to unauthorized publications abroad. On the contrary, the lawyer's statement reemphasized these protests. But rather than disowning everything already published under his name abroad, Solzhenitsyn, through Heeb, made more subtle intentions clear. Without fear of accusations that he was conniving with "foreign enemies," Solzhenitsyn intervened decisively in the unhappy mess caused by the haphazard supply of his works to Western presses. His goal was the highest quality possible in translation and publication of his works. As Heeb's statement put it, part of his brief was "to examine the quality of translations of the works of Alexander Solzhenitsyn and to bring about necessary improvement."

Heeb also undertook to protect Solzhenitsyn's rights as an author. Apart from confirming the world rights of *Cancer Ward* and *The Love Girl and the Innocent,* he also authorized the world premiere of *The Love Girl* in the United States [2] and publication of a volume of short stories, principally those translated earlier from Soviet texts, but in improved translations. And he took steps to legalize the publication of *The First Circle.*

[2] The premiere took place in the Tyrone Guthrie Theater in Minneapolis in October 1970, a few days after Solzhenitsyn was awarded the Nobel Prize.

In these ways Solzhenitsyn's relations with his Western publishers were firmly regularized; he had managed to bring order to a situation that seemed to be festering into menacing, irrevocable worldwide chaos. What he had accomplished in solving these problems was so extraordinary for a Soviet citizen—so bold and, in a deeply isolated country where private citizens do not dream of conducting their own affairs abroad, so imaginative—that this alone would have made him a noteworthy figure in contemporary Soviet life.[3] His plan also required courage on the part of several Russian and foreign friends; but, as always, there was no lack of people near him who, inspired by his integrity and resolution, were happy to help despite real risks to themselves.

No help of this kind, however, would have sufficed to regularize Solzhenitsyn's relations with the Soviet authorities. Sinister rumors about his impending doom continued to circulate in late 1969. One report quoted apprehension of his Moscow friends that he was "in imminent danger of arrest and trial." "The courage he displayed was such," this report continued, "that observers at first thought that [Solzhenitsyn's] letter [protesting against his expulsion to the Writers' Union] was a provocation by the KGB, circulated to provide it with a flimsy excuse for 'legal action' against Solzhenitsyn."

These rumors speak of great nervous strains among certain liberal intellectuals. Actually, a return to the status quo of the years when Solzhenitsyn had carried on his work as a writer but had not yet spoken out as a publicist was taking place. Now extremely eager to finish his long-postponed "principal project" about the First World War, he worked with great intensity on the research and the text—not suspecting the period of relative peace would soon develop into the makings of an ambush.

[3] Solzhenitsyn's action here was not entirely unprecedented. On a smaller scale, Andrei Amalrik, a dissident Soviet writer now serving a three-year sentence in a labor camp, had shortly before entered into direct and open contact with his Western publishers, without the representation of a lawyer.

XXXV

Ambush

THE AMBUSH LAID FOR SOLZHENITSYN IN THE spring of 1970 sought to exploit two apparent chinks in his armor of self-reliance: his irrepressible urge to write—specifically, now, to complete his World War I novel—and his apparent vulnerability to moral imperatives. Even before his expulsion from the Writers' Union, uneasy whispers had begun to steal through both liberal and dissident circles in Moscow. They reproached Solzhenitsyn for selfishness and egoism, and questioned his professed defense of universal freedom of expression. Why, it was asked, had he protested only when *his* novel was suppressed and when *he* was expelled? . . . Why had he never signed even temperate petitions or protests against the persecution of others? He had not even bestirred himself, it was pointed out, during the winter of 1968, when Yury Galanskov, Ginzburg, and other courageous writer-protesters had been sentenced to long terms of imprisonment for mythical anti-Soviet propaganda. Hundreds of Soviet intellectuals risked their careers to appeal for fair trials—but Solzhenitsyn, whose declarations had put him in the forefront of protest, was silent.

To what extent these whispers were sincere is a matter for speculation. They may have expressed genuine disappointment by dissidents who had come to a kind of moral absolutism—and were willing to take grave risks themselves—in the determination to fight lies and corruption in the Soviet system. On the other hand, the talk may have been fanned by the KGB in its eagerness to chip away at Solzhenitsyn's position as "the conscience of the nation."

Whatever the source of these rumors, Solzhenitsyn well knew that as the subject of a particularly vicious campaign of vengefulness and slander by neo-Stalinists, with *Pravda*'s editor at the forefront, he must be exceedingly cautious with his signature. Obviously, he could not conduct a personal investigation of every instance of arrest or persecution that had dismayed other protesters. But to sign without full knowledge of a given case would be to offer himself up to a potential snare. If a case could be found in which the accused was genuinely guilty of something but the facts kept concealed, protests could be manufactured against the conviction in the expectation that Solzhenitsyn would sign, as he would have signed earlier protests. The trap would then be sprung: Solzhenitsyn himself could be convicted of "anti-Soviet slander."

Following Solzhenitsyn's expulsion from the Writers' Union, the whispered censure of him increased in volume. But Solzhenitsyn held to his position: he would not involve himself in protests except about cases known personally to him. In May 1970, the KGB found just such a case.

Their victim was Dr. Zhores Medvedev. He was seized on May 29, in a way which Solzhenitsyn himself has described. "Without warrant for arrest or medical justification, four policemen and two doctors come to a healthy man's house; the doctors declare him insane, the police major shouts: 'We represent an agency of coercion. Get up!' They twist his arms and drive him off to a madhouse."

It was a measure of the determination of the Moscow underground that this incident was reported the very next day in the Western press. Instances of repression even worse than this had gone unreported and unknown by the thousands (perhaps tens of thousands) in the post-Stalin years. Now, however, friends of Medvedev hurried to inform correspondents in Moscow's "foreign ghetto."

But it was also a measure of Medvedev's stature that his case was instantly newsworthy abroad. His reputation in international scientific circles was not much below Rostropovich's in the music world. At forty-five, Medvedev was recognized as one of the world's leading theoretical gerontologists. But as he had shown in recent years, Medvedev's interests went beyond the purely scientific. By education, he was a biologist; and biology had suffered grievously in the manipulation of science and scholarship to swell the power of Stalin and Stalinists.

In general outline the story of the crippling of Soviet biology is widely known. Trofim Lysenko, Stalin's favorite charlatan scientist (and to a lesser extent Khrushchev's), argued that an organism's development was more influenced by environmental than by hereditary factors. It was a theory convenient for the revolutionary goal of creating a New Man, and was twisted for use in Politburo machinations. For decades, Lysenko relied on Stalin's support to deprive Soviet scientists who opposed his notions, some of them brilliant and dedicated men, of research facilities to carry on their work, and further, of their freedom and their very lives.

But it took Medvedev to investigate the destructive years in full detail; and the extent of the evil he uncovered—cynical faking of laboratory data, cold-blooded liquidation of wave after wave of honest scientists—caused pain even to those who thought themselves familiar with the finest nuances of Stalinism. Medvedev whote a full chronicle of Lysenko's crimes in the mid-1960s—and with support from parts of the scientific and even political establishments, since the scientist-author was given access to some official archives. Like *Cancer Ward*, Medvedev's study was on the verge of publication, to be banned after neo-Stalinists had gained ascendancy within the party. The light it shed on men then in influential positions—who had either profited by the "resistible rise" of Trofim Lysenko or shrunk from opposing it—was too explosive.

While Medvedev still had hopes of publishing in Russia, he passed a copy of the manuscript to an American colleague. When it was published in New York in 1969, as *The Rise and Fall of T. D. Lysenko,* the authorities felt that personal contact between Medvedev and foreigners was dangerous, and prohibited him from attending a congress of gerontologists in England.

The circumstances of this restriction were particularly humiliating, not least because Medvedev was to have delivered the key paper at the English congress and now had to disappoint his international colleagues. Medvedev himself later wrote that no Westerner would quite believe what he, a mature scientist, was subjected to in his vain efforts to beg for a passport. The ban prompted him to make a study of unlawful restrictions on Soviet citizens' foreign travel. Meanwhile, refusing to invent the usual diplomatic illness as an excuse for not appearing in England, he wrote to his Western colleagues explaining that he had been prohibited from traveling.

This, in turn, led to intensified interference with his correspondence and to his dismissal, in 1969, from the Obninsk Institute of Medical Radiology. Now at enforced leisure, Medvedev compiled the first study of Soviet postal censorship, including self-gathered statistics about the proportion of letters detained. He also pestered postal authorities for compensation for registered items "lost" en route.

If for no other reason than because it is expressly forbidden by Soviet law, the authorities would not admit the existence of censorship of the post. Medvedev was a thorn in their flesh, all the more exasperating because of its novelty. But the KGB had the increasingly familiar remedy of insane asylums for unaccustomed discomforts of this sort, and the distinguished scientist was committed in the manner Solzhenitsyn described.

The authorities were clearly eager to suppress the meddlesome Medvedev. But the operation may have been simultaneously a provocation against Solzhenitsyn, whom the KGB assumed they had impaled on the horns of a terrible moral dilemma: if he remained silent and did not protest against Medvedev's persecution, his standing would be compromised among the liberals and dissidents for having abandoned a valued friend; if he did protest, he would have opened himself to severe new "adminis-

trative measures." It seemed a deft and cunning maneuver though few
Russians thought of it this way, and some people close to Solzhenitsyn
still deny that Medvedev's detention was in any way motivated by a
scheme to ensnare the writer.

Soviet dissident sources estimate that at this time more than 250 political prisoners were being held in asylums for the criminally insane, including demonstrators against the invasion of Czechoslovakia, journalists who
had disseminated "underground" documentation of repression, and leading
participants in Russia's still tiny protest movements. But Medvedev was
the first member of the scientific establishment to be sent for this "cure,"
and beyond their compassion for him personally many of his colleagues in
all scientific fields were alarmed. Scientists' freedom to harbor, and to a
lesser extent express, "liberal" ideas seemed threatened. By any Western
standard this freedom, painfully won after Stalin's death, was severely
limited, but by measurements of Soviet society it was real enough.

The Medvedev affair had many twists, implications, and consequences
of its own. It is enough to say here that his detention was protested on
the very next day, and at the highest level. As a matter of great urgency,
several prominent scientists were received by the Minister of Health on
Sunday, two days after the seizure, and assured that Medvedev would be
released after a brief investigation of his mental health. He was not. His
colleagues, joined by Tvardovsky and other literary figures, continued to
object and threatened a major public uproar; but Medvedev remained
locked in an insane asylum. His twin brother, Roy, led the campaign for
release and kept Solzhenitsyn fully informed, but Solzhenitsyn made no
public statement.

The reasons for Solzhenitsyn's delay are obscure. But when two weeks
had passed, he arranged a rendezvous with Roy Medvedev—in a public
square so their conversation would not be recorded—and told him that
he "could wait no longer and thought it necessary for him to speak in defense of Zhores and all others imprisoned in psychiatric hospitals for
political reasons." Having been assured that a protest would not harm
Zhores, he quickly wrote an open letter which was delivered to Medvedev's
brother on the next morning, June 15. It was not only a defense of his
friend, but an indictment of the whole of the system that committed sane
men to suppress them, keeping them indefinitely in the company of the
mentally deranged.

No doubt remembering the public description of himself as a "psycho-
logically abnormal man and a schizophrenic" by *Pravda*'s editor-in-chief
two and a half years earlier, Solzhenitsyn now wrote that "this can happen
to any of us," as testified by it having "happened to Zhores Medvedev, a
scientist, geneticist, and publicist, a man of subtle, precise, and brilliant
intellect and of good heart." Having denounced the practice of declaring

dissidents insane, Solzhenitsyn appealed to the common sense and conscience of the men who had resorted to it.

To people familiar with the Soviet government's procedures his appeal might have appeared naïve. But it was consistent with the writer's belief in the essential humanity residing somewhere within even the most corrupt and vicious of men.

> Even in lawlessness, in the doing of evil [Solzhenitsyn wrote], one must remember the line beyond which a man becomes a cannibal.... Even simple common sense should act as a restraint. . . . It is time to recognize that the detention of free-thinking, healthy men in madhouses is spiritual murder; it is a variant of the gas chamber, and even more cruel: the torture of those who are to be killed is more fiendish and more prolonged. Like those of the gas chamber, these crimes will never be forgotten, and all those involved in them will be tried without a statute of limitations, while they are alive and after their deaths.

The language was as emotional as any Solzhenitsyn had used in public. He has told close friends that he is disturbed by the fuss made over his own difficulties in the Western press, compared to the relative silence about martyrs who are tortured in madhouses. He concluded his June statement on a favorite theme: the reassertion of the primacy of conscience. "It is short-sighted to think," he wrote, "that one can live by constantly relying on force alone, constantly scorning the objections of conscience."

On the following day, this appeal was passed to foreign correspondents in Moscow. On the day after that it was featured by the whole of the Western press, finally terminating Solzhenitsyn's short period of non-protest about public matters.

At first, it might have seemed that his appeal was brilliantly successful. For on June 17, just as it was being reproduced everywhere in the world, Medvedev was released. Perhaps this was coincidental; Medvedev's release might have been the result of earlier protests by his scientific colleagues and friends. But there is reason to suspect that the release was hastened because Medvedev's detention had served one of its auxiliary purposes: provoking a vehement response from Solzhenitsyn. The KGB was moved not by his appeal to conscience, but by his newly exposed position.

The authorities had forced Solzhenitsyn's hand, simultaneously demonstrating, at least for their own purposes, that his strong language was wholly out of place. For it was now obvious to everyone, they implied, that cases like Medvedev's were properly reviewed and all mistakes duly rectified. According to this logic Solzhenitsyn had demonstrated his tendency to hurl "anti-Soviet" generalizations, which nicely laid the ground-work for new "administrative measures" against him.

What measures? It might have seemed that after suppression of his works, a panoply of administrative harassment, slander campaigns, and expulsion from the Writers' Union, the bureaucracy had exhausted its arsenal, short of a full-scale trial on charges of "slandering the Soviet Union." But something else might be ventured: banishment from the country. In the summer of 1970, Solzhenitsyn almost fell victim to this measure.

Until 1958, forcible exile abroad was a legal punishment of the Soviet criminal code. Originally drafted (under Lenin) as a means of ridding the country of political opponents or other undesirables without having to kill or imprison them, its last known use was in 1927, during the period before Stalin had begun to murder his political rivals. Instead, he had Leon Trotsky bodily thrown over the border into Turkey.

In a light moment of *The First Circle*, a dormitory of prisoners discusses this punishment with huge merriment. Officially, it was the second severest in the Soviet code, exceeded only by death. The fiction was that any sane man would find separation from the Soviet Union intolerable. For Stalin's prisoners, the facts were so wildly different—exile to freedom would have been such a dazzling blessing—that they roared. It was ironic that the author was now threatened with this measure—and that, for him, it would indeed be a punishment.

Apparently, it could not be applied without altering Soviet law. Deportation was no longer a criminal penalty, as it had been under Stalin; and in any event, Solzhenitsyn had committed no crime. The most recent precedents were those of Svetlana Alliluyeva and the writer Valery Tarsis, who had been deprived of their citizenship while they were abroad. But depriving a person of citizenship, which the Supreme Soviet was author-ized to do under Soviet law, is different from deporting him.

Nevertheless, the Supreme Soviet could have changed Soviet law in any way it wanted—even enacted special legislation for the Solzhenitsyn "case," with contents superseding all earlier laws. One can only speculate on the legal tactics considered by the men determined to rid the country of him. But that plans of some sort to deport him were well advanced is beyond doubt.

To Solzhenitsyn himself, the renewed threat of this punishment first materialized in the form of insinuations. As before, men whose authority could have come only from the highest levels hinted broadly that he might like to emigrate. The implication was that the only realistic deliverance from the extreme difficulties in the Soviet Union caused by his mode of writing—and living—was to leave.

These disingenuous suggestions were first put about after Solzhenitsyn's expulsion from the Writers' Union. But well before this, he had responded

categorically to the officially sponsored rumors of his defection to the
U.A.R. or England. "I should like to assure the slanderers," he declared
publicly, "that it is rather they who will do the running." He explained
his reasons to the Writers' Union in the autumn of 1967. "I've never set
eyes on any 'abroads,'" he then said. "I don't know about such things and
there's too little time in life to learn. . . . All my life the soil of my country
has been under my feet; I hear only her pain; I write only about her."

Some of Solzhenitsyn's Russian admirers see in this vehement attachment to Russia the source of the writer's distinct limitations. However
great his talents, they say, and however shining his purpose and tempered
his courage, Solzhenitsyn will always be restricted by certain strains of a
"village" mentality: parochialism, love-of-native-soil patriotism, and a distinct tendency toward hermitism, both in the personal sense and in the
established pattern of the profoundly "Russian" writer who secludes himself from the strident complexities—and, for broader minds, the challenging realities—of the outside world. Even as a young man, Solzhenitsyn
yearned for retreat to the depths of provincial Russia. Naturally enough,
long years of imprisonment and exile served to intensify his tendency to
withdraw, both geographically and spiritually.

Moreover, Solzhenitsyn is a Russian nationalist. A nationalist in the
best sense of the word, since he wants the highest civilized virtues of justice, goodness, and truth for his country—but a nationalist nevertheless,
with at least some of the narrowness this implies. Other great Russian
writers, after all—Turgenev, Bunin, even Gorky during his best period—
did not suffer impairment to their creativity when they left their native
soil. Solzhenitsyn's dismay at the thought of leaving Russia has something
of the terror of the medieval boyars when forced to shave their beards—
and is all the more Russian for that.

For this "charge" of Russian nationalism, passages in Solzhenitsyn's
writing can serve as evidence. The story "The Bonfire and the Ants" is told
in the first person and clearly reflects Solzhenitsyn's thoughts about these
issues, reduced to some hundred and fifty words.

I tossed a log on the fire, not bothering to notice that inside
it was thickly populated with ants.

The log began to crackle, the ants came tumbling out and
scurried back and forth in desperation. They ran along the top,
writhing as the flames consumed them. I flipped away the log and
rolled it to the fire's edge. Now many of the ants saved themselves
—they ran out onto the sand and pine needles.

But strange: they didn't run away from the fire.

They'd no sooner overcome their terror when they turned,
circled and—some kind of force pulled them back to the homeland

they'd evacuated! And many ran back onto the burning log, dashed about on it and died there.

This microstory strongly implies that Solzhenitsyn not only recognizes his overpowering attachment to Russia, but finds it somewhat irrational, and therefore puzzling. To what extent this bond—virtually inevitable in view of Russia's history and his own—limits him as a man and as a writer is a matter for individual interpretation. But to overlook it is to ignore an important motive force in his life and the reason why the rumors of exile seemed like a grave threat.

There were also wholly "objective" reasons why the thought of life abroad distressed him. He was fully aware of the emasculation of some expatriate writers: contrary to the experience of Turgenev, Bunin, and Gorky, many highly talented Russian writers did suffer artistic disaster in emigration.[1] Solzhenitsyn's own creativity was so enmeshed in Russia's sights and sounds that he feared his ear would inevitably be desensitized abroad, if not his inspiration benumbed.

Beyond this, there was his unique position in Soviet society: that of a free man, as one of his closest friends put it, in a country of slaves. Having liberated himself in Russia despite all his pressures, harassments, and obstacles, Solzhenitsyn need not go abroad to acquire internal freedom. He lived by humanity's laws. He wrote what he perceived, not what censors would print or what stopped short of angering cultural overseers.

In this sense, he was already free—from fear, as well as from lesser inner restrictions; he was his own master, not only as few Russians were, but as were few people anywhere.

There were other "objective" factors. Solzhenitsyn was not a political protester or civil-rights campaigner in the pattern of, say, Alexander Ginzburg or General Grigorenko. But convinced that it was his duty to know about everything else taking place around him, and especially about political developments, he studied current events in Russia with intense interest—and in a way he believed was impossible from abroad.

The sense of duty went further. As Pavel Ličko discovered on his visit to Ryazan in 1967, Solzhenitsyn was nicknamed "the Field Marshal" of the army of former political prisoners. At first a kind of drollery, the nickname acquired real meaning over the years; and Solzhenitsyn needed no reminding that field marshals do not leave their armies—"surely not at this hard time for Russia," as his friends had put it. After 1967 a larger responsibility—to the people who considered him Russia's "mind and conscience"—was imposed on him. He felt that to leave them to struggle

---

[1] The obscurity of such powerful talents as Alexander Kuprin and Ivan Shmelyov testifies to the extent of the disaster for some.

for ideals which he himself helped encourage could be immoral. Close friends of Solzhenitsyn have remarked that life abroad would not be tragic for him, although it might be a hard, lingering punishment, all the more so because of highly personal reasons which would become public later in the year.

After his statement about psychiatric imprisonment, the chances of exile appeared more and more real. In late June 1970, days after Medvedev's release, Soviet diplomats and journalists abroad began discreetly querying several neutral countries about their willingness to receive Solzhenitsyn as a permanent resident. The soundings were never precise nor formally addressed to the governments concerned. But they were unmistakable, especially in Stockholm, where Swedish officials were asked what would happen if Solzhenitsyn were to arrive one day with a one-way ticket.

The notion that Solzhenitsyn might be deported sounded somewhat far-fetched even then, after all that had happened to him. But a month later a Soviet writer with regular access to the *Literary Gazette's* editorial offices claimed confirmation that the move was being planned at the highest level. One day in late June, the writer asserted, he was in the office of the editor-in-chief, Chakovsky, when the telephone rang. The caller was a secretary of the Writers' Union with important instructions to transmit. Chakovsky was told to hold open a page of his paper for a vital story: an imminent government announcement of Solzhenitsyn's banishment from the country. The editor was also instructed to make preparations for organizing and publishing the customary outpouring of "spontaneous" support and felicitations for the action from cooperative writers.

At almost exactly the same time, submissive writers approved another action against Solzhenitsyn, his expulsion from the Literary Fund, which indicated that the authorities were making final preparations for his deportation. Although this meant little to him financially—he was unlikely ever to apply to this organization in the role of a writer fallen on hard times—it severed his last slim link with the official literary world. Theoretically, and until now in practice, the Literary Fund was free from this kind of political manipulation. In the post-Stalin era no writer, whatever his difficulties with the authorities, had been expelled. Even Boris Pasternak remained a member after his severe persecution in the wake of his Nobel Prize, as the terse official announcement of his death so described him in 1960. Unwilling to call him a poet, writer, or even man of letters, the authorities called him starkly "member of the Literary Fund." But Solzhenitsyn was deprived of even this. Whatever measures planned against him now would befall a delinquent, wholly "private" citizen with no recognized or legitimate connections with the uplifting mission of Soviet literature.

Meanwhile, the *Literary Gazette* published nothing about Solzhenitsyn now, and it became clear that if Chakovsky had in fact been instructed to prepare for his deportation, the plan was subsequently abandoned (only after debate in the Politburo, according to the same writer). Soon after this, nothing more was heard of Soviet inquiries abroad about permanent residence for Solzhenitsyn. No clues are available to the authorities' reasoning, but opponents of deportation might well have prevailed on tactical grounds: while it is true that Solzhenitsyn had issued a political protest, Medvedev's release was an admission that there had indeed been a mistake —that Solzhenitsyn and his fellow protesters had been right. It would look weak on record to exile Solzhenitsyn for his vehement language, simultaneously admitting that the substance of his protest was justified.

Another threat had passed. Solzhenitsyn disappeared from world headlines for several months—to reappear in October, in connection with the Nobel Prize.

XXXVI

Prize

EVEN BEFORE *Cancer Ward* AND *The First Circle,* Russians had begun to discuss Solzhenitsyn's place in their literature. Some spoke of a progression beginning with Pushkin, running through Tolstoy and Dostoyevsky and continuing with the author of *One Day.* The slim novel had been enough to convince a body of critics that Solzhenitsyn was the successor to the time-honored school of philosophic realism; and each new story won new converts. "Matryona's Place," for example, convinced Anna Akhmatova, who, despite her admiration for *One Day,* first considered Solzhenitsyn primarily a witness and, like most Western critics, doubted that he would show any great imaginative powers. Until the appearance abroad of Solzhenitsyn's larger novels later that year, the judgment of him as the inheritor of Russia's greatest literary traditions was not widely shared abroad.

With *Cancer Ward* and *The First Circle,* Solzhenitsyn's literary reputation soared and a gush of laudatory reyiews began to appear. "To read Solzhenitsyn's novels is to set up a tension inside oneself," wrote an exhilarated British critic, "a tension of excitement, compassion, and wonder. . . . Our modern literature prepares us for nothing comparable." An American who had been skeptical of Soviet fiction in general and of Solzhenitsyn's literary (as opposed to civic) merits in particular, admitted that while reading *Cancer Ward* he was "gripped by the kind of emotion that only major writing can induce. One has the sense that in these . . . pages are merged immediate apprehensions of beauty, of tragedy, of what is unkillable in the human spirit." The new appreciation of the author was marked most sharply by George Lukács, the veteran Hungarian critic who had greeted *One Day* as a harbinger of socialist literature's renaissance. In his last major work, a long essay on Solzhenitsyn's fiction written in 1969, the octogenarian Marxist critic announced "with joy" that he had underestimated the Russian's artistic significance, and now saw him as "the summit of contemporary world literature."

The torrent of international praise was quickly followed by awards— the first in January 1969, when a jury of French journalists gave a prize for the best foreign book of the previous year to Solzhenitsyn's novels. In March, the American Academy of Arts and Letters elected him an honorary member. The bitterness of the Soviet authorities over the world acclaim was first communicated by the postal censorship, which intercepted information about awards, notifications, and invitations to receive them in person. Solzhenitsyn learned about many through private channels, in the case of the American election with almost two months' delay. Solzhenitsyn did not protest against the meddling with his mail but accepted the awards quietly and "thankfully." By this time, he hardly needed reassurance of his ability to cope with his mission, but the honors were an encouraging measure of the breadth of his impact.

In Russia, the authorities at first appeared bravely unimpressed—surely a difficult stance, for in their extreme isolation, Russian philistines have long harbored an exaggerated fear of criticism by the outside world and of losing face before foreigners. Solzhenitsyn knew that each new honor given him made Russia's rulers yet more anxious about their prestige. But in the present circumstances, each award also decreased the likelihood of their taking some new action against him that would interrupt his work, the eventuality that most concerned him.

Paradoxically, the Writers' Union and KGB were second only to his novels in elevating his international stature: their fumbling attempts to "get him" through expulsion and the Medvedev provocation kept his name in the news, stimulating concern among the general public and messages of solidarity from celebrated intellectuals. Besides guaranteed publicity, the Union and the KGB gave Solzhenitsyn opportunities to state his views which he would otherwise not have enjoyed without abandoning his policy of speaking out only on matters of which he had personal knowledge. With his reputation, the attractiveness of his position and his publicistic powers, these statements could only swell international sympathy for him.

Encouraged by his reception among Russian intellectuals and the wider reading public of the world, Solzhenitsyn was working at near the limit of his capacity, despite his harassment and unsettled domestic conditions. In the winter of 1968–69, he completed a novel which, unlike *The First Circle*, told the story of the lower depths of the concentration-camp world. The novel is entitled *The Gulag Archipelago*, "Gulag" referring to the Russian acronym for the Main Directorate of Corrective Labor Camps (*Gosudarstvennoye Upravleniye Lagerey*). The book marked Solzhenitsyn's final reckoning with camps and prisons, and he turned immediately to his vast project about the First World War and its consequences, conceived over thirty years before. Solzhenitsyn's urged to complete as much of the project as possible in his remaining productive years might have prompted his decision not to publish *Gulag* abroad or allow it to circulate in *samizdat*. For the novel's treatment of some of the harsher aspects of labor camps might well have caused an antitotalitarian sensation, provoking the authorities to interfere with his new work on the historical material.[1]

Honors, however sensational, were clearly a different matter to Solzhenitsyn. The first discreet inquiries from the Swedish Academy about his attitude toward a Nobel Prize reached him in late spring of 1970. His friends were asked whether the prize, if awarded, would make his position even more precarious. Through them, Solzhenitsyn answered unambiguously that he would be stronger with than without it. This was in accordance with the general experience of Russian writers, from Pasternak to Yevtushenko, in the years since Stalin. Although Westerners had not yet fully understood—calculations about what might help or harm Soviet citizens continued to be governed by fear of ruthless, supremely determined autocrats instead of the petty tyrants, anxious to avoid foreign ridicule, who actually ruled—the Russian intelligentsia was by now convinced that international acclaim could only benefit a writer.

That inquiries were made in the spring suggested that Solzhenitsyn was among the half dozen candidates for 1970, although he himself prob-

---

[1] The machinations surrounding *Gulag*'s possible publication in the West were sordid even by comparison to earlier episodes. Again, the NTS-*Grani* organization seems to have been involved. When the novel's existence became known in Moscow early in 1969, rumors spread through émigré circles that a manuscript had been smuggled from Russia. Apparently few publishers remembered that similar doubtful claims had been made about *Cancer Ward*. An old Russian saying warns against "sharing the hide of an unslain bear," but many eager bids were made for *Gulag* and an American firm reportedly acquired the "rights."

During the next eighteen months, the public was informed that the book was "being translated"—but also that it had been "deposited in a bank vault in New York." *Time* magazine reported in March 1970 that Solzhenitsyn had learned of the novel's appearance in the West "with alarm and consternation"—an understandable reaction since he was taking extreme precautions and had never let *Gulag* out of his sight. The following autumn, even some of his closest friends had not yet read it.

How, then, did *Gulag* find its way out of the country? The answer is that it almost certainly did not. Three years after the first whispers about its imminent publication, there is no sign of it anywhere, and the author's trusted Moscow friends hesitate to talk about it. The NTS rumors were probably deliberately spurious: a device to deter publishers who might one day decline a genuine manuscript in the belief that rivals were well advanced in translation. Meanwhile, the NTS could hope that the novel would one day appear in *samizdat* and a copy reach them. Essentially the same maneuver was attempted when *Grani* announced imminent publication of *Cancer Ward* in March 1968, except that this time no manuscript has turned up at all.

ably did not know this. For the selection of the literature laureate is a procedure of considerable duration and complexity. The final selection is made by the Swedish Academy's eighteen members in a simple majority vote, but since the academicians cannot be versed in all literatures of the world, they are advised by experts during a careful preparation. Nominations, usually by distinguished literary figures, close in January, after which the Prize Committee begins a series of weekly meetings to winnow down the average of a hundred names. The "short list" of five or six is usually completed by May, after which the members have until the final vote in October to study their briefs. In Solzhenitsyn's case the vociferous praise for *Cancer Ward* and *The First Circle*—which cut across the political spectrum and included many prominent Communists—helped place him on the short list in the spring.

Although the Academy refused to comment at this stage about any possible nominee, knowledge of Solzhenitsyn's strong candidacy spread through world literary circles in the early summer, generating more support as well as some controversy. The strongest backing came from France, where fifty of the most illustrious intellectuals appealed to the Nobel Prize Committee in July to give Solzhenitsyn the award for the "entirety of his work"—that is, both published and unpublished in Russia. The first signer was François Mauriac, the 1952 laureate. It was among the eighty-four-year-old writer's last public acts—just as Bertrand Russell's protest against Solzhenitsyn's expulsion from the Writers' Union and George Lukács' proclamation of his artistic significance had been among their last—and he died before the selection was made. The concern for Solzhenitsyn by these great octogenarians of European culture was not accidental, for all three had deep roots in Solzhenitsyn's "native" nineteenth century: Mauriac represented its progressive religious tradition; Russell, the rationalist, and Lukács, the Marxist-revolutionary. Each sensed in Solzhenitsyn's strong commitment to humanity's betterment a spirit more kindred to his own than to the prevailing twentieth-century currents, and each could find his intellectual passions reflected in Solzhenitsyn's characters.[2]

But despite his impressive support, Solzhenitsyn hardly had a clear run to the prize. In one international poll, critics strongly favored the Argentinian Jorge Luis Borges, whose sophistication and understated despair put him much more in tune with the Western twentieth century. In early autumn the Australian novelist Patrick White's significant following among the academicians became known.

As the date for selection approached—normally it would have been

---

[2] One thinks of Mauriac when reading about Alyosha, the pure, naïve believer of *One Day;* of Russell in connection with *First Circle's* majestic, almost sovereign mathematicians; and of the parallels between Lukács and Lev Rubin, with his intense intellectuality and fiery love of the revolution, despite its harsh distortions.

October 22—powerful pressures were exerted on the Academy, causing internal tensions. The Swedish press began lauding Solzhenitsyn in unusual volume, indicating that from moderate right to extreme left, public opinion in the country favored him for the prize. On the other hand, the Academy's feelers to the Soviet authorities about their reaction to such a choice provoked a cold fury. Past experience—specifically the award to Boris Pasternak in 1958 and to the Russian émigré Ivan Bunin in 1933— suggested that the fury would probably turn to abuse if Solzhenitsyn were in fact selected. A significant faction of the academicians urged that the problem be solved by avoiding "conflicts entirely unrelated to literature." It became clear that Solzhenitsyn's most active opponent was Arthur Lundqvist, the very member who had canvassed most actively in support of Mikhail Sholokhov, a selection which pleased the Soviet authorities extremely in 1965. Poet, travel writer, Lenin Prize laureate, and "fighter for peace," Lundqvist warned his colleagues of the dangers for neutral Sweden in encouraging the "enemies" of its powerful Eastern neighbor.

In order to resolve this impossible situation the Academy abandoned its usual majestic ways and took the unprecedented step of advancing the date of the first ballot. Normally the first Nobel Prize to be awarded each year is that for medicine, but to everyone's great surprise they announced on October 7 that the final ballot for the literature prize would take place the following day. On the morning of October 8, the eighteen academicians met behind closed doors and struggled to their "difficult" and "not unanimous" decision. In the early afternoon, it was announced that the 1970 Nobel Prize for Literature, consisting of a gold medal, a richly illustrated diploma, and 400,000 Swedish kronor, was awarded to Alexander Solzhenitsyn for "the ethical force with which he has pursued the indispensable traditions of Russian literature." However indecorous some of the Academy's maneuvering might have seemed, its citation had an elegance which succinctly and precisely caught his significance as understood by those who had included him in the progression of great Russian writers.

The evening before the award, Solzhenitsyn was told that he was unlikely to win it. This was a Norwegian journalist's interpretation—passed to him by a mutual friend—of the hurried advance of the date. For some reason, Solzhenitsyn thought that the vote was to come on October 17, and prepared to spend October 8 in his normal fashion. In Rostropovich's converted garage in Zhukovka, curtains closed, leather door padded against the cold and locked, he worked on the final chapters of his novel of World War I, which he had determined to complete within ten days. The deadline had made him increase his ordinary working pace.

Shortly after three o'clock, he was called to the telephone in the main house. A minute's walk put him in touch with a breathless friend and the information, which the friend had heard on a foreign radio station, that he had won the prize. Solzhenitsyn suggested that his friend had misheard the broadcast: it was not the day for the award, and in any case, it would not be going to him. He returned to his desk—but only to get up for a second call several minutes later, then another. Friends who knew he was not to be disturbed during working hours were ringing with the same message; one said his news came directly from a Scandinavian correspondent in Moscow. Still, Solzhenitsyn refused to believe—and was becoming irritated at the unnecessary interruptions.

At three forty-five, he was called to the telephone for the fourth time in thirty minutes. Now it was the Norwegian journalist who knew his friend, and whom the friend, in exasperation, had given his Zhukovka number without permission. Solzhenitsyn did not bother to hide his irritation and his reply to the Norwegian's congratulations was a curt "Where do you have this information from?" Only after the journalist explained that the Academy had officially announced the award at three o'clock did Solzhenitsyn fully comprehend. For a moment, he was speechless.

He had considered his tactics in advance, on the chance that he would win on October 17. "I'd planned to sit still like a mouse for a week," he later explained, "so that no one would know whether I'd accept the prize or not." Once again, he had intended to explore a potentially turbulent situation to the full—in this case, observing the reaction of the embarrassed, edgy authorities under the increasing pressure of publicity generated by an intrigued world. After the curious proceedings in and around the Academy, however, he had no doubt of his final decision: to accept the prize and relinquish it under no circumstances. While digesting the Norwegian's news in silence, Solzhenitsyn's first impulse was to follow his original plan, and he asked the journalist to convey his gratitude to the Academy—only gratitude, and this strictly privately.

Distressed at the prospect of explaining to his editors that his hot story was wholly off the record, the journalist rebelled and pressed Solzhenitsyn for a clear public statement. "You must understand," he said with the courage of despair, "that the whole world is interested in your reaction." In the heat of the moment, Solzhenitsyn abandoned his plans for a waiting game and dictated a statement which fully revealed his attitude. "I am grateful for this decision," he said. "I accept the prize. I intend to go and receive it personally on the traditional day—insofar as this will depend upon me. I am well. The state of my health is no obstacle to my journey." In this, Solzhenitsyn's first ever direct statement to the Western press, three of the five sentences—proclaiming his determination to follow his own course and dismissing all diplomatic excuses beforehand—were clearly addressed to the Soviet authorities. Three days later, four Western journalists, having uncovered his whereabouts, appeared unannounced in

Zhukovka. Solzhenitsyn interrupted their first congratulatory sentences and hurriedly closed the door.

Although not officially announced in Russia for some time, news of the prize had begun to spread in intellectual circles by the time of Solzhenitsyn's conversation with the Norwegian. A friend who went to the Moscow Conservatory to inform Rostropovich found him teaching his cello class. He dismissed his students with joyful exclamations, rang several friends to invite them to an improvised celebration in Zhukovka, collected a few others, and drove to his dacha. After the first group of well-wishers had congratulated Solzhenitsyn excitedly in his usually sacrosanct garage retreat, he peered at them in simulated severity and asked who had "sold his telephone number to the journalist." But although willing to mock himself for his original irritation, he was still reluctant to sacrifice the remnant of his working day, and it was with some effort that Rostropovich enticed him to the house for the party.

That afternoon, the news continued to spread in Russia. Among the intelligentsia, even the cautious and the mildly liberal were elated. The reaction of people who kept portraits of Solzhenitsyn in places of honor in their rooms was even stronger. One underground artist burst into tears upon hearing the news, explaining that it signified recognition by the world of "those of us who have ever suffered in Russia." A prominent literary critic who might have been expected to consider Solzhenitsyn's views extreme echoed this judgment, adding two considerations of his own: the prize would encourage everyone, not only artists, to tell the truth, and discourage those who acted against their conscience, since dishonest behavior would be exposed even during the perpetrators' lives—in descriptions such as Solzhenitsyn's.

Although many instances of moving personal reaction have been recorded, news of only two formal congratulatory messages from within Russia has reached the outside world. One, from thirty-seven Moscow dissidents who constituted the hard core of the "democratic movement," came within a day. The other had longer to travel and was delayed. It was signed by twelve political prisoners, headed by the poet Yury Galanskov, and smuggled from their labor camp in Mordovia. "Barbed wire and automatic weapons," the message read, "prevent us from expressing to you personally the depth of our admiration for your courageous creative work, upholding a sense of human dignity and exposing the trampling of the human soul and destruction of human values."

Official Russia's stunned silence seemed even more telling in contrast to the liberal minority's joy. By now Solzhenitsyn was wholly unpersoned. A huge academic history of Soviet literature—by coincidence, officially approved for printing at this very time—simply excised him from the record, failing even to mention his name. A month-by-month chronicle of literary events reported a Soviet writers' delegation attending a conference in Rome in November 1962; but not the appearance of *One Day*. Too talented to be derided, too tough to crack, too big to handle, Solzhenitsyn was best forgotten. For two days after the Academy's announcement, official Russia made no response. The Writers' Union refused to comment to Western correspondents because Solzhenitsyn "is not a member"; the Foreign Ministry insisted that they knew nothing of the writer since he "does not belong to our department." These pretenses reflected something of the consternation at high levels, where, behind the impassive façade, a spirited debate was taking place over the appropriate reaction.

Since there was no hope of Solzhenitsyn's yielding and renouncing the prize, all the alternatives facing the authorities were unpleasant. Among the speculations in the Western press were two extreme possibilities: that Solzhenitsyn be tried and the subsequent world storm braved, or that he be permitted to collect the prize and return. The latter would of course be at the expense of encouraging hopes for liberalization at home and perhaps inspiring other dissidents to test the leadership's mettle. In the event both courses were apparently felt to be too dangerous for serious discussion by Soviet leaders.

Their debate centered about two different options. Radical reactionaries proposed that Solzhenitsyn be denounced vociferously and, in the absence of recantation, expelled from the country; certainly he should not be allowed to return to Russia if he did go to Stockholm. Perhaps recalling the great harm to Soviet prestige caused by the furious anti-Pasternak campaign twelve years before, moderate conservatives favored a more restrained denunciation which would blame the Nobel Committee more than Solzhenitsyn; later decisions could await Solzhenitsyn's reaction. This course, whose advantage lay in naming foreigners as the guilty parties, thereby obviating the choice of punishing Solzhenitsyn or appearing "soft," eventually prevailed. Late on the evening of October 9, the Writers' Union issued a terse statement in bureaucratic prose attacking "reactionary circles in the West" for using Solzhenitsyn's works "for anti-Soviet purposes" and the Nobel Prize Committee for "an unworthy game . . . dictated by speculative political considerations." But although still unacceptable, Solzhenitsyn himself was not accused of intentional anti-Soviet behavior.

Several days later, an article in Chakovsky's *Literary Gazette* elaborated on the union's statement, informing Russian readers that the Swedish Academy "has allowed itself to be drawn into an unworthy game" initiated by White Russian intriguers and obscure Western organizations. This was the limit of the official Russian reaction—but on October 17, a newspaper known for its fervent neo-Stalinism went much further. Hinting that Solzhenitsyn was insane and had attempted to defend Hitlerite collaborators, *Komsomolskaya Pravda* implied that the way to deflate the "morbidly conceited man" was to "turn him out into the free world." But despite the fears of Solzhenitsyn's friends that this might mark the beginning of a campaign similar to that against Pasternak, the Soviet press confined itself during the following weeks to reproducing occasional adverse opinions from foreign publications. Unlike 1958, there were no mass meetings, denunciations from outraged construction workers and milkmaids, or canvassing of intellectuals. The attacks were confined to closed political indoctrination lectures, where Solzhenitsyn had for years been the subject of slander and vituperation. "Now," the writer himself explained later, "the word from all the speakers' platforms was: the Nobel Prize is Judas's payment for betrayal of one's country." With no consideration for the implied aspersions on earlier laureates, including Communist writers, this "line" was repeated in meeting after meeting. "In effect, they were unreservedly insulting all Nobel laureates and the very institution of the Nobel Prize."

Such as it was, the campaign was difficult to mobilize. Even in Eastern Europe, only the most Stalinist-minded writers' organizations managed to produce official condemnations of the award. In East Germany, as so often, the Writers' Union outdid its elder Soviet brother in zeal; but in Bulgaria, denunciations were issued only after overcoming internal resistance. In the non-Communist world, praise for the Nobel Committee and its laureate was almost universal, and the French Communist *Les Lettres Françaises* said that "the choice of Alexander Solzhenitsyn justifies the existence of the Nobel Prize for Literature." Soviet propagandists could find but two weak anti-Solzhenitsyn voices: the Moscow-line Communist *Daily World* of New York, which accused Solzhenitsyn of serving Hitler's heirs in the persons of American publishers, and the newspaper of a group of admirers of Stalin in the town of Lulea in the north of Sweden (official Communist publications in Stockholm strongly approved the award). The Soviet press restricted its coverage of foreign comment exclusively to substantial excerpts from these two newspapers.

The lack of information given Russian readers kept national debate about the prize at a low intellectual level, but that debate took place at all was significant. The "uncommunicative people," Russia's silent, largely uneducated majority, were not given expression in the Soviet public media, and their thoughts about the matter, if any, are not known. But among the fifteen-odd million who had a higher or technical education, the customary indifference to—or fear of—politics was breached, and discussions took place not only among family and friends but in the outer, more risky, world of state institutions. When provoked by Solzhenitsyn's detractors or on their own initiative, the writer's admirers took a stand, and offices, schools, research establishments, academic institutions, and factory front offices rang with the kind of "public-affairs" conversation which had hardly existed for decades.

Many of the detractors reflected the siege mentality of the 1930s: since "they" (the West) were out to get "us," praise from them meant that Solzhenitsyn had harmed us. Besides, they reasoned, since most of Solzhenitsyn's work was unknown in the Soviet Union, it could not be particularly good or important. Although thousands of copies of *Cancer Ward* and *The First Circle* circulated in Russia, they reached but a fraction of the country's readers, and few of his admirers could argue from knowledge of any work beyond *One Day* and some of the short stories. But beyond defending Solzhenitsyn's talent, they argued that Western appreciation of Sholokhov, Paustovsky, and other writers had not required Soviet readers to reject them. Russian intellectuals who witnessed these exchanges observed that they provided one of the rare occasions when ordinary "white collar" employees spoke up with an independent voice on a sensitive political issue; and when reported to high party officials, the discussions strengthened Solzhenitsyn's position as much as the attention of the world press. It was clear that the writer's popularity had not evaporated, and that millions of citizens cared about his safety.

In the echo of world praise, Solzhenitsyn undertook a difficult decision. Originally, his determination to receive the award personally in Stockholm on "this traditional day" of December 10 overruled all other considerations. He was resolved that nothing except *force majeure* should prevent him from accepting the "tribute to Russian literature and to our arduous history," as he called the prize in a telegram to the Swedish Academy. Such was his resolve to assert Russian literature before the world that he apparently considered accepting the heavy sacrifice of permanent separation from Russia. Close friends told Western journalists that although he deeply desired to return home, he might go to Stockholm even if reentry were barred. The risk was great. He would probably be permitted to travel to Sweden if he made application, but any statement of his while abroad might be branded "anti-Soviet," serving as the pretext for deprivation of citizenship and permission for reentry. The authorities would no doubt construct an explanation around his "voluntary departure from the country."

Yet "wearied," as his friends put it, by "constant harassment . . . and eager for peace and solitude to get on with his work," Solzhenitsyn at first seemed to consider the risk worthwhile. His financial security was now assured and his store of memories for writing unusually large; and much time and energy now spent struggling with the authorities might be saved in emigration. In the end, however, these considerations gave way to his

SOLZHENITSYN

attachment to Russia and belief that he must directly share her people's fate. Doubts about his original plans were reinforced by conversations with friends, among them the academician Andrey Sakharov. A physicist widely reputed to be the father of the Soviet hydrogen bomb who emerged in the mid-1960s as one of the most outspoken opponents of neo-Stalinism, Sakharov believed that the letter of Soviet law gave determined men scope to work for individual rights, and had appealed to the government to reform stultifying attitudes and procedures in its own interest. He was now on the verge of founding a Committee for the Defense of Human Rights, the country's first independent, quasi-political organization since the Communist Party's establishment of monopolistic power. In a long talk with Solzhenitsyn in October, Sakharov and a friend argued that the writer was badly needed in the country as, among other things, an example of the assertion of personal freedom, and urged him to give Russia's need priority over all other considerations. Although unconvinced of the efficacy of Sakharov's legalistic tactics, Solzhenitsyn sympathized deeply with his aims, and in the end assured him that he would not go to Stockholm without iron-clad guarantees of his reentry. Solzhenitsyn understood that this made his trip highly unlikely, but in accordance with his usual tactics of exploring all possible alternatives, proceeded to make discreet inquiries about guarantees and even what conditions to his stay in Stockholm might be asked in return.[3]

There were also strong private reasons militating against his leaving Russia permanently. He had entered a *de facto* marriage with a woman in her early thirties named Natalya Svetlova, a friend of several Moscow protesters and an admirer of his work. A mathematician like himself and, according to widespread Moscow comment, a highly intelligent woman whose intellectual stimulation Solzhenitsyn valued, she had become an important companion in his otherwise reclusive life. At the time of Solzhenitsyn's decision, she was expecting a child within weeks, the heir for which he had longed at least since his early prison years.

Juridical marriage to Svetlova could not easily be arranged without Reshetovskaya's cooperation in an uncontested divorce; and without the legal tie, Svetlova's position would be extremely precarious should Solzhenitsyn not be allowed to return from abroad. Boris Pasternak was finally cowed into refusing the prize less because of personal threats than because of fears for his great love Olga Ivinskaya in the event of his exile; and although, as Solzhenitsyn had put it, those "timid, frosty times" were gone and it was unlikely that the authorities, having refused him reentry, would fan the scandal by preventing his *de facto* wife from joining him, he

[3] Solzhenitsyn's plans at this time have been discussed at length by a Scandinavian in regular contact with him. See *Mellomman i Moskva* by Per Egil Hegge (Oslo: Cappelen, 1971).

could hardly help remembering that when Pasternak died, Ivlinskaya was sentenced to a long term in prison. In these circumstances, even a temporary parting from Svetlova would bring grave anxiety. Not to go abroad was surely the less emotionally taxing decision.[4]

As for receiving the prize, a tentative alternative plan was soon ready, surely made in Solzhenitsyn's recollection of a pleasant ceremony in the Swedish embassy six years earlier for transferring *One Day*'s Swedish royalties to him (the only payment he received for this work's extremely widespread publication in the West). The idea seemed uncomplicated: after all, in 1962 a Soviet physicist in ill health had been presented with his Nobel Prize through the Swedish embassy in Moscow, and three years later, the same Swedish Ambassador who is now in Moscow had invited Mikhail Sholokhov in order to present official congratulations. Solzhenitsyn was so certain that there could be no objection to a similar ceremony that he invited a few close friends to the presentation. In the following months, he was to discover that the attitude of Swedish officials to a Soviet dissident and to officially favored intellectuals differed strikingly; and he would learn something about Western varieties of bureaucratic obliqueness.

The intricate, twisted story of his relationship with the Swedish authorities grew out of the embassy's categorical refusal not only to present the award, but also—on the ground that the embassy did not usually invite private Soviet citizens—to ask him to the building for talks. It was Solzhenitsyn's suggestion, passed through the Norwegian correspondent who had telephoned him in Zhukovka, that he visit the embassy. The intermediary correspondent, Per Egil Hegge, was told that this was inadvisable since any gesture toward Solzhenitsyn might disturb "good relations between Sweden and the U.S.S.R.," the embassy's "first duty." Solzhenitsyn's friends and relatives also say that Swedish authorities wrote him a letter proposing that if he came to Stockholm, he should live not in the Grand Hotel, like other laureates, but in a private, guarded flat. This—and the proposals that he not hold press conferences, not appear on radio or TV, etc.—was suggested supposedly for his own comfort, safety, and peace of mind: to avoid demonstrations, sensations, etc. But Solzhenitsyn was angered. Go to Stockholm for what? To live in a guarded private flat? The very notion of the restrictions nettled him, even if he had no intention of appearing on TV, etc.

[4] That persecution of Natalya Svetlova was a distinct possibility was confirmed by her treatment at work when it became known that she was Solzhenitsyn's wife. No less a personage than a corresponding member of the Academy of Sciences— Solzhenitsyn identified him as Timur Timofeyev, director of Moscow's Institute of the International Workers Movement—dismissed her from her job there "with unseemly haste, although this was just after she had given birth and contrary to all laws" (which provide that no woman may be fired for any reason whatever during the first six weeks after childbirth).

Hegge was the first known Western correspondent to meet Solzhenitsyn, although not in a journalistic capacity but, affecting conspiratorial rendezvous and walking Moscow's frozen streets to avoid bugging, to discuss possible arrangements with the embassy. The Norwegian recorded the bitterness of Solzhenitsyn's friends at the Swedish attitude as well as Solzhenitsyn's own cool, contemptuous "if that's the way it is" upon learning of the embassy's refusal to hold a ceremony. Expelled from Moscow in early 1971 for his contacts with Solzhenitsyn, Hegge described them in a book which provoked considerable indignation in Sweden.[5] After forthright condemnation by Swedish leaders of injustices beyond their power to right—the persecution of Greek intellectuals, for example, and even the invasion of Czechoslovakia—many Swedes were resentful of the apparent cowardice in a case where their government could indeed have "done something," and with little self-sacrifice. The Swedish Prime Minister felt compelled to explain his policy to the nation over television: Solzhenitsyn could receive his prize at the embassy at any time, he said, but since the Soviet government would regard even a modest ceremony as an unfriendly demonstration, there could be none.

Solzhenitsyn rejected this subtle distinction (which had not been put to him during his meetings with Hegge) as "degrading to the prize, regarding it as something shameful which must be hidden." In an angry open letter, he asked the Prime Minister whether the Nobel Prize was "stolen property which must be handed over behind closed doors, with no witnesses." He was prepared to receive the award in Moscow at any time, but "the delivery of the insignia must be made in public." Harried Swedish officials eventually reached a bureaucrat's decision of Solomon: the Nobel Foundation, rather than the embassy itself, would present the prize publicly to Solzhenitsyn. Since Nobel officials were unlikely to be granted a Soviet visa for this purpose, the solution struck critics of the Swedish government as no less devious than its earlier attitude.

By the time Hegge's book appeared, Solzhenitsyn seemed to feel a slight derisive amusement in the Swedish timidness, but in the autumn of 1970, as the time approached for his final decision about the prize, the danger of a collision with the Soviet authorities through misunderstanding made Stockholm's prevarication a source of considerable worry. Although the Soviet press dropped almost all mention of him within a week of the announcement of the award, he knew that there was still strong backing for retribution against him. His inquiries about guarantees of reentry into Russia were never formally answered; officials merely scoffed that the very request was "humiliating" for the Soviet government. This clumsily

---

[5] *Mellomann i Moskva*, by Per Egil Hegge.

hypocritical reaction dissolved any residual hopes Solzhenitsyn had of going to Stockholm.

By mid-November, after the authorities' nerves had been strained by a long month of uncertainty about Solzhenitsyn's plans and by the publication abroad of Rostropovich's letter defending him, new attacks were launched against the writer. Victor Grishin, the chief of the Moscow party organization and an alternate member of the Politburo (thus one of the country's twenty highest leaders), spoke out sharply against him at a confidential party meeting. Several days later, Arkady Vasilyev, the man who had made the first public move leading to Solzhenitsyn's expulsion from the Writers' Union, told a meeting of the party organization of the Moscow branch, which he headed, that "in his personal opinion" Solzhenitsyn should be offered a one-way ticket to Stockholm. Still waiting for a reply from the Swedish government, Solzhenitsyn could not make his position clear. It was only on November 20 that his hands were untied by Hegge's embarrassed report to him of the refusal, decided "on a high level in Stockholm," to present the award at the embassy.

Solzhenitsyn now prepared a letter to the Swedish Academy explaining his final position. He reiterated his gratitude and acceptance of the honor for himself and those of his predecessors "who, because of the difficult conditions of the preceding decades, did not survive" until a prize might be bestowed upon them. It was because of this feeling for Russia's persecuted writers, he implied, that he had been prepared to submit even to the "humiliating procedure" necessary for permission to travel abroad.[6] However, hostility toward the award in the press and persecution of readers of his books (in the form of "dismissal from jobs and expulsion from colleges") "compelled me to suppose that my trip to Stockholm would be used to sever me from my native land, simply by barring my return home." Because of this—and of the largely "ceremonial and festive" nature of the visit to which his "way of life and character" made him "unaccustomed" —he "preferred not to apply for a trip to Stockholm at the present time." Preserving his restraint toward the Swedish authorities, Solzhenitsyn included only a hint for the initiated few about his difficulties in this quarter. He could receive the diploma and gold medal in Moscow from the Academy's representatives, he wrote, "at a mutually convenient time."

While Solzhenitsyn was drafting the letter, Hegge was seeking assurances that it would reach Stockholm by diplomatic post. The Swedish

---

[6] Solzhenitsyn knew that when Sholokhov won the prize in 1965, an exit visa was delivered to him, together with an air ticket. He, by contrast, would have to fill out long questionnaires, request recommendations from petty officials in many offices, seek approval from party secretaries—in short, wade through a long bureaucratic route.

embassy's initial response to the suggestion that it forward the message of a Nobel Prize laureate to the Royal Swedish Academy was that this was "against the rules." After bargaining on points such as whether the envelope should be sealed or open—and barely veiled threats of a worldwide scandal—Hegge achieved a reluctant assent.

On November 27, Solzhenitsyn went to the embassy to deliver the letter. His earlier request for a formal invitation had been prompted by fear that he might be stopped by the policemen normally posted outside Western embassies with orders to intercept Soviet citizens lacking one. Luckily for all concerned, perhaps most of all for the Swedish authorities, he was not stopped, and the KGB men following him in their emblematic sheepskin hats did no more than observe and make themselves observable. The ambassador received him and confirmed Hegge's information in a correct, businesslike tone. When Solzhenitsyn returned to the embassy a week later to pass on the message he had drafted for reading at the Nobel banquet, it was received with extreme reluctance and no assurance of delivery. Sensing that the embassy did not wish to see him again, Solzhenitsyn left in quiet anger and never returned.

On December 10, Solzhenitsyn spent several hours at his radio in Zhukovka, listening to a live broadcast of the prize presentation by the Swedish radio's Russian service. He later expressed his pleasure with the Nobel citation, which summed up his place in Russia's ethical and esthetic traditions—both involving the transformation of suffering into moral insights—and drew attention to his literary technique of polyphonism. After a moving speech by the secretary of the Academy—"Solzhenitsyn," he declared, "seeks not innovations but a renovation"—the King, in normal circumstances, would have presented Solzhenitsyn with his prize insignia. Instead a moment of silence intervened, followed by the secretary's regrets about "the circumstances which have prevented Alexander Solzhenitsyn from appearing in person." After another moment of solemn silence, the King stood to lead the applause in Stockholm's crowded Concert Hall. Only the silence of the trumpets which accompany the applause for attending laureates distinguished this ovation from the others that afternoon.

Solzhenitsyn listened too to the after-dinner speeches, relayed from the Stockholm Town Hall. Traditionally, the laureates speak of their personal feelings—which, on that day, invariably included the absent man. "I speak from the mind," said the American economist Paul Samuelson. "If Alexander Solzhenitsyn had been here to speak from the heart, all of us would be better for it: every individual, every country, without exception." Solzhenitsyn could not fail to be pleased by this tribute and its echoes; but the reading of his own message came as a shock. Although he did not want his "involuntary absence" or his words "to overshadow the festive occasion," he had written, he could not overlook "the portentous coincidence of the Nobel Prize presentation day with Human Rights Day. The Nobel laureates cannot but be aware of their responsibility in view of this coincidence. All those gathered in the Stockholm town hall cannot but see it as a symbol. So at this festive table let us not forget that political prisoners are on hunger strike today to defend their infringed or completely trampled rights."

Solzhenitsyn's responsibility toward Human Rights Day was demonstrated by agreeing to his election, on that very day, as a corresponding member of Sakharov's small Committee on Human Rights, by this time established and functioning. While he had no intention of participating actively in its work, his willingness to lend his name, overcoming his reluctance to involve himself in nonliterary activities, was clear indication of his moral support. It was also an acknowledgment to the political prisoners who had managed to smuggle their congratulations to him in October. Solzhenitsyn particularly wanted to support Vladimir Gershuni, a fellow inmate of his Ekibastuz days who was again imprisoned, this time in a mental hospital, where he was on a hunger strike.

To his dismay, Solzhenitsyn heard his message read at the banquet— with its final sentence excised. The chairman of the Nobel Foundation later admitted that he and the secretary of the Academy (who had spoken so eloquently about Solzhenitsyn's literary significance) had taken this action upon themselves because they thought it might "harm the laureate and present an obstacle for a trip by him to Stockholm at another time." Perhaps Solzhenitsyn's mention of hunger strikes played some part in their considerations too, for it might have been awkward to pronounce after a banquet of smoked salmon and venison accompanied by champagne, especialy in front of an audience of easily embarrassed middle-class Swedes. Whatever its motives, his first censorship in the West incensed Solzhenitsyn, who knew at least as well as the chairman and secretary what risks he was taking and for what reasons. It was not only in Russia, he was discovering, that plain speaking could make him inconvenient.

As for the Soviet authorities, they were predictably angered by Solzhenitsyn's references to exit visas, political prisoners, and hunger strikes, and within a week of prize day their policy of playing down the prize and forgetting the unfortunate episode as quickly as possible gave way to wrath. A long *Pravda* attack against Solzhenitsyn was as significant for its signature—I. Alexandrov, a pseudonym used only for discussing affairs of state of the gravity of Czechoslovakia's course on the eve of the invasion —as for anything in the text. Calling Solzhenitsyn a tool of imperialist propaganda and "a spiritual inner émigré, hostile and alien to the entire life of the Soviet people," the article put the writer in the same context as defectors and imprisoned "anti-Soviet" agitators. On the following day, the world press took up "Alexandrov's" argument and speculated, as the

Times of London put it concisely, that "Solzhenitsyn may face trial or expulsion from Russia." In fact, the "inner émigré" was again close to becoming an actual one. The *Literary Gazette* played its part; this time, according to people with entree to its editorial offices, the newspaper actually set in type materials announcing Solzhenitsyn's expulsion from the country. The reprieve came at the last moment, no doubt lest the action cause a serious crisis in the high establishment intelligentsia. Once again, the Politburo's aversion to disturbance was greater than its pride.

The Alexandrov article was the last but one mention of Solzhenitsyn in the Soviet press for a year. A late isolated attack on him appeared in January 1971, probably permitted because the author, improbably enough an American folk singer called Dean Reed, was too good a trump not to play. Although continuing to imprison other dissidents, the Soviet authorities now tolerated Solzhenitsyn in silence for the time being. His talent and self-assertiveness had made him the country's freest citizen— independent, as events would soon demonstrate, and able to devote himself to his goals in ways he could hardly have believed possible when, half in despair, he wrote his letter to the Writers' Congress less than four years earlier.

XXXVII

Epic

IN THE SENSE THAT IT WAS INTENDED TO EXPLORE how present conditions came into being, the novel which Solzhenitsyn was completing during the Nobel Prize commotion bore closely on current events. The author discussed its genesis in an afterword.

> The general conception . . . came to me in 1936 upon graduation from high school. Since then I have never abandoned it, but thought of it as the principal project of my life. Diverting myself to other books only because of the peculiarities of my life and the richness of present-day impressions, I have been advancing toward this project, preparing myself and collecting materials for it alone.

The great epic was to deal with what Solzhenitsyn considered "the principal theme of our recent history": the disintegration of old Russia and the emergence of the new. Consciously or otherwise, the handling of the vast body of material almost certainly derived from Pushkin, who had conceived of the Decembrists' revolt of 1825, in some ways a precursor of the 1917 revolution, as a gradual weaving of a "secret net" in which "knot follows knot." In this sense, a "knot" or fascicle of events differs significantly from a focus, which suggests a central point of attention: only the accretion of a required number of knots amounts to a net. This approach had a natural appeal for a writer inclined toward literary polyphonism, a dislike for categorizing characters and events into principal and secondary, and a conviction that the "course of time" could be grasped by portraying any significant section of it with sufficient depth and insight.

Solzhenitsyn set about depicting the development of the revolution through a series of events bearing directly and indirectly on families much like his father's and mother's, combining his pervading interest in Russia as a whole and in the fate of his own antecedents. Three to six self-contained knots were planned, each of which would portray Russia at a chosen moment before, during, and after the revolution. The work would take up to twenty years. The task had fallen to him, Solzhenitsyn explained, because

> Russian writers older than I have bypassed the principal theme of our most recent history or slid over its surface. There is even less hope that those younger than I will concern themselves with it, and they would find it even more hopeless to bring those years to life, something almost too difficult even for my generation.

Bringing prerevolutionary society to life was one of Solzhenitsyn's greatest difficulties. With no direct experience of it, his source material was restricted to the memory and memoirs of older people and to publications of those years. Soviet histories since the 1930s were, mildly speaking, less than reliable, and, as with all archives, even those without secret papers, most of the relevant research materials—documents, Western works, and early postrevolutionary Russian studies—were available only to possessors of a permit for the "special depositories" of several larger libraries. Lacking access to these sources, Solzhenitsyn avidly sought out living witnesses of revolutionary and prerevolutionary events. Of these, Irina Shcherbak, the aunt who had remembered his dying father's expecting a son, was one of the most helpful, especially with family lore. Solzhenitsyn visited the aged, near-indigent lady several times—she was living in a small town near Kislovodsk, in a tiny room of six square meters with an earth floor—and spent hours listening to her reminiscences.[1]

Although Solzhenitsyn devoted many more hours to reading prerevolutionary newspapers and magazines and memoirs of the period, he was resentful of the limitations on his sources. "In my own country," he complained, "all collections of materials accessible to others are barred to me." The following year, while working on the epic's second knot, he elaborated on the obstacles to his research, far greater now, he emphasized, than the "special" ones in his youth. Not entitled to a secretary or assistant as a nonmember of the Writers' Union, he could not afford such assistance himself; and even if he could, anyone representing him would be as restricted as he himself. Denied access not only to central and provincial archives but also to historical buildings now occupied by government offices, he was also refused approval and help by local authorities to talk with the last surviving witnesses of his settings and scenes. "And without that permission, everyone shuts up." Attempting to pursue what would elsewhere be the most legitimate and harmless exploration, "I could be arrested at every step of the way. That has already been tested."

I live in my own country. I write a novel about Russia. But it is as

---

[1] She is drawn in the novel as the beautiful, rich, and deeply and unaffectedly religious Irina Tomchak, one of the most attractive characters.

hard for me to gather material as it would be if I were writing about Polynesia.

Despite this, he persevered with his diligent "homemade" research, with the result that *August 1914*'s descriptions of the extinct society were so accurate that only historians and eyewitnesses quibbled with secondary details. He was helped in this by volunteer contributions of well-wishers, often strangers, who knew of his work and sent him—"of course not by mail, which might not reach me"—memoirs and books, including the rarest collector's items. Some of these materials fit his needs precisely, others were less useful—but the fact itself of their being sent "always touches me and gives me the real feeling that I am working for Russia and Russia is helping me." [2]

He was also helped by what he called the "miracle" of the survival of two of his notebooks filled with the research of his student days on the rout of the Russian armies in East Prussia in 1914. Although in 1942 a bomb destroyed the "hut" where he had lived with his mother in Rostov and all their possessions, including books and papers were burned, these two notebooks were not consumed by fire. Preserved, they were returned to him after he was freed from exile, and the fact that it had been easier for him to gather material as an entirely unknown student in provincial Rostov thirty years before enhanced their value to him.

Solzhenitsyn's other difficulties pertained more directly to the creative process. The novel was his first known work not based on personal experience and dealing with an era he did not know. With apprehension that he might lack time or inspiration to complete his task—"perhaps I might be arriving too late," he wrote; "both my life and my creative imagination might by now be insufficient for the twenty years of work"—he began the epic's first knot in early 1969.

How much his ideas had developed during the thirty years since 1936 was suggested by the speed with which they were now put on paper; in less than two years a quarter of a million words were polished in their final draft. Set at the outbreak of World War I, the novel begins as the chronicle of a family in Cossack territory, clearly based on Solzhenitsyn's

---

[2] In his deep attachment to Russia, Solzhenitsyn exposed here, as elsewhere, the limitations to his perception of the West. Comparing the volunteer help given him to the laborious copying of *samizdat* texts, in which money never changes hands and people "sit up nights doing work for which the most they can get is persecution," Solzhenitsyn felt this was so unlike anything to be found in the West that Westerners, who expect payment for all work, might have difficulty understanding. Apparently he was unaware of how youthful political movements, not to speak of more traditional volunteer charities, operate in the West. And while remarkable labor of love is indeed poured into *samizdat*, it requires some idealization (much like that of Russia's nineteenth-century Slavophiles) to claim that the valuable manuscripts are never sold —and for fancy prices—by the people who toil to reproduce them. Nevertheless, he did acknowledge that he may be wrong in his understanding of the West.

own, and develops into a kaleidoscopic view of Russia in the early weeks of war. The narrative core is the chaotic rout of Russian troops among the lakes and forests of East Prussia (less than a hundred miles southeast of Koenigsberg) during twelve days of the month designated in the title: *August 1914*.

A draft which Solzhenitsyn considered adequate to show others was ready in late autumn of 1970. Convinced of the need for evaluation and criticism, Solzhenitsyn knew that there was little chance of this—in his view, society's sole duty to a writer—deriving from official channels, and organized his own critiques by distributing copies of the manuscript, together with a short questionnaire, to half a dozen friends. In addition to his customary broader questions—Did you like the novel in general? Which characters were delineated best? Which appealed to you most?—others pertained to specifics: Are the military passages boring? Have elements of World War II found their way into the battle scenes? Still other queries were related to some of the novel's unusual literary techniques. Awed by the book's sweep, depth, and delineation of scene and character, Solzhenitsyn's friends made suggestions for improving details, and it was only after considering them that Solzhenitsyn offered the manuscript for publication in Russia.

In March 1971 he wrote to the editors of seven publishing houses that he had completed a novel and would like to hear their proposals for publishing it. Feeling that he was established enough to obviate the need —and to guard against unauthorized reproduction, either in *samizdat* or by officials for their own purposes—he did not submit the typescript itself. But several copies were made available to high Soviet authorities, and Solzhenitsyn's friends saw important Central Committee cultural overseers reading them in their offices. Although the friends were assured that the novel was well liked, it became clear that it provoked heated dispute.

That some men close to authority argued determinedly for publication was indicated by the reaction of Konstantin Simonov, the secretary of the Writers' Union, who, behind closed doors, had spoken for *Cancer Ward* (though against *The First Circle*) over three years before. Since many Russians in literary circles identified him, with good reason, with *The First Circle's* devious Galakhov, Simonov had grounds for disliking Solzhenitsyn personally; and despite his occasional liberal statements, he was hardly less cautious than the fictional Galakhov. Nevertheless, in April 1971, Simonov went so far as to plead for publication of *August 1914* before a group of Westerners in West Berlin. Such a stand on a controversial issue before "ideological enemies" suggested the existence of serious support for the novel.

It proved insufficient, however: not one of Solzhenitsyn's letters to the seven editors was so much as acknowledged, clear evidence that orders to ignore the book had been sent down from high authority, and that Solzhenitsyn himself was now anathema no matter what he wrote.[3] Had the manuscript been submitted by someone else, publishers would surely have leapt on it, for from the political point of view, *August 1914* was not only not "anti-Soviet" but in certain senses compatible with official thinking, making many of the statements, with greater power and far more subtlety, that the Soviet regime had dwelt upon incessantly for decades.

Nothing in the vast outpouring of Soviet love-for-the-Motherland literature—indeed, nothing in Russian prose or poetry since Tolstoy's *War and Peace* and Crimean War stories—could elicit such surging patriotism in Russians. Infused with pride for Russia and pain for her terrible hardships, *August 1914* will engulf even Russia's enemies in wave after wave of often involuntary affection and admiration for the Russian people. The novel presents the Soviet leaders with what they have exhorted Soviet writers to produce for decades: a work that could inspire Soviet youth with deep national pride and dedication.

In the rout in East Prussia, of which the high point is an entire regiment's sacrificing itself to certain death in an attempt to save others, the bravery of the Russian soldier is depicted with fierce love. No Russian who reads these scenes will not be profoundly moved. It is the kind of writing that could be used to teach military cadets about spirit and morale.

This theme is wholly acceptable to the Soviet point of view, as are most of the reasons why this "miracle" of bravery was self-sacrificial in the largest sense, leading only to defeat. Solzhenitsyn is as searing in his indictment of the ineptitude of tsarist generals as he is soaring in his praise of the muzhiks who made up the ranks of foot soldiers and the ordinary, educated men who were the field officers. And his exposé of the *ancien régime* goes further, into what had caused the generals to be "the higher in rank, the more hopeless." In Solzhenitsyn's treatment, tsarist Russia's deepest social, political, and psychological attitudes predetermined its downfall.

Old Russia, Solzhenitsyn demonstrates, strangulated in red tape, intrigues, and the stifling of its most inventive and devoted people, potentially the natural leaders. One of the novel's principal characters is a staff colonel who, having witnessed the rout and perceived the fatal flaws of leadership that caused it, tries to break through to his superiors in his certainty that, if uncorrected, the same flaws will soon bring on not only a general military defeat but also the collapse of Russia and its entire

---

[3] "Not one of them wanted to take the manuscript in his hands, let alone read it or even leaf through it," said Solzhenitsyn the following year to correspondents of *The New York Times* and *Washington Post*. "No one answered the letter. No one asked for the manuscript."

social order. The superiors are not only deaf to the colonel's warning, but deprive him of his modest influence. This is the beginning, Solzhenitsyn makes quite plain, of a process which, in the course of the four-year war, will undermine old Russia's self-confidence and "snap the national spirit."

In this as well as many other aspects of the novel, notably the bourgeoisie's vulgar self-seeking, the independent writer offering his own truth confirms official Soviet attitudes: no doubt what led Solzhenitsyn to describe the novel's suppression in terms of "censorship objections that are inaccessible to normal human reasoning." [4] He mentioned only one such objection: the requirement that God not be capitalized, "a humiliation to which I cannot bow in any case."

From the viewpoint of the most orthodox, narrow-minded officials, however, there may have been other objections. Solzhenitsyn's is not a propagandist indictment of tsarism, but a wide-ranging panorama of life at that time, including elements incompatible with the present regime's interpretation. Religious devotion, for example, and prayer in particular, are shown not only masking ineptitude, as they often did in tsarist Russia, but also as the source of genuine relief and ethical inspiration. Revolutionaries are portrayed not exclusively as brave and dedicated, but also as overstepping the limits of civilized decency and callous about individual suffering—indeed, as willing, so as to enhance the chances of revolution, to aggravate wartime suffering and misery already near the limit of human endurance. Thus (although the major revolutionary character is not a Bolshevik and does not directly represent those who seized power) Solzhenitsyn traces the ruthlessness abundantly exhibited after 1917 to the revolutionaries' earlier moral code. And although Russia's present rulers equate political freedom with chaos, Solzhenitsyn clearly demonstrates that it was not freedom which led to confusion and hopeless disorder but its opposite, the suppression of dissident opinion and the consequent irrationality of decisions by the leadership, leading in turn to social and military breakdown.

Though the novel is historical and in no way simply a parable about Soviet conditions, a warning of doom is implicit in the parallels between the rigidity of tsarist and Soviet Russia; moreover, Solzhenitsyn implies that the *ancien régime*'s deep flaws are even more widespread now. But none of these points, or their combined effect, can explain the refusal to publish *August 1914*. Had it been submitted by almost anyone else, its "positive" aspects—the indictment of tsarism and celebration of Russian patriotism—would almost certainly have outweighed its "lapses." But like the reaction of one of Gogol's hysterically superstitious women to the word

---

[4] Censorship here is meant in the general sense. The manuscript never reached a censor's office as such, for this is an advanced stage in Soviet publishing.

"scarecrow," the very name of the man who had exposed Stalinism caused neo-Stalinist authorities to jerk back.

Above all the Soviet authorities feared enhancing Solzhenitsyn's reputation. Had the novel been published in Russia, there is little doubt that he would have become the hero not only of the liberal anti-Stalinist intelligentsia but of the nation as a whole. No military officer would be immune to his voice, no wife of a fallen soldier, no member of a soldier's family —which embraces virtually all of Russia. Solzhenitsyn's influence as the spokesman of all that is unrepresented by the official conception of man, history, and society was already enormous; *August 1914* would have linked in admiration "the other Russia" and the largely apolitical, but fervently patriotic, masses.

War and Peace is a facile comparison, but the only valid one. On its own, *August 1914* does not equal its predecessor in scope and depth, but this first knot is only a beginning, roughly comparable to Tolstoy's opening books. On the basis of this alone, however, parallels between the two epics are obvious.[5] Like Tolstoy, Solzhenitsyn took his characters principally from his family and historical personages, although Tolstoy referred to aristocratic rulers familiar to every educated Russian, whereas Solzhenitsyn wrote of ordinary people unknown outside their own circle. Like Tolstoy, Solzhenitsyn began his work roughly a half a century after the events described, although the distance between him and these events is far greater. Since Russian society remained basically unchanged from the time of the struggle against Napoleon, Tolstoy could draw on his own observations of the manners and social relations he described: Solzhenitsyn, by contrast, depicted a society wholly swept away, involving great difficulties in achieving verisimilitude even in the way Russians communicated with each other. Yet despite isolated linguistic anachronisms, he succeeds impressively.

In technique, too, mainly the mixture of minute description of scene and action with philosophizing about great events, Tolstoy's influence is unmistakable. Here the comparison with *War and Peace* is not only in the reader's mind but in the author's too, for at times Solzhenitsyn steps from the pages to argue directly with his teacher. At least in the twentieth century, Solzhenitsyn maintains, Tolstoy's underlying historical concept— that the final outcome of great events of war and politics is determined not by leaders but unconscious movements of the masses—no longer applies.

Solzhenitsyn is also unfettered by Tolstoy's literary conventions. He uses

[5] Even Solzhenitsyn's description of "the principal project of my life" echoes, perhaps involuntarily, Tolstoy's reference to *War and Peace* as "the aim of my entire life."

any "modernistic" literary device which serves his purpose—selections of official documents and, like John Dos Passos, newspaper clippings and "cinema eyes" for visual images whose impact is too strong for words. Among other things, the novel is a massive documentary study of Russia at this crucial turning point, showing great skill in making exhaustive research come alive. *August 1914* exploded the notion that Solzhenitsyn was limited to describing his personal experiences. As an American analyst of Soviet affairs wrote, its challenge to the Soviet authorities was, "in the first place, that of blindingly superior quality." [6]

Solzhenitsyn himself was described by friends as artistically pleased with the novel; and he was not prepared to allow bureaucrats to determine its future. When a month passed without response to his letters to Soviet editors, he decided to publish the book nevertheless—abroad. In May, a copy of the manuscript was passed to the émigré Y.M.C.A. Press in Paris —publishers of such Russian authors as the Nobel Prize laureate Ivan Bunin, the philosopher Nikolay Berdyayev, and Vladimir Nabokov— whose earlier editions of two of Solzhenitsyn's own novels had pleased him with their typographic quality. In the same month, Dr. Heeb signed a contract with this house giving them Russian-language publication rights in France. When it appeared in June, an afterword left no doubts that the edition was authorized. "I am now publishing the first knot of my work," Solzhenitsyn wrote, "for Russian readers abroad."

This edition secured important advantages for Solzhenitsyn. Since French publication carries automatic copyright, the author and his attorney had complete control of publication in other languages. Houses in other countries were selected for their literary merits, and although some of the highest bids were rejected, the novel was reported to have earned some $2 million in advance royalties alone. When a pirate edition appeared in Germany several months later and another was in preparation in Britain, the lawful publishers, acting in cooperation with Dr. Heeb, promptly obtained court injunctions. This assertion of a Soviet author's rights in the West despite the government's noncooperation certainly brought great satisfaction to the indefatigable campaigner for such rights.

But although the Soviet government did not cooperate, it could not easily prosecute. Despite considerable Western speculation to the contrary, Solzhenitsyn's authorization of the Paris edition was entirely legal under Soviet law; in fact, establishment authors had previously resorted to "Western-first" publication to secure world copyright and earn hard currency. Only a book's alleged "anti-Soviet" content could be prosecuted, and in no sane view could *August 1914* fit that description. All other means

---

[6] This statement was distorted in later anti-Solzhenitsyn polemics in Russia. The analyst, Anatole Shub, was said to have described the novel as "a challenge to Soviet authorities."

of influencing the writer having been exhausted without results, the
authorities could only tolerate his sovereign behavior. But since public
admission of this considerable civic victory would have added self-insult
to Solzhenitsyn's injury, it was pretended that neither the novel nor its
authorized Western publication existed. There was no official Soviet reaction whatever to *August 1914*, neither public nor "private," at home or
abroad—and not a word of it in the Soviet media for six months.

The policy of sullen tolerance of Solzhenitsyn was confirmed at the
Twenty-fourth Congress of the Communist Party in March 1971. Reporting
on the "ideological struggle" in his keynote address, Secretary General
Leonid Brezhnev stated that "if a man of letters slanders Soviet reality, if
he helps our ideological adversaries fight against socialism, then he
deserves only one thing: society's disdain." The reference to Solzhenitsyn
was unmistakable, and in the context, "disdain" was a mild penalty,
seemingly excluding repressive measures.

Yet Solzhenitsyn and his close friends were still subjected to the full
panoply of KGB surveillance methods, no doubt in the hope of discovering
something incriminating; and in August 1971, the spying led to a grave
incident. Solzhenitsyn fell ill in Moscow and asked a friend, Alexander
Gorlov, to fetch a spare part for the car "Denisik" from the cottage at the
eighty-third kilometer. Taking advantage of the owner's indisposition, the
KGB had entered the dwelling to search and make adjustments to their
electronic equipment, and when Gorlov, a young scientist about to defend
his doctoral dissertation, arrived, he heard voices within. Solzhenitsyn
himself described the encounter in an open letter to the chairman of
the KGB.

> Gorlov stepped inside and demanded the robbers' documents. In
> the small structure, where three or four people can barely turn
> around, were about ten men in plain clothes. On the command of
> the senior officer—"to the woods with him and silence him"—they
> bound Gorlov, knocked him to the ground, dragged him face down
> into the woods and beat him viciously. . . . However, Gorlov fought
> back vigorously and shouted, summoning witnesses. Neighbors . . .
> came running . . . and barred the robbers' way to the highway,
> demanding their identification documents. Then one of the robbers
> presented a red [KGB] identification card and the neighbors let
> them pass.

His face "mutilated" and suit "torn to ribbons," Gorlov was taken to a
car—"We are on an operation," he was told, "and on an operation we can
do anything"—and then to the local police station, where the leader of
the KGB team, a Captain Ivanov, was deferentially greeted. Ivanov demanded that Gorlov produce a written explanation of his presence and

what had happened; and despite his condition, the latter gave a full and accurate account.

> After that, the senior robber demanded that Gorlov sign an oath of secrecy. Gorlov flatly refused. Then they set off for Moscow and, on the road, the senior robber bombarded Gorlov with, literally, the following: "If Solzhenitsyn finds out what took place at the dacha, it's all over with you. Your official career will go no further. You won't be defending any dissertation. This will affect your family and children and, if necessary, we will put you in prison." Those who know our way of life understand the full feasibility of these threats. But Gorlov . . . refused to sign the pledge and now is threatened with reprisals.

Gorlov's courage was a sign of the changing times; only a few years earlier, such KGB intimidation was all but totally effective. And Ivanov's seeming panic at being caught in an illegal act marked a corresponding change in the KGB's long indifference to such concerns. As for Solzhenitsyn—to whom Gorlov immediately reported everything—he was shocked at this first application of violence to someone who had helped him. To friends, he kept repeating that "they could have killed him." Ivanov's attempted intimidation had indicated his fear of Solzhenitsyn's *glasnost*, to which the writer turned again in an attempt to protect his friends from further physical injury.

His open letter was written on the following day. Having described Gorlov's treatment, he attacked the entire system of long-standing secret police "lawlessness," which he had "borne in silence" until now, and demanded "public identification of all the robbers, their punishment as criminals and an equally public explanation of this incident. . . . Otherwise I can only believe that you, the chairman of the KGB, sent them." Handed by friends to Western correspondents in Moscow, Solzhenitsyn's protest made world headlines and prompted new speculation about retribution against him. But the storm of unfavorable publicity over the KGB's behavior forced the authorities to retreat. Gorlov was summoned by the KGB several times during the following days and told (despite the "red card") that their organization had had nothing to do with the incident: it was the work of the local police—whose chief later explained that his men had been guarding Solzhenitsyn's cottage, mistook Gorlov for a burglar, and had been duly punished. Although this clumsy apology fell far short of Solzhenitsyn's demands, it was the first time since his rehabilitation that the authorities implicitly admitted doing him wrong.

However, other circumstances indicated that the authorities were far from contrite. With the publication of *August 1914*, another slander campaign had been launched against Solzhenitsyn, and was sustained after the Gorlov affair. Again party instructors briefed small audiences "in confidence" about Solzhenitsyn's immorality and "anti-Sovietism."

Distress returned in mid-December, when Alexander Tvardovsky died after a lengthy struggle with lung cancer. Several days later, the funeral was an occasion for one of Solzhenitsyn's rare public appearances, and another expression of his abhorrence of official hypocrisy. For despite their increasing pressure on Tvardovsky in his last years as *Novy Mir*'s editor —forcing the tenacious campaigner to resign almost two years before, and the magazine to be muffled even more—the Soviet leadership affected profound grief over his death, issuing a glowing obituary signed by the entire Politburo. Visibly moved during the funeral, Solzhenitsyn kissed the corpse's forehead in keeping with the Russian custom and tossed his handful of earth into the coffin; then he is reported to have laid a flower on the grave of Khrushchev, who had been buried nearby in the same Cemetery some three months before. Following the coincidence of the two men's proximate deaths and interments, the gesture seemed to symbolize the final passing of the moment when Solzhenitsyn's attitude toward literature found some place in the structures of party and state.

Solzhenitsyn's affection for Tvardovsky—he called him a man "lit up with a childish trust which he carried with him throughout his life," and his resentment of what he considered the authorities' crocodile tears, were asserted uncompromisingly in a memorial oration which he circulated after the funeral.

> There are many ways of killing a poet—the one chosen for Tvardovsky was to take away his offspring, his passion, his journal. . . . They heaped the coals of disbandment, destruction, and morti- fication upon him, within six months these coals had consumed him . . . [and] he took to his deathbed. . . . And now the whole gang from the Writers' Union has flopped onto the scene. The guard of honor comprises the same flabby crowd that once hunted him down with unholy shrieks and cries. Yes, it's an old, old custom of ours—it was the same with Pushkin.

Despite his long seclusion and the attitude of the public media, his appearance at the funeral, as well as at a concert by Rostropovich the following spring, created a flurry of excitement, especially among young people.

Another remarkable event in late 1971 showed that however dead the period of official accommodation to Solzhenitsyn and despite the growing lopsidedness of the struggle, he continued to inspire some Russians and even to win a few seemingly unlikely converts. Apparently thanks to a routine lapse in the censorship machinery. *Novy Mir*'s November issue included a poem which seemed to honor Solzhenitsyn in oblique allusions.

Its author was Yevgeny Markin, the little-known Ryazan writer who, after succumbing to the enticement of a new flat and joining the vote to expel Solzhenitsyn from the local Writers' Union branch, subsequently roamed the city expressing his remorse. Now, in the poem, he hinted that it was his love of comfort that had undermined his moral stand, and that much of the intelligentsia made shameful compromises for similar reasons: to protect their jobs and well-being. Despite the vagueness of Markin's recantation, he himself was promptly expelled from the Writers' Union, a much more serious punishment for a writer of his caliber than for Solzhenitsyn, quite apart from its special irony after Markin's role two years before.

But despite this kind of harassment and Solzhenitsyn's troubles with what he called "thievish" Western publishers, the year following the Nobel Prize passed in relative calm. Although a source of continuous tension, his "balance of power" with the authorities gave him substantial periods of the quiet life, dedicated to work and his new family, that he desired. In December 1970, a son was born to him and Natalya Svetlova. He was baptized in a church several weeks later and named Yermolai (the pianist Svyatoslav Richter is reported to be his godfather). Yermolai is a somewhat archaic, "common-folks" name, seemingly emphasizing the writer's attachment to "Russianness" and peasant roots. Because Solzhenitsyn was still unable to obtain a quiet, uncontested divorce from Reshetovskaya, he could not legally move into Svetlova's Moscow flat, where she lived with their son: police permission to register permanently at her Moscow address could be obtained only on the basis of proper marriage documents. Rather than risk petty harassment for evading this rule, Solzhenitsyn continued to spend most of the summer at the eighty-third kilometer and his winter with Rostropovich, confining his time in Moscow to temporary visits.

Despite his huge Western earnings, his financial position was delicate. *One Day's* carefully husbanded royalties were exhausted in 1968, after which he had no significant domestic income except for a bequest from the writer Korney Chukovsky, which was also coming to an end. Through Dr. Heeb, he declared that his income from Western royalties, the main bulk of his assets, would remain "inviolate" for use for "humanitarian purposes" in Russia "as soon as a possibility for this appears"; and these arrangements were fixed in a will. For his own subsistence, he would make use only of the Nobel Prize award, but getting small, periodic amounts from a Western bank was made "degrading, difficult, and uncertain," as he put it, by the authorities, who told him that every transaction would require a special decision of the board of the Ministry of Foreign Trade. In any case, they insisted on treating this money as a gift from abroad, withholding roughly a third in taxes.

As for work, in mid-1972 he was well into *October 1916,* the second knot of his epic. A picture of Russia—especially of social and spiritual currents in the rear, where the important events of that month took place —after two years of exhausting war, the book would not be completed soon, for "it turned out to be more complex than I had assumed." The monarchy is about to fall, disintegration of Russian life is advanced on many levels, and Solzhenitsyn's is an attempt to "fix, shape, and color," as an observer remarked, "this primal uphealval . . . for future genera-tions." The significance of this work for Russian posterity, as well as the relative importance of Solzhenitsyn and his persecutors, was reflected in a current joke. In the twenty-first century, a history teacher asks one of her pupils to identify Brezhnev and Kosygin. After puzzled hesitation, the pupil ventures a reply. "Weren't they politicians or something during the time of Solzhenitsyn?"

But 1972 was to give Solzhenitsyn little of the inner calm his work requires. Early in January, Chakovsky's *Literary Gazette* printed the first extensive comment on *August 1914,* an angry reproach which declared that the novel had "turned out to be very helpful for anti-Soviet elements of every description." Charging the writer with putting private ownership of land and private employment of labor in a favorable light (in his descriptions of prerevolutionary country life), the newspaper alleged that the West had rushed to exploit the "rich opportunities" of his challenge to the Soviet system's very essence.

In unmistakable implication that the novel's bourgeois, not to say counterrevolutionary, tendencies grew from Solzhenitsyn's resentment over the revolution's cost to his own family, *Literary Gazette* linked its censure to the writer's personal background. In November 1971, the German magazine *Stern* had published a story about Irina Shcherbak, Solzheni-tsyn's eighty-two-year-old aunt who was living in poverty near Kislovodsk. Entitled "A Boorish Family"—the term attributed to her for Solzhenitsyn's forebears—the article quoted her memory of them as extremely rich landowners with vast estates, moneyed manners, grand foreign tours and feudalist attitudes. The text was accompanied with photographs of a Rolls-Royce and of a large, elaborately carved estate house, both al-legedly belonging to the family before the revolution. Referring to card playing and lewdness, painting Reshetovskaya and Solzhenitsyn's mother unflatteringly and hinting that his father may have committed suicide, the story reported Irina Shcherbak as claiming that the writer himself had spent his early years in her care.

Now *Literary Gazette* seized upon *Stern*'s article to degrade Solzheni-tsyn in a familiar "class-enemy" approach (reinforcing, in the process, the writer's detestation of any biographical investigation conducted outside his own control). It was within weeks that Dr. Heeb made his first protest against Western biographies. Coyly affirming that it would never establish a "direct and vulgar sociological connection" between a person's descent and upbringing, on the one hand, and his adult views on the other, the newspaper accepted the deeply "bourgeois" *Stern*'s report as fact, and reported that local old-timers still remember the wealthy Solzhenitsyn family with its more than 50 farmhands employed early in the century. "His grandfather, Semyon Yefimovich Solzhenitsyn, owned up to 5,400 acres of land and about 20,000 head of sheep . . ." The article went on to give a grotesquely distorted picture of the novel, as if it were some anti-revolutionary pamphlet.

Solzhenitsyn's answer was an immediate, angry, and categorical denial that his family was unusually wealthy or that *August 1914* was a disguised critique of the Soviet Union. Inasmuch as he had long expressed himself directly about contemporary Soviet conditions, he said, he had no need of "allegories, analogies, or tales" to do so. Other Western journalists were unable to confirm the interview's authenticity, and in the circumstances, a certain suspicion was inevitably attached to it: if the authorities' hand, ever grasping to discredit the writer, was not plain in the text itself, the question of how *Stern*'s writer and photographer had found the obscure, elderly woman and made their way to her—in an area normally closed to foreigners—remained unanswered. As to be expected, Solzhenitsyn was obviously stung to the quick by the appearance of such implications about his family.

As if to drive home the *Literary Gazette*'s implied threat in the appropriate setting, Solzhenitsyn was cited a month later during the trial of Vladimir Bukovsky, the young publicist who had made available to foreign correspondents detailed information about the treatment of political dissidents in special "psychiatric hospitals." In her summation to the court, the state prosecutor painted a picture of rabid anti-Communism seeking internal collaborators, in which Solzhenitsyn played a central role with his "tacit consent," by "lampooning" and "blackening" the dignity, exploits and achievements of the Soviet people and their homeland.

> Inwardly a spiritual emigrant, alien and hostile to the entire life of the Soviet people, Solzhenitsyn was invested by imperialist propaganda with the robes of a "great" Russian writer. . . . Extolling Solzhenitsyn not for his "talent" but merely because he had defamed Soviet reality, antisocialist speculators led the Nobel Committee by the bridle. Falsifications and underhand insinuations of isolated renegades are the propaganda weapons of our ideological opponents.

In such a trial—which ended with the sentencing of the twenty-nine-year-

old Bukovsky to a total of twelve years in prison, labor camp, and exile—
the linking of Solzhenitsyn to the Soviet Union's "enemies" could only
have been sanctioned by high authority. If these was meant to intimidate
Solzhenitsyn into silence, it underestimated, once again, his sense of
mission. In March 1972, the full force and sting of his pen was directed
to a question barely raised in the country. In a "Lenten Letter" to the
Patriarch of All Russia (made available to Western correspondents) he
excoriated the Orthodox Church for passivity in the face of—even connivance with—Christianity's relentless destruction in Russia.

He had written before of the degrading spectacle of indignities to the
faith and the faithful tolerated, if not encouraged, by the authorities.
Published in the West in 1969, "The Easter Procession" sketches a group
of young hooligans mocking a frail Easter celebration in the village of
Peredelkino, near Moscow. The story makes note of cigarettes, transistor
radios, and trouser-suited girls in the "procession"—and of the tiny huddle
of believers, pressed against the churchyard's railing in fear of the callous,
cynical youths.

> The legal boundary to crime has not been crossed, the banditry is
> bloodless, the insult to the spirit is in the bandit leer of those
> grinning lips, the brazen talk, the courting, pawing, smoking, spit-
> ting—two paces away from the Passion of Christ. The insult is the
> triumphantly contemptuous expression with which the toughs have
> come to watch their grandfathers reenact their forefathers' rites.

But the Lenten Letter charged Patriarch Pimen himself with counte-
nancing far worse than this. Reproaching him for adding to the burden of
the faithful and of complicity in robbing Russian children of their chance
to experience the pure, youthful perception of worship that he had known
—thereby sealing the doom of Russia's future—the sometimes caustic,
sometimes anguished statement showed the depth of Solzhenitsyn's religious commitment and the extent of his outrage.

> But what are you saying? Why do you address this honest appeal
> [that parents should inculcate their children with love of the
> church] only to Russian émigrés. Why do you appeal only for *those*
> children to be brought up in the Christian faith? Why is it only the
> distant flock which you warn to be "discerning of slander and false-
> hood" and to gird itself with righteousness and truth? What about
> *us* . . . what about *our* children? . . .

Warning that continued bowing to the church's planned destruction
would eventually reduce the flock to the Patriarch's own staff, Solzhenitsyn cited case after grim case in which the patriarchate had capitulated
to dictatorial rule by atheists—"a sight never before seen in two millennia!"
—sacrificing truth, its mission, and the few priests and bishops unwilling

to cooperate in shameful acts. He ended by appealing to stop the "voluntary internal enslavement" by sacrifice, reminding the Patriarch of Russian believers whose martyrdom was "worthy of the early Christians."

Startling as it was, the Lenten Letter was overshadowed by something more unexpected a week later. In late March, Solzhenitsyn invited Moscow correspondents of the *New York Times* and *Washington Post* to interview him, so extraordinary an occurrence in light of his previous relations with the press that the very granting of the audience was in itself a significant event in his life. Had his distaste for journalism, which for a decade had bordered on contempt, somewhat abated? Did he see in the Brezhnev-Kosygin regime's relentless persecution of dissidents and members of the civil rights "movement" a weakening of his first shield—the potential of Soviet liberals to erupt in protest—and a need to strengthen his second by describing his situation to international public opinion? In any case, he again chose his own moment, as he had in March 1967, to tell part of his story to the press and the world. This provided the opportunity for the first close observation of him by a journalist in five years. Posing for photographs in a Moscow apartment, probably that of Natalya Svetlova, the *Times* reporter described him as "all smiles"; but "alone, he was somber and refused to be coaxed into a grin. 'This is a time to be serious,' he explained, evidently thinking of his world image."

While his son Yermolai played cheerfully nearby—Solzhenitsyn's affection for him was described as "lavish"—the writer paused for frequent asides with his new wife, whose opinion he obviously valued; when his words came out in a rush—and in a vigorous but "surprisingly thin" voice for someone of his build—it was she who explained his thoughts. Informal and relaxed—the conversation took place in a typically easy-going "Russian" atmosphere, but with berry juice in place of more customary, stronger refreshment—Solzhenitsyn looked well and said his health was "not bad." The correspondents were struck by his intense, penetrating eyes—and, predictably, by his energy.

The interview itself was fully as purposeful as one would have expected by this time. In keeping with the "basic inclination toward deep analysis and rejection of any kind of superficiality" observed by the Soviet journalist Victor Bukhanov almost ten years earlier, Solzhenitsyn declined, for example, to comment on whether persecution of writers was a permanent feature of Russian life. "It would be indiscreet for me to talk about these things in a few, brief, superficial words." Nor would he discuss Yevtushenko, Voznesensky, and Aksyonov—the young writers who had aroused hope for a more creative literature in the late 1950s—except to say that they were now more popular in the West than in Russia, and that writers who deal with highly topical questions, as opposed to "themes of eternal significance," naturally fade from the limelight together with the issues they have treated. Although he could mention other Russian writers whose work was serious and accomplishments great, he indicated that naming them in a bugged apartment might harm them.

As for his own work, he denied that *One Day* had been an important literary instrument of Khrushchev's de-Stalinization campaign, asserting that such questions were better addressed not to him, a writer, but to political dissidents. About his great fame and the enormous international publicity attached to his every statement, he said simply that he would prefer wide publication in his own country.

But there was as little hope as ever of that. Stressing again and again that his situation was probably beyond the comprehension of Westerners, Solzhenitsyn described a "program to suffocate me," which included the systematic slander of political lecturers, the obstacles surrounding his research, and the general climate of intense pressure and severe intimidation in which he struggled to work and live. Although revealing nothing startlingly new, this was by far his most graphic—and pained—portrayal of his persecution. "A kind of contaminated zone" surrounded his family, he said, and people in Ryazan were to this day losing their jobs for having visited him years before. Conversations on the telephone and in his home were listened to "around the clock," and in "some vast premises" ranking officers analyzed them, together with all his correspondence. And if someone came to visit him with information for his writings,

> we work an hour or two, and as soon as he leaves my house, he will
> be closely followed as if he were a state criminal, and they will
> investigate his background. And then they go on to find out who
> this man meets and then, in turn, who that person is meeting.

Understandably, he seemed profoundly weary and oppressed by his ostracism and remorseless persecution. And although the "new era," as he called it, of Soviet life—that is, the post-Stalin period—permitted him to learn a great deal about the slanders by well-wishers who attended even the most closed meetings (perhaps in party and government agencies), no one could defend him. "No one dares to stand up and object to a party propagandist, because if he does, the next day he may lose his job and even his freedom." Nevertheless, Solzhenitsyn kept a list of the most striking lies, which "might come in handy some day." He might confront the speakers with it; the day might even come when they would be answerable in court for their statements. The search to find incriminating material about his background was still being pursued, together with the sending of ersatz manuscripts abroad to confuse Western publishers and readers.

Solzhenitsyn seemed to feel a special exasperation for the *Stern* article and its exploitation by the *Literary Gazette*. Emphasizing that his grand-fathers had both been simple farmers and not wealthy landowners, he went into uncharacteristic detail about his mother's burdens and his own difficult childhood. Specifically denying that he had ever lived with his Aunt Irina, but had merely spent parts of two or three summer vacations with her, he declared that "the rest is the fruit of her imagination, which already must be fuzzy."

Immediate revenge for the interview took the form of depriving Solzhenitsyn yet again of his Nobel Prize insignia. After some sixteen months of temporizing, presentation of the award had finally been arranged for early April; although the Swedish Embassy was still unwilling to offend the Soviet authorities by using its own premises, a compromise had been arranged under which the prize would be transferred in a simple, private ceremony in a Moscow apartment. The Solzhenitsyns had invited several Western journalists as well as a group of Russian friends and supporters, including Rostropovich, Academician Sakharov, and other leading liberal scientists and cultural figures. Having declared that renewed interference would be a "shameful absurdity" which would keep the prize in Stockholm for another ten or twenty years, he disclosed that correspondents from two Soviet newspapers "which have so far not slandered me" would be among the guests, and Western observers in Moscow saw in the authorities' willingness to give leave for the ceremony, however reluctantly, indication of a somewhat more tolerant attitude toward him.

On the day following publication of the interview, it became known that the Secretary of Swedish Academy, who was to have traveled to Moscow to make the award, had been denied a Soviet visa. The bubble having burst, Solzhenitsyn canceled the ceremony in obvious bitter disappointment, expressing dwindling hopes of ever receiving the insignia in his lifetime and willing it—he stressed that this was within the Academy's rules—to his son.

Puzzled Western correspondents speculated about his motives for granting the interview days before the scheduled presentation: had he been ill advised to believe that it would force the authorities, out of embarrassment, not to deny the visa—when in fact their reaction was opposite? Was he naïve and living "very much in a world of his own," or had he demonstrated a "martyr's streak"? Perhaps it was simply that the pressures on him had become intolerable and he was unwilling to contain himself longer. The fervor with which he had described his hounding to the Western reporters seemed to belie the notion that his stalemate with the authorities somehow assured him of protection or peace of mind. (He even asked that the interview not be published on April 1, for fear that it be dismissed as a joke.) Again and again, he had returned to his lonely struggle to fend off the state's programed molestation.

The plan is either to drive me out of society or out of the country, throw me in a ditch, or send me to Siberia, or to have me dissolve "in an alien fog," as they write.

But still more intense pressures followed swiftly. As if to demonstrate its dissatisfaction at having been cited as one of the newspapers still free of slander against Solzhenitsyn, *Trud*, together with the weekly *Literary Russia*, republished a violent attack on *August 1914* which had appeared a month before in a Polish paper. Likening Solzhenitsyn's view of World War I to Hitler's, charging him with attempting to "prettify German militarism" and with denigrating "everything Russian," accusing him of lack of sympathy for the revolutionary movement and of "indescribable intellectual arrogance," the article made of him a man with treasonable inclinations, whose books were understandably welcomed in the West because they demonstrated "hatred for the Soviet Union." "Alexander Solzhenitsyn . . . is convinced that mankind will remain in utter darkness and remain ignorant if he does not open his mouth."

Extraordinary even by the standards of previous sallies against the writer—the likening ("exactly") of his attitude toward the Russian rout in 1914 to that of "Fascist leaders" was especially pointed—the article made public the real hatred in the Solzhenitsyn case.

In all the tense events of early 1972, elements of Solzhenitsyn's personality came into sharp relief: the thorough knowledge of Swedish Academy regulations and careful reading of the Soviet press to know which newspaper had printed what about him; the irritation at the *New York Times* for having published, shortly after his funeral lament for Tvardovsky, a letter of an official Soviet writer challenging it; the circulating of his own text of the March interview, with passages (said to contain detailed refutation of the *Stern* article) unused by the American newspapers for lack of space and local interest. His determination to defend his rights and assert his viewpoint against any odds and all hindrances seemed to have jumped, even from its previous level. But although more outspoken and wider in his criticism than before, his principal attention remained on his vision of an ethical society, and the "stupidity and shortsightedness" of those who were trying to choke off his evocation of it.

They refuse to acknowledge the complexity and richness of history in its diversity. All they are concerned with is to silence all the voices that they find unpleasant to the ear, or that deprive them of today's calm. And they don't worry about the future. By senselessly silencing *Novy Mir* and Tvardovsky, they themselves were made poorer, they were made blind, and they refuse to understand their loss.

The study of Russian history, which has led me back to the end of the last century, has shown me how valuable peaceful outlets are for a country, how important it is that authority, no matter how autocratic and unlimited, should listen with good will to society, and that society should assume the position of real power: how important it would be to have not strength and violence, but righteousness, guide the country.

One of the most remarkable of Solzhenitsyn's attributes is his combination of talent and capacity for concentrated creative work with the practicality he has needed to survive physically and as a writer. The near-anomaly of his victory over circumstances was implicitly recognized in his 1967 letter to the leadership of the Writers' Union, urging that it at last fulfill its obligations to literature. "More than six hundred [officially registered] writers, guilty of nothing, were obediently handed over to their fate in camps and prisons," he wrote of the Stalin period. "But the roll is even longer and its curled-up end cannot and will not ever be read by our eyes. Among others, it contains the names of young prose writers and poets whom we have come to know about only accidentally through personal encounters, those whose talents perished in the camps before they could blossom and whose works never got farther than the offices of the state security service."

In addition to his practicality, sheer good luck—in war, prison, and hospitals—helped Solzhenitsyn to appear on the Nobel Prize list rather than on that of destroyed writers. But without an unusually powerful urge for survival, his timely strokes of good fortune doubtless would have been wasted. In turn, Solzhenitsyn's determination to prevail over hardship has been based on a visceral optimism underlying all his more cerebral philosophies, from the idealistic Leninism of his youth through the non-cynical skepticism of prison years to the Christian faith of his mature period.

A fundamental optimism about the human condition, clearly revealed in the note of promise with which his major novels end, also pervades his work, even in a setting of extreme trials. Ivan Denisovich's one day closes significantly better than it began. In the course of *The First Circle*'s three days, Gleb Nerzhin wins an important moral victory and an inner freedom. As for *Cancer Ward*, Solzhenitsyn himself explained its central meaning in terms of "life overcoming death" in the form of Kostoglotov's recovery and "the past overcome by the future" as hinted in the exile's possible release. "Were this not the case," he added, "I would not, *because of the elements of my makeup,* have undertaken to write this work." As energy is the primary physical wellspring of Solzhenitsyn's resilience and ability to survive, optimism is its principal psychological source.

His moral beliefs and intellectual position reflect this psychological disposition. Despite the scope and power of evil, goodness—without which optimism would be senseless—survives. Solzhenitsyn finds it in the concept of justness in relations between men, arising from the promptings of individual conscience. Shortly after assuming the stance of a protester, he sketched the foundation of his morality in a letter to three students who had asked for guidance about how to behave in an imperfect society.

> Justness belongs to mankind as it moves through the ages and, even when eclipsed for the majority of people during certain "narrowed" periods, never dies. Apparently this concept is innate to mankind since no outside source of it can be found. Justness exists if people are alive, however few, who sense it. . . . In periods of mass depravity when the questions "For whom should one make an effort? For whom sacrifices?" arise, the answer can be given with certainty: for justness. *There is nothing relative about it,* as there is nothing relative about conscience. Indeed, justness is conscience —not an individual's, but mankind's as a whole. . . . If in any situation in society you act in accordance with justness, you will never err. . . . This makes it possible for us to keep active always without losing heart. And please do not tell me that "everyone understands justness in his own way." No! One can shout, take others by the throat, tear one's own breast, but the tapping inside is as infallible as the promptings of one's conscience (and in our private lives too, we sometimes try to drown our conscience in shouts).

Tested in battle, labor camps, and dissent, this guide to action has helped sustain Solzhenitsyn in his own pursuits when the odds were against him and temptations to compromise were extreme. Its relationship is obvious to the "ethical force" singled out by the Nobel Committee as the outstanding feature of his writing.

His work has also benefited from another quality developed in confrontation with his circumstances. Along with a certain number of the survivors of the purges and World War II, Solzhenitsyn acquired a "fearlessness of death," in the phrase of Venyamin Kaverin. Analyzing its manifestation in *Cancer Ward*, Kaverin called this trait "the foundation of our victory in the hard war, the guarantee of the preservation of science and art during the Stalinist years, the assurance of the survival of human dignity in the hardest and most tragic circumstances in prisons and concentration camps." To Solzhenitsyn, fearlessness has given an inner freedom to write without consideration of what was permissible, something indispensable to his art. "The remarkable merit of Solzhenitsyn's works," commented one Soviet writer, "is primarily the fact that they were written. A man reached the point," he continued, drawing attention to the difference between an author working to his own standards and those of outside authority, "of writing his own books." Solzhenitsyn's faithfulness to himself lifts his writing well above even the better works of tolerated Soviet literature.

Although Solzhenitsyn's character and talent would have made him an important phenomenon in Soviet society whatever his attitude toward literature, a clear conception of the writer's role was essential to achieving his unusual stature. Like much about him, his view is traditional—yet fresh and powerful in his pursuit of it and in the context of the rejection of many traditional values in recent Russian history. Addressing his colleagues in 1967, Solzhenitsyn spoke of their common charge. "The writer's tasks," he argued, "cannot be reduced to defending or criticizing one or another method of distributing the national wealth, to defending or criticizing this or that form of government." He did not deny that such matters should be *among* a writer's interests; and for his own part, he was far from neglecting them. But he went on to insist—contrary to official practice—that literature's principal obligations lay in another area entirely.

> The writer's tasks concern more general and eternal questions—the secrets of the human heart and conscience, the clash between life and death, and the overcoming of inner sorrow. They concern the laws of mankind in its uninterrupted course, conceived in the immemorial depths of time and ceasing only when the sun will be extinguished.

To this conception, Solzhenitsyn has committed himself wholly as a man and as an artist. His belief that art transcends politics and political theory is not unique, even in the Soviet Union. But his powers of living according to his ideals and of giving life to them in his work are rare, and it is their use for what can only be called the sustenance of the human spirit and of civilized values that has inspirited not only Russians but readers only faintly aware of the hardships under which they were developed. As often in the best of Russian literature, his genius is both realistic and visionary.

BIBLIOGRAPHY AND CHRONOLOGY

Bibliography

Solzhenitsyn's published works in chronological order (first Russian, first British, and first American publications).

One Day in the Life of Ivan Denisovich (Odin den' Ivana Denisovicha): *Novy Mir*, Moscow, No. 11, 1962; Victor Gollancz, London, 1963 (tr. by Ralph Parker); Dutton, New York, 1963 (same tr.).

"Matryona's Place" (Matryonin dvor): *Novy Mir*, Moscow, No. 1, 1963; *Encounter*, London, May 1963 (tr. by H. T. Willet); South Carolina University Press, Columbia, 1963 (in a collection *We Never Make Mistakes*, tr. by Paul Blackstock).

"An Incident at Krechetovka Station" (Sluchay na stantsiyi Krechetovka): *Novy Mir*, Moscow, No. 1, 1963; Sphere Books, London, 1972 (tr. by Paul Blackstock); South Carolina University Press, Columbia, 1963 (same tr. and collection as "Matryona's Place").

For the Good of the Cause (Dlya pol'zy dela): *Novy Mir*, Moscow, No. 7, 1963; Pall Mall Press, London, 1964 (tr. by David Floyd and Max Hayward); Praeger, New York, 1964 (same tr.).

"Microstories" (Etudy i krokhotnyye rasskazy): *Grani*, Frankfurt-am-Main, No. 56, 1964; *Encounter*, London, March 1965 (tr. by H. T. Willet); *New Leader*, New York, January 18, 1965.

"It Isn't Done to Put Tar in the Cabbage Soup, You Put Sour Cream in It" (Ne obychai dyogtyom shchi belit', na to smetana)—a literary essay: *Literaturnaya Gazeta*, Moscow, November 4, 1965.

"Zakhar the Pouch" (Zakhar-Kalita): *Novy Mir*, Moscow, No. 1, 1966; the Bodley Head, London, 1971 (in a collection *Stories and Prose Poems*, tr. by Michael Glenny); Stein and Day, New York, 1969 (in a collection *For Freedom: Theirs and Ours*, tr. unnamed).

Cancer Ward (Rakovy korpus): Il Saggiatore, Milan, 1968 (Part I, published anonymously); the Bodley Head, London, 1968 (Part II); the Bodley Head, London, 1968 (Part I, tr. by Nicholas Bethell and David Burg; same publishers and translators, 1969 (Part II); Dial Press, New York, 1968, tr. by Rebecca Frank.

In the First Circle (V kruge pyervom): S. Fischer Verlag, Frankfurt-am-Main, 1968; Collins-Harvill Press, London, 1968 (tr. by Michael Guybon); Harper & Row, New York, 1968 (tr. by Thomas Whitney).

"The Right Hand" (Pravaya kist'): *Grani*, Frankfurt-am-Main, No. 69, 1968; *Sunday Telegraph*, London, December 29, 1968; *Atlantic Monthly*, Boston, May 1969.

A Candle in the Wind (Svecha na vetru): *Student*, London, No. 11–12, 1968.

"Easter Procession (Paskhal'ny krestny khod): *Posev*, Frankfurt-am-Main, No. 2, 1969; *Observer*, London, April 6, 1969 (tr. by Manya Harari); *Time* magazine, March 21, 1969 (same translator).

"They Read 'Ivan Denisovich'" (Chitayut "Ivana Denisovicha"): *Novy Zhurnal*, New York, No. 94, March 1969.

"An Answer to Three Students" (Otvet tryom studentam): *Novy Zhurnal*, New York, No. 94, March 1969.

The Love-Girl and the Innocent (Olen i shalashovka): *Grani*, Frankfurt-am-Main, No. 73, 1969; the Bodley Head, London, 1969 (tr. by Nicholas Bethell and David Burg); Farrar, Straus & Giroux, New York, 1969 (same tr.).

August 1914 (Avgust chetyrnadtsatogo): YMCA-Press, Paris, 1971; the Bodley Head, London, September 1972 (tr. by Michael Glenny); Farrar, Straus & Giroux, New York, 1972 (same tr.).

Chronology

December 11, 1918	Alexander Isaiyevich Solzhenitsyn born in Kislovodsk, in the Caucasus.
1924	Moves with his mother to Rostov-on-Don.
1936	Graduates from high school and enters Rostov University's Faculty of Mathematics and Physics.
1939	Enrolls in correspondence course with Moscow's Institute of Philosophy, Literature, and History.
1940	Marries Natalya Alekseyevna Reshetovskaya, a fellow student at Rostov University.
Summer 1941	Graduates with honors, after holding a Stalin Scholarship. Begins teaching physics at Morozovka, a town near Rostov.
October 1941	Conscripted as a private soldier. After humble duties, his scientific training leads him to a school for artillery officers in early 1942. Emerging as a battery commander, he serves continuously at the front until 1945, winning two high decorations and rising to the rank of captain.
February 1945	Arrested in East Prussia while on active service, after interception of letters to a friend containing unfavorable references to Stalin. Transported to Moscow's Lubyanka prison for interrogation.
July 1945	Sentenced by NKVD tribunal to eight years in labor camps.
Summer 1945– Summer 1946	Shunted through transit prisons and serves first period at hard labor in camps in and near Moscow.
Summer 1946	Transferred to prison research institute in Marfino, near Moscow (subsequently described in *The First Circle*), and assigned work as a mathematician.

Late 1940s
and early 1950s

Composes a long poem, "The Way"—which has remained largely unpublished—and an epic drama, "The Feast of the Victors"—which he later categorically repudiated. He used verse throughout both works to facilitate memorization, because he had to destroy his writings.

May 1950

Dismissed from prison research institute largely on his own initiative. After transport through transit prisons, is delivered to labor camps for political prisoners in northern Kazakhstan. Works as a bricklayer and in a machine shop.

February 1952

Stomach cancer diagnosed and operation performed in labor camp.

March 1953

Released after expiration of eight-year sentence and condemned to "perpetual exile." Delivered to the remote Kazakh settlement of Kok Terek, where he teaches physics and astronomy in the local school.

Autumn 1953

Stomach cancer recurs.

Early 1954

Intensive treatment in a Tashkent oncological hospital (later described in *Cancer Ward*).

1954

First draft of *The Love-Girl and the Innocent*. The play is his first work about labor camps which Solzhenitsyn considered publishable.

Spring 1955

Returns to Tashkent hospital for checkup and is pronounced cured.

1955

Begins *The First Circle*, a novel.

Summer 1956

Released from exile and moves to Vladimir Province in Central Russia, where he continues to teach school.

February 1957

Wholly rehabilitated by decision of the Supreme Court.

Late 1950s

Resumes his marriage with Natalya Reshetovskaya and joins her in Ryazan, where he continues to teach science.

1957–59

Writes "Matryona's Place," a story.
Conceives and writes *One Day in the Life of Ivan Denisovich*, a novel.

Early 1960s

Writes *A Candle in the Wind*, a play.

1961

Writes the first of his "microstories," to which he will add regularly in subsequent years.

1962

Writes "An Incident at Krechetovka Station," a story.

November 1962

At the direction of Nikita Khrushchev, *One Day*, Solzhenitsyn's first published work, appears in *Novy Mir* magazine to universal acclaim.

December 1962	Appearance of first hostile review. Solzhenitsyn gives up teaching to concentrate wholly on writing.
January 1963	Publication of "An Incident at Krechetovka Station" and "Matryona's Place" in *Novy Mir* and first appearance of *One Day* in the West.
1963	Begins *Cancer Ward*, a novel.
August 1963	Publishes "For the Good of the Cause," a story. Hostile criticism continues. *Novy Mir* nominates him for the Lenin Prize for Literature.
1964	Writes "The Right Hand," a story, and completes *The First Circle*.
1965	Personal papers, including the only manuscript of the repudiated "The Feast of the Victors," are seized by the KGB from a friend's apartment.
January 1966	*Novy Mir* publishes "Zakhar the Pouch," Solzhenitsyn's last work to be published in Russia. He submits *Cancer Ward* (Part I) to the magazine.
November 1966	Discussion of *Cancer Ward* (Part I) by the Writers' Union. After most speakers approve the manuscript, publication is recommended.
January 1967	First extract of *Cancer Ward* published in Czechoslovakia.
May 1967	In an open letter to the Fourth Congress of the Writers' Union meeting in Moscow, Solzhenitsyn denounces censorship and demands that the union defend its members.
September 1967	Solzhenitsyn again attacks the Writers' Union, demanding that it refute slanderous gossip circulating about him and authorize publication of *Cancer Ward;* makes clear he will not be responsible if the novel should appear abroad.
January 1968	*Novy Mir* abandons *Cancer Ward* after type has been set.
February 1968	*Cancer Ward* published in Italy.
April 1968	*Cancer Ward* extracts published in England. Solzhenitsyn makes available to writers documentation of his disputes with the authorities.
June 1968	*The First Circle* published in Germany. A Moscow literary newspaper prints Solzhenitsyn's denial of responsibility for publication of his works abroad, accompanying it with a long presentation of the official attitude toward him which provokes widespread protests in literary circles.

December 1968	Solzhenitsyn's fiftieth birthday brings many tributes from the Soviet Union and abroad.
November 1969	Local branch in Ryazan expels Solzhenitsyn from the Writers' Union. Despite protests from the editor of *Novy Mir* and other members, the expulsion is confirmed by the union's governing bodies.
Late 1960s	Separates from Reshetovskaya and enters into a *de facto* marriage with Natalya Svetlova, a scientist.
October 1970	Solzhenitsyn awarded the Nobel Prize for Literature, accepts it but is unable to attend the ceremonies in Stockholm in December.
January 1971	A son born to Solzhenitsyn and Natalya Svetlova.
June 1971	Publication of *August 1914*, the first book of an epic novel, in a Russian edition in France.
Autumn 1972	Publication of *August 1914* in English translation.

INDEX

Index